D0773288

THE SCIENCE OF GIVING

EXPERIMENTAL APPROACHES TO THE STUDY OF CHARITY

SOCIETY FOR JUDGMENT AND DECISION MAKING

Series Editor: **Derek J. Koehler**, *University of Waterloo, Canada*

The purpose of the *Society for Judgment and Decision Making* book series is to convey the general principles and findings of research in judgment and decision making to the many academic and professional fields to which it applies. Because the field of judgment and decision making is largely a formal one (similar to mathematics), its principles and findings are applicable to a wide range of disciplines, including psychology, medicine, social policy, law, management science, economics, and accounting.

The books in this series are aimed at researchers and their upper-level students. Most of the books are multiauthored volumes written by authorities in the field and sponsored by the Publications Committee of the Society for Judgment and Decision Making.

PUBLISHED

Social Psychology and Economics, De Cremer, Zeelenberg & Murnighan

The Science of Giving: Experimental Approaches to the Study of Charity, Oppenheimer & Olivola

Perspectives on Framing, Keren

A Handbook of Process Tracing Methods for Decision Research, Schulte-Mecklenbeck, Kuehberger & Ranyard

For continually updated information about published and forthcoming titles in the *Society for Judgment and Decision Making* series, please visit **www.psypress. com/sjdm**

THE SCIENCE OF GIVING

EXPERIMENTAL APPROACHES TO THE STUDY OF CHARITY

Edited by

Daniel M. Oppenheimer
Christopher Y. Olivola

Psychology Press
Taylor & Francis Group

New York London

Psychology Press
Taylor & Francis Group
711 Third Avenue
New York, NY 10017

Psychology Press
Taylor & Francis Group
27 Church Road
Hove, East Sussex BN3 2FA

© 2011 by Taylor and Francis Group, LLC
Psychology Press is an imprint of Taylor & Francis Group, an Informa business

International Standard Book Number: 978-1-84872-885-1 (Hardback)

Library of Congress Cataloging-in-Publication Data

The science of giving : experimental approaches to the study of charity / editors, Daniel M. Oppenheimer, Christopher Y. Olivola.
    p. cm.
Includes bibliographical references and index.
ISBN 978-1-84872-885-1 (pbk. : alk. paper)
  1. Charities--Psychological aspects. 2. Charity--Psychological aspects.
3. Generosity--Psychological aspects. I. Oppenheimer, Daniel M. II. Olivola, Christopher Yves, 1980-

HV16.S39 2011
179'.9--dc22

2010034067

Visit the Taylor & Francis Web site at
http://www.taylorandfrancis.com

and the Psychology Press Web site at
http://www.psypress.com

Contents

SECTION I   THE VALUE OF GIVING

SECTION II   THE IMPACT OF SOCIAL FACTORS

SECTION III   THE ROLE OF EMOTIONS

SECTION IV   OTHER IMPORTANT INFLUENCES ON CHARITABLE GIVING

Acknowledgments

We would like to thank Paul Brest and the Hewlett Foundation for their financial and logistical support in promoting empirical approaches to the study of charity. We would also like to thank participants of the 2007 Princeton-Hewlett conference, *Experimental Approaches to the Study of Charitable Giving*, for engaging discussions about the factors influencing charitable giving decisions. Special thanks go to Dara Wathanapaisal and Jeff Zemla for excellent research assistance on this project. Thanks also go to Peter Forsberg, Carolyn Hsu, Taylor Numann, Mark Starks, and the members of the Opplab for advice, feedback, and support. Paula Hunchar, Hale Peffall, Nicole Eley, and Adrian Sargeant provided valuable insights from the perspective of fundraisers, for which we are very grateful. Finally, we would like to thank Stephanie Drew, our contact at Taylor and Francis, and the SJDM Book Series committee for their support and guidance through the creation of this book. And of course, we thank our parents, to whom we dedicate this volume, our very first (edited) book.

About the Editors

Danny Oppenheimer is currently an Associate Professor of Psychology and Public Policy at Princeton University. He received his B.A. from Rice University and his Ph.D. from Stanford University. His research focuses on human decision making strategies and their policy implications.

Christopher Olivola is a research fellow at University College London. He received a B.A. in psychology from the University of Chicago and a joint-Ph.D. in psychology and policy from Princeton University. His research focuses on the psychology of human decision making and behavioral economics. He is funded by a Newton International Fellowship and an ESRC grant.

Contributors

Lara B. Aknin
Department of Psychology
University of British Columbia
Vancouver, British Columbia, Canada

Lalin Anik
Harvard Business School
Harvard University
Boston, Massachusetts, USA

Jonathan Baron
Department of Psychology
University of Pennsylvania
Philadelphia, Pennsylvania, USA

Aronte Bennett
Leonard N. Stern School of Business
New York University
New York, New York, USA

Jennifer A. Clarke
Psychology Department
University of Colorado at Colorado
    Springs
Colorado Springs, Colorado, USA

Rachel Croson
School of Economic, Political and
    Policy Sciences
School of Management
University of Texas at Dallas
Richardson, Texas, USA

Cynthia Cryder
Olin School of Business
Washington University in St. Louis
St. Louis, Missouri, USA

Stephan Dickert
Max Planck Institute for Research on
    Collective Goods
Bonn, Germany

Elizabeth W. Dunn
Department of Psychology
University of British Columbia
Vancouver, British Columbia, Canada

Michaela Huber
Department of Psychology and
    Neuroscience
University of Colorado at Boulder
Boulder, Colorado, USA

Tehila Kogut
Department of Education
Ben-Gurion University
Beer Sheva, Israel

Wendy Liu
Anderson School of Management
University of California, Los Angeles
Los Angeles, California, USA

George Loewenstein
Department of Social and Decision
    Sciences
Carnegie Mellon University
Pittsburgh, Pennsylvania, USA

Richard Martin
Department of Economics
University of Regina
Regina, Saskatchewan, Canada

A. Peter McGraw
Leeds School of Business
University of Colorado at Boulder
Boulder, Colorado, USA

Tom Meyvis
Leonard N. Stern School of
  Business
New York University
New York, New York, USA

Michael I. Norton
Harvard Business School
Harvard University
Boston, Massachusetts, USA

Christopher Y. Olivola
Cognitive, Perceptual & Brain
  Sciences
University College London
London, United Kingdom

Daniel M. Oppenheimer
Psychology Department
Princeton University
Princeton, New Jersey, USA

John Randal
School of Economics and Finance
Victoria University of Wellington
Wellington, New Zealand

Rebecca K. Ratner
Robert H. Smith School of Business
University of Maryland
College Park, Maryland, USA

Ilana Ritov
School of Education
Hebrew University
Jerusalem, Israel

Namika Sagara
Fuqua School of Business
Duke University
Durham, North Carolina, USA

Jen Shang
The Center on Philanthropy
School of Public and Environmental
  Affairs
Indiana University at Bloomington
Bloomington, Indiana, USA

Paul Slovic
Decision Research
University of Oregon
Eugene, Oregon, USA

Deborah A. Small
The Wharton School
University of Pennsylvania
Philadelphia, Pennsylvania, USA

Michal Ann Strahilevitz
Ageno School of Business
Golden Gate University
San Francisco, California, USA

Ewa Szymanska
Department of Psychology
University of Pennsylvania
Philadelphia, Pennsylvania, USA

Leaf Van Boven
Department of Psychology and
  Neuroscience
University of Colorado at Boulder
Boulder, Colorado, USA

Min Zhao
Joseph L. Rotman School of
  Management
University of Toronto
Toronto, Ontario, Canada

Introduction

In 2004, a tsunami devastated the Asian coastline, leaving 226,000 dead and 2,500,000 displaced (EM-DAT: The OFDA/CRED International Disaster Database, 2009). The humanitarian response was striking. Americans opened their hearts and their pocketbooks, donating more than $1.8 billion to relief efforts (Center on Philanthropy at Indiana University, 2006). One year later, an earthquake struck the densely populated Kashmir region of Pakistan, killing 79,000 and displacing over 2,800,000 people (EM-DAT: The OFDA/CRED International Disaster Database, 2009). In response to this disaster, less than $130 million was donated (Center on Philanthropy at Indiana University, 2006). While this is by no means a trivial contribution, it is interesting to note that the response per death was more than 5 times higher for the tsunami than for the earthquake ($8,296 vs. $1,635) and the response per affected person was more than 16 times higher for the tsunami ($750 vs. $45).

Of course, even contributions to the tsunami victims pale in comparison to the more than $2.4 billion raised by charities for victims of the terrorist attacks on September 11, 2001 (Chronicle of Philanthropy, 2003), which translate into an astounding $821,184 raised per death (without even counting the more than $5 billion awarded to victims by the U.S. government through the federal September 11 Victim Compensation Fund). And consider that Hurricane Katrina received over $3.5 billion in charitable relief (Center on Philanthropy at Indiana University, 2006)—over 200 times more per death than the tsunami, and 1,100 times more per death than the Kashmir earthquake. These examples showcase a startling level of inconsistency and inefficiency in the way donations for charity are raised and allocated to needy recipients; a tendency that seems to be mirrored by biases in media attention to epidemics and humanitarian crises (Armstrong, Carpenter, & Hojnacki, 2006; Eisensee & Strömberg, 2007; Slovic, 2007).

If the amount that people give isn't based on the amount of need, then perhaps it is based on the efficiency of the charity. Maybe people give on the basis of where the money will be best spent, rather than where it is most needed. This turns out not to be the case either. We randomly sampled 185 charities from across the spectrum of types of causes and compared their efficiency rates and the amount of donations they received from 2006 to 2008 (these data were collected from www.charitynavigator.com). The overall correlation between efficiency and dollars received was quite small: $r(185) = .002$. That is, there is no observable relationship between the quantity of donations a charity receives and how efficiently it spends this money.

So, if people's donation decisions aren't based on the amount of the need or the quality of the organization, what are the factors that govern charitable giving? Can we understand what drives people to respond altruistically, and in doing so help generate donations to help affected victims rebuild their lives and their communities in ways that would be impossible without these charitable contributions?

Understanding when and why people donate is of critical importance in a world where a wealthy minority has the ability to make a large impact on the lives of many who live in difficult and uncertain conditions. The decision to donate money, time, or other resources can be conceptualized as a choice among options, like any other choice about how to spend one's finite assets. Therefore, psychologists and economists specializing in the study of human decision making are well-suited to make contributions to our understanding of charitable giving, as we hope to show in this volume.

The existing research and writing on charitable giving has mainly been correlational in nature and focused on macro-level variables, such as institutions and giving trends (e.g., Clotfelter, 1985; Schiff, 1990). What differentiates this book from other volumes on the topic, and from previous attempts to understand donation giving, is its focus on experimental methods, as well as its analysis of individual donation decisions and the mental processes that underlie these decisions. While many factors have been shown to correlate with charitable giving, correlational methods cannot demonstrate a causal relationship. Thus, if a researcher were to show, for example, that donations increase in the month of December, we couldn't know if that increase was due to the holiday season, last-minute tax deductions, a tendency to give more in cold weather, or even the possibility that the first few letters of December prime the word "decent" and thus the concept of helping others.

By contrast, all of the chapters in this book describe the results of studies in which the variables of interest are experimentally manipulated. The rigorously controlled methodology of these experiments allows researchers to isolate and understand the factors that lead to giving and to make causal attributions about the impact of these variables. As a result, it becomes possible to design effective intervention programs that can increase the likelihood and amount that people contribute to a cause. In this volume we have attempted to highlight some of the most exciting, intriguing, surprising, and enlightening experimental studies on the topic of donation behavior. This work has tended to fall into four broad categories, which form the organizational structure of the book.

THE VALUE OF GIVING

The chapters in this section are concerned with the value that donors place on, and derive from, giving to charity. These chapters explore the psychological costs and benefits of giving, and address questions of how we can increase the benefits and lower the costs. Charities can use these insights to make it more fulfilling and less psychologically painful for donors to give, and thereby increase the number of donors and the magnitude of donations.

The section opens with Lalin Anik, Lara Aknin, Michael Norton, and Elizabeth Dunn's insightful treatment of the relationship between giving and happiness. They review previous investigations and provide novel empirical evidence that giving actually causes people to become happier. They then discuss how charities could help people become aware of this effect, thus encouraging greater giving.

Next, Michal Strahilevitz examines the extent to which increasing the amount a person contributes augments the amount of pleasure he/she gets from doing so. She plots this relationship, showing that smaller gifts lead to more psychological benefits per dollar than larger gifts. Moreover, she shows that the psychological benefits one gets from giving are distinct from the psychological benefits of receiving. She uses these findings to recommend ways in which charities can structure giving opportunities to maximize the amount of psychological value their donors will experience from having made the gift.

Unlike the first two chapters, which look at the benefits of giving, Tom Mevyis, Aronte Bennett, and Danny Oppenheimer consider the psychological costs of giving. Mevyis and his colleagues examine the notion that giving away one's money is psychologically painful, and that this pain can be lessened by creating separation between the decision to give the money and the actual act of giving the money. They show that having people precommit to charity (e.g., pledging to give in the future) can reduce the pain of giving, and thus increase giving rates. They also discuss situations where this strategy backfires, so that asking for immediate donations is more effective than soliciting pledges.

While the first three chapters are mainly focused on either the costs or the benefits of giving to charity, Christopher Olivola explores both variables and how they relate to each other. He suggests that rules of Pareto efficiency—the notion that one should simultaneously try to maximize the benefits of giving without increasing the costs and minimize the costs of giving without decreasing the benefits—do not seem to govern charitable behavior. Instead, he shows that in some situations, people seem to have a preference for painful and effortful means of giving to charity (e.g., running a marathon), rather than easier and more enjoyable alternatives (e.g., going to a picnic). He explores the implications of this preference, both for our understanding of human motivation and for the design of charity fundraisers.

THE IMPACT OF SOCIAL FACTORS

The chapters in this section explore how norms and other social forces influence our decisions of whether, and how much, to give. These chapters show that the actual or expected thoughts and behaviors of others can have an important impact on donations. Charities can use these insights to draw upon existing social pressures to give, and weaken social barriers to giving.

First, Rachel Croson and Jen Shang begin by looking at how the size of a potential donor's gift is influenced by the size of a previous contributor's donation. They show that the impact of this knowledge varies depending on whether the previous contributor is similar, in some way, to the potential donor. They then explore how the size of a person's social network influences how much he/she gives to the charity. They identify several practical interventions that can be used to increase donation magnitude.

Next Richard Martin and John Randal examine the effects of implied social giving norms. They show that the monetary amounts and denominations initially contained in a museum's donation box affect both the likelihood that museum visitors donate to the museum and the amount of each contribution. They further examine the impact of various posted signs and appeals on donation rates and magnitudes. They report some surprising findings concerning the factors that seem to influence donations and those that do not.

While the previous chapters in this section focus on how social information can be used to facilitate donations, Rebecca Ratner, Min Zhao, and Jennifer Clarke explore how social factors can serve as barriers to giving. Ratner and her colleagues examine one aspect of the "norm of self-interest"—that people feel that it is only culturally acceptable to donate to causes in which they have a personal stake. They note how this can prevent people who might want to donate from doing so. For example, men might want to donate to charities that strive to empower women, but don't do so because they feel it is not culturally appropriate. The authors discuss several ways that charities can overcome this barrier, thus potentially allowing fundraisers to expand their donor bases.

Finally, Tehila Kogut and Ilana Ritov examine how a classic phenomenon in charitable giving—that people prefer to donate to a single, identified victim than to a group of many victims—is moderated by certain social factors. They review existing literature demonstrating the prevalence of this phenomenon, and then provide new empirical evidence concerning the moderators of the effect. They suggest some important caveats about how the identifiable victim effect can be used to increase donations.

THE ROLE OF EMOTIONS

The chapters in this section examine the impact of emotions on charitable giving. In particular, they explore what drives our emotional responses, how those emotions influence our decisions of whether and how much to give, and how the impact of these emotions can be overcome. Charities can use this information to develop appeals that elicit donation-promoting emotions, and to help donors resist emotions that hinder their ability to make rational decisions about giving.

Deborah Small opens this section with a discussion of the role of sympathy in donation decisions. She discusses the different factors that induce sympathy and provides evidence that sympathy appeals lead people to be more generous in their charitable giving. She closes with practical advice on how charities can use these types of appeals to increase the success of fundraising campaigns.

While Deborah Small examines sympathy as a case study of emotional influence on giving, Stephan Dickert, Namika Sagara, and Paul Slovic consider the role of emotion more generally. They review a large body of literature on the role of emotion in donation decisions, and provide novel empirical evidence that the choice of whether to donate is guided by different emotional factors than the determination of how much to donate. Thus, different types of emotional appeals might be preferable depending on the nature of a fundraising campaign.

Finally, Michaela Huber, Leaf Van Boven, and Peter McGraw show that emotions can lead people to make impulsive donation decisions in less principled ways than they would normally prefer. They explore several interventions that might be used to better overcome emotional biases in giving, and allow people to donate more efficiently and in line with their charitable goals. They provide suggestions for how organizations can help people resist emotional lures and allocate their limited charity budgets in ways that maximize welfare.

OTHER IMPORTANT INFLUENCES ON CHARITABLE GIVING

The final chapters of the book explore an eclectic range of topics that are important to our understanding of charitable giving but are not covered in the preceding sections. While these chapters do not converge on a single topic or theme, they have important implications for how charities can improve the effectiveness of fundraising and how donors can improve the efficiency of their giving.

First, Wendy Liu notes that people can often donate their time as well as their money. She investigates how requests for time differ from requests for money, and provides intriguing empirical evidence that people are more responsive to either request if they are first asked to consider donating time. She explores the reasons behind this "time-ask effect" and the implications of this phenomenon for charitable organizations.

Next, Jonathan Baron and Ewa Szymanska note that while people desire to donate in ways that maximize welfare, determining how to do so often creates a difficult mental challenge. The authors examine some of the common mental shortcuts that people employ to simplify their donation decisions, and the inefficient patterns of giving that result. They suggest some interventions that charities might consider to help overcome these biases and help people more efficiently allocate their charitable dollars.

Finally, Cynthia Cryder and George Loewenstein look at how the tangibility of donation recipients impacts the amount that is contributed. Drawing upon research on the identifiable victim effect and emotional influences on charity, they theorize that donation decisions may depend critically on the salience of the beneficiary, and provide strong empirical support for this notion. They then discuss how current fundraising strategies could be improved by increasing outcome tangibility.

CONCLUSION

When we first conceived of the idea to put together a volume of this sort, back in 2005, it seemed to us that work on donation behavior was being done in isolated pockets and that the researchers involved were not interacting as much as they could or should be. Thus, one goal of this book is to bring together and showcase some of the newest and most promising lines of research on charitable giving. We hope that this collection of papers will serve as a source of inspiration and ideas for future research on the factors involved in charitable giving decisions.

Each of the chapters not only provides novel experimental findings, but also an overview of the relevant literature in the area. As such, this book can serve as a primer for anyone who is interested in experimental approaches to charity.

Our hope is that this volume will not only increase the interest in charity as a domain of inquiry among experimental social scientists, but that it will also provide charitable organizations with a body of empirical findings that may help them be more successful at fundraising. Moreover, we hope that this book will inspire charitable organizations to approach their fundraising activities with a more empirical mindset and, as a result, promote collaborations between charities and researchers.

In 2007, charities raised more than $300 billion (Giving USA, 2008), an impressive accomplishment, no doubt. By using the insights presented in this book, however, we think they could do much, much better. Together, the chapters in this volume provide a number of social scientific principles for simultaneously improving the welfare of three important groups: the charity organizations who struggle to raise money for worthy causes, the donors who contribute to the fundraising effort, and the targets of those donations who depend on charity for basic support or even survival. As such, we believe this book can contribute substantially to the mission of raising contributions to make the world a better place.

Danny Oppenheimer & Chris Olivola

REFERENCES

Armstrong, E. M., Carpenter, D. P., & Hojnacki, M. (2006). Whose deaths matter? Mortality, advocacy, and attention to disease in the mass media. *Journal of Health Politics, Policy and Law*, *31*, 729–772.

Center on Philanthropy at Indiana University. (2006). Retrieved September 30, 2009, from http://www.philanthropy.iupui.edu/

Charity Navigator. (2009). Retrieved September 30, 2009, from http://www.charitynavigator.com/

Chronicle of Philanthropy. (28 August 2003). Retrieved September 30, 2009, from http://philanthropy.com/free/update/2003/08/2003082801.htm

Clotfelter, C. T. (1985). *Federal tax policy and charitable giving*. Chicago: University of Chicago Press.

Eisensee, T., & Strömberg, D. (2007). News floods, news droughts, and U.S. disaster relief. *Quarterly Journal of Economics*, *122*, 693–728.

EM-DAT: The OFDA/CRED International Disaster Database. (2009). Université catholique de Louvain, Brussels, Belgium. Data retrieved September 30, 2009 from www.emdat.be

Giving USA. (2008). Retrieved September 30, 2009, from http://www.givingusa.org/

Schiff, J. (1990). *Charitable giving and government policy: An economic analysis*. New York: Greenwood.

Slovic, P. (2007). "If I look at the mass I will never act": Psychic numbing and genocide. *Judgment and Decision Making*, *2*, 79–95.

Section *I*

The Value of Giving

1

Feeling Good About Giving
The Benefits (and Costs) of Self-Interested Charitable Behavior

LALIN ANIK, LARA B. AKNIN, MICHAEL I. NORTON,
and ELIZABETH W. DUNN

People see a world out of whack. They see the greatest health crisis of 600 years and they want to do the right thing, but they're not sure what that is. (RED) is about doing what you enjoy and doing good at the same time.

—Bono, "Ethical Shopping: The Red Revolution," *Belfast Telegraph,*
January 27, 2006.

*H*elping others takes countless forms, from giving money to charity to helping a stranger dig his car out of the snow, and springs from countless motivations, from deep-rooted empathy to a more calculated desire for public recognition. Indeed, social scientists have identified a host of ways in which charitable behavior can lead to benefits for the giver, whether economically via tax breaks (Clotfelter, 1985, 1997; Reece & Zieschang 1985), socially via signaling one's wealth or status (Becker 1974; Glazer & Konrad 1996; Griskevicius et al., 2007) or psychologically via experiencing well-being from helping (Andreoni, 1989, 1990; Dunn, Aknin, & Norton, 2008). Charitable organizations have traditionally capitalized on all of these motivations for giving, from attempting to engage consumers with emotion-laden advertising to pushing governments to offer tax incentives. The psychological benefits of giving are underscored by Bono's quote above, referring to the Product (RED) campaign, in which a portion of profits from consumer purchases of luxury goods is donated to the Global Fund for AIDS relief. Giving feels good, so why not advertise the benefits of "self-interested giving," allowing people to experience that good feeling while increasing contributions to charity at the same time?

In this chapter, we have two primary aims. First, we explore whether claims about the benefits of helping are in fact justified: while many appeals for charity center on the notion that helping makes the giver happy, a relatively small amount of research exists to support this causal claim. We review evidence that happy people give more, that giving is associated with and causes happiness, and that these relationships may run in a circular fashion, such that happy people give more, then feel happier, then give more, and so on. Second, however, we consider the possible negative implications of advertising these well-being benefits in an effort to increase charitable behavior. When people start to give for "selfish" reasons—in order to feel good—instead of altruistic reasons—to help others—such extrinsic motivations may crowd out intrinsic motivation to help; as a result, helping behavior might increase in the short term as people seek benefits, but decrease in the long-term as people's inherent interest in the welfare of others declines.

HAPPIER PEOPLE GIVE MORE

One of the first experimental studies to demonstrate that happiness increases charitable behavior was conducted by Isen and Levin (1972), who showed that after experiencing positive events (such as receiving cookies, or finding a dime left in a payphone), participants were more likely to help others. Thus, people who felt good were more likely to provide help. Replicating this effect in a different context, Aderman (1972) induced either an elated or depressed state by having participants read statements designed to induce these moods. Participants in a positive mood were more likely to help with a favor to the researcher during the experiment, and even promised to help by participating in a second experiment. Other positive mood states have also been shown to increase altruism; feelings of competence, for example, have been shown to increase helping and volunteering behavior (Harris & Huang 1973; Kazdin & Bryan 1971), as has succeeding on tasks (Isen, 1970).

Young children exhibit similar effects of mood on helping. Rosenhan, Underwood, and Moore (1974) randomly assigned second and third graders to positive or negative mood conditions by having them reminisce about mood-appropriate memories. To strengthen the mood induction, children were asked to talk about these memories and then think about them once again. Children were then allowed to have some candy from a treasure chest (self-gratification) and also give money to other students if they wished (altruistic behavior). While both happy and sad children ate more candy than those in the control condition, only happy children gave more money away to classmates. These results also suggest that prosocial behavior may not necessitate self-sacrifice, as happy children engaged both in more self-gratification and more altruistic behavior—like those consumers who buy Product (RED) iPods and enjoy the product while also giving to charity. Similar to results for adults, other positive mood states, such as the feeling of success, are related to prosocial behavior in children (Isen, Horn, & Rosenhan, 1973).

While the majority of research has explored the impact of happiness on prosocial behavior via mood inductions, recent extensions have examined how naturally occurring moods influence helping behavior. Wang and Graddy (2008) suggest that happy people are both more emotionally capable to help others and have more optimistic personalities, fostering charitable giving behavior. Using individu-als' self-rated happiness as an indicator of psychological inclination to donate, they found that a feeling of happiness affected religious giving, but not secular giving, which may have stemmed from the association of happiness and religious giving in people's minds. Konow and Earley (2008) also argued that happier people give more because they are fueled by their positive emotions. In the context of a dicta-tor game, where a proposer divided a fixed endowment between himself and one other (the recipient), individuals who were happier at the beginning of the game were more likely to give at least a dollar to their partner.

Positive moods, whether experimentally induced or naturally occurring, have also been shown to facilitate helpful behavior in the workplace. Forgas, Dunn, and Granland (2008) induced a positive, neutral, or negative mood in sales staff at a department store by engineering an interaction with a confederate (posing as a customer) that varied in pleasantness. Next, another confederate approached the sales staff and requested help finding an item that did not in fact exist. While experienced staff members were largely impervious to the effects of mood, inexpe-rienced staff provided more help—by trying to find the item, suggesting alterna-tives, and devoting more time to helping the customer—than did those in a neutral mood. Converging evidence for the benefits of positive mood on prosocial behavior in the workplace comes from research on naturally occurring mood; in a study by Williams and Shiaw (1999), employees who reported being in a good mood were more likely to display organizational citizenship behaviors that were not part of their formal job requirements.

Taken together, the existing evidence suggests that happier people do indeed help more in a variety of contexts. Studies using random assignment to experi-mentally induce positive mood have provided important evidence that happiness *causes* increased helping behavior. Supporting the external validity of these find-ings, naturally occurring positive moods have also been shown to facilitate proso-cial behavior. While we have focused on the impact of positive mood on giving, however, another well-documented area of inquiry has documented the impact of negative mood on helping as well, a seeming contradiction (see Batson, 1987; 1991). For example, Cialdini et al. (1987) showed that watching another person suffer a mild electric shock motivates helping in an observer through a sense of heightened empathy and increased personal sadness. Similarly, Small and Verrochi (2009) found that people were more sympathetic and likely to donate when chari-table appeals contain victims with sad expressions, and the sadness experienced on the part of the donor mediates the effect of emotion expression on sympathy. We suggest that a key difference in the way these two research streams have oper-ationalized mood may account for these seemingly disparate findings. Research exploring the impact of positive moods on helping has generally focused on happi-ness—whether incidental as with finding money, or global as with overall well-be-ing—unrelated to the specific cause or individual in need of charity, as opposed to negative mood directly tied to the victim: "I feel good in general, and so am going to give" rather than "I feel badly for that person, and so am going to give." Future research should manipulate both factors independently to examine the interplay of positive and negative mood on giving.

The research reviewed thus far has examined how moods, both positive and negative, cause people to give, as well as exploring the consequences of this behavior for the victim (i.e., whether they received help or not). This work, however, only addresses one direction of the causal arrow between mood and prosocial behavior. In the following section we review the evidence in the opposite direction. That is, does giving make people happy?

GIVING MAKES PEOPLE HAPPIER

Dialogue on whether prosocial behavior increases well-being dates as far back as ancient Greece, where Aristotle argued that the goal of life was to achieve *eudaemonia*, which is closely tied to modern conceptions of happiness. According to Aristotle, eudaemonia is more than just a pleasurable hedonic experience; eudaemonia is a state in which an individual experiences happiness from the successful performance of their moral duties. In recent years, popular opinion, self-help gurus, and community organizations have endorsed the notion that helping others has mood benefits. Although these claims sometimes outpace the evidence base, a growing body of research provides methodologically diverse support for the hedonic benefits of generosity.

At the most basic level, functional magnetic resonance imaging (fMRI) evidence shows that giving money to charity leads to similar brain activity in regions implicated in the experience of pleasure and reward. In a study conducted by Harbaugh, Mayr, and Burghart (2007), neural activity was recorded while participants decided how to split a $100 sum between themselves and a local food bank. Results showed that donations of the original $100 sum to the food bank led to activation in the ventral striatum, a brain region associated with representing the value of a range of rewarding stimuli, from cocaine to art to attractive faces (Aharon et al., 2001; Vartanian & Goel, 2004; see Elliott, Friston, & Dolan, 2000). Thus, these results suggest that giving (in the form of charitable donations) is inherently rewarding.

At a very different level of analysis—from brain to nation—Meier and Stutzer (2008) demonstrated that volunteering increases life satisfaction, through use of the German Socioeconomic Panel, a longitudinal study of German households. Consistent with other correlational studies of volunteering and well-being, they found that higher levels of volunteer work were associated with higher levels of overall life satisfaction. This study, however, is unique in that it examines the relationship between happiness and volunteer work around the collapse of the German Democratic Republic, providing a quasi-experimental design. Specifically, by looking at data collected shortly after the fall of the Berlin Wall but prior to the German reunification, a time when volunteering opportunities dropped dramatically in Eastern Germany, happiness of East Germans can be compared to a control group who experienced no change in their volunteer status. Using this design, the authors are able to conclude that helping others increases well-being. While this study lacks true random assignment, it does offer intriguing evidence of the impact of volunteer work on well-being in a large, nationally representative dataset.

Additionally, some experimental work hints at a causal relationship between giving and happiness. For example, when Field, Hernandez-Reif, Quintino, Schanberg, and Kuhn (1998) asked a volunteer group of retired senior citizens to give infants a massage three times a week for three weeks, these seniors experienced less anxiety and depression, as well as improved health and a reduction in stress-related hormones. Further support for a causal link comes from recent work by Lyubomirsky, Tkach, and Sheldon (2004), which shows that simply asking people to commit random acts of kindness can significantly increase happiness levels for several weeks. Specifically, in their investigation, Lyubomirsky and colleagues randomly assigned students to a no-treatment control group or to an experimental group, in which students were asked to commit five random acts of kindness a week for six weeks. As predicted, students who engaged in random acts of kindness were significantly happier than controls.

Finally, our own recent research suggests that altruistic financial behavior, such as gift giving and charitable donations, may promote happiness (Dunn, Aknin, & Norton, 2008). In an initial study, we asked a nationally representative sample of Americans to rate their general happiness and provide monthly estimates of personal and prosocial spending. Specifically, participants were asked to report their annual household income and general happiness level and to estimate how much they spent in a typical month on (1) bills/expenses, (2) gifts for themselves, (3) gifts for others and (4) donations to charity. We summed categories 1 and 2 for an index of personal spending and categories 3 and 4 for an index of prosocial spending. Lastly, participants reported their general happiness on a one-item happiness scale (Abdel-Khalek, 2006), which simply asked participants "Do you feel happy, in general?" Analyses revealed that individuals who devoted more money to prosocial spending reported greater happiness, whereas personal spending was unrelated to happiness. Even controlling for income, higher prosocial spending was associated with greater happiness; income had an independent and similar association with happiness. While these results provide a first glimpse of the association between prosocial spending and happiness in the population, the correlational nature of this study restrains discussion of causal claims.

Therefore, we also used an experimental design to test the casual claim that spending money on others leads to higher happiness levels than spending money on oneself (Dunn et al., 2008). Our hypothesis was that participants randomly assigned to spend money in a prosocial fashion would be happier at the end of the day than others assigned to spend money on themselves. Participants were approached in person during the morning hours (approximately 10 a.m.–noon) in public places and asked to report their baseline happiness level. After doing so, participants were randomly assigned to one of four spending conditions, receiving either five or twenty dollars to spend on themselves or others. Specifically, participants in the personal spending condition were asked to use their windfall on a bill, expense, or gift for themselves, while participants in the prosocial spending condition were asked to spend the money on a gift for someone else or donation to charity. All participants were asked to spend the money in line with their assigned spending direction by 5 p.m. that day. Participants were then contacted in the evening hours (between 6 p.m. and 8 p.m.) on the phone by a research assistant to complete a follow-up survey that assessed their current happiness level. As predicted, participants asked to spend their windfall in a prosocial fashion were happier at the end of the day than were participants in the personal spending condition. Interestingly, the amount of money people were given did not influence how happy they were that evening, suggesting that *how* people spent their money was more important than *how much* money they received. Therefore, this experimental study provides support for the causal claim that spending money on others leads to higher happiness than spending money on oneself. Moreover, these results suggest that the spending amount need not be large to facilitate positive hedonic gains, as prosocial purchases made with as little as five dollars were sufficient to boost happiness levels.

DOES HAPPINESS RUN IN A CIRCULAR MOTION?

The streams of research reviewed above—that happy people give more, and that giving makes people happy—beg an obvious question: Is there a positive feedback loop between happiness and giving? Previous research on volunteering and prosocial behavior has suggested that happier people are more likely to engage in these activities and subsequently experience higher happiness levels from doing so (e.g., Thoits & Hewitt, 2001; Piliavin, 2003). Thus, we explored whether the link between happiness and prosocial spending runs in a circular motion, such that recollections of previous prosocial spending make people happier, and in turn, more likely to engage in prosocial spending in the future.

To investigate this question, we asked a sample of students to think back and describe the last time they spent either $20 or $100 on either themselves or someone else. After describing this experience, each participant was asked to report their happiness. Next, each participant was given the opportunity to select the future spending behavior they thought would make them happiest from the four conditions presented in the experimental study described above ($5 or $20 to spend on themselves or others).

Our hypothesis was that recalling a prosocial spending experience would make people happier than recalling a personal spending experience (regardless of how much money was spent) and that this boost in happiness would lead participants to select a prosocial spending choice in the future. To investigate whether recalling specific spending experiences influenced happiness levels, we compared the happiness ratings of participants in the four recall conditions. As expected, participants randomly assigned to recall a purchase made for someone else were significantly happier than participants assigned to recall a purchase made for themselves. We also predicted that this boost in happiness would shape people's future spending choice, such that happier participants would be more likely to spend prosocially in the future. To investigate whether this happiness boost led participants to select a prosocial spending choice in the future, we used the purchase amount ($20 or $100), purchase target (oneself or others), and happiness to predict future spending choices. In line with our hypothesis, happiness was the only significant predictor of future spending choice, suggesting that participants made happier by recalling a previous purchase for someone else were significantly more likely to choose to engage in prosocial spending in the future. Further, mediational analyses confirm that other-oriented spending memories only fostered future prosocial spending choices to the extent that these recollections increase happiness levels in the interim.

These data confirmed our hypothesis that prosocial spending and happiness fuel each other in a circular fashion. By asking participants to recall a previous time they spent money on others, we were able to observe that the prosocial spending recollections led to an increase in happiness. Furthermore, by allowing participants to make a future spending decision, we were able to show that this increase in happiness shaped spending decisions such that happier people were more likely to make to make prosocial spending choices in the future. In addition, we have recently shown that these effects hold cross-culturally, with both North American and African samples, offering preliminary evidence that the reciprocal links between giving and happiness may be a human universal.

WILL INCREASING AWARENESS OF THE BENEFITS OF GIVING LEAD TO MORE, OR LESS, GIVING?

One implication of the research reviewed above is quite clear: if giving makes people happy, and happy people give more, then one means of increasing charitable donations is simply to inform people of this loop, making a rational appeal that self-interested giving can lead to higher well-being. Indeed, Dunn et al. (2008) showed that people erroneously believe that spending money on themselves makes them happier than spending money on others, suggesting that there is ample room for people to be "educated" to the contrary. Recently, many organizations appear to be engaged in efforts to link charitable donations with feel-good campaigns, as opposed to the classic campaigns involving images of in-need individuals designed to elicit sadness and guilt, as the quote with which we opened from Bono suggests: "(RED) is about doing what you enjoy and doing good at the same time." And (RED) is far from alone in this messaging, as slogans from many of the largest charitable organizations reflect these feel-good impulses. The American Red Cross tells prospective blood donors that "The need is constant. The gratification is instant." CARE asks donors to "Help us empower women around the world" with the slogan "I am powerful" applying to both donors and recipients. Susan G. Komen for the Cure asks each donor, "Are you inspired to save a life?" Enjoyment, instant gratification, empowerment, inspiration—all of these sentiments offer powerful emotional incentives for people to donate.

At the same time, however, any social scientist knows the possible costs of tampering with behaviors that arise from intrinsic motivations, as ironic effects often stem from incentivizing such behaviors. In an early demonstration, Lepper, Greene, and Nisbett (1973) showed that rewarding children for their performance— "overjustifying" their interest—undermined those children's intrinsic motivation to do well. Relatedly, Titmuss (1970) argued that paying for blood donation would undermine the social utility of the act. More generally, "crowding out" intrinsic motivation through external incentives (see Frey & Jegen, 2001) carries the risk that incentivizing behaviors that are socially motivated may move those behaviors from the social realm into the economic realm, with sometimes unexpected— and detrimental—results. Indeed, presenting people whose charitable behavior is motivated by altruistic impulses with self-interested appeals can be alienating (Nelson, Brunel, Supphellen, & Manchanda, 2006).

What happens when social behaviors, like helping others, move into the economic realm? In one compelling demonstration, Gneezy and Rustichini (2000a) documented the ironic outcome that emerged when the owners of a childcare center instituted fines for parents who were late to pick up their children. Lateness actually *increased* when fines were instituted; while most parents had made a good-faith effort to arrive on time when not doing so was rude to the owners of the center, the institution of fines made showing up late an economic matter, with parents simply calculating the costs and benefits of tardiness. Most troubling, when the owners discontinued the fines, parents did not revert to their earlier behavior, suggesting that when social markets are made economic, it may be difficult to change them back. The impact of switching from social to economic markets helps to explain some curious results in which people work harder for no money than for low pay (Gneezy & Rustichini, 2000b). People are willing to engage in effort such as helping others or doing favors for them for social reasons; once money is introduced, however, people engage in cost-benefit analysis, and small amounts of money are not sufficient to incentivize them to do the work they were willing to do for free for more altruistic reasons. Moreover, mixed markets, where both social and economic incentives are present, look like economic markets, as though the mere whiff of monetary incentives corrupts social motivations (Heyman & Ariely, 2004).

How might these dynamics play out specifically in the domain of charitable giving? While researchers have only recently devoted attention to this issue, early results suggest that mixing economic incentives with social incentives may have similar effects as in other domains. At a general level, the mere thought of money undermines people's motivation to engage in prosocial behavior (Vohs, Mead, & Goode, 2006), and several investigations have demonstrated the negative impact of mixing incentives with charitable giving. For example, Falk (2007) examined the impact of sending gifts to possible donors on their frequency and amount of donation. Small gifts increased donations by 17% and large gifts by 75%, but people who received large gifts were more likely to donate smaller amounts, while those who received no gift were most likely to donate large amounts; while only suggestive, these results imply that receiving gifts may crowd out some inherent motivation to give. Two investigations that explored the impact of matching donations, in which an employer or other agency matches the amount of one's donation to some charity, showed that matching did increase people's likelihood of contributing (Karlan & List, 2007; Meier, 2007). Importantly, however, Meier (2007) showed that while initial contribution rates increased, contribution rates actually declined after the matching offer ended, leading to a net loss in giving. Again, these results suggest that providing people with external incentives to give—a matching donation or a gift—may undermine some of their intrinsic interest in giving in the longer term.

But does advertising the mood benefits of charitable acts alter the reasons and outcomes of donating? Specifically, we wondered whether the effects we demonstrated in Dunn et al. (2008) might be undermined by adding external incentives to people's reason for giving. In short, we asked two related questions: If people are aware that giving to others makes them happier, will they (a) give more money and (b) will this incentive undermine the happiness they receive from giving to others? In an initial test of this question, we asked a sample of over 1,000 readers of the *New York Times*, who had just read about our research demonstrating the link between giving and happiness, to answer questions about their personal and prosocial spending and their well-being. Compared to our other studies, respondents reported spending a relatively large amount on others (some 40% of their spending). While this difference could be due to the sample (this was a much wealthier sample than would be typical, as approximately half the respondents reported earning $85,000+), an intriguing possibility—and one that deserves further investigation—is that people who read the article may have been spurred to devote more of their money to others versus themselves.

Most importantly, our basic effect was replicated: respondents who reported having spent more so far that day on others reported greater happiness, whereas there was no relationship between spending on oneself and happiness. Thus, the beneficial effects of giving still emerged, suggesting that becoming aware of the emotional benefits of prosocial spending did not undermine its impact on happiness. Because we could not follow up with these individuals, however, we do not know if this momentary increase in charitable behavior would sustain over time, or—as with increases in donations when matching funds are available—self-interested giving might crowd out intrinsic motivation and decrease subsequent giving.

CONCLUSION

In this chapter, we explored whether organizations that seek to increase charitable giving by advertising the benefits of giving are (1) making claims supported by empirical research and most importantly (2) wise to make such claims. To the first point, the evidence we reviewed is quite supportive: happier people give more and giving makes people happier, such that happiness and giving may operate in a positive feedback loop (with happier people giving more, getting happier, and giving even more). To the second point, however, the evidence is less clear. At minimum, charitable organizations should be concerned about the possibility of crowding out their donors' proclivity to donate in the longer term by incentivizing them (via gifts, etc.) in the short term. While offering donors monetary or material incentives for giving may undermine generosity in the long term, our preliminary research suggests that advertising the emotional benefits of prosocial behavior may leave these benefits intact and might even encourage individuals to give more. Future research, both laboratory and field studies, is needed to disentangle the possible costs and benefits of self-interested giving.

REFERENCES

Abdel-Khalek, A. M. (2006). Measuring happiness with a single-item scale. *Social Behavior and Personality*, *34*, 139–150.

Aderman, D. (1972). Elation, depression, and helping behavior. *Journal of Personality and Social Psychology*, *24*, 91–101.

Aharon, I., Etcoff, N., Ariely, D., Chabris, C. F., O'Connor. E., & Breiter, H. C. (2001). Beautiful faces have variable reward value: fMRI and behavioral evidence. *Neuron, 32*, 537–551.

Andreoni, J. (1989). Giving with impure altruism: Application to charity and Ricardian equivalence. *The Journal of Political Economy, 97*, 1447–1458.

Andreoni, J. (1990). Impure altruism and donations to public goods—a theory of warm glow giving. *Economic Journal, 100*, 464–477.

Batson, C. D. (1987). Prosocial motivation: Is it ever truly altruistic? In L. Berkowitz (Ed.), *Advances in experimental social psychology* (Vol. 20, pp. 65–122). New York: Academic Press.

Batson, C. D. (1991). *The altruism question: Toward a social-psychological answer.* Hillsdale, NJ: Erlbaum Associates.

Becker, G. S. (1974). Theory of social interaction. *Journal of Political Economy, 82*, 1064–1093.

Cialdini, R. B., Schaller, M., Houlihan, D., Arps, K., Fultz, J., & Beaman, A. L. (1987). Empathy-based helping: Is it selflessly or selfishly motivated? *Journal of Personality and Social Psychology, 52*, 749–759.

Clotfelter, C. T. (1985). *Federal tax policy and charitable giving.* Chicago: University of Chicago Press (for National Bureau of Economic Research).

Clotfelter, C. T. (1997). The economics of giving. In J. W. Barry & B. V. Manno (Eds.), *Giving better, giving smarter* (pp. 31–55). Washington, DC: National Commission on Philanthropy and Civic Renewal.

Dunn, E. W., Aknin, L. B., & Norton, M. I. (2008). Spending money on others promotes happiness. *Science, 319*, 1687–1688.

Elliott, R., Friston, K. J., & Dolan, R. J. (2000). Dissociable neural responses in human reward systems. *The Journal of Neuroscience, 20*, 6159–6165.

Falk, A. (2007). Gift exchange in the field. *Econometrica, 75*, 1501–1511.

Field, T. M., Hernandez-Reif, M., Quintino, O., Schanberg, S., & Kuhn, C. (1998). Elder retired volunteers benefit from giving massage therapy to infants. *Journal of Applied Gerontology, 17*, 229–239.

Forgas, J.P., Dunn, E., & Granland, S. (2008). Are you being served …? An unobtrusive experiment of affective influences on helping in a department store. *European Journal of Social Psychology, 38*, 333–342.

Frey, B. S., & Jegen, R. (2001). Motivation crowding theory: A survey of empirical evidence. *Journal of Economic Surveys, 15*, 589–611.

Glazer, A., & Konrad, K. A. (1996). A signaling explanation for charity. *American Economic Review, 86*, 1019–1028.

Gneezy, U., & Rustichini, A. (2000a). A fine is a price. *Journal of Legal Studies, 29*, 1–18.

Gneezy, U., & Rustichini, A. (2000b). Pay enough or don't pay at all. *Quarterly Journal of Economics, 115*, 791–810.

Griskevicius, V., Tybur, J. M., Sundie, J. M., Cialdini, R. B., Miller, G. F., & Kenrick, D. T. (2007). Blatant benevolence and conspicuous consumption: When romantic motives elicit strategic costly signals. *Journal of Personality and Social Psychology, 93*, 85–102.

Harbaugh, W. T., Myer, U., & Burghart, D. R. (2007). Neural responses to taxation and voluntary giving reveal motives for charitable donations. *Science, 316*, 1622–1625.

Harris, M. B., & Huang, L. C. (1973). Helping and the attribution process. *Journal of Social Psychology, 90*, 291–297.

Heyman, J., & Ariely, D. (2004). Effort for payment: A tale of two markets. *Psychological Science, 15*, 787–793.

Isen, A. M. (1970). Success, failure, attention and reaction to others: The warm glow of success. *Journal of Personality and Social Psychology, 15*, 294–301.

Isen, A. M., Horn, N., & Rosenhan, D. L. (1997). Effects of success and failure on children's generosity. *Journal of Personality and Social Psychology, 27,* 239–247.

Isen, A. M., & Levin, P. F. (1972). The effect of feeling good on helping: Cookies and kindness. *Journal of Personality and Social Psychology, 21,* 384–388.

Karlan, D., & List, J. A. (2007). Does price matter in charitable giving? Evidence from a large-scale natural field experiment. *American Economic Review, 97,* 1774–1793.

Kazdin, A. E., & Bryan, J. H. (1971). Competence and volunteering. *Journal of Experimental Social Psychology, 7,* 87–97.

Konow, J., & Earley, J. (2008). The hedonistic paradox: Is homo economicus happier? *Journal of Public Economics, 92,* 1–33.

Lepper, M. R., Greene, D., & Nisbett, R. E. (1973). Undermining children's intrinsic interest with extrinsic reward. *Journal of Personality and Social Psychology, 28,* 129–37.

Lyubomirsky, S., Tkach, C., & Sheldon, K. M. (2004). *Pursuing sustained happiness through random acts of kindness and counting one's blessings: Tests of two six-week interventions.* Unpublished data, Department of Psychology, University of California, Riverside.

Meier, S. (2007). *Do subsidies increase charitable giving in the long-run? Matching donations in a field experiment.* Working paper, Boston Federation.

Meier, S., & Stutzer, A. (2008). Is volunteering rewarding in itself? *Economica, 75,* 39–59.

Nelson, M. R., Brunel, F. F. Supphellen, M., & Manchanda, R. J. (2006). Effects of culture, gender, and moral obligations on responses to charity advertising across masculine and feminine cultures. *Journal of Consumer Psychology, 16,* 45–56.

Piliavin, J. A. (2003). Doing well by doing good: Benefits for the benefactor. In M. Keyes & J. Haidt (Eds.), *Flourishing: Positive psychology and the life well lived* (pp. 227–247). Washington, DC: American Psychological Association.

Reece, W. S., & Zieschang, K. D. (1985). Consistent estimation of the impact of tax deductibility on the level of charitable contributions. *Econometrica, 53,* 271–293.

Rosenhan, D. L., Underwood, B., & Moore, B. (1974). Affect moderates self-gratification and altruism. *Journal of Personality and Social Psychology, 30,* 546–52.

Small, D. A., & Verrochi, N. M. (2009). The face of need: Facial emotion expression on charity advertisements. *Journal of Marketing Research, 46,* 777–787.

Thoits, P. A., & Hewitt, L. N. (2001). Volunteer work and well-being. *Journal of Health and Social Behavior, 42,* 115–131.

Titmuss, R. (1970). *The gift relationship: From human blood to social policy.* London: Allen & Unwin.

Vartanian, O., & Goel, V. (2004). Neuroanatomical correlates of aesthetic preferences for paintings. *NeuroReport, 15,* 893–897.

Vohs, K. D., Mead, N. L., & Goode, M. R. (2006). The psychological consequences of money. *Science, 314,* 1154–1156.

Wang, L., & Graddy, E. (2008). Social capital, volunteering, and charitable giving. *Voluntas, 19,* 23–42.

Williams, S., & Shiaw, W. T. (1999). Mood and organizational citizenship behavior: The effects of positive affect on employee organizational citizenship behavior intentions. *Journal of Psychology, 133,* 656–668.

2

A Model of the Value of Giving to Others Compared to the Value of Having More for Oneself

Implications for Fundraisers Seeking to Maximize Donor Satisfaction

MICHAL ANN STRAHILEVITZ

How selfish soever man be supposed, there are evidently some principles in his nature, which interest him in the fortune of others, and render their happiness necessary to him, though he derives nothing from it, except the pleasure of seeing it.

—**Adam Smith**, *The Theory of Moral Sentiments* (1869)

It's a wonderful feeling to know that today many people are alive and some of them married and have their children, and that their children will have children because I did have the courage and the strength.

—**Irene Gut Opdyke,** a Polish gentile woman who was honored by Yad Va Shem for risking her own life to rescue Jews in Nazi Europe (cited in Monroe, Barton, and Klingmann, 1990)

We are the ones who make a brighter day, so let's start giving. There's a choice we're making. We're saving our own lives. It's true we'll make a brighter day, just you and me.

—Chorus from the song "We are the World" by **Michael Jackson** and **Lionel Richie (1985)**

15

INTRODUCTION

As the quotes on the prior page illustrate, scholars, heroes, and artists have all talked about the ways that giving to others help the giver. Every day, people find themselves faced with the choice between keeping resources for themselves and applying those resources to the aid of others. Yet not enough is known regarding how charitable behavior differs from the opposing force of wanting to have more for oneself. This chapter begins to address these issues.

I begin with a brief review of some of the literature on the many benefits that charitable giving offers to donors. Next, a model is proposed that compares the value that donors obtain from giving to a worthy cause to the value of having more resources for themselves. The model is based on the prospect theory value function introduced by Kahneman and Tversky (1979) but includes a second value function for helping others. The chapter focuses on three characteristics of this model and supports them with a series of simple studies that examine the differences and similarities between the value that consumers derive from making contributions to charity and the value they derive from having more wealth. Based on each of the characteristics of the model described, recommendations are offered for fundraisers interested in maximizing the value donors obtain from giving.

UNDERSTANDING CHARITABLE GIVING AND OTHER ACTS OF ALTRUISM

Those who choose to make sacrifices for the benefit of others must derive value from doing so; otherwise, it would not happen. People can pay for this "value" in a variety of ways, including: donating money, contributing their time, giving blood, going through painful bone marrow extraction procedures, and even risking their own lives to rescue others in need. One form of altruistic behavior that is especially interesting to economists is the act of consumers voluntarily giving up wealth to help strangers, without being promised anything in return. Such expenditures can occur in the context of donations supporting a cause that does not directly affect the donor, or donors may agree to help pay for a public good, such as a park, that will be consumed not only by them, but also by the community at large. Although this chapter focuses on financial contributions, to understand what motivates donations to charity, it is worthwhile to review prior research on the motivations for a wide range of altruistic behaviors.

Acts of altruism have been observed throughout history in a wide variety of cultures, among males and females, children and adults, the wealthy and the needy. Why altruism continues to exist in so many forms and in so many cultures has been a topic of scholarly debate throughout the ages. The phenomenon is especially puzzling to economists. If people are all selfish utility maximizers, why should they make sacrifices for others?

Several explanations have been proposed to as to why altruism exists. These include an aspiration to "do the right thing" (Dawes & Thaler, 1988), a quest for moral satisfaction (Kahneman & Knetsch, 1992), a need to view oneself as compassionate and kind (Walster, Berschield, & Walster, 1973; Schlenker, 1980) and the desire to experience a "warm glow" (Andreoni 1990). What these explanations have in common is the underlying assumption that helping others leads to positive emotions such as warmth and happiness, while refusing to do so can lead to negative emotions, such as sadness and guilt (Harvey and Enzle, 1981). Beyond short-term emotions, giving has several long-term benefits as well. Since most individuals like to think of themselves as kindhearted, they experience happiness and an enhanced self- image when they help others. In contrast, selfish or unkind acts can harm one's self-image, thus reducing self-esteem (Walster, Berschield, & Walster 1973; Schlenker, 1980). The emotional impact of changes in self-esteem can affect one's long-term happiness and sense of well-being.

Just as many forms of consumption involve paying a price; in most cases, there is a sacrifice involved in acts of helping others. Cialdini, Darby, and Vincent (1973) point out that the mere fact that one is helping others often causes an otherwise painful sacrifice to feel like an overall hedonically pleasant experience. Many nonprofits appear to be aware of this. A long-running slogan used by the Red Cross illustrates this well—"Feel good. Give blood." Obviously, if all people were purely selfish utility maximizers, the notion that giving blood feels good would be absurd. Yet giving does feel good to those who do it, in part because helping others allows the donors to see themselves as unselfish. In addition to encouraging individuals to contribute blood, the tactic of suggesting a connection between altruism and happiness has been used to encourage financial contributions as well. This is illustrated in a slogan used by the New York Philanthropic Advisory Service of the Better Business Bureau that reads, "Give a gift to charity and make a lot of people happy, including yourself." The basic notion is that helping others can make the givers as well as the recipients feel good.

It is important to note that donors are unlikely to consciously rationalize that giving will improve their self-esteem or make them feel happier. Furthermore, emotions are not the only factor that influences giving. Loewenstein and Small (2007) have pointed out that the choice to give can be affected by both deliberate thought and emotional reactivity. Also, beyond emotional or rational concerns for the welfare of others, some seemingly charitable behavior can have calculated benefits such as gaining approval or esteem from others, improving one's status, or even furthering one's career objectives. In the extreme (e.g., when buildings or schools are named in honor of benefactors), charitable giving can turn into a form of conspicuous consumption offering status, recognition, and possibly opportunities for professional or political advancement for its donors. Still, even these more selfish sides to giving are sought in the pursuit of happiness.

Even in the absence of recognition and status, Dawes and Thaler (1988) have argued that seemingly "altruistic" acts are actually motivated by selfish considerations associated with wanting the positive feelings brought on by being "good" and avoiding the negative feelings associated with being "bad." Regardless of whether individuals give to experience a warm glow (pleasure), feel better about themselves (improve self-image), evade feelings of guilt (pain), or avoid feeling bad about themselves (hurting self-image), it is clear that giving often involves emotional benefits to donors. In the context of consumer behavior, donors can be viewed as consumers seeking the many benefits of giving. This suggests that one way of viewing a choice between donating to others and having more for oneself is to view this as a trade-off between the pleasure and pain associated with each option.

There are several potential applications for research on altruism in general and research on charitable giving in particular. From a fundraiser's perspective, it would be useful to gain insights into strategies for increasing overall donations to their charity. One way to do this is to maximize the value consumers derive from making contributions. In order to truly understand how to maximize the value donors derive from giving, it is helpful to think about how the benefits of giving are both similar to and different from the benefits of having more for ourselves.

COMPARING THE VALUE OF GIVING
TO THE VALUE OF RECEIVING

People obviously derive value from both giving to the needy and acquiring more goods or wealth for themselves. Otherwise, they would not be willing to invest resources in either. Both contributing to charity and receiving more resources or goods for oneself generally involve giving something up (e.g., money, labor, time and/or effort). If we assume that people are value maximizers, then both the decision to acquire something and the decision to make a donation should be based on comparing the cost of the transaction to the positive value to be gained from it.

In this section, a model is developed that examines the differences and similarities between the value that people derive from giving to others and the value they derive from receiving something for themselves. The model described is based on the prospect theory value function proposed by Kahneman and Tversky (1979). Prospect theory proposes that people's decisions are based on how they value the potential gains and losses that result from making decisions. The theory is based on the individual's *value function*. The value function may be thought of as a psychophysical function reflecting the anticipation of pleasure or pain associated with a specific decision outcome. This function has several important properties, each consistent with the preferences that people express when asked to choose between multiple alternatives.

These three properties are:

1. The value function is defined in terms of gains and losses from some natural reference point.
2. The value function is concave for gains and convex for losses (i.e., $v''(x) < 0$, $x > 0$: $v''(x) > 0$, $x < 0$).
3. The value function is steeper for losses than it is for gains (i.e., $v(x) < -v(-x)$). This suggests that the pain of losing x is greater than the pain of not having x to begin with. As Kahneman and Tversky phrase it, "losses loom larger than gains."

These three properties have been supported by a variety of lab experiments (Kahneman & Tversky, 1979; Thaler, 1985; Thaler & Johnson, 1990). However, previous studies of "gains" and "losses" have involved receiving and losing wealth.

However, receiving goods or wealth for oneself is not the only positive outcome of value to individuals. As noted earlier, there are also many benefits that an individual can derive from helping others. Therefore, unlike the prospect theory value function, the model introduced in this chapter includes two value functions. As illustrated in Figure 2.1, the *v(rx)* curve is the original Kahneman and Tversky value function, which characterizes the value individuals derive from changes in personal wealth. This is referred to as the *value function for receiving*. The second value function, introduced here for the first time, characterizes the value that individuals derive from giving to others, *v(gx)*. This is referred to as the *value function for giving*.

The proposed model is based on the notion that the act of giving can be viewed as a positive outcome that is of value to the giver. The model acknowledges that the value derived from giving to others is different from the value derived from acquiring things for oneself. It is for this reason that there are two separate value functions in the proposed model. As shown in Figure 2.1, the function that characterizes the value derived from giving *v(gx)* is similar but not identical to the function that characterizes the value derived from receiving *v(rx)*.

The remainder of this chapter focuses on the positive side of giving *v(gx)* and receiving *v(rx)*, which are depicted in the top right-hand corner of the model in Figure 2.1. The lower left-hand corner of this model characterizes the negative outcomes of losing one's own wealth *v(−rx)* and taking from a worthy cause *v(−gx)*. Research examining the negative value of taking from charity (undoing a donation)

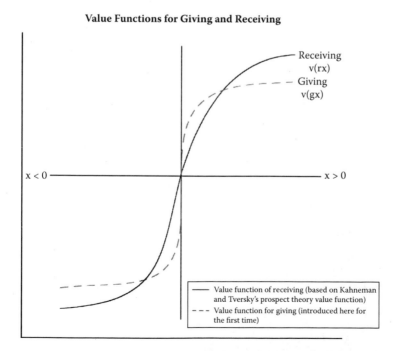

Value Functions for Giving and Receiving

Receiving
v(rx)
Giving
v(gx)

x < 0

x > 0

——— Value function of receiving (based on Kahneman and Tversky's prospect theory value function)

– – – Value function for giving (introduced here for the first time)

Figure 2.1   Value functions for giving and receiving.

and losing one's wealth are not covered here, but rather discussed elsewhere (Strahilevitz, 2008).

Three important characteristics of the positive value of giving and receiving are reviewed:

1. **Shape:** Both the giving and receiving functions are concave, suggesting diminishing marginal value to giving as well as to receiving.
2. **Separateness:** The value function for giving and the value function for receiving are distinct such that neither is a substitute for the other.
3. **Slope:** The value function for receiving is steeper than the value function for giving. This means that the relative appeal of giving to charity rather than having those same resources for oneself is greater for small amounts than for large amounts.

A VALUE FUNCTION FOR GIVING AND RECEIVING

The Shape Characteristic

Both the giving and receiving functions are concave for gains. In other words, there is positive but diminishing marginal value to both giving and receiving.

Diminishing marginal value for receiving implies that the more we receive, the less marginal value there will be to receiving one more unit. Similarly, diminishing marginal value to giving suggests that, holding all else constant, the more we give, the less marginal value there will be to giving one more unit.° The concavity for positive outcomes for both the giving function, $v(gx)$, and the receiving function, $v(rx)$, are illustrated in the top right-hand corner of Figure 2.1. Together, these capture the basic psychophysics of quantity and imply that diminishing marginal value is characteristic of both receiving and giving.[†]

As mentioned earlier, the receiving function $v(rx)$ in the proposed model is identical to the value function from Kahneman and Tversky's prospect theory (1979). The concavity of this value function for gains has been supported by extensive

---

° It is important to note that this is a theoretical model discussing averages. There may be special cases where this does not hold. Most notably, if a donor has a threshold below which he or she thinks a donation is insignificant, then marginal value may increase as one approaches that threshold amount. There also may be special recognition given by a charity for donations at a particular level of giving. Either of these could possibly lead to an increasing marginal value as one approaches the threshold donation magnitude.

† Donations to charity involve two components: (1) losing money (pain) and (2) knowing you have contributed to a good cause (pleasure). Similarly, most cases where we acquire goods or amass additional wealth involve two components: (1) losing money or sacrificing leisure time (pain) and (2) acquiring more for oneself (pleasure). In the current research, a distinction is drawn between the positive values of giving and acquiring, (i.e., the pleasure derived from contributing to a good cause or receiving more for ourselves), rather than the net value of giving and acquiring (i.e., the pleasure of the contribution or acquisition minus the pain of the sacrificed wealth or effort). Thus, the proposed model compares the pure value of giving to the pure value of acquiring, holding the cost (be it effort or money) constant. The negative (loss and take) sides of the model, illustrated in the bottom left-hand corner of the functions, are not covered here.

research (Kahneman & Tversky, 1979, Thaler, 1985, Thaler & Johnson, 1990). What has not been examined is the concavity of the value function for giving. If we accept the notion that the act of giving has value attached to it, then it follows that the same phenomenon that occurs with positive outcomes that involve the value of receiving should occur with positive outcomes that involve the value of giving.

To test the prediction that the value function for giving is concave for $x > 0$, a short study was carried out involving 123 undergraduates at a major American university. The students were asked two questions that directly tested the concavity of the value function for giving. With these two questions, the order of the options listed for each of the two questions was counterbalanced so that each option was listed first in half the cases and second in the other half of the questionnaires. The first question read, "In which of the following cases would the difference be greater: the difference in how good you would feel about raising $5 for your favorite charity as opposed to not raising any money for that charity, or the difference in how good you would feel about raising $30 for your favorite charity as opposed to raising $25 for that same charity?" The word *difference* was underlined to reduce the chance that subjects would misread the question. Concavity would predict that more study participants would choose the first option, and indeed, 92.7% of them indicated that the difference in feeling good that they would experience going from contributing nothing to contributing $5 would be greater than the difference going from contributing $25 to contributing $30. Similarly, when asked if they would feel a greater increase in positive emotions going from a donation of $5 to a donation of $10 than they would going from a donation of $490 to a donation of $495 (again with the word *difference* underlined and the order of the two options counterbalanced), 89.4% of the participants indicated that the jump from $5 to $10 would lead to a greater increase in positive emotions. The responses to these two questions support the proposition that the value function for contributing money to a good cause is concave and thus subject to the law of diminishing marginal value.

Based on the shape of Kahneman and Tversky's value function, Thaler (1985) developed a framework describing how consumers code multiple gains and losses. Most relevant to the current research are the findings suggesting that for instances in which multiple outcomes consist of two gains, separating these two positive outcomes in time creates more happiness or value than having them happen together. In other words, if x and y are both gains, then segregation of those gains leads to greater utility than does integration (i.e., $x > 0$ and $y > 0$, then $v(x) + v(y) > v(x + y)$). In the new model proposed here, this would translate to: for $x > 0$ and $y > 0$, then $v(rx) + v(ry) > v(r(x + y))$. In other words, since the value of receiving is concave for gains, one will experience more happiness if two gains occur separately than together. This prediction for gains (involving receiving) was supported by Thaler's experiments (1985).

If the value of giving is also concave, then it follows that the good feelings of making two separate contributions will be greater than the value of giving the same total amount all at once. In equation form, this implies that, in the absence of transaction costs, the emotional benefits of giving the amount $(x + y)$ will be maximized by encouraging the mental segregation of the contributions. This suggests that if we allow $v(gx + gy)$ to denote the value we derive from giving x and y at the same time, and $v(gx) + v(gy)$ to denote the value we derive from giving x and y on separate occasions, then for all $x > 0$ and $y > 0$: $v(gx) + v(gy) > v(gx + gy)$.

A second study involving 104 undergraduate student participants from an American university was carried out to test if, as predicted by the proposed model, the separation of contribution experiences over time would lead to more happiness than contributing the total amount all at once. To control for order effects, the order in which the options were listed was varied so that each option appeared first in 1/3 of the conditions, second in 1/3 of the conditions, and last in 1/3 of the conditions. Participants in this study were first asked to indicate if they would prefer to raise money for the World Wildlife Fund, the March of Dimes, or the United Way.° Next, they were asked to imagine working as volunteers at a phone-a-thon to raise money for their chosen charity. Specifically, the scenario called for them to spend two hours a day for two days working the phone lines to raise money for their chosen cause. They were also told to imagine that they had worked very hard for the entire two-hour shift on each of the two days they had volunteered. They were then asked to indicate which of three options would make them happier, given their completion of all four of their assigned hours of volunteer work. The options included: (a) raising $100 for your chosen charity on the first day and another $100 on the second day, for a total of $200; (b) raising nothing for your chosen charity on the first day and $200 on the second day, for a total of $200; (c) raising $200 for your chosen charity on the first day and nothing on the second day, for a total of $200.

Of the 104 participants in this study, 73.1% preferred to raise $100 on two different days. Only 16.3% preferred to raise all the money the second day. Finally, a mere 10.6% preferred to have raised all the money on the first day. In short, separation was preferred by the vast majority of the study participants. The second question in this survey asked them to imagine they had won $120 in a raffle and had decided to give all of it to their favorite charity using a debit card linked to their checking account. They were asked if they would prefer using their debit card to give the $120 (a) all at once, immediately, (b) all at once, in exactly one year, or (c) over the next 12 months, in increments of $10 a month. It was made clear that the scheduled deductions would happen without their needing to take any additional actions and that the total cost would be $120 regardless of which option they selected. Surprisingly, 29.8% of the participants wanted to give the money away at the start of the year. Also surprisingly, given that these were all business students, only 8.7% of the participants wanted to hold onto the money and contribute it at the end of the year (this would have been the wisest option if you consider present value). Finally, 61.5% wanted the deduction spread out over the 12 months. In short, separation of contributions over time was preferred by the majority of study participants in both of the questions.

° Having the study participants choose a charity was done to make the charity more relevant to them. A list of three was given because in a pretest without a list, many participants had trouble coming up with an actual charity. The list of charities was chosen based on a survey asking another group of students to rate their familiarity with ten charities. The three charities with the highest familiarity scores were used in the final study.

Of course, if separation did not affect overall happiness and present value did not matter, all these options should have been equally appealing. However, if present value were factored in, then in the second question, the option where all the contribution was donated at the start would be best for the charity, and the option where the money would all be donated at the end of the year would be best for the students. Still, both in the contexts of fundraising (no financial cost) and donation (financial cost of $120), the majority of our study participants preferred to have their donations separated over time.° These results parallel those obtained in prior research (Gourville, 1998).

Clearly, there are implications for fundraisers. Scholars have noted that in the absence of some method of legitimizing paltry donations, many potential donors who cannot afford to make large donations may shy away from making small contributions for fear of appearing cheap (Brockner et al., 1984; Cialdini, & Schroeder, 1976; Reingen, 1978). The two studies described here suggest that allowing donors to make small contributions over time, rather than one large donation all at once, may not only help legitimize paltry donations, it may also help them to feel more happiness as the result of their contribution. While many charities offer the option of signing up for a series of multiple small donations over the course of a year, there are many charities that do not offer this option. The concavity of the value function suggests that more charities could benefit from allowing potential donors to precommit to making multiple small contributions over time.

The Separateness Characteristic

Giving and receiving offer two separate and distinct types of value, such that the value of giving and the value of receiving are not substitutes for one another. Therefore, the giving and receiving functions take the form of two separate curves.

As mentioned earlier, the concavity of both giving and receiving implies that the more we receive, the less marginal value there will be to receiving one more unit, and that the more we give, the less marginal value there will be to giving one more unit. This leads to the question, what happens when an opportunity to receive is combined with an opportunity to give? If giving and receiving are in fact separate and distinct types of value that cannot substitute for one another, this suggests that for multiple positive outcomes that involve both giving to a good cause and acquiring more for oneself, the whole will not have less value than the sum of its parts. Specifically, diminishing marginal value should not hold when one is discussing the marginal value that giving will add to receiving or the marginal value that receiving will add to giving. More formally, the model predicts that for positive experiences that combine giving with receiving, it will not be the case that the more one receives, the less marginal value there will be to giving

---

° Thaler's 1985 article also suggested that financial losses should be integrated (or combined) rather than segregated (or separated). This means that if donations are seen as a loss, most consumers would prefer integration. The results of the second question suggest that donors do not experience contributions to charity as losses. Indeed, the preferences observed suggest that donations are in fact more analogous to purchasing the good feelings associated with helping others.

to a good cause, nor that the more one gives to a good cause, the less marginal value there will be to acquiring something for oneself. This is operationalized in the model by making the value of giving and the value of receiving two separate functions.

To illustrate, helping a needy child and winning the lottery would both make a person feel good. However, having one would not reduce the ability to feel good about the other. A far more impactful example is the quotation from the Holocaust hero that is cited at the start this chapter. Irene, the gentile woman who risked her life to save Jews, describes the "wonderful feeling" that she experiences knowing the tremendous positive impact her actions have had on the lives of so many others. The specific "wonderful feeling" she describes would be impossible to replicate by any sort of material gains in wealth. In effect, receiving and giving to others can both make us happy, but neither is a substitute for the other.

Beyond anecdotes, there is also theoretical support that combining distinct types of value is more beneficial than combining similar types of value. Prior research suggests that humans have a limited ability to appreciate multiple pleasant outcomes that are similar in nature when they occur at the same time (Linville & Fischer, 1991). Although Linville and Fischer (1991) did not examine pleasant outcomes that offer the warm glow of giving, they did examine people's preferences for combining multiple positive outcomes from different domains (i.e., social, career, and financial). The results of their work suggest that in the case of two pleasant outcomes from different domains (e.g., a social triumph and a financial gain), individuals tend to prefer that the two events occur on the same day as opposed to having them occur on two different days. In contrast, with two positive outcomes from the same domain (e.g., receiving an unexpected holiday bonus in your paycheck, finding $20 cash in the street) most individuals preferred that the positive experiences be separated. Their results suggest that "gain-savoring resources," a term they use to describe an ability to fully appreciate and enjoy pleasant events, may be limited for each specific type of pleasurable outcome being experienced. They conclude that more happiness is derived from bundling diverse pleasant experiences together than from bundling similar positive experiences together. Applied to our model, this suggests that combining the positive experiences of receiving something for oneself and helping others may lead to more value than bundling receiving something for oneself with receiving more for oneself or giving to others with giving more to others. In equation form:

$$v(gx + ry) - v(ry) > v(gx + gy) - v(gy)$$

and

$$v(rx + gy) - v(gy) > v(rx + ry) - v(ry).$$

In words, these equations imply that the value that giving x adds to receiving y will be greater than the value that giving x adds to giving y, and that the value that receiving x adds to giving y will be greater than the value that receiving x adds to receiving y.

To test if this is the case, an experiment was carried out with 108 undergraduates at a major American university. None of the students who had participated in the prior studies participated in this experiment. Subjects were randomly assigned to one of two conditions in a simple between-subjects design. The first condition involved choosing between a giving situation and a receiving situation, assuming you had just received a substantial amount of wealth. The second condition involved choosing between the same giving and receiving situation, assuming you had just made a substantial contribution to charity. Below is an example of one of the questions that were used:

Subjects in the first condition answered this question: "Which of the following pair of events would make you happier if they both happened on the same day?"

A. Raising a thousand dollars for your second-favorite charity and then raising $100 for your favorite charity.
B. Raising a thousand dollars for your second-favorite charity and then finding $50 in the street.

Subjects in the second condition answered this question: "Which of the following pair of events would make you happier if they both happened on the same day?"

A. Winning a thousand dollars in a raffle and then raising $100 for your favorite charity.
B. Winning a thousand dollars in a raffle and then finding $50 in the street.

The results supported the notion that giving and receiving are more powerful together than giving and giving or receiving and receiving. Specifically, 64.8% of the subjects preferred finding the money in the street after raising the money, while only 26.8% of the subjects preferred finding the money in the street after winning the lottery. This pattern was replicated in three additional questions involving combinations of giving and receiving. In all four cases, the warm glow of helping a good cause was less popular when paired with a contribution to charity than when paired with an increase in wealth. Similarly, receiving something was more popular after having contributed to a good cause than after having an increase in wealth. This supports the model's separate value functions for giving and receiving. It also suggests that mixing the good feelings of giving to others with the good feelings of gaining more for oneself can be a winning combination.

The separateness of the value functions for giving and receiving have important implications for nonprofits as well as businesses. For fundraisers, offering gifts to major donors may be one way to combine the good feelings of giving and receiving into one transaction. The model suggests that this tactic makes sense. However, fundraisers may wonder what type of gifts will make the most sense. Although not explored in the current model, prior research suggests that gifts or experiences that are pleasure oriented (as opposed to functional or practical) may add the most value to a charitable contribution (Strahilevitz & Myers, 1998; Strahilevitz, 1999).° The reason is that the emotions of guilt and happiness that are often elicited while consuming pleasurable products and experiences may complement the warm glow of giving in such a way that the combination creates more value than the individual components. This phenomenon is referred to as *affective complementarity*. Many charities already mix the joy of self-indulgent pleasure with large contributions to their cause. Lavish fundraising banquets and concerts are great examples of this.

Just as charities can offer gifts, marketers of products can also offer charity incentives. Cause-related marketing allows marketers to bundle the sale of their products with a donation to a specific charity. Using this tool, marketers can offer their customers the added value of knowing they are helping a good cause when they purchase their products. As our model suggests, there is great appeal in offering customers a chance to obtain the value of giving to a good cause and the value of acquiring a new product, all in one transaction. The increasing popularity of cause-related marketing offers fundraisers another potential source for raising money for their cause. By choosing the right partner and securing the right terms, nonprofits can help assure that the partnership will be a win-win for both parties (Harvey & Strahilevitz, 2009).

The Slope Characteristic

As mentioned earlier, one could view the act of donating a given amount to charity as an indication that for the giver, the value derived from giving that amount is greater than the value derived from keeping that same amount. This section explores the effect of the magnitude of x on the relative value of giving x as opposed to receiving x.

As Figure 2.1 illustrates, the receiving function has a steeper slope than the giving function. This indicates that the relationship between how good we feel about giving and how much we give is weaker than the relationship between how good we feel about receiving and how much we receive. One reason for this is that when individuals contribute to a charity, they rarely have an opportunity to personally experience the difference between the results of their giving a great deal and the results of their giving only a little. Individuals who acquire things or money for themselves, on the other hand, actually experience a difference based on magnitude when they consume (or spend) what they receive. To illustrate, a donor may feel more warm glow if she contributes $1,000 for charity than if she contributes $1 for charity. However, if she is not present to witness how this money is actually used to help people, then she will not be able to experience the magnitude of either

---

° The research cited focused on cause-related marketing, where donations are used by marketers to appeal to consumers, rather than on fundraising rewards (where gifts are given to large donors). Still, the results do suggest that the combination of pleasurable products and donations to charity is potentially a powerful one.

the large or the small contribution. In contrast, if a consumer earns $1,000 rather than $1 for herself, she is likely to experience pleasure when receiving the check and to experience additional enjoyment as the money is spent. As a result, the incremental value of receiving more is likely to be more vivid than the incremental value of giving more.

In terms of the model, this suggests that for $x > 0$, the slope for the receiving function $v(rx)$, will be steeper than the slope for the giving function, $v(gx)$. In other words, the relationship between how good we feel about receiving something for ourselves and how much we receive is stronger than the relationship between how good we feel about giving and how much we give. This would predict that if forced to choose between receiving money or having it donated to a charity, individuals will be more likely to donate with small amounts than with large amounts. In terms of the model, this means that $v(gx) - v(rx)$ decreases as x increases. In terms of human behavior, this predicts that the proportion of subjects who prefer donating x dollars to charity as opposed to keeping x dollars for themselves should decrease as the magnitude of x increases.

This prediction was supported by the results of a simple survey involving 154 undergraduates at a major American university. Each subject was given a question-naire consisting of eight questions. The first question was, "What is your favorite charity?" Each of the questions after that involved a choice between receiving a given amount and having that same amount donated to their favorite charity. The amounts ranged from one cent to $1,000. Although each subject received exactly the same questions, the order in which they were presented was varied so that each of the seven questions appeared first in 22 out of 154 of the question-naires. The choice shares for this questionnaire appear in Table 2.1. As expected, the proportion of subjects who preferred to have a penny donated to their favor-ite charity, as opposed to receiving a penny (92%), was greater than the propor-tion of subjects who preferred to have $1,000 donated to their favorite charity, as opposed to receiving $1,000 for themselves (0%). As predicted for the magnitudes in between a penny and $1,000, the greater the magnitude in question, the greater

TABLE 2.1   Willingness to Give as a Function of Amount

Specified Amount	Percentage of Subjects Who Preferred Donating Specified Amount to Favorite Charity Over Receiving That Amount in Cash[a]
$0.01	92.2%
$0.10	56.5%
$0.25	38.3%
$1.00	22.1%
$5.00	5.2%
$100.00	0.0%
$1,000.00	0.0%

[a] $N = 154$; Order of the choices varied, and all combinations were equally represented.

the proportion of respondents who chose to receive the money rather than have it donated to charity.

The results indicate a strong positive correlation between the amount of money in question and the percentage of study participants who preferred receiving the money over having it donated to their favorite charity. The observation that receiving was more likely to be preferred to giving for relatively large amounts than for relatively small amounts supports the proposed model's prediction that $v(gx) - v(rx)$ decreases as x increases.

There are several recommendations that these results suggest. First, the findings add further support to the idea that commitments to frequent small donations will be easier to solicit. However, the issue of slope also raises the question of whether it might be possible for fundraisers to strengthen the relationship between how much we give to their charity and how good we feel about giving.

Fundraisers who wish to increase the size of the average donation made by their current donor base may benefit from thinking about ways they can steepen the giving function of their target audience. This basically means increasing the correlation between how much donors give to a specific charity and how good they feel as a result. Understanding how giving and receiving differ actually suggests ways for steepening the value function for giving. Of course, offering special recognition or awards for large donors is one strategy, but this really only helps with certain threshold or target amounts. A more comprehensive approach takes into account that people may be more inclined to make larger donations in situations where they are able to witness the benefits to the recipients of aid. In a sense, this brings them closer to experiencing the positive incremental impact of making larger donations.

To illustrate, a volunteer in charge of distributing food to Sudanese children is likely to have a strong sense of the relationship between how much food is purchased and how many hungry children are fed. In contrast, the individual donors whose contributions have paid for that food may not have as clear of a sense of this. While charities cannot realistically bring all donors to the sight of the beneficiaries, it might be possible to bring the donors psychologically closer by giving them specific details on the impact their individual contributions have made.

Such a method has been utilized by many charities that help underprivileged children. Indeed, it has been common for such charities to give donors an opportunity to receive monthly updates on the children they are sponsoring. By using strategies such as having the benefited children write regular personal letters to their sponsors, many charities have succeeded in strengthening the connection between the magnitude of the donation and the good feelings the donors derive from their contributions. Such tactics can be used by other types of charities as well. For example, a charity that rescues animals might allow a donor to sponsor a specific puppy, or an organization that is trying to save the rain forests might allow you to sponsor a specific number of trees in a specific forest in Brazil. By making the connection between the donation magnitude and the subsequent impact more concrete, fundraisers may in fact be able make the value function associated with their charity steeper for the donor base they target.

While many charities use such methods, many still do not. The relative steepness of receiving over giving suggests that by communicating the results of contributions with the actual donors, fundraisers can in fact bring these donors closer to the fruits of their own contributions. This type of slope steepening could also be achieved by creating marketing communications that clarify what impact each added dollar will have.

Two real-world examples illustrate how fundraisers can accomplish this or fail to accomplish this via advertising. The first example has plenty of numbers, but is still abstract about what one's donation dollars will buy: "This holiday season, let no child, woman, or man feel the gnaw of hunger or the chill of homelessness. Help our network of 260 human service agencies assist more than 2 million New Yorkers of every age …" (placed by the Federation of Protestant Welfare Agencies). In contrast, here is an example of an appeal that is much more specific: "Give a Christmas Dinner to a Homeless Person … $15.70 helps 10 people, $31.40 cares for 20 people, $62.80 helps 40 people, $157 provides 100 meals— and more" (New York City Rescue Mission). At first glance, the latter message seems repetitious and perhaps targeted toward those who are not so good at math. However, more seriously, the second message gives potential donors a much clearer sense of what will happen as a result of their contributions, as well as how much more will happen if they give more. This illustrates how a concrete image can be created to convey how each additional dollar helps make a difference. Indeed, through appropriate messaging and imagery, marketing communications could help make giving to a specific charity a far more vivid experience, with a steeper value function.

GENERAL DISCUSSION

Donating to charity is a type of consumer behavior, and fundraisers can benefit from understanding factors that affect donor satisfaction. As outlined in the proposed model, giving and acquiring share some similarities but are also different. As discussed in this chapter, both the giving and receiving functions are concave in the positive domain. However, giving and receiving are not substitutes for one another. The emotions generated by each are not the same. Furthermore, those who contribute to a charity rarely have an opportunity to personally experience the difference that their donation will make. In contrast, when consumers obtain more for themselves, they are more easily able to experience acquisition as well as consumption. This is illustrated in the relative slope of giving and receiving. In this discussion section, I review the implications of the model presented here along with some general recommendations for viewing giving to charity as a consumption experience that offers value to donors. I also offer a few suggestions for possible extensions and directions for future research.

Summary of Implications

The three characteristics of the model of the value of giving and receiving introduced here each offered implications for fundraisers. The concavity of the giving function (for $x > 0$), referred to as the characteristic of *shape*, suggests that charities may end up increasing overall donations if they offer potential donors the opportunity to make regular smaller donations rather than one large donation at once. The *separateness* of the giving and receiving value functions, indicating one type of value cannot substitute for the other, also has important implications. This characteristic suggests that there are benefits to combining the value of helping a good cause with the value of receiving. The third characteristic of the model reviewed in this paper was *slope* (for $x > 0$). This had to do with the relationship between how much a donor gives and how good they feel about that donation. It was observed that the receiving function is steeper than the giving function. This characteristic adds further support to the notion that regular small donations may be easier to sell than large single-shot donations.

Perhaps more importantly, the relatively flatter curve for giving implies that there is much to be gained from thinking of ways to steepen the slope associated with the giving function for a specific charity. In simple terms, this would involve increasing the relationship between how much one gives and how good one feels about giving. This can be accomplished by helping the donors visualize how larger donations will lead to a greater positive impact on the cause being supported.

Marketers and fundraisers have many goals in common. For example, they share a desire to attract new customers/donors and retain existing ones. Yet there are key differences between giving and receiving that can make this a particularly large challenge for charities. When a consumer acquires a material good, such as a new MP3 player, this is just the first step in a long process. The consumer interacts with the MP3 player over a period of time and derives enjoyment anytime that he uses it. In contrast, often when a donor gives to charity, that act is the end of the experience. Yet more can be done to make giving a more vivid and rewarding experience. Some charities already offer extensive feedback and updates to donors, along with opportunities for greater involvement. Such activities allow the act of giving to become more like a long-term relationship than a stand-alone event. Whether they realize it or not, fundraisers who use such tools may be creating a steeper value function for giving to their organization.

POSSIBLE EXTENSIONS TO THE EXISTING MODEL

The Pain of Undoing a Donation

This chapter focused on the positive value of charitable giving. However, there are also negative emotions associated with not giving, and those emotions may be even stronger if one was initially "endowed" with a donation. Research suggests that taking away from a charity looms larger than not giving to that same charity (Strahilevitz, 2008). This phenomenon is referred to as *take-aversion*. Take-aversion has been observed both when individuals have a chance to turn a donation into cash for themselves and when they have a chance to switch funds from one charity to another. Guilt has been found to play a mediating role in aversion to undoing donations. Take-aversion further supports the development of charity contracts where donors sign long-term commitments to sponsor a specific unit of need. This fund-raising tool allows charities to play on the powerful negative emotions associated with undoing a commitment to a cause, which may lead donors to contribute a far greater total amount over time.

Combining Different Types of Value with Donations to Charity

The model described in this chapter clearly suggests that there are benefits to mixing two different kinds of value together in one transaction. Two types of value were compared in this chapter: giving and receiving. Yet there are many other types of activities that bring value to consumers. Winning a competition, achieving a goal, and getting in better physical shape can all create value. These types of value can also be combined with charitable giving. Indeed, in recent years, there has been a huge increase in the popularity and success of fundraising athletic events that include walking, running, biking, and swimming for a cause. Although there was no value function in the current model for athletic events, it is clear that such activities also offer value to participants (Olivola & Shafir, 2010; see also Olivola in this volume). This value includes pride, a sense of accomplishment, an increase in confidence, possible social aspects to training, as well as both the short- and long-term health benefits of physical exercise. Future research could examine the mixing of athletic events with charitable giving from a value maximizing perspective.

Giving Time vs. Giving Money

While the studies described in this paper compared the value of giving to the value of receiving money, time is also a scarce resource that can be used either for gaining more for oneself or in the service of others. In our current recession, donations are down, but volunteering is up (Bosman, 2009). How will this translate into long-term donor behavior? A clue comes from recent research examining the relationship between giving time and giving money. Specifically, work by Liu and Aaker (2008) reveals that first asking individuals to think about "how much time they would like to donate" to a charity (as opposed to "how much money they would like to donate") actually increases the amount of money that they ultimately donate to the charity. Their findings suggest that getting the donor base to volunteer time may be another way to steepen their value function for donating money to a cause. In a recession fueled by rising unemployment, it is intuitive that the shift will continue toward giving time rather than giving money. Liu and Aaker's work suggests that this short-term shift toward more volunteering may be especially beneficial in the long term because the experience of volunteering may lead to greater future engagement with and commitment to the causes being supported. As the economy improves, it is quite possible that volunteers of today may become the donors of tomorrow. Liu and Aaker's work suggests that it would be advantageous for charities to track the relationship between volunteering time and donating money in their donor-base over time. Future academic research can further examine the relationship between the value consumers derive from different ways of investing time and money in the pursuit of helping others as opposed to accumulating more wealth for themselves.

FINAL THOUGHTS

The fundraising climate in the United States is increasingly competitive. In recent years, there has been a growing awareness on the part of charities that smart marketing is just as relevant in fundraising as in the selling of products and services. Part of that smart marketing involves maximizing both the anticipated and experienced value donors derive from giving. This chapter began with a review of ample evidence that charitable giving can make donors feel good. Most fundraisers probably do not think of themselves as being in the business of selling happiness to donors but, to some extent, that may be part of the job. Just as marketers of products and services strive to satisfy their customers, fundraisers should strive to help donors to feel as good as possible about the contributions they make.

I have presented a model for the value functions of giving and receiving with several suggestions for maximizing the value donors derive from giving. However, the model proposed here is an aggregate one. Obviously, some people are more altruistic than others. Similarly, some have far greater financial resources, making it easier for them to make large contributions. Indeed, both the concavity of the receiving function, and the fact that the value of giving and the value of receiving cannot substitute for one another, suggest that if you are extremely wealthy, the marginal value to having more wealth may be small relative to the good feelings derived from giving more to causes they care about.

Beyond individual differences between donors, individual charities may have different curves for the value donors derive from contributing to them. For example, if donations at a certain level lead to having one's name on a wall, we might expect the curve to be steeper approaching that level and then relatively flatter after that. Fundraisers have much to gain from thinking about ways to improve their own value curve. After all, charities do not just need to persuade people to give their time or money rather than use these resources for some other purpose (e.g., acquisition of material things). They also must convince potential donors who wish to make a contribution to give to their specific charity rather than to another charity. By suggesting ways to maximize the value donors derive from the act of giving, it is my hope that the issues covered in this chapter will help charitable organizations in their fundraising efforts.

REFERENCES

Andreoni, J. (1990). Impure altruism and donations to public goods: A theory of warm glow giving. *Economic Journal, 100*, 464–477.

Bosman, J. (2009, March 15). From ranks of jobless, a flood of volunteers. *New York Times*, A1.

Brockner, J., Guzzi, B., Kane, J., Levine, E., & Shaplen, K. (1984). Organization fundraising: Further evidence on the effect of the legitimizing of small donations. *Journal of Consumer Research, 11*, 611–614.

Cialdini, R. B., Darby, B. L., & Vincent, J. E. (1973). Transgression and altruism: A case of hedonism. *Journal of Experimental Social Psychology, 9*, 502–516.

Cialdini, R. B., & Schroeder, D. A. (1976). Increasing compliance by legitimizing paltry contributions: When even a penny helps. *Journal of Personality and Social Psychology, 34,* 599–603.

Dawes, R., & Thaler, R. (1988). Anomalies: Cooperation. *Journal of Economic Perspectives, 2*(3), 187–197.

Gourville, J. T. (1998). Pennies-a-day: The effect of temporal reframing on transaction evaluation. *Journal of Consumer Research, 24*(4), 395–408.

Harvey, J., & Strahilevitz, M. (2009). The power of pink: Cause-related marketing and the impact on breast cancer. *Journal of the American College of Radiology, 6*(1), 26–32.

Harvey, M. D., & Enzle, M. E. (1981). A cognitive model of social norms for understanding the transgression-helping effect. *Journal of Personality and Social Psychology, 41,* 866–875.

Isen, A. M. (1970). Success, failure, attention and reaction to others: The warm glow of success. *Journal of Personality and Social Psychology, 15,* 294–301.

Jackson, M., & Richie, L. (1985, January 28). We are the world [USA for Africa]. On *We are the world* [CD]. Los Angeles: Columbia Records.

Jacoby, S. (1997, December 9). Why do we donate? It's personal. *New York Times,* G1 & G18.

Kahneman, D., & Knetsch, J. L. (1992). Valuing public goods: The purchase of moral satisfaction. *Journal of Environmental Economics and Management, 22,* 57–70.

Kahneman, D., & Tversky, A. (1979). Prospect theory: An analysis of decision under risk. *Econometrica, 47,* 263–291.

Latane, B., & Darley, J. M. (1970). *The unresponsive bystander: Why doesn't he help?* New York: Appleton-Crofts.

Linville, P. W., & Fischer, G. W. (1991). Preferences for separating or combining events. *Journal of Personality and Social Psychology, 60*(1), 5–23.

Liu, W., & Aaker, J. (2008). The happiness of giving: The time-ask effect. *Journal of Consumer Research, 35*(3), 543–557.

Loewenstein, G., & Small, D. (2007). The Scarecrow and the Tinman: The vicissitudes of human sympathy and caring. *Review of General Psychology, 2*(1), 112–126.

Monroe, K. R., Barton, M. C., & Klingemann, U. (1990). Altruism and the theory of rational action: Rescuers of Jews in Nazi Europe, *Ethics, 101,* 103–122.

Olivola, C. Y., & Shafir, E. (2010). The martyrdom effect: When pain and effort increase prosocial contributions. Manuscript submitted for publication.

Olson, R. G. (1965). *The morality of self interest.* New York: Harcourt Brace.

Piliavin, J. A., Dovidio, J. F., Gaertner, S. L., & Clark, R. D. (1981). *Emergency intervention.* New York: Academic Press.

Reingen, P. H. (1982). Test of a list procedure for inducing compliance with a request to donate money. *Journal of Applied Psychology, 67,* 110–118.

Schlenker, B. R., Forsyth, D. R., Leary, M. R., & Miller, R .S. (1980). Self-presentational analysis of the effects of incentives on attitude change following counterattitudinal behavior. *Journal of Personality and Social Psychology, 39*(4), 553–577.

Schwartz, S. H. (1977). Normative influences on altruism. In L. Berkowitz (Ed.), *Advances in experimental and social psychology* (Vol. 10). New York: Academic Press.

Small, D. A., & Simonsohn, U. (2008). Friends of victims: Personal experience and prosocial behavior. *Journal of Consumer Research, 35*(3), 532–542.

Smith, A. (1869). The theory of moral sentiments. *Prometheus Books.*

Strahilevitz, M. (1999). The effects of product type and donation magnitude on willingness to pay more for a charity-linked brand. *Journal of Consumer Psychology, 8,* 215–241.

Strahilevitz, M., (2008). "Why would I feel bad about giving a homeless guy a dollar? Take-aversion and the guilt associated with undoing a donation. Talk presented at the Association for Consumer Research Latin America Conference, Sao Paulo Brazil, July 2008.

Strahilevitz, M., & Myers, J. G. (1998). Donations to charity as purchase incentives: How well it works may depend on what you are trying to sell. *Journal of Consumer Research, 24.*

Thaler, R. H. (1985). Mental accounting and consumer choice. *Marketing Science, 4,* 199–214.

Thaler, R. H., & Johnson, E. J. (1990). Gambling with the house money and trying to break even: The effects of prior outcomes on risky choice. *Management Science, 36,* 643–660.

Walster, E., Berschield, E., & Walster, W. G. (1973). New directions in equity research. *Journal of Personality and Social Psychology, 25*(2), 151–176.

3

Precommitment to Charity

TOM MEYVIS, ARONTE BENNETT, and
DANIEL M. OPPENHEIMER

*T*he efficacy of fundraising solicitations is a topic of both theoretical and practical importance. In an effort to increase donations, prior research has examined different ways to increase the desire to give and the perceived benefit of giving. For instance, researchers have studied the roles of increased sympathy (Small, Loewenstein, & Slovic 2007; Small, this volume), moral imperatives (Freeman, Aquino, & McFerran, 2009), perceived effectiveness of donations (Chen, 2009), social factors (Croson & Shang, this volume; Martin & Randal, this volume), and a number of other contextual variables (Hung & Wyer, 2009; Liu, this volume; White & Peloza, 2009).

However, the amount that people donate does not just depend on their desire to donate, but also on the anticipated pain associated with parting with their money. Prior research has mostly focused on increasing the perceived *benefit* of the act of donating, without considering lowering the perceived *cost* of donating. Yet, in many cases, people desire to be charitable and are interested in making a donation but fail to do so. For example, we asked participants to compare the amount that they intended to donate in the past year to the amount that they had actually donated in the past year on a 7 point scale (1 = donated significantly less than intended, 4 = exactly the same amount, 7 = donated significantly more than intended). Two out of three participants reported donating less than they wanted to and the average donation rate across all participants was significantly below the level of intention (mean rating = 2.9, standard deviation = 1.6, $t(29) = 3.6, p < .001$). This indicates that while people would like to give, there are impediments preventing them from achieving their charitable goals.

We propose that one major obstacle to increasing charitable donations is the perceived pain of parting with one's money. Furthermore, we propose *precommitment* to the donation as a mechanism for reducing this pain—and thus increasing donations. In particular, we argue that precommitment reduces the aversiveness of the donation by distancing people from the money with which they are parting. Although not often discussed in terms of precommitment, there are several examples of strategies that are commonly employed by charities and fundraisers that rely on this principle. For instance, the United Way permits donors to precommit to donations through paycheck deductions; because donors never "possess" the money (psychologically speaking), they are spared the pain of having to part with it. Charitable reward programs, such as affinity cards, rely on a similar mechanism to allow donors to precommit to charitable behavior. Rather than redeem points for gifts, flights, or electronic gadgets, consumers enrolled in these programs precommit to using them toward a charitable end and do not experience the pain of parting with money. A different type of precommitment is used by telethons, such as Jerry Lewis's annual fundraising campaign, which encourage donors to call and pledge to make donations at a later time. This method reduces the pain of paying by distancing the decision to contribute from the actual act of contributing.

In this chapter, we will discuss the challenges and possibilities of precommitment as a method for increasing charitable donations. We will first discuss the general strategy of precommitment and how it is used to alter behavior in other (noncharity) domains. Next, we will discuss the different psychological mechanisms through which precommitment can operate. We will then outline the ways in which precommitment may increase charitable contributions, while also identifying situations in which precommitment may actually decrease contributions. Finally, we will present a series of recent studies that empirically test the impact of precommitment on charitable donations. We observe that precommitment can indeed increase charitable donations when it distances people from the act of donating, but that it can also reduce donations when it *only* distances them from the act of donating but *not* from the money being donated. We will discuss the opportunities and challenges implied by these results as well as limitations and future directions.

SELF-CONTROL AND PRECOMMITMENT

We have argued that although people desire to be charitable, they are often dissuaded from acting on this desire by the pain associated with having to part with their hard-earned money. This conflict between a long-term goal and more salient, short-term concerns suggests that managing charitable donations can be thought of as a problem of exerting *self-control*. Self-control failures are often characterized by "myopia," the tendency to prefer short-term pleasure over long-term satisfaction, and are present in a wide variety of domains. Myopic dieters go ahead and eat the tempting chocolate cake despite their weight loss goals, myopic savers buy a new coat rather than place the money in the savings account they wish to establish, and myopic students attend a party rather than study for the final exam they are aiming to pass.

People can generally exert self-control in one of two ways: by changing the options that are available to them or by changing the costs associated with these available options (Read, 2007). Precommitment operates through the first method: it involves committing to the future act by limiting options now in order to avoid temptations later. More generally, the need to precommit occurs when preferences are inconsistent over time; that is, when current preferences for future acts are different from future preferences for these same acts. Time-inconsistent preferences are typical for choices between vices and virtues. We often wish to behave virtuously at a future date; however, when that date approaches, we are torn between the previously desired virtue and a presently tempting vice. By precommitting to the virtue, we can avoid being tempted by the vice (Wertenbroch, 1998).

There are many examples of people precommitting to virtuous behavior to avoid the pitfalls of time-inconsistent preferences. For instance, a person on a diet may recognize that when faced with alluring desserts he will be tempted to indulge. In order to avoid the temptation associated with an alluring dessert menu, the person may select a restaurant with less appealing dessert options in order to make it easier to adhere to his diet. Similarly, Wertenbroch (1998) observed that consumers will forgo quantity discounts to reduce the consumption of vices. For example, rather than purchasing three bags of potato chips for $2, a consumer may opt to buy one bag for $1, forgoing a per-unit savings of 33¢ in an effort to restrict consumption. This precommitment technique is known as *rationing* and it permits consumers limited amounts of a vice but prevents them from fully indulging. Other examples of using precommitment to deal with time-inconsistent preferences include hiring a personal trainer, purchasing an opera subscription, renting "high-brow" DVDs, and committing future income to retirement savings.

Many people hold the long-term goal of improving their health and getting in shape. Yet, at any given time, there are likely to be more tempting options than going to the gym to work out. One way to deal with this conflict is to purchase sessions with a personal trainer, which serves as a prior commitment to the long-term goal of getting in shape at a point when the painful effort involved in working out is less salient. Once the (already paid for) trainer arrives for a session, it is too late to decide not to exercise that day. Another, milder form of precommitment is the simple act of purchasing a gym membership—even when you know that paying per visit would likely cost you less. For example, Della Vigna and Malmendier (2006) observed that gym members paid, on average, 58% more than they would if they purchased access with a pay-per-visit plan. Although purchasing a gym membership is not a guarantee that one will actually go to the gym, the purchase of a membership increases commitment to future workouts and often does increase gym attendance for the first few months of membership (Gourville & Soman, 1998).

Another long-term goal that conflicts with short-term temptations is the desire to partake in high-brow culture. People may feel they should attend plays and operas or watch critically acclaimed dramas and documentaries, yet this desire often conflicts with the easy entertainment offered by blockbuster action movies or watching television at home instead. For instance, Read, Loewenstein, and Kalyanaraman (1999) observed that movie viewers plan to watch movies they feel they *should* watch (e.g., *Shindler's List*), but when movie watching opportunities arise, instead select movies they *want* to watch (e.g. *Spider-Man*). People can deal with this conflict by precommitting to the high-brow cultural options. This precommitment mechanism is revealed in research on DVD renting behavior by Milkman, Rogers, and Bazerman (2009). Using data from a rental subscription service, they observe that people include both *should* and *want* movies in their queue of desired films, yet hold on to *should* films longer than *want* films, indicating that they are delaying the consumption of the *should* films while quickly consuming the *want* films. Thus, although people's immediate preference clearly favors the *want* films, they precommit to the *should* films by including them in their queues. Upon receipt, they delay watching them, causing a delay in the receipt of subsequent movies, and thus exerting pressure on the consumer to actually watch and return them.

A fourth area in which precommitment can resolve time-inconsistent preferences is that of retirement savings. Choi, Laibson, Madrian, and Metrick (2001) found that a large portion of households believe their savings rate is too low and hope to increase this rate in the near future. However, when the same households were surveyed at a later date, they had not yet implemented the desired changes in their behavior. To address this problem, Thaler and Benartzi (2003) propose a mechanism that permits households to precommit to saving for retirement. The investment tool they propose, Save More Tomorrow (SMarT), allows households to precommit to increasing savings allotments when they receive a raise in income at a later date. Since the decision is made well before the raise becomes effective, people are parting with money that is not theirs yet, which substantially reduces the aversiveness of the decision. Results indicate that households that opt to enroll in SMarT programs significantly increase their rate of savings compared to those who decide to manage their retirement savings without assistance.

Finally, aside from increasing self-control, precommitment can also be used to strategically *reduce* an excess of self-control. Indeed, under some conditions, people are overly virtuous and may benefit from precommitting to a relative vice. Although consumers are cast as indulgent and wanton creatures, they often select necessities over luxuries more frequently than they would prefer. This condition is known as *hyperopia*, which refers to excessive self-control that leads to *under*indulgence. Kivetz and Simonson (2002) show that people can choose to precommit to luxuries or relative vices to combat such hyperopia. For instance, they observe that when choosing between a lottery with the chance of winning a luxury (e.g., a restaurant voucher, a cruise, or a spa service) versus a chance of winning an equal or greater amount of cash, a significant number of people prefer the luxury lottery over the cash lottery. By thus constraining their future activities, these people effectively precommit to indulging (rather than taking the cash and risk feeling compelled to spend it on necessities). Thus, by selecting the luxury lottery, people obtain the possibility of indulging in a cruise without having to feel guilty for actually paying for it.

In sum, precommitment can help people overcome current concerns and temptations so as to achieve their long-term goals, be they greater self-control or greater indulgence. In the next section, we will discuss *how* precommitment helps achieve these goals. In particular, we will address why it is easier for people to commit in advance, rather than at the time of the required action.

HOW PRECOMMITMENT LEADS TO GOAL ACHIEVEMENT

As we mentioned earlier, the need to precommit arises when there is a conflict between a long-term goal and immediate concerns. Examples not only include the earlier discussed conflicts between the general goals of dieting and saving for retirement and the immediate temptations to eat and spend, but also (as we will discuss in the following sections) the conflict between the general desire to be charitable and the immediate pain of parting with one's money.

We have argued that asking people to precommit can make it easier for them to overcome these immediate concerns and achieve their long-term goals. However, for precommitment to be a viable strategy, it must be substantially easier for people to commit to their goal at an earlier point in time than to do so at the time of action. Why is it easier to choose a restaurant without desserts than to not order dessert in the restaurant? There are several reasons why the prior commitment is easier to make.

First, people are myopic because they engage in time discounting—they value positive outcomes less the longer they have to wait for those outcomes. However, people discount much more steeply in the near future than in the far future, a pattern of behavior that approximates a hyperbolic function (Kirby & Herrnstein, 1995). Many people would prefer a 10-minute massage now over a 15-minute massage 2 hours from now, but few would prefer a 10-minute massage in 6 hours to a 15-minute massage in 8 hours. As a result of this hyperbolic discounting, our desire to cheat on our diet and eat dessert right now is considerably stronger than our desire to eat a dessert in two hours.

Second, the cost of pursuing the long-term goal will also be much more vivid and salient at the time of the action than at the time of precommitment. Since people are more likely to be influenced and persuaded by information that is more vivid and salient (Nisbett & Ross, 1980), they are more likely to focus on those costs at the time of action than at the time of precommitment. The diet-disrupting dessert is much more seductive when read from a menu in all its luscious detail (or seeing it on the dessert cart) than when contemplated as an abstract possibility before entering the restaurant.

Third, and related to the previous point, the temporal distance from the time of action will also determine the level of abstraction at which the action is being construed. According to construal level theory (Trope & Liberman, 2003), actions that are psychologically distant (including temporally distant) are construed at a more abstract level than actions that are psychologically near. Thus, the choice between sticking to the diet and ordering dessert will be construed more abstractly when it is made before entering the restaurant than when it is made at the end of the meal. This level of abstraction matters because people have been shown to be more likely to follow their general principles and ideals when making decisions in an abstract mindset than when making decisions in a concrete mindset (Liberman, Trope, & Stephan, 2007). In other words, our dieter is more likely to adhere to his general dieting goal when contemplating the dessert choice at an abstract level before dinner than when contemplating it at a concrete level during dinner. In sum, because of these three mechanisms, it is substantially easier for people to commit to long-term goals in advance than it is in the face of temptation.

PRECOMMITTING TO DONATIONS TO CHARITIES

Like the earlier examples, decisions about whether or not to donate pit a general long-term goal against specific immediate concerns. The general goal is people's desire to be altruistic and charitable. Although we certainly tend to act out of self-interest, we also have been socialized into a society that values altruism and, to some extent, have internalized that norm. However, this desire to be charitable conflicts with the immediate negative consequences of donating: the foregoing of alternative uses of that money (e.g., purchasing a specific product or experience), but also the immediate *pain of paying* (Prelec & Loewenstein, 1998; Zellermayer, 1996). Zellermayer (1996, p. 2) refers to the pain of paying as "direct and immediate displeasure or pain from the act of making a payment." Notably, the pain of paying is not synonymous with the reduction of utility that will occur in the future as a result of reduced wealth; rather it is the "psychological, or hedonic, vexation connected with spending money" (Zellermayer, 1996, p. 2).

This pain of paying can reduce the enjoyment one derives from the purchase (in this case, the satisfaction of having contributed to a worthy cause), but can itself also be reduced by being linked to the benefits the money has purchased (Prelec & Loewenstein, 1998). That is, the pain associated with the payment can be *buffered* by thoughts of the future benefits it will finance (in this case, thoughts of the charity's activities). Yet the automatic and pervasive nature of the pain of paying guarantees that it will remain a serious impediment to people's pursuit of their desire to be charitable. Indeed, although the pain of paying is typically credited with reducing impulsive resource spending, beneficial expenditures are also occasionally avoided because the immediate pain of paying outweighs the delayed benefit. In instances where consumers possess lay theories about their susceptibility to the pain of paying, they may seek ways to circumvent the debilitating effects of the pain in order to make payments they believe to be worthwhile.

As such, tools to precommit to donating may be a welcome solution to reduce the pain of paying when pursuing the desire to be charitable. But is it indeed easier to precommit to a charitable donation than to donate immediately? This will only be the case if people's preferences are time-inconsistent; that is, if the dominance of the pain of paying over the desire to be charitable disappears when one is further removed from the act of paying. For the three reasons listed in the previous section, we propose that the pain of paying will indeed be generally reduced as the potential donor is further removed from the act of paying. First, because of hyperbolic discounting, any temporal distancing from the immediate act of donating will result in sharp discounting of the pain of paying. Second, the pain of paying should also be less pronounced at the time of precommitment because of reduced vividness and salience (i.e., not yet having to write a check or hand over cash). Third, at the time of precommitment, people will be more psychologically distant from the act of donating and therefore should construe it at a more abstract level, resulting in greater reliance on the general principle of altruism.

Not surprisingly, many charitable organizations have implicitly relied on this mechanism by using a variety of strategies that distance potential donors from the actual donations—and thus potentially reduce the pain of paying. These strategies include asking them to later donate money that is not theirs yet (such as future paychecks or points they may accrue on affinity cards), to later donate money they already have (i.e., asking them to pledge future donations), to later donate their time (i.e., to precommit to volunteering), or to donate money that is uncertain (such as donations based on sports performances). In all these situations, people are psychologically distant from the act of paying, potentially reducing the pain of paying and making it easier for them to precommit to the charitable behavior they are pursuing.

Unfortunately, there is little systematic research on whether precommitment indeed increases charitable donations. One exception is work by Breman (2006), who specifically examined the influence of time-inconsistent preferences on repeated charitable giving. In a field experiment designed to mirror work on precommitment to savings by Thaler and Benartzi (2003), the author observed a 32% increase in donations when monthly contributors to a charity were asked to increase their donations two months from now, rather than today. Although the scope of this study was limited to changing donations from current donors, it does indicate that it can be more effective to ask donors to *precommit* to a future increase in donations rather than commit to an increase at the present time.

In sum, there are many reasons to believe that precommitment should be able to increase charitable donations: several psychological processes should reduce the impact of the pain of paying at a later point in time, various precommitment strategies are already frequently used by charitable organizations, and an empirical study that directly examined the impact of precommitment found convincing evidence of its beneficial effect. Indeed, we predict that people should generally be more likely to donate to charities when they are more removed from the actual donation. However, there may be boundary conditions for this effect, and even times when it may backfire. In particular, precommitment may only be effective when donors are more distant from the money being donated rather than simply more distant from the act of donating. That is, asking people to delay donating money that they already have (as is common with pledges) may result in decreased rather than increased donations.

We expect that people will be reluctant to delay donating the money they already have because they anticipate that this future payment will be particularly painful. This prediction is in line with work by Zellermayer (1996), who demonstrated that people anticipate greater pain of paying when having to make drawn out (delayed) payments for a purchase rather than paying everything at the time of purchase. That is, precommitting money you already have may be particularly painful because of the anticipated dread of knowing you will have to part with it. As Zellermayer (1996) states in the context of delayed payments for purchases: "drawn-out purchases generate immediate pain due to the consumer's anticipation of their future financial drag" (p. 51).

Additional support for this prediction is offered by Prelec and Loewenstein's (1998) work on the pain of paying. As these authors point out, the pain of paying can be buffered by connecting the payment to the benefits it was used for. However, the mental accounting system that connects the payments to the benefits is *prospective* in nature: we are more likely to connect payments to future benefits than to past benefits. To the extent that donors derive a major benefit from the mere act of agreeing to donate (i.e., the "warm glow of giving," Andreoni, 1990), the link between this benefit and the payment will be much stronger if the payment occurs at the same time as this agreement rather than some time after the agreement. In a pledging situation, the actual payment occurs a substantial time after the agreement to donate, making it harder to connect it to this agree-ment and thus increasing the pain of paying. Potential donors would be expected to pay after already having "consumed" the warm glow accompanying their pledge to donate, making the payment particularly painful. Of course, this mechanism would only affect pledges if people actually *anticipate* the painfulness of delayed payments. In fact, past research indicates that people indeed do anticipate that payments will be more painful when made after the benefit of the payment has already been incurred, as reflected in a general preference to make payments before consumption rather than after consumption (Prelec & Loewenstein, 1998; Zellermayer, 1996).

Moreover, the primary goal of precommitment is increasing one's psycholo-gical distance from the money one will have to surrender. It isn't painful to pledge money one doesn't have. However, once a person has the money, it is too late to precommit. Just as once one is staring at the dessert cart, it is too late to precommit *not* to look at the desserts—overcoming myopia will already be too painful. In sum, delayed donations of money one already has seem particularly painful because (1) people anticipate dreading the payment, (2) the payment is disconnected from one of the critical benefits (the warm glow of giving), and (3) the money is psychologi-cally near and thus harder to part with.

Some preliminary evidence for this hypothesis comes from Pronin, Olivola, and Kennedy (2008). They showed that people were less likely to agree to pledge to receive emails on behalf of a charity in the future than they were to agree to receiving emails in the present. While Pronin and her colleagues (2008) were looking at donations of time and inbox space as opposed to money (see Liu, this volume, for a discussion of how requests for time differ from requests for money), this nonetheless suggests that asking for pledges in the future can, under the right circumstances, backfire.

Thus, on the one hand, compared to immediate donation requests, people should be *more likely* to precommit money that they have not earned yet or that is uncer-tain. For instance, people should be more likely to precommit to donating future pay or credit card points than they are to currently donate an equivalent amount in cash. However, on the other hand, people may be *less likely* to donate when they are asked to precommit money that they currently have rather than simply donate the money right now. For instance, people may be less likely to *pledge* to donate their current money than they would be to simply *donate* their current money.

EMPIRICAL STUDIES

We empirically tested these predictions in a set of three laboratory experiments. In the first study, we show that a significant proportion of participants prefer to precommit to a donation over a cash prize that normatively dominates it, indicat-ing that people sometimes feel the need to precommit to charitable donations. In the second study, we present people with hypothetical lotteries and ask them how much of their winnings they would precommit to donate to charities in case they won the lottery. Participants are only willing to donate a substantial portion of their winnings when they are in an abstract mindset *and* the odds of winning the lottery are low, indicating that psychological distance from the money is a critical condition for donation. Finally, in the third study, participants are asked to imagine that they have just won a lottery and are asked to donate some of the winnings. Participants are willing to part with more of their winnings when they are simply asked to donate than when they are asked to pledge to donate later, indicating that distancing potential donors from the act of donating can backfire when they are asked to pledge money they already have.

Study 1: Precommitting Raffle Winnings to a Charity

If, as we have argued, people would like to donate more than they do but are prevented from doing so because of the pain of paying, then people ought to spontaneously precommit to donating to a charity when given the opportunity. We tested this in a study in which participants were entered in a raffle that would occur approximately one week later and offered the chance to win $25. Participants were asked to decide in advance whether to donate the $25 to United Way or to receive the $25 in cash, which they could then "donate or spend on whatever you would like, including the charity of your choice." Importantly, the latter option dominates the former option; a participant who wants to donate to charity should still choose the cash option because that offers more flexibility about where the money is donated, and the percent of the winnings that are donated. However, if participants want to donate, but are aware that once they have the money it will be too painful to part with it, then they might precommit as a self-control mechanism (cf. Kivetz & Simonson, 2002). Indeed, nearly 40% of participants (53 out of 143 participants) preferred to precommit to the donation rather than receive the cash. This suggests that precommitment is indeed an attractive strategy for helping people overcome their myopia when it comes to charitable giving, and that giving campaigns that make use of precommitment might be quite effective.

Study 2: Donating Money When It Is Psychologically Distant

We have argued that precommitment to charitable donations is effective because people are less likely to experience the pain from paying when they are more removed from the money they are parting with. In the second study, we therefore manipulated people's psychological distance from the money. Two hundred university students were asked to imagine that they held a ticket for a lottery that offered a chance at winning $100, and were asked, before the results were announced, to indicate how much of their winnings they would precommit to donate to a charity.

We manipulated participants' psychological distance in two different ways. First, we varied the alleged probability of winning the lottery. In the high-probability condition, participants were told that they had a 90% chance of winning the lottery, whereas in the low-probability condition, they were told that they only had a 10% chance of winning the lottery. Because psychological distance increases with uncertainty (Liberman, Trope, & Stephan, 2007), people in the low-probability condition should feel more distant from the money than those in the high-probability condition. In addition, we also manipulated psychological distance using a mindset manipulation. A more abstract mindset tends to increase psychological distance whereas a more concrete mindset tends to decrease psychological distance (Liberman et al., 2007). We manipulated participants' mindset prior to the presentation of the lottery scenario using a procedure adapted from Fujita, Trope, Liberman, and Levin-Sagi (2006). Participants were asked to either generate superordinate category labels (abstract mindset) or subordinate exemplars (concrete mindset) for 16 different words, such as singer, king, chair, and car. For instance, those in the abstract mindset condition were asked to indicate what a chair is an example of (e.g., furniture), whereas those in the concrete mindset condition were asked to provide an example of a chair (e.g., a desk chair).

Since both inducing an abstract mindset and lowering the probability of winning the lottery should increase the psychological distance from the money (and hence reduce the anticipated pain of parting with the money), we expected that both manipulations would increase the proportion allocated to the charity. Participants indicated how much of their winnings they were willing to donate to a charity using an 11-point scale anchored by "Nothing" (1) and "Everything" (11).

As expected, the extent of precommitment to the charity reliably increased as the probability of winning decreased ($M_{90\%} = 3.15$, $M_{10\%} = 3.74$, F (1, 196) = 4.90, $p = .028$). However, contrary to our expectations, on its own, the mindset manipulation did not reliably influence participants' allocation decisions ($M_{Abstract} = 3.55$, $M_{Concrete} = 3.56$, $F < 1$, ns). Yet, interestingly, the mindset manipulation did moderate the effect of the probability of winning the lottery (F (1, 196) = 5.21, $p = .023$). Lowering the probability did not increase the amount of winnings allocated to the charity when people were in a concrete mindset ($M_{90\%} = 3.37$, $M_{10\%} = 3.35$, $F < 1$, ns), but substantially increased the charitable allocation when they were in an abstract mindset ($M_{90\%} = 2.91$, $M_{10\%} = 4.16$, F (1, 196) = 9.72, $p = .002$, see Figure 3.1). These results suggest a nonlinear relationship between psychological distance and willingness to donate the winnings to a charity (cf. Jones & Rachlin, 2006). Simply (but dramatically) lowering the probability of winning in the concrete mindset condition was not sufficient to increase donations to the charity. Instead, participants only increased their charitable donations when their psychological distance from the money was increased both by lowering the probability of winning the money and by being in an abstract mindset. Indeed, testing the contrast of the abstract/low-probability condition against the combination of the three other conditions reveals that this first condition reliably differs from the other ones (F (1, 196) = 4.71, $p = .031$). These results indicate that even in a hypothetical lottery context, it is essential to sufficiently distance people from the money if one wants to increase their willingness to precommit this money to a charity.

Study 3: Reluctance to Pledge Your Current Wealth

In the third and final study, we manipulated the distance from the donation itself rather than from the money being donated. As we discussed earlier, we expect that although distancing people from the money to be donated should increase

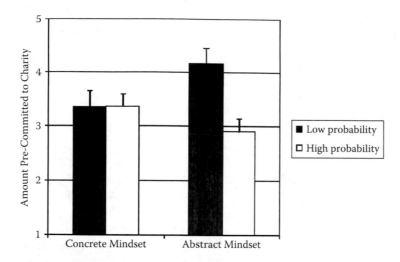

Figure 3.1 Study 2: Amount of the winnings precommitted to charity as a function of mindset and probability of winning the lottery (1 = Nothing, 11 = Everything).

donations (as demonstrated in the previous study), distancing them from the act of donating can backfire and decrease donations if the money they are precommitting to donate is already in their possession.

To test this last prediction, we again asked university students (N = 138) to imagine that they participated in a lottery (for $1,000), but this time we instructed them to also imagine that they *had just found out that they won the lottery*. We then asked them either how much of their winnings they would want to donate now (*donate* condition) or how much of their winnings they would pledge now to donate two months from now (*pledge* condition). As in Study 2, participants used an 11-point scale (anchored by "Nothing" [1] and "Everything" [11]) to indicate how much of their winnings they wanted to allocate to a charity. Given the anticipated painfulness of a delayed payment, we expected that participants would allocate less money to the charity when they were asked to pledge a later donation than when asked to donate now. In addition, we also administered a modified version of Vallacher and Wegner's (1989) Behavioral Identification Form (BIF), which measures the level of abstraction at which participants construe personal actions. We expected that participants who construed the situation more abstractly would feel more distant from the lottery winning scenario, anticipate less pain of paying, and thus donate more.

As expected, participants who were asked to pledge to donate money two months after winning the lottery were willing to part with less of their winnings than participants who were asked to donate some of their winnings immediately after winning the lottery (M_{Pledge} = 3.60, M_{Donate} = 4.16, F (1, 134) = 4.96, p = .027). Furthermore, participants who, based on the BIF scale, were classified as having a more abstract mindset donated (or pledged) more of their winnings than those who were classified as having a more concrete mindset ($M_{Abstract}$ = 4.32, $M_{Concrete}$ = 3.50, F (1, 134) = 5.65, p = .019). Thus, whereas increasing the psychological distance

from the entire situation (including the winnings) again resulted in greater donations to the charity (as evidenced by the BIF effect), increasing the distance to
the actual donation without changing the distance to the money backfired and
resulted in fewer donations (as evidenced by the pledge effect). In sum, whereas
pledging to later donate *future* earnings may be *less* painful than donating money
now, pledging to later donate *current* earnings may in fact be *more* painful than
donating money now.

CONCLUSION

Whereas most charity research has focused on increasing people's motivation to
help a cause, we propose that many people already feel they should donate more
than they currently do, but are prevented from doing so by the immediate pain of
parting with their money. Furthermore, the conflict between the general goal of
being charitable and the immediate pain of paying is resolved differently depending on people's distance from the time of donation. When people are contemplating
future donations, the anticipated pain of paying is less vivid and easily overcome
by people's desire to be charitable. However, at the time of donation, the pain of
paying gains power through its immediacy and can make potential donors give up
on their charitable intentions.

This pattern of time-inconsistent preferences is hardly unique to charitable
giving. It is in fact an essential characteristic of problems of self-control—and has
been studied extensively in that context. One way to exert self-control in light of
time-inconsistent preferences is to commit well in advance to actions consistent
with the long-term goal, that is, well before the immediate temptations become
sufficiently vivid to block any progress toward the goal. This is why people sometimes avoid restaurants with wonderful desserts, commit to painful workout sessions with a personal trainer, include educational but tedious documentaries in
their movie rental queues, and precommit to increasing their retirement savings
after receiving a raise. We propose that potential donors may similarly wish to precommit to charitable donations.

Our first study demonstrated that many people were indeed willing to precommit their potential winnings from a raffle to a charitable cause, even though this
option was strictly dominated by the possibility of receiving the winnings in cash.
However, people's willingness to precommit their future earnings to a charitable
cause is certainly not universal. As the second study showed, distancing people
from their future earnings made them more likely to precommit these earnings:
participants allocated a greater proportion of possible winnings to a charity if they
were both thinking abstractly and had small likelihood of winning, than if they
were either thinking concretely or had a high likelihood of winning. This qualifi-
cation that people only like to precommit money to charities *as long as they feel
sufficiently removed from this money* is absolutely critical. In fact, as the results
of the third and final study demonstrate, asking people to precommit money that
they already have can actually backfire: when people were asked to pledge some
of their current winnings for future donation, they actually allocated less of their
winnings to charity than if they were simply asked to donate right now.

Our results do not imply that asking people to pledge to a charity is always a bad strategy. Indeed, our results suggest that asking potential donors to pledge to donate *future* earnings will result in more donations than asking them to donate right now. However, asking potential donors to pledge to donate *current* earnings will result in fewer donations than asking them to donate right now. This distinction between future and current earnings is of course not absolute given that money is inherently fungible. When someone is asked to pledge to donate $100 a month from now, it should really not matter whether this money comes from next month's paycheck or from the current savings account (in the absence of severe budget restrictions). Indeed, the amount to be pledged can be construed both ways by the potential donor—and this construal can be influenced by the framing of the pledge request. In other words, it is in the interest of the charity to explicitly frame requests for pledges as pledges of future earnings rather than pledges of current savings. In cases in which this framing is unlikely to be successful (e.g., if future earnings of that magnitude are unlikely in that time span), it would be better to ask people to donate right now rather than pledge to donate in the future.

REFERENCES

Andreoni, J. (1990). Impure altruism and donations to public goods: A theory of warm-glow giving. *The Economic Journal, 100*, 464–477.

Breman, A. (2006). Give more tomorrow: Evidence from a randomized field experiment. Working Paper, Stockholm School of Economics.

Chen, G. (2009). Does meeting standards affect charitable giving? An empirical study of New York metropolitan area charities. *Nonprofit Management and Leadership, 19*, 349–365.

Choi, J. J., Laibson, D., Madrian, B. C., & Metrick, A. (2001). Defined contribution pensions: Plan rules, participant decisions and the path of least resistance. Working Paper No. 8655, National Bureau of Economic Research, Stanford, CA, 94305.

Della Vigna, S., & Malmendier, U. (2006). Paying not to go to the gym. *American Economic Review, 96*, 694–719.

Freeman, D., Aquino, K., & McFerran, B. (2009). Overcoming beneficiary race as an impediment to charitable donations: Social dominance orientation, the experience of moral elevation, and donation behavior. *Personality and Social Psychology Bulletin, 35*, 72–84.

Fujita, K., Trope, Y., Liberman, N., & Levin-Sagi, M. (2006). Construal levels and self-control. *Journal of Personality and Social Psychology, 90*, 351–367.

Gourville, J. T., & Soman, D. (1998). Payment depreciation: The behavioral effects of temporally separating payments from consumption. *Journal of Consumer Research, 25*, 160–174.

Hung, I. W., & Wyer, R. S. (2009). Differences in perspective and the influence of charitable appeals: When imagining oneself as the victim is not beneficial. *Journal of Marketing Research, 46*(3), 421–434.

Jones, B., & Rachlin, H. (2006). Social discounting. *Psychological Science, 4*, 283–286.

Kirby, K. N., & Herrnstein, R. J. (1995). Preference reversals due to myopic discounting of delayed reward. *Psychological Science, 6*, 83–89.

Kivetz, R., & Simonson, I. (2002). Self-control for the righteous: Toward a theory of pre-commitment to indulgence. *Journal of Consumer Research, 29*, 199–217.

Liberman, N., Trope, Y., & Stephan, E. (2007). Psychological distance. In A. W. Kruglanski & E. T. Higgins (Eds.), *Social psychology: Handbook of basic principles* (2nd ed.). New York: Guilford Press.

Milkman, K. L., Rogers, T., & Bazerman, M. H. (2009). Highbrow films gather dust: Time-inconsistent preferences and online DVD rentals. *Management Science, 55*, 1047–1059.

Nisbett, R. E., & Ross, L. (1980). *Human inference: Strategies and shortcomings of social judgment.* Englewood Cliffs, NJ: Prentice-Hall.

Prelec, D., & Loewenstein, G. (1998). The red and the black: Mental accounting of savings and debt. *Marketing Science, 17*, 4–28.

Pronin, E., Olivola, C. Y., & Kennedy, K. A. (2008). Doing unto future selves as you would do unto others: Psychological distance and decision making. *Personality and Social Psychology Bulletin, 34*, 224–236.

Read, D. (2007). Time and the marketplace. *Marketing Theory, 7*(1), 59–74.

Read, D., Loewenstein, G., & Kalyanaraman, S. (1999). Mixing virtue and vice: Combining the immediacy effect and the diversification heuristic. *Journal of Behavioral Decision Making, 12*, 257–273.

Small, D. A., Loewenstein, G. & Slovic, P. (2007). Sympathy and callousness: The impact of deliberative thought on donations to identifiable and statistical victims. *Organizational Behavior and Human Decision Processes, 102*, 143–153.

Thaler, R. H., & Benartzi, S. (2004). Save More Tomorrow (STM): Using behavioral economics to increase employee saving. *The Journal of Political Economy: Papers in Honor of Sherwin Rosen Part 2, 112*, S164–S187.

Trope, Y., & Liberman, N. (2003). Temporal construal. *Psychological Review, 110*, 403–421.

Vallacher, R. R., & Wegner, D. M. (1989). Levels of personal agency: Individual variation in action identification. *Journal of Personality and Social Psychology, 57*, 660–671.

Wertenbroch, K. (1998). Consumption self-control by rationing purchase quantities of virtue and vice. *Marketing Science, 17*, 317–337.

White, K., & Peloza, J. (2009). Self-benefit versus other-benefit marketing appeals: Their effectiveness in generating charitable support. *Journal of Marketing, 73*(4), 109–124.

Zellermayer, O. (1996). The pain of paying. Unpublished dissertation. Department of Social and Decision Sciences, Carnegie Mellon University, Pittsburgh, PA.

4

When Noble Means Hinder Noble Ends

The Benefits and Costs of a Preference for Martyrdom in Altruism

CHRISTOPHER Y. OLIVOLA

*T*he decision to donate one's money and time is a particularly interesting kind of choice because it involves trade-offs between personal, self-interested goals (i.e., goals that primarily benefit the decision maker) on the one hand, and collective, altruistic goals (i.e., goals that contribute to the greater good) on the other. Why and how people make altruistic choices has been a topic of great interest in many fields, including philosophy, biology, economics, sociology, political science, and psychology. As a result, plenty of intellectual energy has gone into devising models and theories that can explain altruistic behaviors or provide normative standards for how we *should* make decisions when faced with trade-offs between personal well-being and collective welfare. In this chapter, I start by considering two normative standards for making donation choices, which I call *Pareto hedonism* and *Pareto utilitarianism*. Next, I briefly review literature that suggests that people may not always be motivated to follow these standards, instead preferring means of charitable giving that involve significant pain and effort—a phenomenon called the *martyrdom effect*. I then discuss recent research showing that, as a result of the martyrdom effect, donation decisions often violate both Pareto hedonism and Pareto utilitarianism. I conclude by discussing the implications and dilemmas that result from this preference for challenging forms of altruism.

THE *SHOULD* OF GIVING: NORMATIVE
CONSIDERATIONS IN DONATION DECISIONS

Most theories of decision making have focused on the consequences of people's choices (Baron, 1994; Hastie, 2001; Messick, 1999). Although they come in many flavors, we can distinguish two broad types of *consequentialist* theories. At one extreme, theories such as the standard neoclassical economic model assume that decision makers only care about maximizing their own personal utility, not the utility of others (Rabin, 2002). In these models, rationality implies very little or no altruism and the prototypical *rational actor* is a purely selfish decision maker (in the narrow sense). Of course, we know this isn't the case in reality. Most people are often willing to donate some of their time and money to help others. Consider, for example, the fact that private giving in the United States totaled $295 billion in 2006 (Wing, Pollak, & Blackwood, 2008). Thus, people seem to be characterized by what Mullainathan and Thaler (2001) call "bounded self-interest." At the other extreme, utilitarian theories prescribe bringing about the greatest total good by maximizing aggregate utility (i.e., collective welfare). The most stringent utilitarian models typically imply that people should sacrifice as many of their own resources (including time and money) as possible until the cost of doing so exceeds the total benefit they provide to others (for a discussion of utilitarian models, see Baron & Szymanska in this volume). But we know this doesn't occur either. As utilitarian moral philosophers have correctly pointed out, many of us could be doing more to help others in need at relatively negligible costs to ourselves (Singer, 1993, 2009; Unger, 1996). Thus people are also characterized by bounded altruism.

Since people are limited both in their selfishness and their altruism, it is unrealistic to expect that they will always follow the prescriptions of neoclassical economic theories or those of utilitarian moral theories. Decisions about whether, when, how, and how much to donate are more likely to be governed by a mix of personal and prosocial goals than by either set of goals alone. In fact, many behavioral economic models of decision making now include parameters for other-regarding utility, in addition to standard self-regarding utility (e.g., Charness & Rabin, 2002). In doing so, they have formalized the combined influence of selfish and prosocial considerations in shaping people's choices. As a result, these models can account for a much larger variety of choices, both selfish and altruistic, than their more traditional neoclassical predecessors. Under these models, the concept of rationality encompasses a much broader set of behaviors. Similarly, not all utilitarian models require us to make heavy personal sacrifices. As Baron and Szymanska (in this volume) explain, some versions of utilitarianism recognize that most people are not willing to give away most of their resources, even if doing so brings about more collective good than personal harm. Under these more relaxed utilitarian models, a larger set of choices can be considered morally acceptable. In sum, the traditional and normatively stringent economic and utilitarian models of decision making have given way to more complex and flexible normative theories. Consequently, more choices are normatively defensible.

Nonetheless, we might still expect decision makers to abide by some minimal normative standards, even within these newer models. In particular, trade-offs between

selfish (personal) and altruistic (prosocial) goals should be constrained by two principles, Pareto hedonism and Pareto utilitarianism, which I define as follows:

1. *Pareto hedonism*: Whenever decision makers can increase their personal
   utility without decreasing the benefits to others, they should do so.
2. *Pareto utilitarianism*: Whenever decision makers can increase the utility of
   others without decreasing the benefits to themselves, they should do so.

These principles borrow from the economic concept of *Pareto efficiency* (or
Pareto optimality), by which a state of affairs is considered efficient if no transactions (i.e., reallocations of resources) can make at least one person better off without making anyone else worse off. While pure self-interest or pure altruism may be
too stringent for most people to follow or even to accept in principle, Pareto hedonism (the notion that a person should strive to improve their own state of affairs
if they can do so without sacrificing others' welfare) and Pareto utilitarianism (the
notion that a person should strive to improve others' states of affairs if they can
do so without sacrificing their own resources) should be easy to follow since they
don't require any sacrifices. Furthermore, these principles have a nice normative
characteristic: they neither violate rational-choice models that assume pure self-
interest nor moral codes of conduct that prescribe pure altruism. We should therefore expect all decisions to follow the principles of Pareto hedonism and Pareto
utilitarianism. In this chapter, however, I will review recent evidence that people
violate both of these principles, sometimes simultaneously. But first, I present a
brief discussion of some existing literature that helps explain why this happens.

EVIDENCE OF A GENERAL PREFERENCE FOR MARTYRDOM

Our everyday experiences show us that we often gain more satisfaction from
achieving difficult goals (i.e., those involving effort and pain) than we do from
those we achieve with ease. Indeed, a number of researchers have argued that
people derive meaning and value from having to work hard and suffer for their
chosen goals (Baumeister, 1991; Berns, 2005; Higgins, 2006; Kaufman, 1999;
Lane, 1992; Loewenstein, 1999). These assertions are supported by various lines
of research showing, for example, that people assign more value to objects they
have worked hard to earn than those they have obtained with minimal effort
(Lewis, 1965; Loewenstein & Issacharoff, 1994), that actively obtained rewards
are associated with greater activation of certain brain reward systems than those
obtained passively (Elliott, Newman, Longe, & Deakin, 2004; Tricomi, Delgado,
& Fiez, 2004; Zink, Pagnoni, Martin-Skurski, Chappelow, & Berns, 2004), and
that consumers are more hesitant to frivolously spend their earned income than
their unearned income (Abdel-Ghany, Bivens, Keeler, & James, 1983; Arkes et al.,
1994; Henderson & Peterson, 1992; Keeler, James, & Abdel-Ghany, 1985).

Our own research (Olivola & Shafir, submitted), which I discuss below, shows
that in some cases, people will contribute more to a cause if doing so is painful and

effortful (either for themselves or for a friend) than if the contribution process is easy and enjoyable. We call this phenomenon the *martyrdom effect*, as it essentially involves people suffering for a cause they believe in and care about. Much as martyrs are often assigned a special symbolic status (Cormack, 2002; DeSoucey, Pozner, Fields, Dobransky, & Fine, 2008; Fields, 2004; Glas, Spero, Verhagen, & van Praag, 2007), people seem to derive additional meaning and value from the pain-effort that they (or close others) anticipate enduring for a chosen cause. For many, the word *martyrdom* is associated with religion and fanaticism. However, there is a more general definition: According to the *Oxford English Dictionary* (2008) a *martyr*, in its broadest sense, is "a person who undergoes death or great suffering for a faith, belief, or cause," while *martyrdom* is "the act of becoming or the condition of being a martyr." We can simplify and combine these definitions to obtain the following definition of *martyrdom*: The act of suffering for a cause. Thus, by martyrdom, I simply mean the act of engaging in hedonically aversive activities (i.e., involving various kinds of difficulties and discomforts, such as pain, effort, and/or the risk of death) for a chosen cause.

As the above literature suggests, human beings often seem to show a preference for difficult and dangerous means of achieving goals and supporting causes. In the next few sections, I show how this tendency to value and reward martyrdom in altruism leads to violations of both Pareto hedonism and Pareto utilitarianism.

VIOLATIONS OF PARETO HEDONISM: THE SUCCESS OF PAINFUL-EFFORTFUL FUNDRAISERS

When it comes to decisions about how to donate to a charitable cause, the principle of Pareto hedonism implies that people should always prefer less costly methods of donating money over more costly ones, all else being equal. Yet this doesn't seem to be the case. Some of the most popular and successful fundraisers involve a good deal of pain and effort (Symonds, 2005). Many people, it seems, aren't just willing to give to charity; they'll go to great lengths to do so—literally! Popular fundraising events include walk-a-thons, marathons, bike-a-thons, swim-a-thons, triathlons, and other endurance events where donors must exert physical effort over an extensive period of time to help raise money for charity. Contrary to what we might expect, a large proportion of the participants in these events are not athletes; many of them are inspired by the charitable cause to participate in a dauntingly effortful event that they would otherwise avoid (Sweeney, 2005). In fact, this approach to raising money for charity seems to be growing in popularity at an astonishing rate (Williams, 1995). As an illustrative example, consider the March of Dimes. In 1970, when its first walk-a-thon fundraiser was organized, approximately 1,000 walkers participated and raised a total of $75,000. By 2003, the March of Dimes was holding well over 1,000 walk-a-thons per year and raising more than $100 million through these events (Napoli, 2003). Moreover, painful-effortful fundraisers are not limited to endurance events. Other variants include walking barefoot on burning coals ("Firewalkers," 2004; "Pub-goers," 2002) and broken glass (Barry, 2006; Birks, 2006), fasting for an extended period (Gardiner,

2007; Russell, 2004), and jumping out of planes (Lee, Williams, & Hadden, 1999) to raise money for charity.

Not only are painful-effortful fundraisers quite popular (i.e., attract many donors), they may also increase the amount of money that charities raise per donor, relative to less painful-effortful events. To explore this hypothesis, I examined data on the average amount of money raised, per participant, by endurance fundraising events that vary quantitatively in terms of physical effort involved. This data was obtained from two large national health-related charity organizations in the United States, each of which focuses on combating different diseases. Both charities organized regular endurance fundraising events to raise money for their respective causes and kindly shared some of their data with me.

The first charity organized an endurance cycling event in the northeastern United States, and provided data on the mean amounts raised, per cyclist, between 2005 and 2007. One characteristic of this bike-a-thon is that participants could vary the amount of effort they put into raising money, by cycling either 25, 50, or 170 miles (40.2, 80.5, or 273.6 km). These data automatically control for a range of possible factors since all cyclists started from the same physical location on the same day, and were cycling for the same cause, regardless of the distance they chose. Figure 4.1 shows the mean donations raised by cyclists for each distance in 2005, 2006, and 2007. For all three years, there is a positive correlation between the distance cycled and the amount of money raised. Those who cycled the shortest distance (25 miles) raised an average of $239.49, those who cycled twice as far (50 miles) raised an average of $426.00, while those who chose the most effortful option (170 miles) raised the most: an average of $1,085.69. Although the minimum

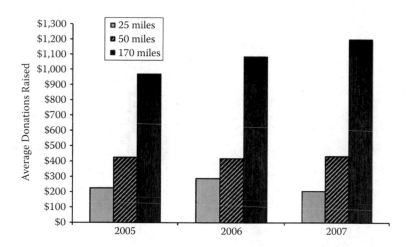

Figure 4.1   Mean donations raised per charity fundraising cyclist as a function of cycling distance and event year. Individual donations could not be obtained (only means were available), so calculation of the error bars was not possible. However, sample sizes were available for each bar and are as follows (from left to right): N = 438, 705, 500, 433, 700, 478, 391, 554, and 374.

contribution required to enter the bike-a-thon did correlate with distance ($75, $150, and $300, to cycle 25, 50, and 170 miles, respectively), it doesn't fully account for the differences in donations raised. For example, although one had to contribute $75 more to enter the 50-mile bike-a-thon than the 25-mile one, the former raised $186.51 more than the latter. Similarly, although one had to contribute $150 more to enter the 170-mile bike-a-thon than the 50-mile one, the former raised $659.69 more than the latter one. It should also be noted that the willingness to participate did not vary linearly with distance: Substantially more people chose to cycle 50 miles than either 25 or 170 miles (the latter two distances were comparable in terms of their popularity). This suggests that although people may be motivated to suffer for a cause, there are (not surprisingly) limits to the distance they are willing to go.

The second charity organized a variety of endurance events (e.g., walk-a-thons, marathons, and triathlons) across several locations in the United States, and provided some data on the individual-level amounts raised by participants between 2004 and 2008. These events differed both qualitatively (i.e., they involved walking, running, cycling, swimming, or a combination thereof) and quantitatively (i.e., the distance to run, walk, etc., varied across events). To control for qualitative differences, I only compared events that differed primarily in terms of the distance traveled. For example, this charity organized both marathons and half-marathons, which differ mainly in terms of the distance participants must run (26.2 miles vs. 13.1 miles). Figure 4.2 shows the mean donations raised by participants as a function of the distance traveled (i.e., effort invested) and the type of endurance event (only nonzero donations were considered). Again, we see that the amount raised by participants correlated positively with the effort they invested. Furthermore, this was true for all three types of events that I considered (i.e., those for which variations in distance existed).

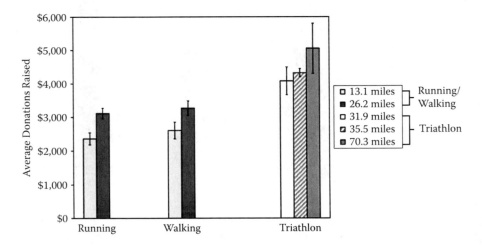

Figure 4.2   Mean donations raised per charity fundraising participant as a function of event type and event distance. Error bars represent standard error. The sample sizes associated with each bar are (from left to right): N = 79, 89, 62, 49, 20, 55, and 16.

These results are suggestive and offer real-world (i.e., nonlaboratory) evidence that making charity fundraisers more challenging increases the amount that participants are willing and able to raise. However, these data lack explanatory power. A number of factors could account for the positive relationship between the amount of effort invested by fundraising participants and the amount of money they raised. This is where experimental approaches can significantly advance our understanding. In contrast to observational and correlational methods, experiments can be used to isolate and manipulate the factors that may be responsible for the success of painful-effortful fundraising events. In doing so, they allow us to determine the causal relations linking these factors. Below I review experimental evidence that the addition of pain and effort can increase willingness to contribute to a prosocial cause.

EXPERIMENTAL EVIDENCE OF THE MARTYRDOM EFFECT IN CHARITABLE GIVING

In order to clarify the factors and causal links underlying the success of painful-effortful fundraisers, my colleagues and I carried out a number of experimental studies (Olivola & Foddy, submitted; Olivola & Shafir, submitted). In one set of studies (Olivola & Shafir, submitted), we found that participants who imagined the prospect of participating in a charity fundraiser were willing to donate more to the charitable cause when the hypothetical fundraiser was expected to be painful and effortful (e.g., a charity endurance run) than when it was expected to be easy and enjoyable (e.g., a charity picnic), even though both events were said to be equally popular (i.e., the same number of people were said to participate in both cases). In another study involving real money and actual pain, participants each made an anonymous decision about how to divide a budget between themselves (a personally beneficial allocation) and a collective financial pool where money was doubled and evenly redistributed to all members of the group (a collectively beneficial allocation). Participants allocated significantly more of their budgets to the collective cause when doing so required keeping their hands immersed in near-freezing cold water for 60 seconds (a rather painful task) than when no such task was involved. As a result, participants in the painful, cold condition ended up with higher payoffs than those in the control condition. Critically, the former participants made their allocation decisions *before* experiencing any pain, which rules out a number of alternative explanations for our results, such as cognitive dissonance theory (Festinger, 1957) and self-perception theory (Bem, 1967). One interesting result was that this manipulation had no effect on their beliefs about what other members of their group would do, which suggests that they were not drawing inferences about the perceived value of donating from the presence of the painful task. Furthermore, the anonymity of their decisions meant that they could not convey signals or gain status through their allocation choices, so these were not the driving factors behind their allocation preferences.

These studies also showed that the martyrdom effect extends from the self to others. Specifically, participants indicated a greater willingness to donate to a charity, following a hypothetical friend's solicitation for contributions, when she anticipated participating in a painful-effortful fundraising process for the same charity (as opposed to when she asked them for contributions without anticipating a painful-effortful fundraising experience). Moreover, the effect was not attributable to the friend's perceived dedication, since participants were willing to contribute more when the friend had a difficult fundraising experience than if she happened to enjoy the event, even though in both conditions she initially anticipated that it would be quite unpleasant. And the effect held only when the money donated was *directly associated* with the pain and effort (to be) experienced by the friend: When the friend was going to suffer for a charity unrelated to the one for which she solicited donations (thereby dissociating participants' contributions from her pain-effort), donations were the same as when she asked for donations without anticipating a painful-effortful fundraiser. This suggests that the martyrdom effect is not just about feelings of obligation or pity for a friend about to suffer for a worthy cause.

Finally, additional studies showed that the martyrdom effect could be moderated by the nature of the charitable cause: When the nature of the cause and the type of fundraiser were congruent, willingness to donate was higher than when both were incongruent. In other words, a painful-effortful fundraiser was more successful than an easy, enjoyable one when the charitable cause was associated with human suffering (starving children in developing nations), but not when it was associated with enjoyment (a public park). The importance of congruency in promoting charitable giving is interesting and seems to extend beyond the cause–fundraiser relationship. For example, Croson and Shang (in this volume) review evidence that the tendency for potential donors to be influenced by another donor's contributions increases when the latter is somehow similar to the former (e.g., same gender), so congruency between current and previous donors seems to also play a role. Ratner, Zhao, and Clarke (in this volume) review evidence that people show more deference toward to an advocate or volunteer for a cause when this person has a personal stake in the cause. For example, in one study, participants were more likely to respond positively to an advocate/volunteer for a cause related to disease A when that person had a parent who died from disease A, but not when the same person had a parent who died from disease B. This suggests a potential role for a form of advocate-cause congruency in donation decisions.

In sum, these studies show that people clearly seem to be violating the principle of Pareto hedonism by choosing to suffer for a cause when they could make the same contribution without doing so (e.g., by simply sending a check). What about the principle of Pareto utilitarianism?

VIOLATIONS OF PARETO UTILITARIANISM: WHY PAINFUL-EFFORTFUL FUNDRAISING IS INEFFICIENT

The principle of Pareto utilitarianism implies that charities and donors alike should always prefer the most efficient method of raising money for a cause, all else being equal. In other words, the goal should be to produce the highest contribution-to-cost ratio, so that limited resources of money and time can produce the largest possible benefits for the recipients of these donations. However, and despite the fact that willingly suffering for a noble cause may seem praiseworthy (a *noble means*), this approach to charitable fundraising is often highly inefficient, and thus violates Pareto utilitarianism.

For one thing, painful-effortful fundraising events are very costly means of raising money for charity. A study of charitable fundraising activities in 2007 (Charity Navigator, 2007) found that special event fundraisers (of which painful-effortful fundraisers are a special case) on average cost charities $1.33 per dollar raised, representing a net loss (by contrast, the overall average cost of fundraising was only $0.13 per dollar raised). In fact, for only 15% of the charities in the study sample did special events seem more beneficial than regular fundraising activities. One conclusion of the study was that many health charities would benefit from relying less on special events as means to raise money.

Painful-effortful fundraisers are also inefficient in terms of energy and time usage. The calories that participants burn to complete endurance events do not generate direct benefits for the charitable cause. As I argue in the concluding section, this energy could be put to better use. Similarly, the hours spent training for these events and participating in them constitute another important opportunity cost, which might be better spent at work, earning money for the cause. Through their efforts to raise money for charity, which include months of training for painful-effortful events and door-to-door fundraising, participants are failing to make full use of their professional skills and earning potentials.

Finally, these events can pose serious health hazards (Sweeney, 2005), adding medical expenses to the cost of organizing these events. In one illustrative study (Lee, Williams, & Hadden, 1999), researchers performed a cost-benefit analysis of parachuting for charity in a region of Scotland. They found that, rather than producing a net benefit, each pound raised for charity cost the National Health Service (NHS) £13.75 in parachute-related injuries. Ironically, approximately 70% of these donations were for NHS-related causes. As the study's authors aptly note: "Parachute jumping for charity is not cost-effective in raising money, as the cost of treatment of the 11% who are injured is far in excess of any money raised by the rest" (p. 286).

In sum, a preference for martyrdom in altruism not only leads people to seek out painful, effortful, and sometimes dangerous means of raising money for charity (a violation of Pareto hedonism). It also violates the principle of Pareto utilitarianism, since many painful-effortful fundraising practices are highly *in*efficient, with some even producing net losses (despite the fact that they often attract larger donations, on average).

In nearly all of our experiments, however, participants were *either* presented with a painful-effortful fundraiser *or* an easy, enjoyable one, but not both options at once. One might therefore object that in these studies (and in the examples presented so far), the opportunity costs associated with painful-effortful fundraising may not have been salient at the time of the donation decision (Frederick, Novemsky, Wang, Dhar, & Nowlis, 2009). In a separate, but related, line of work (Olivola & Foddy, submitted), we made these trade-offs and opportunity costs quite prominent for participants, to see whether this would reduce their preferences for altruistic martyrdom. To do so, we developed an ethical dilemma scenario involving two hypothetical American physicians: One who joins *Médecins Sans Frontières* (*Doctors*

Without Borders)[*], earns \$18,000 per year, and saves 200 lives each year through his work; another who starts a private practice in Hollywood, earns \$700,000 per year, but donates \$20,000 to *Médecins Sans Frontières* and, in doing so, saves 500 lives each year. We asked a sample of students, researchers, and professionals, all working in the fields of medicine, health, or humanitarian aid, to directly compare the decisions made by these two physicians and to indicate which career choice they would prefer. Barring "exotic" preferences, the Hollywood private practice clearly dominates, since it offers a higher salary (i.e., greater personal utility) and saves more lives (i.e., greater total welfare). And yet, the majority of our respondents considered the *Médecins Sans Frontières* career (which involves living in very poor and often dangerous parts of the world) to be preferable. In other words, they considered it better to live in a harsh environment, lead a challenging lifestyle, and be directly involved in humanitarian health efforts than to lead a comfortable lifestyle and contribute indirectly through donations, even though the former option ultimately leads to many fewer lives being saved. This provides a striking demonstration that people can hold preferences that simultaneously violate Pareto hedonism and Pareto utilitarianism, despite being made keenly aware of the opportunity costs involved.

WHAT DO WE DO ABOUT ALTRUISTIC MARTYRDOM? IMPLICATIONS FOR CHARITY FUNDRAISING

People are clearly motivated to partake in painful, effortful, and sometimes dangerous efforts to raise money for charity and to support others who engage in such efforts—a phenomenon we refer to as the martyrdom effect. Our own research suggests ways that charities can harness this paradoxical preference for martyrdom in altruism, while also pointing to some boundary conditions on this tendency. These studies show that organizing painful-effortful fundraisers can often increase the amount that participants and their sponsors are willing to donate for a cause, relative to easy and purely enjoyable means of raising contributions. However, adding pain and effort to the fundraising process seems to be more effective when the target cause is associated with human suffering (e.g., raising money for the victims of disease, malnutrition, or war) than when it is associated with human pleasure (e.g., raising money for a museum, a children's sports team, or an orchestra). Thus, health-related and humanitarian aid charities are the most likely to benefit from painful-effortful fundraising. We also noticed that adding pain-effort to the fundraising process had a small, but systematic, effect on decisions about *whether* or not to participate (and thus to donate), such that a consistent fraction of potential donors in our studies seemed to be deterred by the prospect of having to endure great pain and effort. Charities, therefore, are likely to maximize contributions by organizing fundraisers that are painful-effortful enough to be perceived as challenging (so as to boost donations from participants and their sponsors), yet

---

[*] *Médecins Sans Frontières* (also known as *Doctors Without Borders*) is an independent international medical humanitarian organization that delivers emergency aid to people affected by armed conflict, epidemics, natural or man-made disasters, or exclusion from health care in nearly 60 countries. *Médecins Sans Frontières* employs hundreds of doctors, as well as other medical and non-medical professionals, who work alongside locally hired staff to provide medical care.

not so daunting that large numbers of potential donors are deterred from even participating.

Although the specific mental processes underlying the martyrdom effect have yet to be fully elucidated, some of the research I have reviewed suggests that it occurs because people derive satisfaction and symbolic value from engaging in, or supporting, painful-effortful activities that contribute to a charitable cause. Simply put, the act of donating may seem more "special" when it involves great personal sacrifice and, in particular, some amount of suffering (Ramos, 1999). The implication seems to be that people care a lot about the *means* of achieving altruistic goals. In doing so, however, they may lose sight of the *consequences* and *opportunity costs* involved. Indeed, I have provided evidence that altruistic martyrdom can be highly inefficient in terms of organizational costs, health costs, and time spent preparing and engaging in painful-effortful events. This highlights an important dilemma. In many cases, much more money could be raised if in place of the hours training for and participating in endurance events, donors spent that time at work and donated the resulting wage. However, if people are motivated by the challenges inherent in painful-effortful fundraisers, then they may be resistant to replacing those events with easier means of contributing, even if the latter are more cost-efficient. One solution might be to replace running, biking, and other popular endurance events that do not, in themselves, contribute to charity, with more useful, but equally challenging, activities. Imagine, for example, an event where participants must plant trees, help build (or rebuild) homes, serve food, pick-up trash, or package medical supplies, to raise money for charitable causes. These activities could be just as physically engaging as standard endurance events, provided that participants set challenging goals for themselves (e.g., planting a certain number of trees within a specified time limit). By participating in fundraisers of this sort, participants would have a dual positive impact through their donations *and* the fundraising act itself. Furthermore, this bundling of altruistic goals, whereby donors and sponsors can simultaneously contribute to two charities for the cost of one, might prove highly appealing (see Strahilevitz, in this volume).

CONCLUSION

The research covered in this chapter shows that people violate two very basic, but important, consequentialist principles of rationality and morality: *Pareto hedonism* (the notion that decision makers should always opt to reduce the disutility they experience from helping others whenever they can do so without decreasing their altruistic contributions) and *Pareto utilitarianism* (the notion that decision makers should always opt to increase their altruistic contributions whenever they can do so without increasing the disutility they experience from helping). These violations pose theoretical and practical problems. On a theoretical level, even modern consequentialist economic models of decision making, which incorporate both selfish and altruistic goals, fail to explain these violations of self- and other-regarding utility. On a practical level, a preference of martyrdom in charitable giving often leads to highly inefficient means of raising contributions. A challenge for future researchers, policy makers, and charities will be to devise fundraising practices that tap into our motivation to suffer for altruistic causes, while also minimizing the opportunity costs involved.

REFERENCES

Abdel–Ghany, M., Bivens, G. E., Keeler, J. P., & James, W. L. (1983). Windfall income and the permanent income hypothesis: New evidence. *Journal of Consumer Affairs, 17,* 262–276.

Arkes, H. L., Joyner, C. A., Pezzo, M. A., Nash, J. G., Siegel–Jacobs, K., & Stone, E. (1994). The psychology of windfall gains. *Organizational Behavior and Human Decision Processes, 59,* 331–347.

Baron J. (1994). Nonconsequentialist decisions. *Behavioral and Brain Sciences, 17,* 1–10.

Barry, P. (2006, November 29). Glass act! *Surrey & Hants Star.* Retrieved March 29, 2008, from http://www.shstar.co.uk/

Baumeister, R. F. (1991) *Meanings of life.* New York: Guilford Press.

Bem, D. J. (1967). Self–perception: An alternative interpretation of cognitive dissonance phenomena. *Psychological Review, 74,* 183–200.

Berns, G. (2005). *Satisfaction: The science of finding true fulfillment.* New York: Henry Holt.

Birks, B. (2006, October 25). Sedgley firewalk. *BBC Black Country.* Retrieved March 29, 2008, from http://www.bbc.co.uk/blackcountry/

Charity Navigator (2007, May 1). *2007 Special events study.* Retrieved July 31, 2008, from http://www.charitynavigator.org/index.cfm?bay=studies.events

Charness, G., & Rabin, M. (2002). Understanding social preferences with simple tests. *Quarterly Journal of Economics, 117,* 817–869.

Cormack, M. (Ed.). (2002). *Sacrificing the self: Perspectives on martyrdom and religion.* Oxford: Oxford University Press.

DeSoucey, M., Pozner, J. E., Fields, C., Dobransky, K., & Fine, G. A. (2008). Memory and sacrifice: An embodied theory of martyrdom. *Cultural Sociology, 2,* 99–121.

Elliott, R., Newman, J. L., Longe, O. A., & Deakin, J. F. W. (2004). Instrumental responding for rewards is associated with enhanced neuronal response in subcortical reward systems. *NeuroImage, 21,* 984–990.

Festinger, L. (1957). *A theory of cognitive dissonance.* Stanford, CA: Stanford University Press.

Fields, R. M. (2004). *Martyrdom: The psychology, theology, and politics of self–sacrifice.* Westport, CT: Praeger.

Firewalkers blaze a trail for charity. (2004, October 21). *Haverhill Weekly News.* Retrieved March 29, 2008, from http://www.haverhill-news.com

Frederick, S., Novemsky, N., Wang, J., Dhar, R., & Nowlis, S. (2009). Opportunity cost neglect. *Journal of Consumer Research, 36,* 553–561.

Gardiner, R. (2007, July 16). Discovering how lucky we are. *Times Online.* Retrieved January 11, 2009, from http://www.times.co.nz/

Glas, G., Spero, M. H., Verhagen, P. J., & van Praag, H. M. (Eds). (2007). *Hearing visions and seeing voices: Psychological aspects of biblical concepts and personalities.* Dordrecht, The Netherlands: Springer.

Hastie, R. (2001). Problems for judgment and decision making. *Annual Review of Psychology, 52,* 653–683.

Henderson, P. W., & Peterson, R. A. (1992). Mental accounting and categorization. *Organizational Behavior and Human Decision Processes, 51,* 92–117.

Higgins, E. T. (2006). Value from hedonic experience and engagement. *Psychological Review, 113*, 439–460.

Kaufman, B. E. (1999). Exploring the behavioral foundations of labor economics. *Industrial and Labor Review, 52*, 361–392.

Keeler, J. P., James, W. L., & Abdel–Ghany, M. (1985). The relative size of windfall income and the permanent income hypothesis. *Journal of Business & Economic Statistics, 3*, 209–215.

Lane, R. E. (1992). Work as "disutility" and money as "happiness": Cultural origins of a basic market error. *Journal of Socio-Economics, 21*, 43–64.

Lee, C. T., Williams, P., & Hadden, W. A. (1999). Parachuting for charity: Is it worth the money? A 5-year audit of parachute injuries in Tayside and the cost to the NHS. *Injury, 30*, 283–287.

Lewis, M. (1965). Psychological effect of effort. *Psychological Bulletin, 64*, 183–190.

Liu, W., & Aaker, J. (2008). The happiness of giving: The time–ask effect. *Journal of Consumer Research, 35*, 543–557.

Loewenstein, G. (1999). Because it is there: The challenge of mountaineering … for Utility Theory. *Kyklos, 52*, 315–344.

Loewenstein, G., & Issacharoff, S. (1994). Source dependence in the valuation of objects. *Journal of Behavioral Decision Making, 7*, 157–168.

Messick, D. M. (1999). Alternative logics for decision making in social settings. *Journal of Economic Behavior and Organization, 39*, 11–28.

Mullainathan, S., & Thaler, R. H. (2001). Behavioral economics. In N. J. Smelser & P. B. Baltes (Eds.), *International encyclopaedia of the social and behavioral sciences*. Oxford: Elsevier.

Napoli, L. (2003, November 17). Why walking in circles gets charities going. *New York Times*. Retrieved September 30, 2009, from http://www.nytimes.com/

Olivola, C. Y., & Foddy, B. (submitted). The "Médecins Sans Frontières" ("Doctors Without Borders") dilemma: Evidence that medical martyrdom appeals to moral intuitions more than rational cost-benefit analyses.

Olivola, C. Y., & Shafir, E. (submitted). The martyrdom effect: When pain and effort increase prosocial contributions.

Oxford English Dictionary Online. (2008, June). Oxford University Press. Retrieved August 4, 2008, from http://dictionary.oed.com/

Pub-goers walk on fire for charity. (2002, December 6). *BBC News*. Retrieved March 29, 2008, from http://news.bbc.co.uk

Rabin, M. (2002). A perspective on psychology and economics. *European Economic Review, 46*, 657–685.

Ramos, G. (1999, March 11). For marathoners, 26 miles and thousands of reasons to run them. *Los Angeles Times*. Retrieved September 30, 2009, from http://articles.latimes.com/

Russell, A. (2004, October 18). Students hungry to help. *The Age*. Retrieved January 11, 2009, from http://www.theage.com.au/

Singer, P. (1993). *Practical ethics.* (2nd ed.). Cambridge: Cambridge University Press.

Singer, P. (2009). *The life you can save: Acting now to end world poverty*. New York: Random House.

Sweeney, C. (2005, July 7). The latest in fitness: Millions for charity. *New York Times*. Retrieved September 30, 2009, from http://www.nytimes.com/

Symonds, W. C. (2005, September 19). Sweating for dollars. *Business Week*. Retrieved March 29, 2008, from http://www.businessweek.com

Tricomi, E. M., Delgado, M. R., & Fiez, J. A. (2004). Modulation of caudate activity by action contingency. *Neuron, 41*, 281–292.

Unger, P. (1996). *Living high and letting die: Our illusion of innocence*. Oxford: Oxford University Press.

Williams, L. (1995, May 7). New charity strategy: Get up and go. *New York Times*. Retrieved September 30, 2009, from http://www.nytimes.com/

Wing, K. T., Pollak, T. H., & Blackwood, A. (2008). *The nonprofit almanac 2008*. Washington, D.C.: Urban Institute Press.

Zink, C. F., Pagnoni, G., Martin–Skurski, M. E., Chappelow, J. C., & Berns, G. S. (2004). Human striatal responses to monetary reward depend on saliency. *Neuron, 42*, 509–517.

Section *II*

The Impact of Social Factors

5

Social Influences in Giving
Field Experiments in Public Radio

RACHEL CROSON and JEN (YUE) SHANG

INTRODUCTION

*A*cademics from multiple disciplines, as well as nonprofit practitioners, have examined the internal motivations of individuals to make charitable contributions and voluntarily provide public goods. These scholars include economists (e.g., Kolm & Ythier, 2006; Powell & Steinberg, 2006), psychologists (e.g., Batson, 1990; Carlson, Charlin, & Miller, 1988; Clary, Snyder, Ridge, Copeland, Stukas, Haugen, & Miene, 1998; Penner, Dovidio, Piliavin, & Schroeder, 2005; Piaget, 1932; Weber, Kopelman, & Messick, 2004), sociologists (e.g., Havens, O'Herlihy, & Schervish, 2006), and nonprofit marketing and management scholars (e.g., Bennett & Sargeant, 2005). In economics, models of altruism (e.g., Becker, 1974), impure and warm-glow altruism (e.g., Andreoni, 1989, 1990), conditional cooperation (e.g., Fischbacher, Gachter, & Fehr, 2001), and reciprocity (e.g., Sugden, 1984) have been developed and tested in the experimental laboratory (e.g., Croson, 2007).

We examine the setting of individual contributions to public radio. Individual donations are the bread and butter of the public broadcasting industry in the United States. Over 800 member radio stations collected $275 million from individual donors in 2006 (Corporation for Public Broadcasting Revenue Report, 2006). These donations were collected using the fundraising principle that public services drive public support (Audience Research Analysis, 1988, 1998, 2010). That is, people listen, so they give; when audiences decline, so do donations.

This fundraising wisdom inspires sophisticated practices like distinguishing between core listeners and fringe listeners, understanding how listener loyalty translates into donations, and how to design fundraising appeals to remind people of the importance of listening to public radio in their lives. This mental model of fundraising, however, assumes a one-to-one relationship between a station and a donor in the transaction of service and support. However, these practices do not typically incorporate the social environment surrounding listeners and donors into the equation.

In contrast, our research expands the vision of giving to include the social environment of donors to public radio. The focus of this research is to understand the social environment surrounding both listening and donating behavior. Our research highlights the observation that listeners and donors are not only individuals who act on their own; they are also social animals (Aronson, 2007). They live in connection with each other. Audience research (Audience Research Analysis. 1988, 1998, 2010) can tell us how much each individual listens, but it does not tell us how long they listen with friends, how much they talk with others about the programs they listen to, how often they discuss their donation decisions with their family, how their donations are influenced by others' donations, or how much listening and donating constitute an important part of who they are (their self-identity). It is this social context surrounding listening and donating that our research sets out to study.

A relevant stream of literature (and one to which these authors have contributed) goes beyond internal motivations of donors and investigates the impact of *social information*—knowing whether and what others contribute—on one's own contribution. The first part of our chapter ("Social Information") reviews this literature and draws practical implications from it that will be of interest to fundraisers.

While this previous work demonstrates that social information about others' *giving* can influence one's own, in the second part of this chapter ("Social Networks") we discuss the impact of a different type of social information on giving: information about others' *use* or *value for* the organization. Models of charitable giving typically balance these two factors within the individual. In deciding whether or how much to give, the individual compares his value for the services the organization provides with the contribution he is considering. He contributes up to the amount that he values the work the organization is doing. In the "Social Networks" section we suggest an expanded conception of the individual's value of the organization, which includes not only the value the individual receives, but also the value his social network receives. What they value and what is important to them increases their happiness, and thus our own. Thus supporting services that provide value to one's social network in turn supports one's own values.

SOCIAL INFORMATION

The body of research described in this section studied the effects of social information on giving. Previous research on social information and social norms suggests that people's behavior is driven by their perceptions of others' behavior (Crutchfield, 1955). Cialdini, Reno and Kallgren (1990) describe these perceptions as *descriptive social norms*, which specify what is typically done in a given setting (what most people do), and differentiate these from *injunctive social norms*, which specify what behaviors garner approval in society (what people ought to do).

Many studies have demonstrated the influence of descriptive and injunctive social norms on subsequent behavior in varying situations. For example, they have been shown to influence the choice of exercising during leisure time (Okun, Karoly, & Lutz, 2002; Okun, Ruehlman, Karoly, Lutz, Fairholme, & Schaub, 2003; Rhodes & Courneya, 2003); communication styles during wedding ceremonies (Strano, 2006); team-based innovations in the workplace (Caldwell & O'Reilly, 2003); littering (Cialdini, Reno, & Kallgren, 1990); and stereotyping, prejudice, and discrimination (Mackie & Smith, 1998). The relationship between social norms and behavior has also been shown for specific subpopulations, including breakfast food choice among children (Berg, Jonsson, & Conner, 2000), alcohol misuse among college students (Walters & Neighbors, 2005), smoking cessation among smokers (Van de Putte, Yzer, & Brunsting, 2005), and condom use among drug users (Van Empelen, Kok, Jansen, & Hoebe, 2001). In this body of research we are the first to look at the influence of social norms, and descriptive social norms in particular, in the domain of donations to public radio. Our variable of interest is the level of giving by individual donors.

In Shang and Croson (2009), we amended the script that volunteers used when listeners called in to make their donation. After being greeted by the volunteer, callers were randomly assigned to a control condition (where they were given no social information) or were told "We had another donor who gave $X dollars. How much would you like to give today?" The amounts that callers were told another donor had given were varied ($75, the median gift level of this station; $180, the 80th percentile of gifts to the station; and $300, the 95th percentile of gifts to the station) to examine their impact on giving.

We found that providing social information increased the amounts that people donated, but that there was an optimal "specimen" amount that was most effective. This is illustrated in Figure 5.1 where the average gift from new donors in the control condition (i.e., where donors are given no social information) is shown alongside the cases where the caller is told about another donor having made a gift

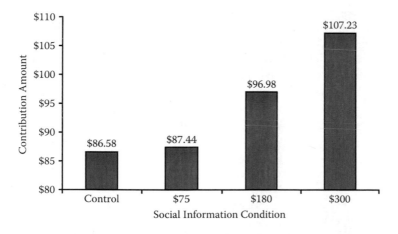

Figure 5.1   Social information increases the contribution levels of new donors.

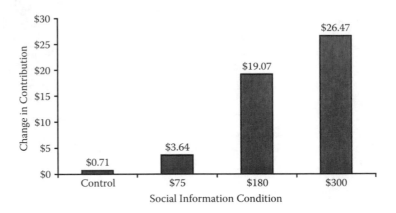

Figure 5.2   Social information increases the contribution levels of renewing donors over previous year's contribution.

of $75, $180, or $300. In this case, citing a prior donation of $300 was the most profitable, and increased giving by an average of 29%.

A similar picture was obtained with donors who were calling in to renew their existing membership. Figure 5.2 shows that donors not exposed to the social information gave almost the same amount as they had given last year (up only 71 cents). Those donors exposed to social information, however, gave markedly more than they had previously given, and in the $300 condition, their contributions increased by $26.47.

These results raise the natural question of the optimal level of social information to provide. After some further studies and calibration exercises (Shang & Croson, 2006), we conclude that the ideal amount to choose is between the 90th and 95th percentile of the value of previous gifts to the station. Croson and Shang (2009) find that higher levels of social information actually decrease individual giving.

These first three studies all examine the impact of *upward* social information (another donor is giving more than the target). But what is the impact of *downward* social information? Shang and Croson (2008) answered this question using a direct mail campaign for the same radio station.

In this study, solicitations were sent to existing donors asking them to renew their memberships. We collected the previous year's contribution of each donor from the station. Some donors received materials that indicated that another donor had contributed exactly the amount that they had contributed in the previous year (although they were not reminded of what that contribution had been). Others received materials that indicated that another donor had contributed more than their previous year's contribution. Still others received materials that indicated that another donor had contributed less than their previous year's contribution.

Figure 5.3 describes the change in contribution exhibited by donors in each of the three conditions. Donors who received social information higher than their previous year's contribution increased their contribution by $12 on average. Donors who received social information that was the same as their previous year's contribution increased their contribution by $5.45 on average. However, donors who

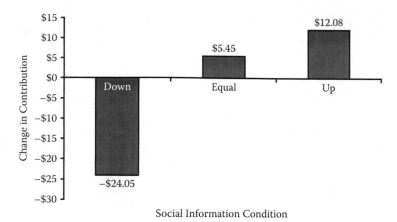

Figure 5.3   Social information influences contributions via mail.

received social information lower than their previous year's contribution decreased their contribution by $24 on average.

This research illustrates two important features of social information. First, social information is as robustly effective at influencing contributions when delivered via mail (or in writing) as when it is delivered over the phone (or in person). This provides an important robustness check to the results from the previous studies. Second, downward social information is about twice as impactful as upward social information; the reduction in contributions as a result of downward social informa-tion is twice as large as the increase in contributions as a result of upward social information. This suggests an important caveat to the use of social information in fundraising. Appeals need to be customized to the donor so they do not represent (too much) downward social information, which will likely decrease contributions.

Intuitively, one might imagine that causing someone to increase their giving this year might reduce it the next (intertemporal crowding out). This turns out not to be the case, and in fact, quite the opposite effect occurs. Contributions one year later from new donors who received information about a previous donor's contribu-tion are approximately $20 higher than contributions from donors in the control condition without such information.

Even with this result, we do not conclude that the script that donors receive in one year influences their giving in the following year. In a follow-up experi-ment, very few (if any) donors remembered the script they heard one year earlier, and it is not reasonable for us to assume that the effect of the script itself is that long-lasting. Instead, the effect seems to be one of giving "stickiness." The donor remembers giving more in the previous year (although not *why* they gave more), and this increases giving in the current year. Similarly, we anticipate that if the organization follows up with these donors with personalized ask strings, this strat-egy has the potential of keeping donors at this higher level of giving.

While the research up until now has demonstrated the impact of social infor-mation on individual giving, we can further ask why it works. Croson, Handy, and

Shang (2008) investigated this question using a survey of public radio donors. In the survey we asked for self-reports of their current and previous contributions. We also asked for individuals' perceptions of the descriptive social norm—what they believed others contributed to the station on average. We find that the perceived descriptive social norm is significantly related to self-reported contributions. Respondents who believe that others contribute high amounts self-report their own contributions as high.

We next collected data from the radio station itself about these donors' actual contributions. Again, we find a significant relationship between the donors' beliefs about the descriptive social norm and the amount they actually give to the station. This work thus provides support for the proposed mechanism through which social information influences behavior—the desire to conform to the descriptive norm induced by the information.

In a final study in this stream of research, Shang, Reed, and Croson (2008) examine the interaction between social information and social identity on public radio contributions. In particular, theories of social influence from psychology predict that the more similarities exist between the potential donor and the other donor who has made the contribution, the more impactful the social information about the other donor's contribution will be. This project investigates whether donors give more money if told that a previous donor *who shares their identity* also made a large contribution.

In consumer behavior, there is extensive literature showing that identity impacts the effectiveness of social information (Smith, Bruner, & White, 1956). This can occur for a number of different reasons. First, social identities may be diagnostic of the decisions or judgments at hand, and thus other consumers' behavior can become more relevant to a judgment (Feldman & Lynch, 1988) when aspects of these consumers are similar to the target consumer's identity (Reed, 2004). Second, individuals may want to conform to the behavior of others like themselves, but feel no desire or need to conform to the behavior of those different than themselves. For either of these reasons, the more similar the individual is to the source of the social information, the stronger its impact is likely to be.

In this study we used gender match or mismatch between the target donor and a previous donor. We chose gender because it is a well-established dimension of social identity in the psychological literature (Bem, 1981; Deaux et al., 1995). Males and females have been shown to behave in ways that are consistent with the social targets of the same gender in other settings (Mussweiler, Ruter, & Epstude, 2004). Therefore, in the domain of charitable contributions, we believed that identity along the gender dimension can influence the strength of the social information effect demonstrated above.

From an implementation point of view, gender is also an attractive possibility because it is easily identifiable (Cialdini, 2001). Previous research has used incidental similarities such as first names, birthdays, or fingerprints; however, that information is not available to us in typical phone or even mailing campaigns. Gender, on the other hand, is applicable to all potential donors, and callers' gender is identifiable from their voice, with only a few exceptions.

In this study we changed the wording of the telephone script from "we had another *who* gave $300" to "we had another donor; *he/she* gave $300." We then compared contributions of callers whose gender was the same as that of "another donor" and those whose gender was different than "another donor." No callers received the control condition, or any other dollar amounts. The results are shown in Figure 5.4.

In cases where the gender of the caller was matched with the gender of the example, the amount of the gift was increased by an average of 34%. This result tells us that individuals pay attention to social information and in particular social information from others who are similar in some way to themselves. It also tells us that this information has the capacity to dramatically increase giving.

In theory, this effect is more likely to occur when donors have high social identity. In Shang, Reed, and Croson (2008) we go on to show that this prediction is upheld. Individuals who more positively identified with being male (or female) showed this effect more strongly.

In summary, results from the first set of papers illustrate the strong impact of social influence on individual giving. Informing donors of the donations of others has the potential to significantly increase (or decrease) their own donation. Choosing the appropriate level of social information to communicate is critical; our research indicates that contributions in the 90th to 95th percentile of the contribution distribution are high enough to induce increased giving but not so high as to scare off low donors. Social information that is lower than what the donor would have given significantly lowers donations. Results from our second set of papers further investigate the mechanisms behind this result. One paper demonstrates that conformity to the descriptive norm is causing the result, rather than anchoring or other cognitive biases. Another paper shows that as the social similarity between the target donor and the example donor increases, the effect of social information increases. Taken together, this research highlights the importance of the social environment in which the

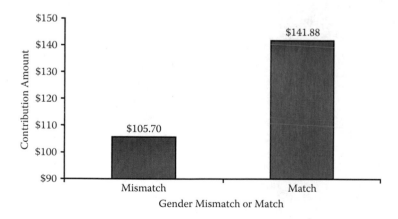

Figure 5.4   Social information is more impactful for matched gender.

donor finds him- or herself, as well as the other, previously identified factors that influence giving.[°]

SOCIAL NETWORKS

Background and Motivation

The effect of social information on giving described previously is situational; that is, donors are told about another donor's previous contribution right before they make a donation and the influence of social information on giving occurs instantly. Other effects of social interaction on giving may involve a more stable social environment of the donor. In this section, we will study a more stable social factor: social networks.

The power of social capital in civil engagement has recently become well known among academics and practitioners (Putnam, 1993, 2000). Fundraising professionals know that people do not give to causes; people give to people (Tempel, 2003). This has spawned a large literature and practice of peer-to-peer giving and solicitation, where current donors solicit or recruit new donors using their existing social networks.

Previous research has identified the importance of social networks on behaviors as varied as the formation of online communities (Yu, Lang, & Kumar, 2009), perceptions on the quality of life by drug users (De Maeyer, Vanderplasschen, & Browkaert, 2009), the level of innovation in management teams (Hung, Wu, Wen, & Wu, 2008), and poverty reduction (Simmons & Birchall, 2008). In this research, we investigate the impact of the social network on giving to public radio stations.

In this (new) study, we will be testing two hypotheses.

H1: The size of the potential donor's social network is correlated with the level of contribution (a main effect of social network size).

H2: This relationship is driven by the *priming* of the social network.

The first hypothesis draws directly from previous research, which demonstrates that larger networks impact behavior in other domains. In particular, we hypothesize that the value an individual receives from the radio station depends not only on the value (s)he receives individually from listening to the station, but the value the people they care about (their social network) receive from the services that the station provides. As the social network grows, the individual's total value from the station's services also grows, which increases their willingness to contribute toward the station's continued operation. Note that this hypothesis expands the notion of individual value (or exchange) that we described in the beginning of this chapter to include value received both directly (as previous work has hypothesized) and indirectly (via the social network).

The second hypothesis provides a limitation to this observation, however. Here we hypothesize that the value a potential donor receives indirectly is not naturally

---

[°] Further details on the experiments, implementation, or other issues can be found in the papers cited in this section.

and immediately considered when they make their donation decision. However, if a potential donor is *primed* to consider their social network, this indirect value will be highlighted and included in their calculation of how much to give. Thus we expect that the social network size will be related to the contribution only (or especially) in a setting where it is primed before the individual makes their contribution decision.

We test these hypotheses in a field experiment with a public radio station. This station has three on-air fund drives per year. DJs on the air ask for donations and suggest a variety of contribution levels. A $120 gift makes the donor a basic member; listeners who give $150 and $180 receive additional gifts. Other gift levels occur at $240, $365, $500, $1000, $1200, $2500, and $5000. Listeners call into the station to make contributions in response to these appeals.

In the experiment reported here, we ask callers about their social networks either before or after they have made their contribution. We then examine the relationship between the size of the network and the amount contributed.

The Experiment

This experiment was conducted in an anonymous public radio station in the Midwest in 2006 and 2007. During the on-air drive, the station DJs interspersed news and informational programs with appeals for donations. Listeners responded to the on-air appeals during the drive and called the station to make a pledge. Experimenters answered the phone as volunteers for the station, asked the routine questions for the station, and implemented the manipulation in the appropriate place in the conversation. We collected data on 547 callers.

We used a between-subject design with two conditions. We asked all the callers how many of their friends and family also listened to the station, and recorded the outcome (the size of their network). For half of the callers (randomly selected) we asked this question before they made their contribution; for the other half, we asked them after. All experimental conditions were randomized within each experimenter and within each hour. As expected from this randomization process, we find no systematic effects of the experimenter (who answered the phone) or of the hour (which might be linked to the particular programming for the time slot).

Other information collected by the station during the phone conversation included the caller's name, phone number, email address, billing address, city, zip code, credit card or check information, and the thank-you gifts they would like to receive. However, for confidentiality reasons, and to conform to human subjects protocols, only research-related information was copied and kept by the researchers.

Results

Descriptive Statistics   The average pledge received in our experiment was $153.31 (standard error 8.18; median $120), with a minimum of $5 and a maximum of $2000. The average reported network size was 13 (standard error 1.29; median 5), with a minimum of 0 and a maximum of 500. A simple correlation demonstrates that these two measures are significantly correlated ($\rho = 0.129$, $p = .0024$).

This provides preliminary evidence in favor of H1 (see the "Social Information" section for statistical analyses), suggesting an overall effect of the size of the social network on the amounts contributed.

Of the 547 callers, 302 were asked for network information before they made their donation. For this subsample, the average pledge received was $151 (standard error 9.95; median $120), and the average reported network size was 20.9 (standard error 2.22; median 10). A simple correlation demonstrates that these two measures are significantly correlated ($\rho = 0.194$, $p = .0006$).

In contrast, 245 callers were asked for network information after they had made their donation. For this subsample, the average pledge received was $156 (standard error 13.58; median $120), and the average reported network size was 3.2 (standard error 0.13; median 3). A simple correlation demonstrates that these two measures are *not* correlated ($\rho = 0.076$, $p = .2377$). These two results together support H2 (see the "Social Information" section for statistical analyses), suggesting that the impact of social network size on contribution amount is contingent on when the social network size is elicited.

We find no effect of elicitation order on contribution amounts. The average contribution amount when social network size is elicited before the contribution is made is $151, and when social network size is elicited after the contribution is made is $156. These are not significantly different, using either a parametric t-test ($t = 0.25$, $p = .4010$), or a nonparametric Wilcoxon test ($Z = 0.18$, $p = .8545$).

Interestingly, we also find (although not hypothesized) that elicitation impacts the reported size of the social network. The average reported social network size when the question is asked before the contribution is made is 20.9, while the average reported social network size when the question is asked after the contribution is made is 3.2. These are significantly different using either a parametric t-test ($t = 7.17$, $p < .0001$), or a nonparametric Wilcoxon test ($Z = 14.41$, $p < .0001$). This surprising result is discussed further below.

Statistical Analyses   Table 5.1 reports the results of three regressions. The dependent variable is the amount contributed. Independent variables include the size of the individual's network and their gender.

Column (1) supports our first hypothesis. Overall, we find a significant (and large) effect of the size of the social network on giving. For each additional person in a caller's social network, (s)he contributed slightly more than $1 ($1.32). Furthermore, this effect is statistically significant.

Columns (2) and (3) report the same regressions as Column (1), but separated by whether the donor was asked about their network before or after their contribution. As can be seen, the relationship between the size of the caller's network and the amount they contributed is significant and positive when the network size is elicited *before* the contribution is made (Column [2]), but not significant when it is elicited after (Column [3]). This comparison supports our second hypothesis.

To further support our second hypothesis that the size of people's social network is not a naturally occurring decision-making factor in determining the level of charitable donations, we can compare the R-squares of regressions in Columns (2) and (3). When the size of the network is asked before a donation is made, the model

TABLE 5.1   OLS Regressions of Contributions on Social Network Size

	All Data (1)	Network Before (2)	Network After (3)
Constant	137.19[a]	134.18[a]	150.16[a]
	(9.571)	(16.92)	(28.42)
Network size	1.32[a]	1.14[b]	−0.771
	(0.38)	(0.45)	(6.52)
Male	2.67	14.44	18.216
	(8.45)	(19.56)	(27.67)
N	547	302	245
R-squared	.022	.025	.002

[a] $p < .01$
[b] $p < .05$

explains 2.5% of the variance in giving, while the same model explains close to no variance when the size of the network is asked after the decision.

This relationship can be seen in Figure 5.5, which graphs in a scatterplot the reported network size on the X-axis, and the average contribution received (by callers reporting this size of network) on the Y-axis. The lines (labeled Linear (Before) and Linear (After)) show the univariate best-fit relationships in the two treatments. Consistent with the data reported in Table 5.1, the relationship among callers who are asked after their donation is not significant (and even slightly negative) while the relationship among callers who are asked before their donation is significant and positive, as predicted.

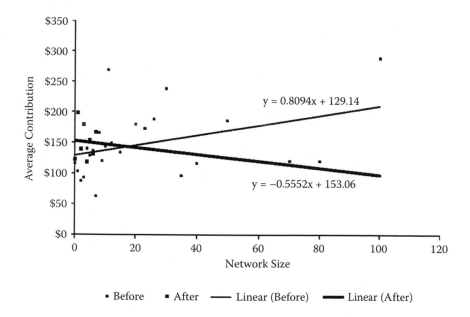

Figure 5.5   Univariate relationship between network size and contribution.

Summary

The results from this research suggest both that social networks matter (a main effect of the social network on giving) and that they affect giving primarily (only) when primed (when elicited before the contribution decision). The average contributions do not change when this priming is in place (thus one might consider it costless). However, surprisingly, individuals report having larger social networks when they are primed (asked before their contribution) than when they are not (asked after their contribution). This was an unhypothesized finding, and while we can speculate on its underlying cause, clearly more research is needed to understand the mechanisms through which this occurred.

Our results have interesting and important implications for fundraising practitioners. As can be seen from Figure 5.5, when individuals have small social networks, priming is likely to be ineffective, and may even lower their contribution relative to what it would have been had they not been primed. When social networks are below 20, callers who are not primed give more than those who are primed. However, when individuals have large social networks (above 20), priming increases contributions. Thus one recommendation might be for fundraising practitioners to *selectively* prime individuals who they believe to be well connected, and to avoid priming others.

A second recommendation from this research is for the organization to increase the size of the donor's social network. This can be done in a number of ways, including inducing the potential donor to introduce their existing friends and family to the organization and what it does (a variant on recruiting), or providing opportunities for existing organization members to become friends and thus join each other's networks (perhaps via social events among donors). Our research suggests that these activities can increase the social networks of the existing donors which, when primed, will subsequently increase their giving.

CONCLUSIONS

In this chapter we expanded the existing model of charitable giving beyond a transactional account (comparing the costs of contributing with the benefits gained from the contribution) and incorporated social factors into considerations of giving—social information, and social networks. We used the setting of individual contributions to public radio.

Public radio provides a particularly interesting setting to study. First, the public radio industry (and individual giving in this industry) is large; in 2006, over 800 member radio stations collected $275 million from individual donors (Corporation for Public Broadcasting Revenue Report, 2006). Second, public radio provides a "pure" public good; individuals can enjoy the benefits of the radio station (listening) without paying (contributing), unlike other nonprofit organizations like museums or opera companies. Finally, public radio is a relatively private activity; individuals listen in their cars or at their homes, rather than consuming the service provided publicly or in the presence of others. Thus both usage and contribution decisions are made in private and (one might think), in relative absence of social factors. As a result, this setting provides a stringent test of the impact of social information and social networks. If they matter here, one might imagine they will matter even more in more "socially" oriented contexts.

We reviewed previously published research demonstrating a positive impact of social information on contributions. When donors are told that others contributed a (relatively) high amount, they give more. We parameterized this effect, and suggest that the most efficacious level of social information to use is that drawn from the 90th to the 95th percentile of the contribution distribution. We also showed that increased contributions caused by social information do not "crowd out" or decrease contributions in the future. Individuals who were provided with social information were significantly more likely to renew their membership, and their contributions were (if anything) larger than those who were not provided with this information. Similarly, donors decreased their contributions when others donated less, and the downward effect was twice as large as the upward effect. We showed that this effect is robust to multiple fundraising channels (phone and mail). We further showed that the mechanism through which this effect operates is conformity to the (descriptive) norm. Finally, as the social similarity between the target and the other donor increases, the impact of social information increases as well.

We also presented new data on the impact of social network size on contributions. We found, as hypothesized, that individuals who had larger social networks gave more overall. However, the effect was significant only for those who were *primed* with their social network (who reported their social network size before they made their contribution). We also found, surprisingly, that those who were primed reported significantly larger social networks than those who were not. This result remains a puzzle for future research.

Like any research, this body of work has limitations. First, as mentioned above, public radio is an interesting and important domain to investigate social influences, but generalizability is always a concern with field experiments. Testing similar interventions in other nonprofit settings would be a useful endeavor. Second, we have reported on two particular social influences on giving (social information and social networks). But there are certainly others, possibly even more effective, which have yet to be tested (see the other chapters in this volume for some examples). With these limitations in mind, we hope that this research has convincingly demonstrated the importance of introducing the social dimension into fundraising theory and practice, and has introduced some new ideas for practitioners to consider in designing their appeals.

REFERENCES

Andreoni, J. (1989). Giving with impure altruism: Applications to charity and Ricardian equivalence. *Journal of Political Economy, 97,* 1447–1458.

Andreoni, J. (1990). Impure altruism and donations to public goods: A theory of warm-glow giving. *Economic Journal, 100,* 464–477.

Aronson, E. (2007). *The social animal* (10th ed.). New York: Worth Publishers.

Audience Research Analysis. Audience 1988. Retrieved December 5, 2007, from http://www.aranet.com/

Audience Research Analysis. Audience 1998. Retrieved December 5, 2007, from http://www.aranet.com/

Audience Research Analysis. Audience 2010. Retrieved December 5, 2007, http://www.aranet.com/

Batson, C. D. (1990). How social an animal? The human capacity for caring. *American Psychologist, 45*(3), 336–346.

Becker, G. (1974). A theory of social interactions. *Journal of Political Economy, 82,* 1063–1093.

Bem, S. L. (1981). Gender schema theory: A cognitive account of sex typing. *Psychological Review, 88*(4), 354–364.

Bennett, R., & Sargeant, A. (2005). The nonprofit marketing landscape: Guest editors' introduction to a special section. *Journal of Business Research, 58*(6), 797–805.

Berg, C., Jonsson, I., & Conner, M. (2000). Understanding choice of milk and bread for breakfast among Swedish children aged 11–15 years: An application of the theory of planned behavior. *Appetite, 34*(1), 5–19.

Caldwell, D. F., & O'Reilly III, C. A. (2003). The determinants of team-based innovation in organizations: The role of social influence. *Small Group Research, 34*(4), 497–517.

Carlson, M., Charlin, V., & Miller, N. (1988). Positive mood and helping behavior: A test of six hypotheses. *Journal of Personality and Social Psychology, 55*(2), 211–229.

Clary, E. G., Snyder, M., Ridge, R. D., Copeland, J., Stukas, A. A., Haugen, J., & Miene, P. Understanding and assessing the motivations of volunteers: A functional approach. *Journal of Personality and Social Psychology, 74,* 1516–1530.

Cialdini, R. B., Reno, R. R., & Kallgren, C. A. (1990). A focus theory of normative conduct: Recycling the concept of norms to reduce littering in public places. *Journal of Personality and Social Psychology, 58*(6), 1015–1026.

Cialdini, R. B. (2001). *Influence: Science and practice* (4th ed.). New York: HarperCollins.

Corporation for Public Broadcasting. (2006). Corporation for public broadcasting annual report 2006. Retrieved April 2009, from http://www.cpb.org/stations/reports/revenue/2006PublicBroadcastingRevenue.pdf

Croson, R. (2007). Theories of commitment, altruism and reciprocity: Evidence from linear public goods games. *Economic Inquiry, 45,* 199–216

Croson, R., Handy, F., & Shang, J. (2009). Keeping up with the Joneses: The relationship between norms, social information and subsequent charitable giving. *Nonprofit Management and Leadership, 14*(9), 467–489.

Croson, R., & Shang, J. (2008). The impact of downward social information on contribution decisions. *Experimental Economics. Special Issue on Field Experiments, 11,* 221–233.

Croson, R., & Shang, J. (2009). Limits of social influence on the voluntary provision of public goods: Evidence from field experiments. Working paper.

Crutchfield, R. S. (1955). Conformity and character. *American Psychologist, 10*(5), 191–198.

Deaux, K., Reid, A., Mizrahi, K., & Ethier, K. A. (1995). Parameters of social identity. *Journal of Personality and Social Psychology, 68*(2), 280–291.

De Maeyer, J., Vanderplasschen, W., & Broekaert, E. (2009). Exploratory study on drug users' perspectives on quality of life: More than health-related quality of life? *Social Indicators Research, 90*(1), 107–127.

Feldman, J. M., & Lynch, J. G. (1988). Self-generated validity and other effects of measurement on belief, attitude, intention, and behavior, *Journal of Applied Psychology, 73*(3), 421–435.

Fishbacher, U., Gachter, S., & Fehr, E. (2001). Are people conditionally cooperative? Evidence from a public goods experiment. *Economics Letters, 71,* 397–404.

Havens, J. J., O'Herlihy, M. A., & Schervish, P. G. (2006). Charitable giving: How much, by whom, to what, and how? In W. W. Powell & R. Steinberg (Eds.), *The nonprofit sector: A research handbook* (pp. 542–567). New Haven, CT: Yale University Press.

Hung, H., Wu, S., Wen, C., & Wu, F. (2008). Competitive advantages of managing an effective social network structure to stimulate innovation from a knowledge management perspective. *International Journal of Technology Management, 43*(4), 363–382.

Kolm, S., & Ythier, J. M. (2006). *The handbook on the economics of giving, reciprocity and altruism.* The Netherlands: Elsevier.

Mackie, D. M., & Smith, E. R. (1999). Intergroup relations: Insights from a theoretically integrative approach. *Psychological Review, 105*(3), 499–529.

Mussweiler, T., Ruter, K., & Epstude, K. (2004). The ups and downs of social comparison: Mechanisms of assimilation and contrast. *Journal of Personality and Social Psychology, 87*(6), 832–844.

Okun, M. A., Karoly, P., & Lutz, R. (2002). Clarifying the contribution of subjective norm or predicting leisure-time exercise. *American Journal of Health Behavior, 26*(4), 296–305.

Okun, M. A., Ruehlman, L., Karoly, P., Lutz, R., Fairholme, C., & Schaub, R. (2003). Social support and social norms: Do both contribute to predicting leisure-time exercise? *American Journal of Health Behavior, 27*(5), 493–507.

Penner, L. A., Dovidio, J. F., Piliavin, J. A., & Schroeder, D. A. (2005). Prosocial behavior: Multilevel perspectives. *Annual Review of Psychology, 56,* 365–392.

Piaget, J. (1932). *Social evolution and the new education.* London: New Education Fellowship.

Powell, W. W., & Steinberg, R. (2006). *The nonprofit sector: A research handbook.* New Haven, CT: Yale University Press.

Putnam, R. D. (1993). *Making democracy work: Civic traditions in modern Italy.* Princeton, NJ: Princeton University Press.

Putnam, R. D. (2000). *Bowling alone: The collapse and revival of American community.* New York: Simon & Schuster.

Reed II, A. (2004). Activating the self-importance of consumer selves: Exploring identity salience effects on judgments. *Journal of Consumer Research, 31*(2), 286–295.

Rhodes, R. E., & Courneya, K. S. (2003). Relationships between personality, an extended theory of planned behaviour model and exercise behaviour. *British Journal of Health Psychology, 8*(1), 19–36.

Strano, M. M. (2006). Ritualized transmission of social norms through wedding photographs. *Communication Theory, 16*(1), 31–46.

Shang, J., & Croson, R. (2006). The impact of social comparisons on nonprofit fundraising. *Research in Experimental Economics, 11,* 143–156.

Shang, J., & Croson, R. (2008). The impact of downward social information on contribution decisions. *Experimental Economics, 11*(3), 221–233.

Shang, J., & Croson, R. (2009). A field experiment in charitable contribution: The impact of social information on the voluntary provision of public goods. *The Economic Journal, 119,* 1422–1439.

Shang, J., Reed, A., & Croson, R. (2008). Identity congruency effects on donations. *Journal of Marketing Research, 45*(3), 351–361.

Smith, M. B., Bruner, J. S., & White, R. W. (1956). *Opinions and personality.* New York: Wiley.

Sugden, R. (1984). Reciprocity: The supply of public goods through voluntary contributions. *Economic Journal, 94,* 772–787.

Simmons, R., & Birchall, J. (2008). The role of co-operatives in poverty reduction: Network perspectives. *Journal of Socio- Economics, 37*(6), 2131–2140.

Tempel, E. (2003). *Achieving excellence in fund raising* (2nd ed.). San Francisco, CA: Jossey-Bass.

Van Empelen, P., Kok, G., Jansen, M. W. J., & Hoebe, C. J. P. A. (2001). The additional value of anticipated regret and psychopathology in explaining intended condom use among drug users. *AIDS Care, 13*(3), 309–318.

Van de Putte, B., Yzer, M. C., & Brunsting, S. (2005). Social influences on smoking cessation: A comparison of the effect of six social influence variables. *Preventive Medicine: An International Journal Devoted to Practice and Theory, 41*(1), 186–193.

Walters, S. T., & Neighbors, C. (2005). Feedback interventions for college alcohol misuse: What, why and for whom? *Addictive Behaviors, 30*(6), 1168–1182.

Weber, J. M., Kopelman, S., & Messick, D. M. (2004). A conceptual review of decision making in social dilemmas: Applying a logic of appropriateness. *Personality and Social Psychology Review, 8*(3), 281–307.

Yu, M. Y., Lang, K. R., & Kumar, N. (2009). Internationalization of online professional communities: An empirical investigation of AIS-ISWorld. *International Journal of E-Collaboration, 5*(1), 13–32.

6

How Social Norms, Price, and Scrutiny Influence Donation Behavior
Evidence From Four Natural Field Experiments

RICHARD MARTIN and JOHN RANDAL

INTRODUCTION

*I*n 2007 American charitable donations were 2.8% of gross domestic product (GDP).° One of the first lessons economics students are taught is that people live in a world of scarcity, where unlimited wants will always exceed limited means. That individuals give away significant resources, rather than consuming, contradicts one of the most basic axioms of neoclassical economics. In the face of this divergence between theory and empirical evidence, various theories of prosocial behavior have been developed, such as impure altruism (Andreoni, 1990), fairness equilibria (Rabin, 1993), conditional cooperation (Fischbacher, Gachter, & Fehr, 2001) and inequity aversion (Fehr & Schmidt, 1999).

In parallel with the development of these theories, thousands of laboratory experiments investigating prosocial behavior have been undertaken. Such a degree of replication leaves no room for doubt that the results are robust: subjects in social dilemma experiments undertaken in the laboratory invariably exhibit behavior that is inconsistent with pure self-interest. While it is clear that pure self-interest fails to explain many interactions among friends and family, the converse is not obviously true. For instance, neither of the authors has been approached in the street and

---

° Charitable donations were estimated to be $306 billion (Giving USA Foundation, 2008) and nominal GDP was $13.8 trillion (International Monetary Fund, 2008).

offered 20% of the contents of a stranger's wallet, despite the fact that it is the most common offer when the dictator game° is played in the laboratory.

At least three biases taint the results of laboratory experiments. First, people who agree to participate in laboratory experiments may be more socially motivated than average. In a social dilemma, this would tend to increase *both* the level of prosocial behavior and the size of the treatment effects. Second, even the most oblivious subject in a laboratory experiment will realize that their behavior is being studied and this scrutiny might influence their behavior. Note that this problem exists even in a double-blind[†] laboratory experiment (Loewenstein, 1999). One could imagine a subject thinking: wow, the researcher has gone to great lengths to ensure my anonymity. Maybe the researcher wants me to behave in a way that I would not if my choices were not anonymous. Third, behavior in the laboratory might not be representative simply because of the artificial context, setting, and stakes.

Because of these weaknesses, field experiments are an increasingly popular complement to laboratory experiments. Using the taxonomy of Harrison and List (2004), the experiments documented in this chapter are all natural field experiments. They benefit from having a representative sample of individuals untainted by self-selection, and whose behavior is observed in a natural setting, generally without the subject realizing they are being studied. As any economist knows, there is no such thing as a free lunch. The cost of leaving the laboratory is some loss of control over the experiment. For example, visitor characteristics (with the exception of gender in Experiment 4) could not be linked to donation behavior without people becoming aware that their donation behavior was being studied.

The experiments took place at an art gallery where admission was free, but donations could be deposited into a transparent box in the foyer. Social information was manipulated by changing the initial contents of the donation box, influencing the visitors' beliefs concerning the "normal" frequency and size of donation. In addition, in Experiment 2, in some treatments donations were matched by corporate sponsors, and in Experiments 3 and 4 the experiment was disclosed in some treatments.

The experiments are not the first to investigate the influence of social information on charitable behavior in the field. However, previous studies have either focused on the propensity to donate *or* the amount donated. For instance, Frey and Meier (2004) document how providing potential donors with information regarding the historical donation frequency influences the propensity to donate. In an alternative approach, Shang and Croson (2005) focus on how providing information about donation size influences both donation size and the probability of contributing again the following year. Using the City Gallery Wellington donation box, we are able to simultaneously manipulate both aspects of the norm, and measure all visitors' responses to these manipulations.

° A "dictator" is given some amount of money (typically $10), and anonymously chooses how much to keep, with the remainder going to another subject in the experiment.

† The term double-blind has a nonstandard meaning in experimental economics: neither the other subjects nor the researcher can attribute choices to the individual.

Hypotheses

Using the results from the four experiments, the following potential explanations of donor behavior can be tested.

- **Homo Economicus** If people are purely self-interested, the treatments should have no impact on behavior and no donations should be observed.
- **Conditional cooperation** (Fischbacher, Gachter, & Fehr, 2001): Donations should be positively related to the initial value of the seed money. Furthermore, altering the composition of the seed money but holding the value constant should have no influence on donation behavior.
- **Impure altruism** (Andreoni 1988, 1989, 1990): City Gallery Wellington receives approximately $2 million of public funding per year. Private donations have virtually no affect on the "size" or quality of the public good, and thus have no impact on the marginal utility that an individual derives from private consumption, "warm-glow" giving, or even the public good itself. If people are impurely altruistic, then the contents of the donation box should not influence behavior. Scrutiny may enhance the warm glow associated with giving, leading to larger and more frequent donations. Nevertheless, no interaction between the contents of the donation box and the degree of scrutiny should be expected.
- **Social norms** (Bernheim, 1994; Akerlof, 1982): Donation behavior will be influenced by the initial contents of the donation box and the degree of scrutiny. The contents of the donation box provide signals of the norms of giving. Norm violators are assumed to suffer a nonpecuniary cost, which is increasing in both the size of the norm violation and the degree of scrutiny. If people conform to social norms, then the prediction is that the norm manipulations will be more effective at influencing behavior when scrutiny is high.

In the first experiment, only the initial contents of the box were manipulated. Holding the total value constant but varying the composition allowed for the comparison between the implications of conditional versus social norms. Conditional cooperation predicts that donation behavior is influenced by the aggregate donations of others, but is not influenced by the composition of the donations. In contrast, visitors attempting to conform to social norms should be influenced by the composition of the donations. Evidence of numerous small donations should cause actual donations to be more frequent and smaller than in the treatments with a small number of bills with the same total value.

In Experiment 2, donation matching from corporate sponsors was also investigated. A one-for-one match effectively halves the "price"° of making a donation. For normal goods, a price decrease always causes an increase in consumption.

° For instance, in many countries, charitable donations reduce taxable income. In effect, this is a rebate from the government on the "purchase" of a donation, making the donation less costly. Similarly, a one-for-one donation match reduces the "purchase price" of a donation by fifty percent. In other words, it costs half as much to put a dollar in the hands of the charity.

In the case of donations, a similar response to a price decrease is anticipated. A decrease in the price of a donation is expected to make donations more frequent and larger in all cases except Homo Economicus. In addition, donors were thanked on signs visually identical to the matching signs. The effect of the signs differs, and therefore the effect is due to the message on, rather than the presence of, the signs. While interesting, this has important implications for the final experiments.

Experiments 3 and 4 investigate a potential reason why behavior might differ between the laboratory and the street—*experimenter scrutiny*. Experimenter scrutiny may encourage prosocial behavior unconditionally, or it could lead to greater conformity to perceived social norms. By manipulating both the level of scrutiny (disclosure of the study vs. nondisclosure) and the visitors' perceptions of the social norms of giving, it is possible to differentiate between the predictions of impure altruism and social norms.

Data Collection

The four separate experiments were conducted in City Gallery Wellington (henceforth, the gallery). The gallery is public with no admission fee and is managed by the Wellington Museums Trust with major funding support from Wellington City Council. The gallery has a single major entry point into a large foyer, while a secondary entrance, via a cafe, also feeds into this foyer. A small donation box resides near the center of this foyer, and all visitors to the gallery must pass within a few meters of it to make their way into the exhibition spaces. The gallery agreed to remove a second donation box in an upstairs foyer for the duration of the experiments.

The construction of the donation box itself was also ideal for these experiments. It is a transparent glass cube, sitting on a wooden base. The sides are approximately 40 cm, and donations are made through a small slot in the top surface. Traditionally, the box had been emptied once a week and the entire contents banked.

The following variables were observed on a daily basis:

- **Donation composition**, defined as the frequency of each type of coin or note.
- **Donation propensity**, defined as the proportion of visitors to make a donation.
- **Average donation per donor**, defined as the total dollar value donated divided by the number of individual donations.
- **Average donation per visitor**, defined as the total dollar value donated divided by the number of visitors.

Of most interest to a myopic fundraiser is the average donation per visitor. Small and frequent, or large and infrequent donations are equally good if the donation revenue is the same. Nevertheless, there are two benefits of decomposing the average donation per visitor into size and propensity. First, it allows us to distinguish between the predictions of conditional cooperation and a model of social norms. Second, a trade-off between donation size and propensity is important in *ongoing* charitable fundraising. Manipulations that increase the propensity will help augment the charity's warm lists (the pool of active donors). Those who have given to a charity in the past are much more likely to give again in the future (Landry, Lange, List, Price, Rupp, & Building, 2008). For both of these reasons, the evidence is presented at both the macro level (average donation per visitor) as well as at the micro level (donation composition, propensity, and the average donation per donor).

The gallery was visited daily to count the contents added to the box on the previous day, and to reset the box. The gallery had equipment in place to count the number of visitors per day, and they were happy to share these data with us. This left the problem of counting the number of donations. Initially, a microphone was installed connected to an electronic counter under the box, but this tended to under-report the number of donations (even after correcting for the silent paper note donations, assumed to happen individually). Subsequently, a rather more high-tech and expensive solution was implemented.

Permission from the gallery and Victoria University of Wellington's Human Ethics Committee was obtained to install a video camera above the donation box. This streamed video to a computer running ZoneMinder° software. The video camera was set up so that the top of the donation box filled virtually the entire field of view of the camera. A "zone" was then defined on the top of the donation box, centered on the donation slot, and the software monitored this zone for any change. Upon detecting a change, it would record images at 25 frames per second on either side of this event. The software would buffer the images, so the event would consist of the past, the trigger (a donation), and the future. The event detection was set to be very sensitive, and many false positives were observed, often triggered by a visitor's shadow passing across the top of the donation box. Based on the numbers and types of false positives, one can be confident that all donations were being recorded.

As the research program progressed, the quality of the captured images improved, due to improvements in both the camera and the processing power of the computer. By Experiment 4, higher resolution color images were available for analysis, allowing for the determination of the exact size of a majority of donations.

Treatments

Contents   The contents of the donation box provide information concerning the norms of giving including the frequency of donations and the typical donation size. In Experiment 1, four contents treatments were utilized: the empty treatment, the $50 treatment, the $5 treatment, and the 50¢ treatment. In Experiment 2, two contents treatments were utilized: the "half" treatment, and the "double" treatment. In Experiments 3 and 4, the $5 treatment and the 50¢ treatments were utilized. See Figure 6.1 for the typical appearance of the treatments, and Table 6.1 for a list of the contents. The lower bound average (LBA) donation in Table 6.1 is the average donation if every previous donor had only put in a single piece of money.

° See http://www.zoneminder.com/

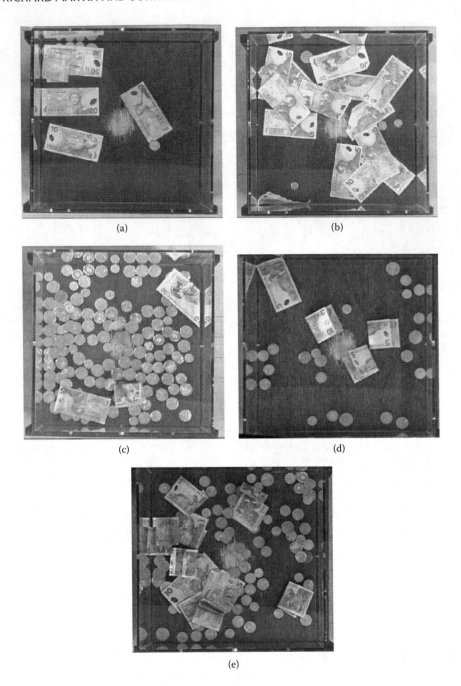

Figure 6.1   The typical appearance of the initial contents of the donation box for the five nonempty treatments: (a) the $50 treatment, (b) the $5 treatment, (c) the 50¢ treatment, (d) the half treatment (total value $50), and (e) the double treatment (total value $200). In (a)-(c) the total value is constant at $100 but the composition varies. In (d) and (e) the relative composition is constant.

TABLE 6.1   The Initial Contents of the Donation Box for the Nonempty Treatments

Treatment	Denomination										Lower Bound Average
	$50	$20	$10	$5	$2	$1	50¢	20¢	10¢	5¢	
$50	1	1	2	1	1	2	2	0	0	0	$10.00
$5	0	1	1	13	1	2	1	1	2	2	$4.17
50¢	0	1	1	1	3	15	71	36	12	2	$0.70
Half	0	0	1	3	9	5	2	5	0	0	$2
Double	0	0	4	12	36	20	8	20	0	0	$2

Note: The aggregate value is $100 for the first three treatments, but the composition varies. For the last two treatments the composition is constant and instead it is the value that varies. The half treatment has a total value of $50, whereas the double treatment has a total value of $200. The lower bound average (LBA) is the average donation if every previous donor had only put in a single piece of money.

In the context of the table, this would be the total value, divided by the number of items in the box; for example, in the $50 treatment there is $100 in the box, and 10 individual pieces of money: five notes, three gold coins, and two silver coins. There can have been no more than ten previous donors, so the smallest average donation must have been $10 per donor. If there were fewer previous donors, the average donation size must have been larger.

By virtue of the transparent donation box, the contents manipulation influenced the visitors' perceptions of two norms of giving simultaneously: the proportion of visitors who donate and the typical donation size. In the three nonempty treatments of Experiment 1, as well as Experiments 3 and 4, the total value of the initial contents was held constant but the composition was varied. Holding the total value of the contents constant allowed the investigation of norm manipulations in a setting where the theory of conditional cooperation predicts no differences in behavior across treatments. Regarding the norms of giving, the 50¢ treatment suggests small but frequent donations, the $50 treatment suggests large but infrequent donations, and the $5 treatment is intermediate. In the empty treatment of Experiment 1, the donation box started the day empty and was emptied throughout the day. The empty treatment signaled that the propensity to donate was very low, but gave no indication of the typical donation size. This empty treatment involved a lot of support from gallery staff, who would empty the box (by releasing a small catch in the base) whenever they noticed a donation had been made.

In Experiment 2, the relative composition of the initial contents was held constant, but the total value was varied in order to test the converse of Experiment 1. Specifically, if there is no difference in relative composition of the seed money, will no difference in the relative composition of the actual donations be observed?

Ideally, every donation made would be under exactly the same conditions. Unfortunately, the seed contents could not remain constant during each day, nor could the donation box be reset during the day (the exception being the empty treatment in Experiment 1). The assumption that the general appearance of the box would be unchanged throughout the day was necessary. The total value of the seed contents (typically $100) was chosen to try to make this assumption as reasonable as possible. Observed donation behavior also helped in this regard, as the composition of contributions tended to mimic the composition of the seed contents.

Signage   In addition to manipulating the initial contents, in Experiments 2, 3, and 4, signs were placed on all four sides of the base of the donation box. In Experiment 2, permission was obtained to use the corporate logos of two of the gallery's sponsors: Telecom New Zealand (the largest company in New Zealand, and a provider of a wide range of telecommunication services), and Ernst and Young (a multinational professional services firm, and one of the "big four" auditors). These two firms are among the members of City Gallery Wellington Foundation who help "underwrite the financial risk associated with major national and international exhibitions."[*] Three treatments were used. The "control" had no signs at all. The "thank you" treatment had signs with logos of two corporate members of this foundation reading:

City Gallery Wellington Foundation thanks you for your donation,

And finally, the "matching" treatment had signs including the two corporate logos reading:

Cash donations today will be matched by City Gallery Wellington Foundation.

The two sets of signs were visually very similar, differing only in the message, apparently made by the corporate sponsors of the gallery and directed at the visitors/potential private donors. The latter treatment was facilitated by the gallery's intention to make a large drawdown from the foundation, though the possibility of the box being filled with cash was worrisome. This didn't happen.

Thanking the visitors for their donation was anticipated to enhance the warm glow associated with a contribution, or alternatively call attention to the existence of corporate sponsorship, thus providing a signal concerning the quality of the public good (Vesterlund, 2003). Matching was expected to induce a negative relationship between the donation price and both the propensity to donate and the average donation per donor. In other words, the price effect of the match was predicted to dominate the potentially perverse income effect, yielding a downward sloping donation curve. Since average donations at City Gallery are typically between $2 and $3, and survey data indicated 47% of visitors had household incomes in excess of $40,000, it is reasonable to expect that the income effect of the match will be small relative to the price effect.

In Experiment 3, potential donors were informed of the experiment using large signs placed on a prominently displayed donation box stating:

Donations are being counted as part of research into donation behavior.

This statement implies researcher scrutiny, but an individual's choice is not attributable. When compared to the no sign treatments, these treatments should give an indication of the impact of researcher scrutiny on the behavior of subjects in laboratory experiments where choices are anonymous.

---

[*] http://www.citygallery.org.nz/mainsite/Foundation.html

In Experiment 4, the language was strengthened and it suggests attribution of actions back to the individual:

Your donation behavior is being monitored and analyzed for research purposes.

This statement implies researcher scrutiny and an individual's choice is attributable. When compared to the no sign treatments, these treatments should give an indication of the impact of researcher scrutiny on the behavior of subjects in laboratory experiments where choices are not anonymous. Both of the statements above were accompanied by a large logo of the local university, Victoria University of Wellington.

The goal in Experiments 3 and 4 was to isolate the effect of researcher scrutiny by leaving all other aspects of the environment constant. This measure should give an indication of the effect of researcher scrutiny on behavior in decision environments featuring a tension between private and social interests. One theory is that people simply behave more altruistically when their decisions are subject to scrutiny, regardless of their perception regarding the behavior of others. In the context of the present study, this would correspond to larger and more frequent donations in the disclosure treatments, regardless of the initial contents of the donation box. A second theory is that scrutiny increases the social cost of norm violations, leading to greater conformity to perceived social norms. Thus adding scrutiny would accentuate the effect of the contents manipulation, but would not necessarily be associated with more frequent or larger donations.

That dictator allocations in the laboratory are decreasing in social distance (Hoffman, McCabe, & Schmidt, 1996) is consistent with either increased scrutiny causing (1) a shift toward more altruistic preferences or (2) increased conformity. The problem is that 95+% of allocations in both the single and double-blind games were at or below the hypothesized social norm (even division of the $10), which makes it impossible to distinguish between the implications of the two theories. By manipulating both scrutiny and social norms in the same experiment, it should be possible to distinguish the implications of the two theories.

One might wonder if visitors paid any attention to the message the signs conveyed. Strong results from Experiment 2 served as the manipulation check for Experiments 3 and 4. In particular, in Experiment 2 the offer to match donations yielded a 34% increase in the average donation per visitor, whereas visually similar signs thanking donors had no significant impact on the donation revenue per visitor. The message on the sign was read, and it was not just the presence of the sign that was influencing behavior.

In summary, four separate experiments were conducted with the following treatments (crossing contents and signage) and durations:

Experiment 1 {empty, 50¢, $5, $50} × {no-sign}   01/12/05–03/06/05

Experiment 2 {half, double} × {no-sign, thank-you, matching}   11/14/05–02/06/06

Experiment 3 {50¢, $5} × {no-sign, anonymous disclosure}   02/21/06–04/19/06

Experiment 4 {50¢, $5} × {no-sign, attributable disclosure}   08/28/06–09/24/06

Experiments 1, 3, and 4 have two treatments in common, that is, {50¢, $5}#{no-sign} treatments. Direct comparison of these is of course possible, but making causal statements is not. Contaminating effects may include, but are not limited to, the time of year, the prevailing economic climate, and the actual art on display.

Independent Variables   For every daily observation, the day of the week was observed (obviously), as well as the total number of visitors to the gallery on that day. In the regression-based analyses that follow, the busyness of the gallery was included in the regression as a binary (dummy) variable, despite the underlying counts being essentially continuous. In Experiment 2, Christmas resulted in an unbalanced sample, which warranted an investigation of the daily pattern of donations.

In Experiment 4, a second camera was installed, capturing a wide angle image of the entrance foyer at the time of a donation. Using these additional images, the gender of the donor was identified (which was next to impossible when only images of the donor's hand and wrist were available). In addition, the number of other people visible in the foyer at the time of the donation was recorded. The donation patterns in Experiment 4 were analyzed for sensitivity to these variables.

There are many other variables that were not recorded and not included in the analysis. A crucial one appears to be the art itself. In all cases, this is constant within an experiment, but the fact that it changes between experiments makes comparison difficult (as mentioned above). The general passing of time is linked to this, and as such cannot be controlled. To some extent, the daily number of visitors can proxy for things such as seasonal (time of year) variation in the number of visitors to Wellington and the gallery, and type of visitor, since there may be a difference in donation behavior between Wellington residents (who partially fund the gallery already through local government taxes), and nonresidents. Some sensitivity to fluctuations in the number of visitors was eliminated by analyzing average donations per visitor and per donor rather than total revenue.

Results

The results for the four experiments are now presented. These are arranged by analysis, and results are discussed for each individual experiment, and where possible, compared across experiments.

Composition

This first analysis gives the most robust result of the whole program.

> *Donation composition tends to mimic the composition of the existing contents of the donation box.*

More specifically, notes are more prevalent in the collection from the $5 (and $50) treatments than in the 50¢ treatment, and silver coins are less prevalent in the collection from the $5 (and $50) treatments than in the 50¢ treatment. Meanwhile, the half and double treatments give collections with the same distribution across notes ($50, $20, $10, and $5), gold coins ($2 and $1), and silver coins (50¢, 20¢, 10¢, and 5¢).

Put another way, when there are differences in seed composition, statistically significant differences in donation composition are observed. When there are not

TABLE 6.2   The Donation Composition for Each of the Four Experiments

	$20	$10	$5	$2	$1	50¢	20¢	10¢	5¢	Bills	Gold	Silver
						Denomination						
						Experiment 1						
$50	0	3	19	55	28	36	41	30	32	22(9.0%)	83(34.0%)	139(57.0%)
$5	1	1	17	63	37	46	54	29	39	19(6.6%)	100(34.8%)	168(58.5%)
50¢	0	1	6	70	56	81	112	59	64	7(1.5%)	126(28.0%)	316(70.4%)
Empty	0	1	9	50	25	24	42	35	27	10(4.7%)	75(35.2%)	128(60.1%)
						Experiment 2						
			(D = double, H = half; M = matching, NS = no-sign, TY = thank-you)									
D, M	0	1	18	66	43	59	57	36	51	19(5.7%)	109(32.9%)	203(61.3%)
D, NS	0	2	9	45	28	37	39	32	35	11(4.8%)	73(32.2%)	143(63.0%)
D, TY	0	3	11	57	35	28	77	41	44	14(4.7%)	92(31.1%)	190(64.2%)
H, M	0	1	13	50	39	44	90	33	48	14(4.4%)	89(28.0%)	215(67.6%)
H, NS	0	0	9	37	37	43	48	36	57	9(3.3%)	74(27.7%)	184(68.9%)
H, TY	0	0	5	56	45	51	78	55	56	5(1.4%)	101(29.2%)	240(69.3%)
						Experiment 3						
						(NS = no-sign, S = sign)						
$5, NS	2	7	42	119	97	122	142	88	81	51(7.1%)	216(30.9%)	433(61.9%)
$5, S	4	4	35	116	107	115	134	98	112	43(5.9%)	223(30.8%)	459(63.3%)
50¢, NS	0	5	20	129	97	136	173	124	110	25(3.1%)	226(28.5%)	543(68.4%)
50¢, S	1	6	23	171	103	145	203	137	105	30(3.4%)	274(30.6%)	590(66.0%)
						Experiment 4						
						(NS = no-sign, S = sign)						
$5, NS	1	3	15	34	33	27	29	20	1	19(11.7%)	67(41.1%)	77(47.2%)
$5, S	2	1	14	22	25	22	36	20	1	17(11.9%)	47(32.9%)	79(55.2%)
50¢, NS	0	0	9	49	27	49	68	73	12	9(3.1%)	76(26.5%)	202(70.4%)
50¢, S	0	0	9	52	54	60	66	74	10	9(2.8%)	106(32.6%)	210(64.6%)

Note: Bills includes the $20, $10, and $5 contributions; Gold, the $2 and $1; and Silver the 50¢, 20¢, 10¢ and 5c. The percentages listed are the proportion of items in each category.

differences in seed composition, no statistically significant differences in donation composition are observed. These formal conclusions are obtained by doing contingency table tests for independence between the treatment and the donation composition, where the latter has been amalgamated to give three categories: notes, gold, and silver as above. The null hypothesis of independence is rejected in all but Experiment 2, where of course the composition is constant across treatments.

Table 6.2 gives the donation compositions across all experiments.

Experiment 1   The results for Experiment 1 show the monotonic relationship between the lower bound average (LBA) and the proportions of notes and silver coins. As the LBA increases, the proportion of notes in the donations increases from 1.5% in the 50¢ treatment to 9% in the $50 treatment. Offsetting this difference, the proportion of silver coins decreases from 70.4% in the 50¢ treatment to 57% in the $50 treatment. In both cases the $5 treatment is intermediate.

Conducting a formal hypothesis test for independence using the observed frequencies yields a highly significant result ($p < 0.01\%$). The same qualitative behavior is observed in the no-sign treatments in Experiments 3 and 4, though the absolute level is quite different. This indicates the importance of the actual art on display for the level of donations, and will be reflected in higher average donations.

The patterns for Experiment 1 are also shown in Figure 6.2. The left-hand plot shows the relative frequencies of bills, gold coins, and silver coins. It is clear from this plot that the most commonly donated object is a silver coin, though this is most striking under the 50¢ treatment, where roughly an additional 10% of the contributions are silver. Bills are most commonly donated in the $50 treatment, followed by the $5 treatment. Very few bills are donated in the 50¢ treatment, but more in the empty treatment. Gold coin contributions are roughly equal in the $50, $5, and empty treatments, but are clearly lower in the 50¢ treatment.

The right-hand plot of Figure 6.2 shows the proportion of the various contributions by value. While the bills have high value, these contributions are relatively infrequent, and for no treatment do they contribute the most value. In each treatment, the gold coin donations are responsible for the largest proportion of the revenue, and this is higher than 50% in all but the $50 treatment. Due to their low values, the common silver coins contribute only in a minor way to the revenue, with the exception of the 50¢ treatment, where they are more important than the bills.

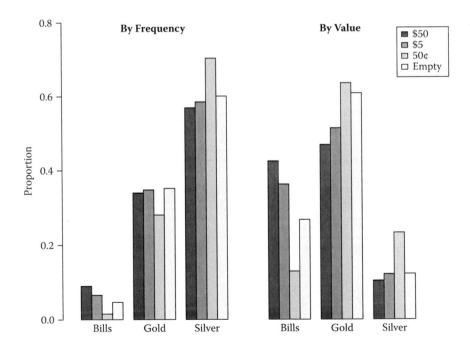

Figure 6.2 Composition of the donations for each treatment. On the left, the composition is plotted by relative frequency. On the right, it is plotted on a value-weighted basis. Bills include the $20, $10, and $5 contributions; Gold, the $2 and $1; and Silver the 50¢, 20¢, 10¢, and 5¢.

TABLE 6.3   Comparison of Composition Details for
the Aggregate Donations (on the left) and the Seed
Contents (on the right) in Experiment 1

	Donation Proportions			Seed Proportions		
	Bills	Gold	Silver	Bills	Gold	Silver
$50	9.0%	34.0%	57.0%	50%	30%	20%
$5	6.6%	34.8%	58.5%	62.5%	12.5%	25%
50¢	1.5%	28.0%	70.4%	2.1%	12.7%	85.2%

Note: Bills includes the $20, $10, and $5 contributions; Gold, the $2 and
$1; and Silver the 50¢, 20¢, 10¢ and 5¢.

Note that although the composition of the donations mimics the composition
of the initial seed money, the distributions are not the same. Formal goodness of
fit tests are rejected in each instance, where the higher-value items are overrepresented in the seed contents. Table 6.3 compares the observed and "expected"
proportions for Experiment 1, where the expected proportions are those in the
seed contents. Notes are underrepresented in donations in all treatments, while
the silver coins tend to be overrepresented (except in the 50¢ treatment).

Experiment 2   The proportions in Table 6.2 show much less variation for
Experiment 2 than they did for Experiment 1. Although there are some minor
systematic patterns, these are not statistically significant. Testing the entire table
for independence between treatment (with six categories) and composition (with
three categories) provides no evidence against the null of independence ($p > 10\%$).
Subsetting the table allows further tests for independence: among the double
treatments only, among the half treatments only, among the no-sign treatments
only, among the matching treatments only, and among the thank-you treatments
only. Even at the 10% level of significance, the data do not allow for the rejection
of independence in any instance.

Consequently, the observations that note proportions all decrease from the
double treatment to the corresponding half treatment, and that the silver proportions all increase from the double treatment to the corresponding half treatment,
are not particularly valid, as the differences are within sampling variation. The
composition of the donations does not change when the amount of money in the
box is scaled, but the composition of seed money remains fixed.

The proportions of the seed money are: 16% notes, 56% gold coins, and 28%
silver coins for all six treatments. As with most of the treatments in Experiment 1,
notes are overrepresented in the seed contents, and silver is underrepresented.

Experiment 3   The proportions from Experiment 3 shown in Table 6.2
indicate a significant lack of independence between treatment and composition
($p < 10\%$). Subgroups are again considered: the two no-sign treatments, the two
sign treatments, the two $5 treatments, and the two 50¢ treatments. In the latter
two cases, the seed contents are identical, and no significant effect is found. The
results for the two no-sign treatments are qualitatively very similar to the same

treatments in Experiment 1, and the sets of observed proportions are very similar. The test for independence is soundly rejected ($p < 0.1\%$). Weakening of the compositional effect is observed when scrutiny is introduced, despite the observed differences in the proportions for the two sign treatments being significant ($p = 4.2\%$). Fewer notes are donated in the $5 treatment when the study is disclosed, and more are donated in the 50¢ treatment (relative to the no-sign treatments). This behavior suggests the donors may feel that they are being manipulated, due to the unnatural appearance of the $5 treatment, and the confirmation that a study is in place.

Experiment 4   The donation compositions in Experiment 4 are dramatically different than those in Experiments 1 and 3. Whether this is due to the art on display, the time of year, or the data collection period is unclear, though the first possibility seems most likely. Note donations are much more common in the $5 treatment in Experiment 4 than in any other treatment during the study.

All treatments yield highly significant differences in composition ($p < 0.01\%$), while the no-sign and sign subgroups are both now highly significant ($p < 0.01\%$ and $p < 0.1\%$, respectively). In this instance, the higher degree of scrutiny implied by the signs had a lesser effect on the composition of the donations. Neither the $5 treatments nor the 50¢ treatments had a significant compositional effect testing across the sign treatment.

These results are largely consistent with Experiment 3, and also the qualitative patterns in Experiment 1, in that note donations are more prevalent in the $5 treatment, and less prevalent in the 50¢ treatment.

Summary   In aggregate, the results show that when seed composition is held fixed, donation composition is unlikely to differ across sign treatments or across the total value of money in the donation box. However, when seed composition changes, donation composition is highly likely to change—the composition of the donations mimics the composition of the existing contents of the box. Thus this aspect of the data is consistent with a model of conformity, but is not consistent with neoclassical preferences, conditional cooperation, or impure altruism.

Donation Propensity

The donation propensity is defined to be the proportion of visitors who make a donation, and is the number of donations divided by the number of visitors. This is calculated for each treatment within each experiment based on the entire time series of donation counts and visitor counts. If $n_{i,t}$ is the number of donations on day t of treatment i, and $N_{i,t}$ is the number of visitors on day t of treatment i, then the estimated propensity for treatment i is $P_i = S_t n_{i,t} / S_t N_{i,t}$. The daily propensities are subject to a larger degree of variation than the single estimate for the entire treatment, and are not analyzed.

The general result for donation propensity is as follows.

The decision to donate appears to be driven by the "cost" of a favorable social comparison.

TABLE 6.4   Number of Donations, Number of Visitors, and Donation Propensity for each Treatment

	Donors	Visitors	Propensity		Donors	Visitors	Propensity
			Experiment 1				
$50	123	5249	2.3%	50¢	182	5394	3.4%
$5	133	5031	2.6%	Empty	104	5585	1.9%
			Experiment 2				
		(D = double, H = half; M = matching, NS = no-sign, TY = thank-you)					
D, M	109	5890	1.85%	H, M	121	5307	2.28%
D, NS	91	5350	1.70%	H, NS	108	5510	1.96%
D, TY	96	6702	1.68%	H, TY	130	5487	2.37%
			Experiment 3				
		(NS = no-sign, S = sign)					
$5, NS	286	14495	1.97%	50¢, NS	288	14704	1.96%
$5, S	273	14414	1.89%	50¢, S	329	14915	2.21%
			Experiment 4				
		(NS = no-sign, S = sign)					
$5, NS	75	3460	2.17%	50¢, NS	87	5182	1.68%
$5, S	59	5526	1.07%	50¢, S	122	4291	2.84%

For instance, in the 50¢ treatment, the cost of looking relatively generous is small. The seed money in this case has an LBA of 70¢. Previous donors have given at least this on average, and to compare favorably to this average, the required donation is relatively small. Giving $2 would make a donor look roughly 3 times as generous as the LBA (70¢) implies. In contrast, in the $50 treatment, the LBA is $10, and looking generous relative to these past "donors" is relatively expensive. On this basis, the cost of a favorable social comparison can be ranked from lowest to highest as 50¢, half, double, $5, $50. In the Empty case, the social comparison is not available (there is no evidence of previous donations with which to compare your donation), so people tend to abstain from making "wasteful" donations.

This general pattern is not completely robust to the noncontents treatment variables as discussed below. The propensities and associated statistics are given for all experiments in Table 6.4.

Experiment 1   As seen in Table 6.4, the propensities observed in Experiment 1 increase through empty, $50, $5, and 50¢. Empty has the smallest propensity at 1.9% of visitors making a donation, whereas 3.4% donated into the 50¢ box, almost double that of the empty box.

A contingency table test is used to formally test these differences for statistical significance. The two categorical variables are the treatment variable, and a donation variable taking on either "donate" or "not." The number of visitors who do not donate is inferred from the difference between the number of visitors and the number of donors. The test is highly significant indicating a lack of independence between these two variables ($p < 0.01\%$).

Experiment 2   Experiment 1 provided compelling evidence that the initial contents of the box had a significant impact on the propensity to donate. The pattern was consistent with conditional cooperation, where the propensity to donate was positively related to the perceived frequency of previous donations. Unfortunately, the perceived frequency of donation was confounded with the differences in the perceived donation size when comparing the 50¢, $5, and $50 treatments.

In Experiment 2, the half and double contents treatments were designed in a way that, in theory, would signal no difference in the typical donation size, but a significant difference in the frequency of previous donations. Hindsight being 20/20, it is now obvious that this is not how most visitors perceived the difference in the contents. This may be apparent to the reader by comparing the two images in the bottom row of Figure 6.1. It is more natural to think of the difference in the contents being due to both an increase in the frequency *and* the typical donation size. In other words, even though the LBA donation was the same in the half and double treatments, the perceived typical donation was in fact larger in the double treatment.

Regardless of the ambiguity described above, evidence was found in Experiment 2 that was unambiguously *inconsistent* with the predictions of conditional cooperation. Referring to Table 6.4, the propensity to donate is always lower in the double treatment than in the half treatment. Holding the sign treatment constant and comparing the half treatment to the double treatment, the donation propensity decreases: from 2.0% to 1.7% in the case of no-sign; from 2.4% to 1.7% in the case of the thank-you sign; and from 2.3% to 1.9% in the case of the matching sign.

Testing the observed differences in the propensities for statistical significance using the contingency table test described above, the overall differences are significant ($p = 3.4\%$). Differences are not significant among the half treatments alone, the double treatments alone (both testing across sign), nor the no-sign treatments alone, and the matching treatments alone, testing across value. The significant difference appears to be restricted to the thank-you treatments, that is, the 1.7% of visitors who donate into the double contents with a sign thanking them for their donation is significantly less than the 2.4% of visitors who donate in the half treatment when the same sign thanks them.

If the perceived typical donation size was larger in the double treatment, then the theory that the decision to donate is driven by the "cost" of a favorable social comparison fits the data quite well. Regarding the fact that the difference is enhanced when visitors were thanked for their donation, it seems plausible that being thanked enhances the value of a favorable social comparison.

Experiment 3   The observed propensities for Experiment 3 shown in Table 6.4 exhibit very little variation, and statistical testing confirms that these proportions are not significantly different. The null result for the no-sign treatments in this case conflicts with the comparison of the 50¢ and $5 propensities in Experiment 1, where a significant result was found ($p = 4.0\%$ for the direct comparison of those two treatments alone).

The biggest observed difference was between the two sign treatments, where although not significant, the propensity was higher for the 50¢ treatment than the $5 treatment, as predicted.

Experiment 4   In contrast, there are quite distinct patterns in the propensities shown in Table 6.4 for Experiment 4, though these are at odds with earlier results.

Independence is rejected using all four treatment categories ($p < 0.01\%$). Similarly, significant differences are found across signs for both the 50¢ treatments ($p < 0.1\%$) and for both the $5 treatments, and significant differences are found across contents for the sign treatments ($p < 0.01\%$). The only insignificant result is for the no-sign treatments ($p = 11.9\%$).

Recall that in the first experiment, there was a significant increase in propensity when going from the $5 treatment to the 50¢ treatment (2.6% to 3.4%), whereas in Experiment 3, the propensities were almost identical (1.97% and 1.96% for the $5 and 50¢ treatments, respectively). In Experiment 4, a sizable, but not significant, *decrease* in propensity is observed, at odds with both the previous results. Specifically, the proportion of donors is 1.7% in the 50¢ treatment, and 2.2% with the $5 treatment.

In the case of the scrutiny signs being placed on the box, the behavior is reversed, and anticipated given previous results. A 2.8% propensity in the 50¢ treatment is more than halved to give a 1.1% propensity in the $5 treatment. In the context of donation boxes commonly seen in New Zealand, the appearance of the 50¢ treatment was very natural, and in contrast, the $5 contents were surprising. Disclosure of the researcher scrutiny may have alerted potential donors to the manipulation, and they chose not to donate as a result. The box certainly looked "fake." On the other hand, the 50¢ sign treatment yielded the highest propensity observed in over two years, perhaps indicating people's willingness to be part of a study if the costs of looking relatively generous are low.

Summary   The decision to donate appears to be driven by the "cost" of a favorable social comparison, where the LBA is a proxy for the typical donation size. The data is consistent with the following scenario: the donors estimate how much money is in the box, estimate how many people have given this money, and calculate an average donation size. They decide whether or not to donate depending on how much they are prepared to give—their intrinsic donation—and how this compares to previous donations. If their intrinsic donation is small relative to previous (estimated) donations, they may choose to not make the donation, as they don't want to appear cheap. If their intrinsic donation is large relative to the previous donations, they will more likely donate, and enjoy appearing generous.

The results are consistent with this scenario. For instance, it is relatively cheap to look generous in the 50¢ treatment, more expensive to look generous in the $5 treatment, and most expensive in the $50 treatment. Furthermore, there is no social comparison possible when the box is empty, which discourages "wasteful" donations. In Experiment 2, a smaller donation is *apparently* necessary to look relatively generous in the half treatments, when compared to the double treatments. Scrutiny did have a small effect on the propensity to donate. An interesting result was that offering to match donations did *not* lead to a significant increase in the donation propensity.

Thus none of the four hypotheses fit the propensity data particularly well. Social norms perhaps comes the closest, but fails to explain (1) why in Experiment

2 donations are far less frequent in the double than in the half treatments, (2) the lack of a significant contents effect in Experiment 3, and (3) the lack of a significant contents effect in the no-sign treatments of Experiment 4.

Our results do have some policy implications for users of donation boxes though—it is clear that an empty box is not good for business. Nor, for that matter, is a donation box with contents that make a favorable social comparison too costly for potential donors.

Average Donation per Donor

Having made the decision to donate, the donor must then decide how much to give. The data is now analyzed to estimate whether or not the treatments affect this decision. The evidence obtained suggests the treatments do influence the size of the donation, and the following broad statement can be made.

As the apparent size of previous donations increases, donation size tends to increase.

The analysis is done in a regression framework, with a number of complications. The most important of these is that the individual donations are not observed. Luckily, this merely hampers the estimation of the standard errors. Optimal estimators for means are based on the sums of donations, and these are observed, even though the individual donations are not. Thus, the estimates are as if all the individual donations were observed and the point estimates are the same with or without the data limitation. Only the inference is affected via the estimate of variance, and the degrees of freedom of the estimators.

In Experiments 1 to 3, all analysis is done on daily totals. However, in Experiment 4, roughly 70% of the donations were identified. This was done by a complicated process of image manipulation, and sometimes hearty debate. The "video" footage was actually a series of .jpg images sampled at 25 frames per second. The negative image of the first shot in the sequence was digitally obtained, and then mathematically "added" to the last. In theory, this yielded a clear image of the individual contribution, though movement in the existing contributions often made life very difficult!

Unobserved donations were replaced by the average of the remaining unobserved donations for that day; that is, the sum of the observed donations was deducted from the daily total, and the number of observed donations was deducted from the daily number of donations. Without the first level of averaging for the majority of the data, a log transformation is employed to enhance the inference. This imposes a nice symmetry on the transformed data, since the log of the minimum donation of 5¢ is equal to the log of the maximum observed donation of $20. The point estimates reported for Experiment 4 are based on the untransformed data, but their significance levels are from the transformed data. Ultimately, the regression is simply a tool to determine where significant differences lie.

The average donations per donor are shown in Table 6.5. The regression results are now summarized for each experiment, with reference to the sample statistics given in the table.

TABLE 6.5   Total Donations, Number of Donors, and Average Donation per Donor for Each Treatment

	Total	Donors	Average		Total	Donors	Average
			Experiment 1				
$50	$293.80	123	$2.39	50¢	$308.00	182	$1.69
$5	$316.65	133	$2.38	Empty	$205.25	104	$1.97
			Experiment 2				
	(D = double, H = half; M = matching, NS = no-sign, TY = thank-you)						
D, M	$322.05	109	$2.95	H, M	$259.70	121	$2.15
D, NS	$214.25	91	$2.35	H, NS	$193.55	108	$1.79
D, TY	$257.00	96	$2.68	H, TY	$231.40	130	$1.78
			Experiment 3				
	(NS = no-sign, S = sign)						
$5, NS	$717.25	286	$2.51	50¢, NS	$625.50	288	$2.17
$5, S	$653.70	273	$2.39	50¢, S	$753.05	329	$2.29
			Experiment 4				
	(NS = no-sign, S = sign)						
$5, NS	$247.35	75	$3.05	50¢, NS	$185.70	87	$2.13
$5, S	$203.35	59	$3.45	50¢, S	$254.10	122	$1.99

Experiment 1   In Experiment 1, a monotonic relationship was observed between the actual donation sizes and the LBA of the treatment, that is, the average donation size if every past donor had put in only a single coin or note. The average per donor was largest in the $50 treatment, at $2.39, where the LBA was $10. Next largest was the $5 treatment, at $2.38 with an LBA of $4.17. Finally, the 50¢ treatment had an average per donor of $1.69, and an LBA of 70¢. The empty treatment had an undefined LBA, and yielded an intermediate average per donor of $1.97.

Due to having only a single treatment variable, a single F-test was able to confirm the treatment means were significantly different from one another ($p = 3.7\%$), with post-hoc tests indicating that the average for the 50¢ treatment was significantly lower than each of the $5 and $50 averages.

Consequently, the perceived actions of past donors did influence new donors, but the effect was not a linear one. A preponderance of notes tended to yield large individual donations, and a preponderance of coins yielded smaller donations. The perceived generosity of individual donors, via the apparent average size, tended to encourage larger donations.

Experiment 2   In Experiment 2, the composition was held constant, and it was the link between total value and donation size that was of interest. The averages listed in Table 6.5 show clearly that the averages for the double treatments (on the left) are all higher than the corresponding averages for the half treatments (on the right). So, holding the sign treatment constant, the box with the larger sum of money yielded larger donations than the relatively empty box. In Experiment 1, generosity was embodied in the apparent average donation, in other words, the prior individuals' generosity. Here, the perceived generosity of *aggregate* donors, in this case via the apparent total, tended to encourage larger donations.

Formally, the regression with an interaction term between the value and sign treatments was estimated. The interaction term was insignificant, so it is omitted, and the regression re-estimated. As discussed above, the value main effect was significant and estimated to be 76¢ per donor ($p < 0.01\%$). In other words, donations to the double treatment are expected to be 76¢ higher than those to the half treatment. Relative to the no-sign treatment, the thank-you sign did not have a significant main effect; however, the matching sign increased donations by 47¢ on average ($p = 1.04\%$).

These results were in many ways key for Experiments 3 and 4. The matching and thank-you signs were visually identical, yet their effects were quite different. The thank-you signs made no difference to the size of donations, yet donors realized that the promise of a match made their donation more valuable, and gave them an incentive to increase it.

Experiment 3 Analyzing the averages reported in Table 6.5 for Experiment 3 indicates a decrease from the $5 treatment (on the left) to the 50¢ treatment (on the right). This is consistent with the results of Experiment 1, although the sizes of the (no-sign) averages and the difference between them are qualitatively different between experiments.

When the regression is estimated, the interaction between the contents treatment and the sign treatment is insignificant, so it is omitted, and the regression re-estimated. The contents main effect was only marginally significant ($p = 5.8\%$), and is estimated to be 25¢; that is, the donations to the 50¢ treatment are on average 25¢ less than those in the $5 treatment. As mentioned, this is somewhat smaller than the 69¢ difference in Experiment 1.

The sign main effect was not significant. The level of scrutiny implied by researchers "counting" the donations was not sufficient to influence donation sizes.

Experiment 4 Experiment 4 shares the general trend of Experiments 1 and 3, as seen in Table 6.5. The averages reported for the $5 treatments, $3.45 and $3.05 for the sign treatments and no-sign treatments respectively, are the highest per-donor averages in the experimental program. The average donations for the 50¢ treatments, $1.99 and $2.13 for signs and no-signs respectively, are considerably lower.

The formal results mimic those of Experiment 3 exactly. The interaction term was not significant, nor was the sign main effect when the reduced model is estimated. The contents main effect was significant ($p < 0.1\%$), and amounts to $1.20 per donation in the $5 treatment over the 50¢ treatment. There is some evidence that the disclosure sign encourages subjects (as they now realize themselves to be) to estimate the cost of a favorable social comparison.

Summary The aggregate evidence certainly favors a link between the LBA of the donation box, and the likely donation size. Large *average* contents are more likely to net a large donation. Additionally, there is some evidence that a larger *total* amount of money in the donation box might further increase the size of donations. Lastly, donors do appear to read signs placed on the donation box, insofar as a matching sign yielded significantly larger donations over a complete absence of any sign, or a sign merely thanking donors for their contribution. It can be safely concluded that the signs were read, but were unimportant in determining donation size.

Both conditional cooperation and a model of social norms are consistent with this aspect of the data, while the other two theories (Homo Economicus and impure altruism) are not. Both conditional cooperation and social norms predict a positive relationship between donation size and the perceived typical donation (proxied by the LBA). In contrast, Homo Economicus should never donate, regardless of the contents of the box. Regarding impure altruism, there are two possible cases. If a visitor is aware of how inconsequential private donations are, then their donation behavior should not be influenced by other private donations. Alternatively, if a visitor is unaware, then incomplete crowding-out would predict smaller donations in the double treatments.

Average Donation per Visitor

The average donation per visitor is the product of the average donation per donor and the propensity to donate. A myopic fundraiser will be most interested in this composite statistic, rather than the individual components. In a one-shot fundraising effort, a charity should be indifferent between low propensity and large donations vs. high propensity and small donations if they yield the same average donation per visitor.

The analysis is based on the average donation per visitor rather than the total donation revenue because the number of visitors exposed to each treatment could not be controlled. If more visitors were exposed to one treatment than another, it would be natural to see a difference in the total revenue, even if the treatments had no effect on individual behavior. Fortunately, none of the treatments influenced the number of visitors to the gallery: people had to enter the gallery before seeing the donation box. Thus the number of visitors (potential donors) can be treated as a constant, implying the total donation revenue is determined solely by the average donation per visitor.

The results for this crucial variable are difficult to summarize, as they are most sensitive to the manipulations.

1. The average donation per visitor is sensitive to whether or not others have given in the past, with donations into an empty box significantly lower than into a non-empty box.
2. An offer to match increases donations.
3. Disclosure of the study affects the way visitors interpret the existing contents of the box.

The analysis is again conducted in a regression framework, with aggregate or individual donations supplemented by the zero donations of the nondonating visitors (i.e., the number of visitors, less the number of donors). In Experiment 4, a square root transformation on the available donations is used to shorten the right tail of the distribution and improve the inference. (Note that the log transformation is unavailable due to the zero donations.)

Experiment 1 The significant differences in donation propensities across the four contents treatments were previously discussed. Empty gave the lowest propensity, and it increased as the LBA for the box decreased. Similarly, there were significant differences in the average donation per donor, with the empty box yielding an intermediate amount, but the 50¢ treatment was significantly different from the $5 and $50 treatments (which were almost identical). The important composite average donation per visitor sees these two patterns cancel out, and all three averages from nonempty boxes are similar. In contrast, the average per visitor for the empty treatment is significantly less.

The observed differences in the average donation per visitor—3.7¢ for the empty treatment, and 5.3¢, 6.3¢, and 5.7¢ for the $50, $5, and 50¢ treatments, respectively—are significant ($p = 0.07\%$). Post-hoc tests indicate that the empty treatment's mean is significantly lower than the other means (p-values of 2.4%, 0.08%, and 1.4% for the $50, $5, and 50¢ treatments, respectively). The averages of the three nonempty treatments are not significantly different.

These results give a clear indication that an empty donation box is very bad for business. Revenue per visitor in the empty treatment was less than 60% of the revenue per visitor in the $5 treatment—a sizable difference. Also interesting is the trade-off between propensity (larger in the 50¢ treatment), and average donation per donor (smallest in the 50¢ treatment). The $5 treatment, which had an intermediate propensity, and intermediate average donation per donor, yielded the largest revenue per visitor.

Experiment 2 The average donations per visitor listed in Table 6.6 for Experiment 2 suggest that donation matching has a positive effect on per-visitor revenue. The averages per visitor with matching are 5.5¢ and 4.9¢ in the half and double treatments, respectively. In contrast, the remaining four treatment averages lie between 3.5¢ per visitor for the half treatment with no-sign, and 4.7¢ per visitor for the double treatment with a thank-you sign. The matching appears to have a positive effect, this time via an increase in the average donation per donor, and with neither an offsetting nor amplifying effect in the propensities.

As was common in the per-donor analyses, the interaction terms were insignificant, so these were omitted, and the regression re-estimated. The resulting estimates indicated a significant matching main effect with an additional 1.4¢ per visitor expected over the no-sign treatment. The thank-you main effect was not significant, nor was there a significant contents main effect.

Note that the propensities were different across contents for the thank-you sign, but this is offset by the value main effect in the average donation per donor. High propensities and high average donations per donor in the matching treatments reinforce each other, leading to significantly high donations per visitor.

Experiment 3 Recall that the donation propensities for Experiment 3 were apparently constant, and that there was only a mild contents effect in the average

TABLE 6.6   Total Donations, Number of Visitors, and Average Donation per Visitor for Each Treatment

	Total	Donors	Average		Total	Donors	Average
			Experiment 1				
$50	$293.80	5249	$0.056	50¢	$308.00	5394	$0.057
$5	$316.65	5031	$0.063	Empty	$205.25	5585	$0.037
			Experiment 2				
		(D = double, H = half; M = matching, NS = no-sign, TY = thank-you)					
D, M	$322.05	5890	$0.055	H, M	$259.70	5307	$0.049
D, NS	$214.25	5350	$0.040	H, NS	$193.55	5510	$0.035
D, TY	$269.70	5702	$0.047	H, TY	$231.40	5487	$0.042
			Experiment 3				
		(NS = no-sign, S = sign)					
$5, NS	$717.25	14495	$0.049	50¢, NS	$625.50	14704	$0.043
$5, S	$653.70	14414	$0.045	50¢, S	$753.05	14915	$0.050
			Experiment 4				
		(NS = no-sign, S = sign)					
$5, NS	$247.35	4758	$0.052	50¢, NS	$216.00	5182	$0.042
$5, S	$209.25	5526	$0.038	50¢, S	$254.10	5847	$0.043

donations per donor. No sign effect was present in either of these variables. The composite average donations per visitor are shown in Table 6.6. The two no-sign averages have direction consistent with the earlier results for Experiment 1; that is, the $5 treatment average is larger than the 50¢ treatment average.

Here, evidence of a significant interaction between the sign and contents treatments ($p = 0.9\%$) is observed, indicating that there are significant differences in the means due to the *combination* of contents and sign. The $5 no-sign treatment and the 50¢ sign treatment both have high (approximately equal) averages per visitor, while the $5 sign and 50¢ no-sign treatments are lower, and also approximately equal. Thus, the differences in expected levels cannot be accommodated by either of the main effects, and the interaction steps in. The estimated value is sensitive to the coding of each of the treatment variables, so focusing on the estimated size of the interaction can be confusing.

Donations per visitor decrease in the $5 treatment when the sign is introduced as a result of a combination of high-propensity (though within sampling error) and high average donation per donor (again, perhaps within sampling error). Perhaps visitors sense the manipulation and distrust the "false" appearance of the box's contents. In contrast, the presence of the sign increases the average donation per visitor in the 50¢ treatment. The cost of a favorable social comparison is low, and people feel more willing to contribute as a result.

Experiment 4   The propensities and average donations per donor in Experiment 4 both exhibited an interaction between contents and sign treatments (although a significant effect was not estimated in the per-donor case). The results shown in Table 6.6 are qualitatively very similar to the results from Experiment 3. The highest average is again for the $5 no-sign treatment, though the 50¢ sign treatment has an average comparable with the $5 sign and 50¢ no-sign treatments. The very high average donation per donor in the $5 sign case has been well and truly offset by a very low donation propensity.

As with the regression in Experiment 3, the interaction term here is highly significant ($p = 0.16\%$). While in Experiment 3, two means were significantly higher than another pair, in this case a single mean is high, while the other three are statistically indistinguishable.

The conclusions of Experiment 3 are echoed: perhaps visitors sense the manipulation in the $5 treatment, and distrust the "false" appearance of the box's contents. The naturally high average donation per visitor (as per Experiment 1) is stifled when the study is disclosed (in this case via the propensity), and this more than offsets the higher contribution per donor.

Summary   To a large extent, differences in the donation propensities and average donations per donor are offset in the average donations per visitor. This, however, is the key statistic for the operator of the donation box, who would choose to maximize revenue via the average donation per visitor regardless of whether it is a single visitor making a huge donation, or every visitor making a tiny donation. It was fascinating to see that the observed averages were typically smaller than the lowest denomination coin (5¢ until Experiment 4, and 10¢ thereafter).

Anything in the donation box was found to be (significantly) better than nothing, a fact of which most street performers around the world seem to be aware! This result is consistent with either conditional cooperation or a model of social norms. However, the lack of a significant contents main effect in Experiment 2 demonstrates that one cannot conclude that more is always better.

The actual contents of the cash-laden boxes appear less important, though. Most, if not all, observed differences were statistically insignificant. The contents were only important when combined with the effects of the various signs introduced, particularly when the study was disclosed, in Experiments 3 and 4.

The offer to match donations yielded a significant increase in the average per visitor, as predicted by all hypotheses except Homo Economicus. This result has the expected policy implication: conditional funding typically results in less free riding than unconditional funding.

Additional Control Variables

Estimating the expected donations per donor and per visitor of course admits inclusion of control variables. The effects (if any) of several candidates are examined in the following sections.

Congestion Effects   Visitor satisfaction, and therefore the donation they are willing to give (nonzero or otherwise), could be influenced by the number of other visitors to the gallery on that day.

The results are reasonably robust across the four experiments. Congestion does not seem to have a major effect on the average donations per donor. The only significant coefficient appears in Experiment 3, where the average donation is 34¢ higher on busy days than when the gallery is not busy. On the per-visitor basis, two distinct patterns were observed. In Experiments 1 and 2, the effect is negative, and amounts to approximately 1¢ per visitor on average ($p = 2.62\%$ and $p = 1.2\%$). In contrast, in Experiments 3 and 4, the marginal effect is positive, and in this case average donations per visitor are approximately 1¢ *higher* ($p < 0.1\%$ and $p = 0.19\%$). The lack of a clear direction for this result is complicated by the passing of time, changes in the art on display, and to some extent methodological constraints vis-à-vis the aggregate size of the contributions on a day being linked to the number of visitors on that day, and the influences of total contents on donation propensity and size.

All previously reported regression results did take this variable into account, and significance levels were reported based on inclusion of the busyness variable where appropriate.

Peer and Gender Effects   In Experiment 4, a second camera was used to record activity around the donation box at the time of a donation. Use of a wide-angle camera in the gallery, in addition to the overhead camera utilized to count the donations, allowed counting of how many other visitors were present in the foyer at the time the donation was made, as well as the gender of the donor. A restricted sample of the data was used in the analysis of these variables, since it was crucial that the donation size was observed.

Observed donations totaled 344, of which 170 (49%) were made by females. During Experiment 4, City Gallery independently conducted random on-the-spot visitor satisfaction surveys, recording among other things, the gender of visitors. Their sample of 221 visitors included 135 females, representing a proportion of 61%. The observed difference between the two female proportions is highly significant ($p = 0.9\%$, with a two-sided alternative). In particular, assuming that survey respondents were truly randomly selected from the population of visitors, female visitors appear to be underrepresented in the population of donors.

Eliminating the donations whose value could not be determined, 226 observations remain. In the regression analysis of this subset of observed donations, differences in gender and whether or not other visitors were present at the time of the donation are modeled. Neither the peer nor the gender variables are significant determinants of *mean* donation behavior. However, although the mean peer and gender effects are not statistically significant, the donations do show some response to whether or not the donor is alone in the foyer when the donation is made. Only 35 out of 226 donations (approximately 15%) are made when there is no other visitor in the foyer.

Figure 6.3 shows quantile–quantile plots for the raw and log donations separated according to whether or not the donor is in an empty foyer. In this case, points corresponding to donations below $5 tend to lie below the line, indicating that when the donor is not alone (i.e., when there are onlookers), donations tend to

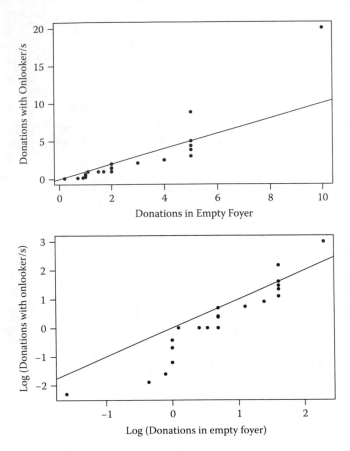

Figure 6.3   Quantile–quantile plots of the donations made when the donor is in an empty foyer, and when other visitors are present, on the raw and log scales, plotting sample quantiles against one another. If drawn from the same population, all points should lie on the line $y = x$.

be smaller. This indicates that when there are onlookers, the act of donating may be more important than how much is given, and consequently visitors are more likely to give, but give a small amount. Put another way, the act of donating is highly visible, yet the amount given is not. Again, the median donation in each case is $2, while the average donation is 21¢ higher when the donor is alone (although again, not statistically significant).

Meier (2005) finds evidence that men are more sensitive to group-level social comparisons than women. Meier studies students paying their tuition at the University of Zurich who were asked if they wished to donate to two social funds. The provision of social information concerning the donation behavior of others was found to have a large impact on the donation behavior of males, but had no significant impact on the donation behavior of females.

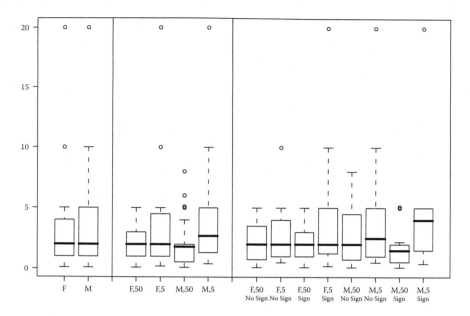

Figure 6.4   Boxplots of the female (F) and male (M) donations, disaggregated by contents (50 for the 50¢, and 5 for the $5 treatments, respectively) and by both contents and signage.

Figure 6.4 gives the sample distributions of the donations disaggregated according to various classifications. In the first panel, the distributions of the female and male donors are displayed. There is a hint that the males give slightly larger donations; however, a Kolmogorov-Smirnov test for equality of distribution cannot reject the null hypothesis that the underlying distributions are identical. The second panel in Figure 6.4 further disaggregates the donations according to the contents treatment. Here, no significant difference between the females' donations exists; however, the males give significantly lower donations in the 50¢ treatment than in the $5 treatment ($p = 0.86\%$ in the Kolmogorov-Smirnov test). Disaggregating further using the sign treatment, the source of this difference is restricted to males in instances when the study is disclosed; that is, there are no significant differences in the underlying distributions of the males' donations when there is no sign, but when the sign is present, males behave very differently in the 50¢ and $5 treatments ($p = 4.5\%$). Males conform to the social norm under scrutiny, but all other gender–scrutiny combinations show little variation in behavior across content treatments. That males react to scrutiny in a way that females do not is consistent with the results of Meier (2005).

In laboratory experiments it is often difficult to establish whether observed gender differences are real or are merely a result of self-selection biases. In the experiments described here, *every* visitor to the gallery during the study was a subject. Furthermore, the decision on whether or not to visit the gallery was made without knowledge of the experiment. As a result, these visitor-subjects are a highly representative sample of the people who visit art galleries, and the results will generalize to this subpopulation. However, females are clearly overrepresented as visitor-subjects (61%), which precludes extrapolation to the general population.

The Sunday Effect   This final analysis looks at seasonal effects in the data. An imbalance in Experiment 2 caused by the Christmas festival suggested the analysis of a potential day-of-the-week effect. Viewing the average donations per donor as a time series is not particularly helpful due to the small length of the series; however, including day-of-the-week dummy variables in the regression equations used yields some insight.

The composition of the donations made on a Sunday is now analyzed. Based on the general absence of compositional effects across treatments, the data is amalgamated by day of the week to yield the information shown in Table 6.7. Testing the composition and the day of the week for independence yields a significant result ($p = 2.8\%$), indicating that the larger numbers of high-denomination currency (bills and gold coins) given on Sunday relative to the "average non-Sunday" are indeed statistically significant.

Comparing the donation propensities observed on Sundays to those on other days of the week, it is apparent that visitors are also more willing to give on a Sunday. The sample distributions of daily propensities are shown in Figure 6.5, along with the averages per day. The boxplots indicate that the propensities may differ across days, although the sample sizes are quite small, and the standard errors on the medians high. The contingency table approach is used as before, focusing particularly on the Sunday propensity.

Since the propensities are (statistically) constant across signs, but not values, they are analyzed separately for the half and double treatments. The data are shown in Table 6.8 along with the average counts per day from Monday to Saturday, and with propensities. When testing for independence with respect to whether or not someone donates and the day of the week, independence is observed in the case of the double treatments, but there is a high degree of significance in the half treatments, indicating strong dependence ($p = 0.03\%$). People seem to be much more willing to donate on a Sunday when there is little money in the donation box, indicating an interaction between the day of the week and the value main effect.

Figure 6.5 indicates the average donations per donor are systematically higher on Sundays. Regression analysis confirms this difference to be statistically

TABLE 6.7   Composition of Donations Made on Sundays Compared to the Other Days of the Week

Day	Bills	Gold	Silver
Monday–Saturday	72	538	1175
Average			
Monday–Saturday	12	89	196
Sunday	21	126	210

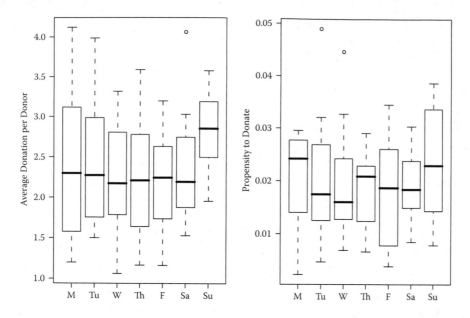

Figure 6.5   Average donation per donor and propensity: "The Sunday" effect.

significant. Repeating the per-donor analysis with the full data set of 84 days, and an added dummy variable equal to one on a Sunday and zero otherwise, a Sunday is estimated to yield donations 54¢ higher than other days on average ($p = 0.4\%$), or approximately 21% of the intercept term. The value main effect is almost identical to the restricted sample result, while the matching sign main effect diminished to 34¢ ($p = 4.6\%$). There is no estimated interaction between the value treatment and the day of the week, unlike with the propensities.

Finally, replicating the per-visitor regression with the full sample of 84 days and including a dummy variable for Sunday, suggests the average donation per visitor is 2.3¢ higher on a Sunday ($p < 0.01\%$), representing approximately 55% of the constant term. Again, all other parameter estimates are qualitatively the same as in the restricted sample. Busyness results in a smaller donation, and the matching sign increases donations by 1.6¢ per visitor on average ($p = 0.02\%$). Note that the Sunday main effect is 46% greater than the matching sign main effect, and almost

TABLE 6.8   The Propensity to Donate by Day of the Week and Value Treatment

Day	$50 Treatments			$200 Treatments		
	Donations	Visitors	Propensity	Donations	Visitors	Propensity
Monday–Saturday Average	359	17229	2.08%	296	18450	1.60%
Monday–Saturday	60	2872	2.08%	49	3075	1.60%
Sunday	93	2933	3.17%	40	2660	1.50%

12 times larger than the (insignificant) thank-you sign main effect. The analysis on the propensities strongly motivates the inclusion of an interaction between the Sunday dummy variable and the value treatment. Including this in the model and re-estimating, a significant interaction effect is observed ($p < 0.01\%$), confirming the fact that the much higher propensity to donate on a Sunday spills over into the average donation per visitor, despite the value main effect being insignificant when Sundays are excluded.

CONCLUSIONS

Voluntary contributions to a public good were studied in a natural setting where free riding was almost universal. Specifically, the propensity to donate in all of the experiments was in the range of 1 to 3%. This is of course very low relative to behavior observed in the laboratory, but perhaps not surprising to practitioners, given that charitable contributions are estimated at 2 to 3% of GDP. Either pure self-interest or crowding out does a good job of explaining the behavior of the majority of individuals, but gives little indication as to why *some* people give. In this series of experiments, several manipulations were studied that affected charitable behavior at the margin.

Donation composition tends to mimic the composition of the initial contents of the donation box. The decision to donate appears to be driven by the "cost" of a favorable social comparison. Linked to this, as the apparent size of previous donations increases, the observed donation size tends to increase. These two measurements tend to interact though, such that the average donation per visitor is based on a trade-off between high-propensity donations and large donations. It seems that the manipulation of one is always at the expense of the other.

Economists rejoice! Even socially motivated individuals respond to incentives. An offer to match donations one for one caused a 37% increase in the average donation per visitor. It is conceivable that other messages placed on the donation box might also have had a positive influence on donation behavior (e.g., fundraising targets, fundraising purposes).

Researcher scrutiny *alone* cannot be responsible for the differences in behavior observed in the field versus the laboratory. Researcher scrutiny did not (1) lead to appreciably more altruistic behavior unconditionally or (2) lead to greater conformity to the perceived social norms. Furthermore, the interaction between researcher scrutiny and the norm manipulation had a much larger influence on the behavior of males than females.

Unexpectedly, donations on Sundays were significantly larger than for any other day of the week. Furthermore, this temporal difference dwarfed most of the treatment effects. It is not clear what causes the Sunday effect. One possibility is that on Sundays people have just been primed in church to be more generous. In New Zealand, most Sunday church services are in the morning, yielding predictions that (1) Sunday morning donations will be lower or comparable to Saturday morning donations and (2) Sunday afternoon donations will be higher than Saturday afternoon donations. A temporal analysis of the data from Experiment 4 does not support these predictions. Another possibility is that the weekend leads people to be more relaxed or more likely to be with friends. This yields a prediction of a weekend rather than a Sunday effect. It may just be that a different population visits museums on Sundays. Unfortunately, with the data available, it is impossible to test this theory.

Overall, the data is best fit by a mixed-motives model of behavior, where impurely altruistic visitors suffer disutility upon violation of perceived social norms. No standard economic model is sufficiently rich to encapsulate the complex human behavior documented using this series of natural field experiments.

While the experiments were primarily conducted to contribute to the growing academic literature on charitable contribution, the results give plenty of food for thought for fundraisers. Contrasting the effects of the matching sign (increasing donations) and the thank-you sign (no effect) indicates that a message on the donation box *can* affect donation revenue. A framework for experimentation is also provided. Conduct an experiment[*]: control all but one variable, and over a period of time, measure the total revenue and the number of visitors exposed to the treatment. In the future, favor treatments with a high average donation per visitor.

Finally, in a controlled setting it is demonstrated what every busker the world over knows instinctively—people are reluctant to donate into an empty donation box.

REFERENCES

Akerlof, G. (1982). Labor contracts as partial gift exchange. *The Quarterly Journal of Economics, 97*(4), 543–569.

Andreoni, J. (1988). Privately provided public goods in a large economy: The limits of altruism. *Journal of Public Economics, 35*(1), 57–73.

Andreoni, J. (1989). Giving with impure altruism: Applications to charity and Ricardian equivalence. *Journal of Political Economy, 97*(6), 1447–1458.

Andreoni, J. (1990). Impure altruism and donations to public goods: A theory of warm-glow giving?. *The Economic Journal, 100*, 464–477.

Bernheim, B. D. (1994). A theory of conformity. *Journal of Political Economy, 102*(5), 841–877.

Fehr, E., & Schmidt, K. M. (1999). A theory of fairness, competition, and cooperation. *Quarterly Journal of Economics, 114*(3), 817–868.

Fischbacher, U., Gachter, S., & Fehr, E. (2001). Are people conditionally cooperative? Evidence from a public goods experiment. *Economics Letters, 71*(3), 397–404.

Frey, B. S., & Meier, S. (2004). Social comparisons and pro-social behavior: Testing "conditional cooperation" in a field experiment. *American Economic Review, 94*(5), 1717–1722.

Giving USA, 2008, a publication of Giving USA Foundation, Center on Philanthropy at Indiana University.

Harrison, G. W., & List, J. A. (2004). Field experiments. *Journal of Economic Literature, 42*(4), 1009–1055.

---

[*] Note that the most difficult aspect of the experiments was measuring the number of donors. For fundraisers, this variable is irrelevant, as donation revenue is maximized when average donation per visitor is maximized.

Hoffman, E., McCabe, K., & Smith, V. L. (1996). Social distance and other-regarding behavior in dictator games. *American Economic Review, 86*(3), 653–660.

International Monetary Fund World Economic Outlook Database, April 2008. http://www.imf.org

Landry, C., Lange, A., List, J., Price, M., Rupp, N., & Building, B. (2008). Is a donor in hand better than two in the bush? Evidence from a natural field experiment. *NBER Working Paper.*

Loewenstein, G. (1999). Experimental economics from the vantage-point of behavioural economics. *The Economic Journal, 109*(453), 25–34.

Meier, S. (2005). Conditions under which women behave less/more pro-socially than men. Unpublished manuscript.

Rabin, M. (1993). Incorporating fairness into game theory and economics. *American Economic Review, 83*(5), 1281–1302.

Shang, J., & Croson, R. (2005). Field experiments in charitable contribution: The impact of social influence on the voluntary provision of public goods. Unpublished manuscript.

Vesterlund, L. (2003). The informational value of sequential fundraising. *Journal of Public Economics, 87*(3–4), 627–657.

7

The Norm of Self-Interest
Implications for Charitable Giving

REBECCA K. RATNER, MIN ZHAO, and JENNIFER A. CLARKE

C onsider the following examples: Michael J. Fox suffered from Parkinson's disease and became a highly visible booster of research on Parkinson's disease. Cicely Tyson lost her sister to lung cancer and was featured in a nationwide ad campaign to encourage women to stop smoking. Many who give to help AIDS patients are themselves members of the gay community (Snyder & Omoto, 1992). Do all of these examples confirm the widespread perception that people are primarily self-interested and care most about those causes to which they have a personal connection (Miller & Ratner, 1996, 1998; Wuthnow, 1991)? That people often explain their own acts of compassion in self-interested terms further implies a central role of self-interest in charitable giving and volunteerism behaviors (Wuthnow, 1991).

In this chapter, we invoke a norms-based explanation for the link between self-interest and support for social causes. Specifically, we describe evidence for a *norm of self-interest*, whereby people expect that others' attitudes and behaviors will be guided by personal stake (Miller, 1999; Miller & Ratner, 1996, 1998; Ratner & Miller, 2001). We argue that these expectations can have profound implications for charitable donations of both money and time. For example, we find that when a spokesperson for a cause solicits support from others, the targets of the advocacy requests feel that it is harder to say no when the advocate indicates a personal connection to the cause. Further, members of a nonprofit organization respond with greater skepticism toward volunteers who do not have a clear personal tie to the cause than to those who do. In fact, we find that people even go so far as to discourage others from volunteering for causes to which they do not have a clear personal connection.

We begin by describing previous research on the role of personal stake in charitable giving and review our own work on this topic, including presenting in detail the results of new evidence related to (1) the impact of the self-interest norm on reactions toward advocates for a cause, (2) the impact of the self-interest norm on reactions toward those who indicate they would like to get involved in supporting a cause, and (3) the impact of the self-interest norm on potential supporters' willingness to act. We discuss implications of these findings for how to increase charitable giving and suggest several avenues for future research.

PREVIOUS RESEARCH: PERSONAL CONNECTION TO CAUSES AND CHARITABLE GIVING

Why are people more likely to support causes to which they have a clear personal connection? The explanation typically put forth is quite intuitive. Specifically, having a personal connection to the cause leads one to have more supportive attitudes toward it: people *care* more about an issue when it affects them personally. For example, when smokers and nonsmokers were asked to indicate their attitudes toward a number of bans on smoking (e.g., in restaurants and other places), smokers were more opposed than nonsmokers to restrictions on smoking (Miller & Ratner, 1998), indicating that their personal stake in the cause can impact their attitudes.

Other research shows that caring about an issue does not require being affected by it personally. For example, even simply feeling that one has a friendship with a victim was sufficient to increase people's sympathy toward other victims of the same cause and willingness to donate money to help them (Small & Simonsohn, 2008, and in this volume). Indeed, even simply knowing that the identity of the victim has been determined leads people to donate more to the cause (Jenni & Loewenstein, 1997), presumably because it increases the sympathy that people feel toward the victim. Other research suggests that a single victim is better at inducing a strong affective response than a large number of victims presented in statistical form (Slovic, 2007, and this volume). It therefore seems that caring about a cause does not require that a person have had a firsthand experience with it; knowing that others have been affected by it can be sufficient. Yet other research shows that attitudes toward causes are often driven by values unrelated to the extent to which the issue is personally relevant (Sears & Funk, 1990).

However, whether individuals' sympathetic attitudes toward a cause will translate into cause-supportive behaviors is another question (Fishbein & Ajzen, 1972). A number of factors have been shown to impact whether people will take action based on their attitudes, including personal experience with the target issue (Green & Cowden, 1992; Regan & Fazio, 1977; Sivacek & Crano, 1982). In one study, both students who were older than a new drinking age and those who were under the new drinking age had similar attitudes toward the increase in the drinking age. However, those who were under the new age, and therefore the most affected by it, were more likely to join a group to oppose it (Sivacek & Crano, 1982). Similarly, another study demonstrated that whether one did or did not have children who would be affected by busing (to achieve desegregation) did not impact people's attitudes toward busing, but it did impact people's actions (Green & Cowden, 1992). One straightforward explanation for such findings is that costly behaviors prompt people to consider "Is it worth it?" to get involved, and only conclude that it does when they have a personal connection to the cause (Green & Cowden, 1992).

In sum, previous research has investigated the actual impact of having a personal connection to a cause on individuals' involvement in supporting those causes. The results suggest that having a connection to the cause (even simply knowing someone who was impacted by it) can lead people to be more supportive toward the cause, and that regardless of the attitudes that people hold, they will be more likely to engage in supportive behaviors when they have a clear personal connection to the cause. We now turn to our norms-based explanation about the impact of personal connection to a cause on social action, and develop our ideas about the relevance for charitable giving.

THE NORM OF SELF-INTEREST

Norms reflect beliefs about what behaviors others engage in and what behaviors are appropriate (descriptive and prescriptive norms; Cialdini, Kallgren, & Reno, 1991). People tend to feel that they should do what others like them do, and therefore engage in the behaviors that they perceive others to perform (Cialdini, Reno, & Kallgren, 1990; Goldstein, Cialdini, & Griskevicius, 2008).

The particular norm that we focus on here pertains to beliefs about the extent to which the attitudes and behaviors of others are dictated by self-interest. Previous research documenting a norm of self-interest indicates that members of Western, individualistic cultures perceive that it is common and rational to hold attitudes—and engage in behaviors—that reflect one's own narrowly defined self-interest (Miller, 1999; Miller & Ratner, 1996, 1998). People expect others' attitudes toward social causes to be guided by material stake, and these lay beliefs in the power of self-interest are so strong that people consistently overestimate the role that personal stake plays (Miller & Ratner, 1998). For example, although smokers were more opposed to bans on smoking than were nonsmokers in the study mentioned earlier, these same respondents overestimated by a sizable margin the impact that self-interest would play: 85% of the smokers and 95% of nonsmokers in the study were in favor of a ban on smoking in restaurants, whereas these same respondents estimated that only 28% of smokers versus 84% of nonsmokers would favor such a ban (Miller & Ratner, 1998, Study 4).

In another study, participants were given an opportunity to assist an (ostensibly real) organization by providing a statement of their attitudes toward the organization's cause that they had written as part of a previous research study (Miller & Ratner, 1998, Study 5). The cause pertained to funding research on an illness that participants were told primarily affected either their own sex or the opposite sex. In that study, there was no effect of which sex they were told was directly affected on individuals' own attitudes toward the cause or willingness to release their written statement to the organization (85% of the participants who read their own sex was at risk and 81% of the participants who read the opposite sex was at risk did so). However, participants overestimated the impact of which sex was at risk on others' willingness to provide their statement to the organization, anticipating that whereas 79% of their vested peers would do so, only 63% of their nonvested peers would do so.

We argue that this strong belief that people will care about causes that affect them personally can have important consequences (Miller, 1999; Miller & Ratner, 1996, 1998; Ratner & Miller, 2001). In the sections that follow, we discuss consequences of this norm of self-interest for charitable giving.

IMPACT OF SELF-INTEREST NORM ON REACTIONS TOWARD ADVOCATES FOR THE CAUSE

One broad set of consequences of the self-interest norm pertains to how the target audience for a persuasive appeal will respond to an advocate who does versus does not have a clear personal connection to the cause. Indeed, the previous research reviewed earlier suggests that having been affected personally by the issue would enhance one's effectiveness as an advocate (e.g., due to the persuasiveness of victims). However, other research suggests that a personal connection to a cause might actually undermine one's effectiveness as an advocate. For example, the literature on self-interest and persuasion (e.g., Eagly, Wood, & Chaiken, 1978; Walster, Aronson, & Abrahams, 1966) shows that acknowledging a personal stake in a cause can render a spokesperson less persuasive. The logic of this claim points to the ambiguity associated with the advocacy of those who might be biased by their personal stake. If a speaker stands to benefit in some way from the advocated policy, the audience cannot confidently determine if the act of advocacy reflects an objective representation of reality or a distorted one (Kelley, 1972). We would note, however, that the effectiveness of an advocate who has a personal connection to the cause need not be defined exclusively by his or her capacity to change attitudes about the merits of the cause. Instead, we propose that having a connection to the cause might not produce more persuasiveness or greater attitude change, but it might cause more prosocial behavior changes, such that an audience will be more deferential to a spokesperson who has a clear stake in their cause. More generally, we argue that a personal connection to a cause grants people (e.g., Michael Fox, Cicely Tyson) psychological standing to make requests of others to support the cause. Our concept of psychological standing is analogous to the judicial concept of *legal standing* (*Sierra Club v. Morton*, 1972), which requires that a party demonstrate they have been harmed before they can initiate a lawsuit.

For example, consider a study that investigated how people would respond to an individual who either did or did not have a clear personal connection to the target issue. In this study, respondents were asked how they would feel about an individual (identified as either male or female) who voiced a position in favor of health plan coverage of abortions or in opposition to health plan coverage of abortions (Ratner & Miller, 2001, Study 2). Participants in this study indicated that they perceived this cause to be of greater personal relevance to women than to men. Consistent with the idea that people would react more favorably to the person with the clear personal connection to the cause, participants in this study reported more confusion when a man showed support for the issue than when a woman did (and greater anger if a man was opposed to the issue than if a woman was). Acting on attitudes without having an obvious personal connection to the cause deviates from what people expect: such behavior violates the norm of self-interest.

A subsequent series of studies tested the idea that people defer more to requests made by victims than by others who care about the cause but have themselves no personal connection to it—even if the audience is not persuaded more by the victims (Miller, Ratner, & Zhao, 2009). A preliminary study showed that people thought that a spokesperson in an ad campaign to encourage women to quit smoking would be more effective when the spokesperson lost a sister to lung cancer than when they did not learn of any personal connection to the cause. Further, people anticipated that this effect would be driven by greater attitude change about the merits of the cause. A follow-up study presented participants with one of two versions of this same actual ad campaign: respondents either saw an ad in which Cicely Tyson mentioned the loss of her sister to lung cancer or in which Brooke Shields voiced her concern about smoking-related deaths but did not identify a direct link to the cause. This follow-up study revealed that the expectations of those in the preliminary study were partially right: those who viewed the Cicely Tyson ad reported a greater interest in taking action to support the cause (i.e., sending an electronic card to their women friends to encourage them to quit smoking) than those who viewed the Brooke Shields ad. However, contrary to the previous participants' expectations, the effects were not driven by changes in perceptions of the merits of the cause. Respondents in both conditions reported to the same degree that smoking puts one at risk of smoking-related illness.

Why, then, are people deferential to the person who has a stake in the cause, if that person is not more effective at changing their attitudes? The reason, we believe, resides in people's belief that they will feel guilty and disrespectful if they were to say no to this person. Doing so would be dishonoring this advocate's personal connection to the cause (i.e., their victimhood experience) (Goffman, 1959). Consider, for example, a situation in which someone comes to your door who suffered from a respiratory illness generated by factory-generated pollution. The person at your door asks for 10 minutes of your time to talk to you about the factory and their proposal that the factory be shut down immediately. How likely would you be to agree to listen to this person? We presented this question to a group of respondents, who reported they would be more likely to talk to this person than one who was not from the town where the factory was located and did not suffer any respiratory symptoms (Miller, Ratner, & Zhao, 2009). Further, they would agree to talk to the victim of the pollution even if their own attitude about what should be done with the factory differed from that of the person who came to their door (e.g., even if they thought less drastic measures should be taken than closing down the factory completely). Respondents said they would find it harder to "say no" to the person who had a clear stake in the cause; they did not want to turn this person away.

One possible explanation for the desire not to say no to someone who has personally been affected by an issue (e.g., a victim) is a general feeling of sympathy. Perhaps people just do not like to disappoint those who have suffered a personal hardship. Our prediction, however, was that people's desire not to say no to a victim would be cause specific: they would not turn down requests made by a victim when those requests related to the person's victimhood, but this deference granted to the victim would not extend to other causes (Miller, Ratner, & Zhao, 2009).

To test this, we told participants about a college student whose "most challenging experience while in college" was having a parent who suffered a heart attack or was diagnosed with cancer. Next, participants read about the person's plans postgraduation, which included a manipulation of the organization for which the person intended to volunteer: half of the participants read that the person wants to volunteer doing clerical work for the American Cancer Society, and half read the identical sentence except that her chosen volunteer organization was the American Heart Association. Thus, half of the respondents read that the student was going to volunteer for the organization to which she had a clear personal connection (i.e., her parent had suffered from that particular illness), and half read that she was to volunteer for another organization. Respondents in the study reported how they would feel saying no to this classmate if she asked them if they wanted to join her at a meeting of a volunteer organization to support her chosen cause.

As predicted, people reported that it would be harder to say no to a request to attend the meeting when the parent suffered from the disease for which the advocate sought their support. Having a parent with cancer licensed one to make requests of others pertaining to cancer, but not heart disease; having a parent with heart disease licensed one to make requests of others pertaining to heart disease, but not cancer. People felt it would be far easier to deny requests made by an advocate who lacked a clear connection to the cause, even when this advocate evoked the same level of sympathy overall.

A skeptic could note that the studies reported thus far involved only hypothetical scenarios and reports of anticipated emotions and behavioral intentions. What would happen if we presented people with a real opportunity to donate money to support a cause? To test this, we gave people the chance to donate money to the Canadian Cancer Society, after they read a pitch for the Canadian Cancer Society made by someone who allegedly lost a parent either to cancer or heart disease (Miller, Ratner, & Zhao, 2009). In addition, we varied the format in which they were to report their donation decision. Half of the respondents indicated whether they wanted to donate $0 or $10 to the cause, and the others indicated whether they wanted to donate $0 to $10, in any one dollar increment (e.g., $1, $2, $3, and so on up to $10). Our prediction was that the biggest impact of the advocate's personal connection to the cause would emerge in the condition in which people needed to decide whether to donate $0 (a complete rejection of their request) or $10 (showing support for the cause), rather than in the condition in which people could support the cause in any amount up to $10. As expected, people did not want to engage in outright rejection of the request made by a victim: when they had to choose between honoring the request or refusing to help at all (i.e., in the $0 vs. $10 binary choice condition), a higher percentage of respondents donated $10 to the Cancer Society when the father died of cancer than when he died of heart disease (95% vs. 73%). However, also as expected, no difference emerged in the percentage of respondents who chose to donate $10 to the Cancer Society as a function of the advocate's father's cause of death when presented with the scale format (61% vs. 64%).

Together, the results of these studies suggest that advocates for a cause are granted standing to make requests of others when they have a clear personal connection to the cause. Advocates who lack such a connection to the cause are not granted this same level of deference. For this reason, organizations will benefit from using advocates who clearly identify their connection the cause. Regardless of whether such spokespersons change people's attitudes toward the cause, it is more likely that the audience will agree to the advocate's requests. In the next section, we consider another way in which the norm of self-interest can impact charitable giving: it can impact how people respond to those who offer to become a supporter of the cause.

IMPACT OF SELF-INTEREST NORM ON REACTIONS TOWARD WOULD-BE SUPPORTERS

Whereas the previous section focused on the effectiveness of advocates who do or do not identify a personal connection to the cause, we turn now to consider what leads people to become an advocate for the cause in the first place. What is the likely response that people will have to someone who is interested in volunteering to help a cause (i.e., seeking to donate their time)? Will people be pleasantly surprised by the unexpected support from someone who does not identify a personal connection to the cause, or is the norm of self-interest sufficiently strong that people will respond with suspicion or negativity to those who lack a clear personal connection to the cause? For example, if someone says they would like to volunteer their time, people might not trust that these individuals will be sufficiently dependable and dedicated to the cause.

In a series of studies, we tested the hypothesis that people express greater feelings of confusion and negativity toward potential volunteers who lack a clear personal connection to a cause than toward those who do (Clarke, 2005; Ratner & Clarke, 2004). Further, we tested the prediction that people would go so far as to *explicitly discourage* others from getting involved in causes for which the would-be volunteer lacks a personal connection. As we will describe next, our findings support these predictions and demonstrate the prescriptive component of the norm of self-interest: people not only expect others to engage in self-interested ways (the descriptive norm) but believe it is rational for them to do so. In the remainder of this section, we will describe in detail the results of three studies that demonstrate the negativity conveyed to would-be volunteers who lack a personal connection to their cause.

Study 1: Questioning the Motivation of Prospective Volunteers Who Do Not Identify a Personal Connection to the Cause

In the first study, participants reviewed a single volunteer application from an individual who did or did not reveal a personal connection (i.e., via a related victimhood experience) to the target organization (Clarke, 2005).* The organization was Students Against Drunk Driving (SADD), and participants in the study were 30 adult volunteers in the Arizona chapter of SADD and the Colorado Springs Junior League (a women's volunteer organization).

Participants completed the study in exchange for a small monetary donation to their organization. Each participant examined one volunteer application allegedly completed by an undergraduate who was applying to the University of North Carolina's Community Service Board, described as an organization that solicits volunteer applications for area organizations. We presented the application as though it was real, although in fact we created the materials so that we could alter the key parts of the application form that we wanted to control. All participants read that the applicant identified SADD (Students Against Drunk Driving) as their intended organization. The application included the applicant's first name ("Amy"), as well as a last name and school address, which we obscured to enhance the perception that we sought to preserve the anonymity of the (real) person who had submitted this application. Sections indicating the applicant's academic major and previous work experience were completed and left visible. The key manipulation was included in the applicant's answer to the question: "Why have you chosen the above organization?" Participants randomly assigned to the *personal connection* condition read the response, "My sister was killed by a drunk driver," whereas those in the *no personal connection* condition read, "I think it is a very important cause" (i.e., intended to reflect the value-expressive function of volunteerism, Snyder, 1993; Snyder & Omoto, 1992). Finally, the applicant indicated prior experience volunteering for "DARE (drug and alcohol education)." All participants were therefore presented with background information about the applicant other than the statement containing the manipulation of a personal connection to the cause.

After reading this information, each respondent completed an evaluation form, on which they rated the applicant from 1 (*not at all*) to 7 (*extremely*) on a number of measures: how dedicated the applicant would be to volunteering, how clear the reason is for the applicant wanting to volunteer for SADD, how well the applicant would understand the SADD mission, how knowledgeable the applicant is about SADD, how much training the applicant would require, and the extent to which the participant would encourage North Carolina's SADD coordinator to select the applicant.

In addition, respondents provided open-ended responses to the following questions:

1. In your opinion, based on the information given in the application, would this applicant be a good volunteer? Why or why not?
2. If you were interviewing the applicant for a volunteer position with SADD, what types of things would you try to find out about him/her during the interview?
3. Please list typical SADD volunteer tasks, and indicate which of the listed tasks you would assign to this volunteer and why.

---

* The third author of this chapter conducted this study as part of her dissertation under the guidance of the first author.

A multivariate analysis of variance (MANOVA) was performed to test the effects of whether the applicant mentioned a personal connection to the cause (i.e., the applicant's sister's death) or not (i.e., no personal loss), and the organization to which the study participant belonged (SADD vs. Junior League) on the respondent's ratings of how suitable a volunteer the applicant seemed to be. This analysis indicated no differences between the responses given by those who were currently members of SADD versus the Junior League. However, as predicted, there was a significant overall effect of mentioning the personal connection to the cause on people's evaluations of the applicant ($F(7, 20) = 5.46$, $p = 0.001$).

Participants rated the applicant more favorably on a number of dimensions when the applicant identified a personal connection to the cause (see Table 7.1). Consistent with predictions, it was significantly clearer to participants why the applicant with the personal connection to the cause than the applicant without a personal connection was interested in volunteering for SADD ($F(1, 26) = 44.94$, $p < 0.001$). Further, the applicant whose sister was killed in the drunk driving accident was rated as significantly more likely than the other applicant to be dedicated to SADD ($F(1, 26) = 14.32$, $p = .001$) and more likely to understand the SADD mission ($F(1, 26) = 24.68$, $p < 0.001$). The applicant with this personal connection to the cause was seen as more knowledgeable about SADD issues ($F(1, 26) = 24.99$, $p < .001$), although it is noteworthy that there was no difference in how much training respondents believed would be required for the two applicants ($F(1, 26) = 1.87$, ns). Consistent with their overall more favorable evaluations of the person who lost her sister to the drunk driving accident, participants were significantly more likely to recommend that that this person be selected as a volunteer ($F(1, 26) = 26.75$, $p < 0.001$).

In order to analyze the results of the three open-ended questions, we trained two coders to read and evaluate participants' responses. Question 1 responses were coded for mentions of the applicant's motivation and dedication (scored as either –1 if mentioned negatively, 0 if not mentioned, 1 if mentioned positively). Question 2 was coded for the extent to which questions arose regarding the applicant's knowledge, commitment, abilities, and motivation to volunteer as well as

TABLE 7.1 Evaluations of Prospective Volunteers as a Function of Whether Victimhood Experience Provided Personal Connection to Organization

Measure	Sister Killed		No Personal Loss	
	M	SD	M	SD
Clarity of reason to volunteer	6.00	0.93	2.57	1.64
Will be dedicated	5.64	0.93	3.88	1.31
Will understand mission	6.21	0.97	3.50	1.63
Encourage SADD to choose	6.29	0.83	4.19	1.22
Knowledgeable about SADD	5.57	1.16	2.94	1.48
Will require training	4.29	1.33	4.69	1.35

Source: Clarke, J. A. (2005). The effect of vested interest on the evaluation of potential volunteers (Doctoral dissertation, University of North Carolina). *Dissertation Abstracts International*, 65(7-B), 3771.

the extent to which the respondent appears to be encouraging the applicant to volunteer through the questions they would pose in the interview (1 = *not at all* to 5 = *very much*). Question 3 was coded for the extent to which the applicant would be given tasks that would make the applicant a "face of the organization" (e.g., public tasks such as counseling families or serving as a community representative of SADD at a public event rather than clerical tasks such as stuffing envelopes; 1 = *not at all* to 5 = *very much*). The two coders' ratings were significantly positively correlated for all measures (intraclass rs = .48 to .82), and analyses were performed on the mean ratings of the two judges for each item.

We performed an analysis (MANOVA) on these coded values for the three open-ended questions. As was the case with the closed-ended measures, participants' responses to these open-ended measures did not reveal any effects of the respondents' organization (SADD vs. Junior League). However, the analysis revealed that people's open-ended responses were significantly more favorable when evaluating the prospective volunteer for SADD who indicated the personal connection to the cause than the one who did not ($F(8, 12)$ = 5.00, $p < .01$). Specifically, respondents voiced more concerns about the motivation of the participant who did not identify a personal connection to the cause (Ms = −.41 vs. 0.38, $F(1, 21)$ = 33.69, $p < .001$) and questioned to a greater extent the motivation of the applicant who did not identify a personal connection than the applicant who did (Ms = 3.23 vs. 1.58, $F(1, 21)$ = 9.66, p = .006). In addition, respondents' open-ended responses were more encouraging toward the applicant with the personal connection (Ms = 2.96 vs. 1.50, $F(1, 21)$ = 16.37, p = .001), and they listed tasks that were rated as containing "face of the organization" opportunities to a greater extent for the applicant with the personal connection to the cause (Ms = 4.12 *vs.* 3.18, $F(1, 21)$ = 7.70, p = .01).

In sum, consistent with our predictions, study participants evaluated more favorably on almost all dimensions the applicant who indicated that she had a personal connection to SADD (due to the death of her sister) than the one who did not mention a personal connection to it. Open-ended responses also were consistent with predictions: participants' interview questions reflected more encouragement—and less confusion and negativity—toward the applicant who indicated a victimhood experience that connected her to the cause than toward an applicant who was not a victim but said the cause was an important one.

Study 2: Perceiving Unreliability and Lack of Commitment When Volunteer Lacks Victimhood Experience

We designed a second study to test whether the skeptical attitudes toward someone who does not identify a personal connection to the cause via a victimhood experience are so strong that they persist even when the volunteer has a track record of helping their chosen organization in the past (Ratner & Clarke, 2004). In this study, 199 undergraduates at a southeastern university evaluated a volunteer application in exchange for money. As in the previous study, half of the participants were randomly assigned to learn the volunteer's sister was killed in a drunk-driving accident, and the other half did not learn of any victimhood experience that connected the volunteer to the cause.

Each participant considered a single SADD application that included the same manipulation of personal connection to the cause that was used in the previous study, embedded within the same application form used in the previous study. In addition, in this second study, participants also read that volunteer applicants were asked to assist the organization at the same day and time each week and read that the applicant had checked off Tuesday mornings as her preferred time slot. Next, a one-page Volunteer Tracking Sheet summarized "Amy's" assistance at SADD over the past semester. It began with her start date one Tuesday in early March and reported whether she had attended each Tuesday until the end of the semester nine weeks later. Each entry in the time sheet noted the date, time in, time out, supervisor's initials, and a short explanation in a "comments" column for any missed days. Half of the participants were randomly assigned to see that Amy had a strong track record of attendance over the past semester, whereas the other half saw that she had a spotty track record over the past semester. Specifically, participants in the *strong track record* condition saw a time sheet in which Amy volunteered at SADD every Tuesday morning from 10 a.m. until noon, and her only missed day was noted as occurring during Spring Break. Participants in the *weak track record* condition saw the same time sheet, with two of the attended days replaced by two additional missed days, identified by the words "no show" in the comments column.

After examining Amy's application form and time sheet, participants reported to what extent they would encourage the supervisors at SADD to retain her as a volunteer in the next semester, how likely it is that she will volunteer the next time she is scheduled, how reliable she was over the past semester assisting SADD on a weekly basis, and to what extent the SADD mission was personally relevant to Amy. Respondents completed all items on 7-point scales, where $1 = not\ at\ all$ and $7 = extremely$.

We performed an analysis (MANOVA) to test the effects of the strength of the volunteer's track record and personal connection to the cause on how favorably the volunteer was rated. The results indicated both an overall effect of having a victim-hood experience that connects her to the cause ($F(1, 191) = 52.55$, $p < .0001$) as well as an overall effect of the strength of track record ($F(1, 191) = 31.27, p < .0001$) on evaluations of the volunteer. As expected, the track record information signifi-cantly impacted people's ratings of how reliable the volunteer had been ($Ms = 5.81$ vs. 3.63, in the strong and weak track record conditions, respectively, $F(1, 194) = 111.44, p < .0001$), and that the SADD mission was judged to be more relevant to the person who identified a victimhood experience that connected her to the cause ($Ms = 6.15$ vs. 3.15, $F(1, 195) = 202.96, p < .0001$).

Moreover, as predicted, respondents' ratings favored the volunteer who had a personal connection to the cause over the one who did not, even when the informa-tion provided about the volunteer's past track record of work for the target organiza-tion was identical. Participants were more likely to recommend that the individual with a personal connection to the cause be retained as a volunteer for the following year ($Ms = 5.28$ vs. 3.84, $F(1, 194) = 45.66, p < .0001$) and perceived that this per-son would be more likely to come in next time than the one who lacked a personal connection to the cause ($Ms = 5.48$ vs. 4.54, $F(1, 194) = 24.65, p < .0001$).

We also found that participants rated the volunteer with the personal connection to the cause as having been more reliable in the past year than the one who did not identify a personal connection to the cause ($Ms = 5.13$ vs. 4.33), even though the track records of the two were identical, $F(1, 194) = 14.99$, $p < .0001$. This suggests that the perceptions of the volunteer who identified the cause as important—though lacking a victimhood experience to connect her to the cause—are more negative than warranted. Indeed, that people perceived the volunteer without a victimhood experience that connected her to the cause as less reliable in the past despite identical track records demonstrates the difficulty such a person will have in demonstrating their commitment to help an organization.

The design of this study also allowed us to test whether individuals' more negative evaluations of the volunteers without the personal connection to the cause were attenuated when they received behavioral evidence that the person's track record had been strong over the preceding months. Analyses revealed that the behavioral information did not reduce the gap in perceptions of the two volunteers on any of the measures (i.e., the "strength of the track record" × "personal connection to the cause" interaction did not approach significance on any of the items, $Fs < 2.10$, $ps > .26$). Indeed, for the measure assessing the extent to which the participant would recommend that this person be retained as a future volunteer, participants provided directionally more favorable responses for the person with a weak track record who had a personal connection to the cause ($M = 4.80$) than a person with a strong track record who lacked a personal connection to the cause ($M = 4.58$). In sum, having a clear personal connection to the cause seems to carry even more weight than several months of engaging in cause-supportive actions when it comes to convincing others of one's commitment to the cause.

Study 3: Discouraging Volunteerism That Is Not Motivated by Personal History

In the two studies just described, respondents were more encouraging to someone volunteering for SADD who lost a sibling to a drunk-driving accident than someone who did not identify how their personal history connects them to the cause. We designed a third study to demonstrate that the favorable attitudes toward the volunteer who lost the sibling emerged because she had a clear personal connection to her chosen cause, rather than due to an overall feeling of sympathy toward the individual who suffered this tragedy (Ratner & Clarke, 2004). For example, losing one's parent to cancer would be perceived to make one an appropriate volunteer for the American Cancer Society (but not the American Heart Association). A second purpose of this study was to test whether participants would go so far as to explicitly *discourage* others from making a substantial time commitment to causes in which the would-be volunteer lacks a clear personal connection (i.e., that they *should* show support for those causes that have affected them personally).

Eighty introductory psychology students at a southeastern university completed the study in partial fulfillment of a course requirement. As in one of the studies described earlier, participants read that a graduating senior was interested in volunteering for either the American Cancer Society or the American Heart Association, and learned either that the prospective volunteer's father suffered a heart attack or a battle with cancer. Participants in this study were not presented with an application form (as in the two preceding studies that investigated evaluations of the volunteer), but rather were asked to imagine that they were in a group of graduating seniors that had gathered to discuss postgraduation plans.

After reading the background information about this student (again identified as "Amy"), participants were asked to indicate how dedicated to the volunteer position they think the volunteer will be, how clear the reason is for Amy's interest in this work, how well they think she understands the organization's mission (on 7-point scales where 1 = *not at all* and 7 = *extremely*), and to what extent they would encourage Amy to volunteer at her chosen organization (1 = *not at all*, 7 = *very much*). In addition, they were asked what time commitment they would recommend that Amy make in volunteering for this organization by checking one of the following options: under 6 months, 6 months to 1 year, 1 to 2 years, or more than 2 years. Finally, they were asked to what extent they would encourage her to think about other organizations that she could volunteer for instead of the one she selected and to what extent the volunteer organization is personally relevant for Amy (on 7-point scales where 1 = *not at all* and 7 = *very much*).

An analysis (MANOVA) was conducted to determine the effects of Amy's parents' illness (cancer vs. heart disease) and Amy's chosen organization (American Cancer Society vs. American Heart Association) on participants' reactions to the volunteer activity. As expected, participants' reactions did not vary simply as a function of the would-be volunteer's background or the organization for which they sought to volunteer. What mattered was whether the volunteer's background (parent had cancer vs. heart disease) and the focus of the organization matched (the omnibus "background" × "organization" interaction was significant, $F(7, 69) = 14.30$, $p < .0001$).[*] Across almost all of the dimensions on which reactions to the would-be volunteer were measured, people had more favorable perceptions of the volunteer and were more encouraging when the volunteer's chosen organization matched the illness in the volunteer's family (see Table 7.2). For example, participants perceived that the volunteer would be more dedicated to the organization when the father's illness was the focus of the chosen organization. Moreover, participants were more likely to recommend that the person consider *another* organization to volunteer for rather than their chosen organization if their illness in the family did not match the chosen organization, and to encourage the person to reduce their intended time commitment for the chosen organization if their illness in the family did not match the focus of the organization.

---

[*] Univariate analyses indicated that the interaction was significant at the p < .01 level for all measures, and simple effects tests indicated significant differences at the p < .05 level for comparisons of the participants with and without the personal connection to the cause for both the Heart Association and American Cancer Society for all of the dependent measures except for two (responses for the "encourage" and "time commitment" measures were directionally consistent with predictions but not significant for the American Heart Association when the person's father had heart disease vs. cancer).

TABLE 7.2   Perceptions of and Recommendations to Volunteer As a Function of Whether Volunteer's Personal Experience Matched Chosen Organization

| Parental Illness | Cancer Society | | | | Heart Association | | | |
| | Cancer | | Heart Attack | | Cancer | | Heart Attack | |
Measure	M	SD	M	SD	M	SD	M	SD
Perceptions of volunteer								
Dedicated to cause	5.75	1.02	4.40	1.47	4.20	1.24	5.25	1.25
Clear reason to volunteer	6.40	0.75	3.45	1.96	3.50	2.06	4.75	2.05
Understand mission	5.60	1.10	4.20	1.20	3.90	1.45	4.75	1.16
Personal relevance	6.45	0.83	3.40	1.88	3.85	1.60	6.15	1.09
Recommendations to Volunteer								
Encourage volunteer	5.95	1.28	4.05	1.64	4.85	1.46	5.50	1.24
Approve time commitment	2.70	1.08	1.70	0.73	1.84	0.83	2.15	0.93
Recommend a different organization	3.25	1.45	5.35	1.50	4.90	1.37	3.50	1.57

Source: Ratner, R. K., & Clarke, J. (2004). Perceptions of potential volunteers who lack a personal connection to the cause. Unpublished raw data.

This pattern of findings replicates our earlier results that people evaluate the person more favorably as a potential volunteer if the person indicates a clear personal connection to their chosen cause. We find that having a clear personal connection to the cause influences evaluations of volunteer applicants beyond the effects of sympathy toward someone who has suffered a personal hardship (in which case it would not matter whether the illness in the family matched the focus of the organization). Significant interactions between background and the chosen organization support the idea that the applicants are evaluated more favorably as volunteers for the organization to which they have a personal connection and further that people encourage others to minimize their involvement in a cause to which the volunteer lacks an obvious personal connection.

The results of these three studies indicate that people evaluate would-be volunteers as more dedicated when they have clear personal connections (via a family member's victimhood experience) to the cause, even when they see the volunteer had a track record of supporting that same cause in the past. Moreover, people said that the would-be volunteer *should* focus on a cause in which they have a personal stake. As a result, the expectation that others will act in self-interested ways can lead observers both internal and external to a nonprofit organization to respond with greater negativity toward supporters of a cause who do not have a victimhood experience that connects them to the cause than to those who do. It will be important for organizations or causes that seek support to be careful not to discourage—and perhaps to explicitly *encourage*—the involvement of those who do not have a direct personal (e.g., victimhood) experience that connects them to the issue.

IMPACT OF SELF-INTEREST NORM ON POTENTIAL SUPPORTERS' WILLINGNESS TO ACT

One clear implication of the present analysis is that people might be reluctant to take action to support a cause to which they lack a clear personal connection. Individuals who lack a personal link to a cause might anticipate that if they show support for a cause, their interest will be questioned. Indeed, research suggests this is exactly what happens: people anticipate that others won't value their input and will wonder why they are involved in supporting the cause if they lack a clear connection to it (Ratner & Miller, 2001). We turn next to describing the results of two such studies.

In one study, respondents learned about a gastrointestinal disease for which they believed either their same sex or the opposite sex was at risk. They considered their opinion about a proposed reallocation of resources that would follow a budget cut away from research on that illness. The manipulation of whether their own sex or the opposite sex was at risk for the illness did not impact people's attitudes—people were overall somewhat negative toward the budget cut, regardless of whether their own sex or the opposite sex was at risk—but they did feel more uncomfortable and expected more confusion if they were to attend a meeting in support of their attitude on this issue if they believed it directly affected the opposite sex rather than their own sex (Ratner & Miller, 2001, Study 3). Moreover, they anticipated that their input at such a meeting would be valued less if the disease affected the opposite sex rather than their own sex.

If individuals' reluctance to show support for a cause stems from the fact that they expect their support would not be fully appreciated, then framing the cause more inclusively could increase the support given by those who perceive they do not have a direct connection to the issue. Another study tested this idea. As before, respondents either read that their own sex or the opposite sex suffered from a disease for which a proposed budget cut would reduce research spending and then read about a local group that had organized to oppose the budget cut. To vary whether the organization was framed inclusively (i.e., embracing both those with and without a direct stake in the cause) the researchers manipulated whether the group protesting the change called itself "Princeton Opponents of Proposition 174" or as more inclusive "Princeton Men and Women Opposed to Proposition 174" (Ratner & Miller, 2001, Study 4).

Results indicated that framing the organization inclusively impacted potential supporters' actions. Among those who believed the opposite sex was at risk for the illness, those in the inclusive framing condition ("Princeton Men & Women ...") were much more likely to write a statement in support of their position about the budget cut (72%) than those in the standard, noninclusive framing condition (22%). The frame did not impact the willingness to write the statement of those whose *own* sex was at risk (50% vs. 53% did so in the standard and inclusive framing conditions, respectively).° In addition, all were willing to complete a survey indicating

---

° Further, no effect of the inclusiveness manipulation (only a main effect of whether one's own sex or the opposite sex was at risk) emerged on willingness to sign a petition, perhaps suggesting a reluctance to be publicly associated with the cause, even when it was framed inclusively.

their attitudes regardless of the name of the group and which sex was afflicted, suggesting an overall willingness to expend effort related to the issue. Together, these results suggest that those who lack a personal connection to the cause can feel inhibited from showing certain types of support but can be encouraged to do so if they feel their support will be welcomed by an inclusive organization.

IMPLICATIONS FOR INCREASING CHARITABLE GIVING

The present findings suggest a number of implications for how to increase charitable giving. Specifically, the results suggest there are three key issues to consider: (1) What are the attitudes that a would-be supporter has toward the cause? (2) Will the person engage in behaviors to support the cause (e.g., expenditures of time, money)? (3) How will others react to their actions?

First, considerable evidence suggests that attitudes are driven by many things (values, etc.) other than one's personal connection to the cause (e.g., Miller & Ratner, 1998; Sears & Funk, 1990). Indeed, people tend to overestimate how much others' attitudes will be driven by their personal connection to the issue (Miller & Ratner, 1998). The implication here is that there might be more potential supporters for any given cause than one might think. Overestimating the impact of self-interest on others' attitudes could mean that people who might be supportive will never be approached. Organizations that desire the support of individuals regardless of those individuals' own personal connection to the issue should be explicit that the organizations needs—and welcomes—that broad support.

Second, the norm of self-interest can impact whether people act on their attitudes to support a cause. Even those who do not hold attitudes supporting the cause could end up engaging in cause-supportive behaviors, such as when the person making the request to them is a victim of the cause (Miller, Ratner & Zhao, 2009). Moreover, results indicated that not everyone who has a positive attitude will feel comfortable supporting the cause (Ratner & Miller, 2001), although they can be encouraged to do so if the appeal is explicitly framed to include them. For example, when a cause is perceived to affect one group (e.g., men or women) specifically, including other groups in the appeals for support (e.g., "Men and Women Supporting Breast Cancer Research") can increase the likelihood that the group perceived to have less of a personal connection to the cause will feel their support will be welcomed.

Third, our findings suggest that people who want to become involved in supporting a cause benefit from making their connection to the cause clear if they have one: doing so normalizes their behavior in the eyes of others. Responses will tend to be more favorable to both spokespersons and potential volunteers who identify a connection to the cause, and would-be supporters who lack a clear connection to the cause will often encounter skepticism and be encouraged to do something else. To counter this, it will be helpful for those within the charitable organization to show encouragement and appreciation to those who do not have a clear personal connection to the cause but want to get involved.

FUTURE DIRECTIONS

The present analysis raises a number of interesting avenues for future research. For example, the present investigations were all conducted in North America and did not examine cross-cultural generalizability. It would be interesting to explore how these dynamics unfold in Western vs. non-Western cultures. In collectivistic cultures, in which the high-level interest of the entire group and interconnectedness between groups is emphasized over the self-interest of a subgroup (Nisbett, Peng, Choi, & Norenzayan, 2001), the effects of an individual's personal connection to the cause might be attenuated.

Other questions for future research pertain to how degrees of connection to the cause are perceived by observers and turn people into compelling advocates. For example, how close to a direct victim does one need to be to justify one's support for a cause? Many of the studies reported here focused on personal connections to the cause created by being relatives of victims; can similar standing be granted to friends of victims? Or can simply knowing of a specific victim be sufficient to license effortful involvement to support the cause?

Along these lines, questions for future research pertain to what factors will attenuate the negativity toward those who do not have any direct connection to a cause. Will individuals without a clear connection to the cause be more accepted as advocates or volunteers if they have been invited to participate in the cause than if they seek it out? Will they feel more comfortable showing their support in private rather than in public ways, as the results of one of our studies suggested (e.g., that people without a direct connection to the cause were more willing to engage in the effortful task of completing a survey than in the public task of signing a petition)?

Conversely, it would be interesting to examine what factors attenuate the effectiveness as advocates of those who are direct victims. Because those with a personal connection to an issue lead people to feel guilty if they don't offer to help, would people choose to avoid contact with those who have a personal connection to a cause? And what would be the long-term impact of having a connection to a cause when the moment of feeling guilty is gone?

We encourage future research that examines what types of connections to causes license what types of behaviors, and what framing of the charitable giving will maximize the likelihood of achieving the desired response (e.g., donations of money, time). For example, does the means by which one developed a personal connection to the cause impact one's standing? Does a victim of lung cancer who chose to smoke fully aware of the risks have the same degree of standing as a gunshot victim who happened to be in the wrong place at the wrong time? Moreover, when does a victim have standing to make requests that only help them individually and not help victims of their cause more generally?

CONCLUSION

People expect supporters of a cause to have a clear personal connection to it (Miller & Ratner, 1998). Individuals expect that an advocate for cancer research will have experienced cancer firsthand, and that someone who appears in ads for

Parkinson's disease will likewise have been affected by the disease personally. However, the findings we presented in this chapter also suggest that people perceive that it is both rational and compelling for those who engage in charitable action to be motivated by personal experience. Across a number of studies, we find that individuals provide more positive feedback to those who engage in charitable action because of a personal connection to the cause than to those who do not identify such a connection (e.g., who lack a victimhood experience related to the cause). We argue that these reactions can discourage people from supporting causes that do not affect them personally and reinforce people's desire to support those causes that are personally relevant. Whereas previous research focuses on how to change people's attitudes toward the cause for which charitable action is desired, we argue that rather than asking themselves "Is this my responsibility?" in some cases people contemplating donations of money or time will ask themselves "Is this my place?" Sometimes what these prospective volunteers or donors will need is simply encouragement that such actions will be welcomed rather than questioned.

REFERENCES

Cialdini, R., Kallgren, C. A., & Reno, R. R. (1991). A focus theory of normative conduct: A theoretical refinement and reevaluation of the role of norms in human behavior. *Advances in Experimental Social Psychology, 24,* 201–234.

Cialdini, R. B., Reno, R. R., & Kallgren, C. A. (1990). A focus theory of normative conduct: Recycling the concept of norms to reduce littering in public places. *Journal of Personality and Social Psychology, 58,* 1015–1026.

Clarke, J. A. (2005). The effect of vested interest on the evaluation of potential volunteers (Doctoral dissertation, University of North Carolina). *Dissertation Abstracts International, 65(7-B),* 3771.

Eagly, A. H., Wood, W., & Chaiken, S. (1978). Causal inferences about communicators and their effect on opinion change. *Journal of Personality and Social Psychology, 36,* 424–435.

Fishbein, M., & Ajzen, I. (1972). Attitudes and opinions. *Annual Review of Psychology, 23,* 487–544.

Goffman, E. (1959). *The presentation of self in everyday life.* New York: Doubleday-Anchor Books.

Goldstein, N. J., Cialdini, R. B., & Griskevicius, V. (2008). A room with a viewpoint: Using social norms to motivate environmental conservation in hotels. *Journal of Consumer Research, 35,* 472–482.

Green, D. P., & Cowden, J. A. (1992). Who protests: Self-interest and white opposition to busing. *Journal of Politics, 54,* 471–496.

Jenni, K. E., & Loewenstein, G. (1997). Explaining the "identifiable victim effect." *Journal of Risk and Uncertainty, 14,* 235–257.

Kelley, H. H. (1972). Causal schemata and the attribution process. In E. E. Jones, D. E. Kanouse, H. H. Kelley, R. E. Nisbett, S. Valins, & B. Weiner (Eds.), *Attribution: Perceiving the causes of behavior* (pp. 79–94). Morristown, NJ: General Learning Press.

Miller, D. T. (1999). The norm of self-interest. *American Psychologist, 54,* 1053–1060.

Miller, D. T., & Ratner, R. K. (1996). The power of the myth of self-interest. In L. Montada & M. J. Lerner (Eds.), *Current societal issues in justice* (pp. 25–48). New York: Plenum Press.

Miller, D. T., & Ratner, R. K. (1998). The disparity between the actual and assumed power of self-interest. *Journal of Personality and Social Psychology, 74*, 53–62.

Miller, D. T., Ratner, R. K., & Zhao, M. (2009). How can you say "no"? Deference granted to advocates who are victims. Unpublished manuscript.

Nisbett, R. E., Peng, K., Choi, I., & Norenzayan, A. (2001). Culture and systems of thought: Holistic vs. analytic cognition. *Psychological Review, 108*, 291–310.

Ratner, R. K., & Clarke, J. (2004). Perceptions of potential volunteers who lack a personal connection to the cause. Unpublished raw data.

Ratner, R. K., & Miller, D. T. (2001). The norm of self-interest and its impact on social action. *Journal of Personality and Social Psychology, 81*, 5–16.

Regan, D. T., & Fazio, R. (1977). On the consistency between attitudes and behavior: Look to the method of attitude formation. *Journal of Experimental Social Psychology, 13*, 28–45.

Sears, D. O., & Funk, C. L. (1990). Self-interest in Americans' political opinions. In J. J. Mansbridge (Ed.), *Beyond self-interest* (pp. 147–170). Chicago: University of Chicago Press.

Sierra Club v. Morton, 405 U.S. 727 (9th Cir. 1972).

Sivacek, J., & Crano, W. D. (1982). Vested interest as a moderator of attitude-behavior consistency. *Journal of Personality and Social Psychology, 43*, 210–221.

Slovic, P. (2007). "If I look at the mass I will never act": Psychic numbing and genocide. *Judgment and Decision Making, 2*, 79–95.

Small, D. A., & Simonsohn, U. (2008). Friends of victims: Personal experience and prosocial behavior. *Journal of Consumer Research, 35*, 532–542.

Snyder M. (1993). Basic research and practical problems: The promise of a "functional" personality and social psychology. *Personality and Social Psychology Bulletin, 19*, 251–264.

Snyder, M., & Omoto, A. M. (1992). Who helps and why? The psychology of AIDS volunteerism. In S. Spacapan & S. Oskamp (Eds.), *Helping and being helped: Naturalistic studies* (pp. 213–239). Newbury Park, CA: Sage.

Walster, E., Aronson, E., & Abrahams, D. (1966). On increasing the persuasiveness of a low prestige communicator. *Journal of Experimental Social Psychology, 2*, 325–342.

Wuthnow, R. (1991). *Acts of compassion: Caring for others and helping ourselves.* Princeton, NJ: Princeton University Press.

8

The Identifiable Victim Effect
Causes and Boundary Conditions

TEHILA KOGUT and ILANA RITOV

INTRODUCTION

Why do people engage in charitable giving? Certainly there are many reasons for this. Social norms, social perceptions, religious convictions, and other considerations may all play a role. However, beyond all those reasons, the wish to help other people, particularly when those people are in need of external help, is the core motivation for charitable giving and helping behavior. Thus, in order to better understand the psychological motivation of charitable giving, it is important to explore the factors that may increase or decrease the fundamental wish to extend help. One of the main factors that affects the wish to aid is the characteristics of the target—the recipient of the help. Why do some targets elicit outpourings of sympathy and aid, while other targets do not? This chapter focuses on an important characteristic of the targets that affect people's willingness to help: the identifiability of the recipient.

The notion that people are sometimes willing to contribute more to save an identified victim than a nonidentified one has a strong intuitive appeal. Schelling, in his seminal economic analysis of the worth of preventing human death (Schelling, 1968) noted the distinction between individual lives and statistical lives. Because he recognized that the death of an individual is a unique event, Schelling applied his analysis only to nonidentified lives. Schelling's assumption concerning the different reactions to identified and nonidentified lives has been experimentally tested in the last decade (Jenni & Loewenstein, 1997; Small & Loewenstein, 2003; Kogut & Ritov, 2005a, 2005b; Small, Loewenstein, & Slovic, 2007; Slovic, 2007). These carefully controlled studies show that people are more generous toward an identifiable victim than toward unidentifiable or statistical victims, even when the identification of a specific victim does not convey any relevant individuating information.

For example, Small and Loewenstein (2003) found that participants playing the allocator in a dictator game contributed more money to recipients who had lost theirs, when the recipient was identified by a number than when the recipient's number was as yet undetermined.

The identified victim effect represents an apparent deviation from the principle of economic rationality, as it is unlikely that social benefits will be maximized when resources are made available to identified victims more than to unidentified ones. Furthermore, unless willingness to contribute is driven either by a special personal attachment to the particular identified victim, or by an assessment (biased as it may be) of the need for one's contribution, the greater contribution to an identified victim may also not serve the contributor's goals to the best extent (see Baron & Szymanska, this volume). Thus, understanding the sources and boundaries for this effect is of great importance. In this chapter we review experimental and theoretical work on the effect of victim's identifiability on charitable giving. We integrate recent findings, concentrating on the psychological processes underlying the effect and its boundary conditions.

THE SINGULARITY EFFECT OF IDENTIFIED VICTIMS

One feature that often distinguishes identified victims from unidentified ones is the fact that the former are typically encountered as single individuals: John, who needs a costly treatment to be cured of a rare disease; Miriam, the little girl who just lost her parents, and so on. The very fact that identified victims are usually single individuals, rather than groups, may affect people's tendency to invest in helping them.

In our own earlier research (Kogut & Ritov, 2005a, 2005b), we argued that the identifiable victim effect is largely restricted to single victims. Drawing upon research on the processes involved in perceiving individuals versus perceiving groups (Hamilton & Sherman, 1996; Susskind, Maurer, Thakkar, Hamilton, & Sherman, 1999), we hypothesized that the processing of information related to a single victim might be fundamentally different from the processing of information concerning a group of victims. According to the above research examining perceptions of individuals and groups (Hamilton & Sherman, 1996; Susskind et al., 1999), a single individual, unlike a group of individuals, is viewed as a psychologically coherent unit. Expectancy of coherence leads to a more extensive processing of information, and to active integration of the information in real time. Thus, people more readily make extreme attributions about individuals than about groups, they respond more quickly and with greater confidence when asked to make a judgment, and they recall more information when it pertains to an individual rather than to group members. The distinction between the two processes, that of perceiving individuals and that of perceiving groups, is likely to become clearer the more extensive the available information (e.g., the name of the targets, pictures or any additional details). Hence, identifying information is expected to play a greater role in the case of a single victim than in the case of a group of victims.

In a series of studies, we tested the prediction that willingness to extend help is greatly affected by the victims' identifiability when the target includes a single victim, but not when several victims are involved, by eliciting contributions for sick children in need of an expensive medicine. In these studies, a group portrait of eight children (four boys and four girls) was used for the identification of the group. In order to control for possible reactions to specific children in the picture, we used eight separate pictures of the same eight children for the identification of the single individual. Each individual child was presented an equal number of times in the identified single victim condition (so that the attractiveness of a specific child could not affect the results). We found that a single identified victim elicited higher contributions (real donations as well as hypothetical willingness to donate) than a nonidentified individual, while a group of eight identified individuals did not elicit significantly higher contributions than a group of unidentified individuals, even when the amount of money needed to save the children remained the same in all conditions (1.5 million Israeli Shekels; about $300,000). Thus, the sick children in need of an expensive medicine yielded consistent interactions between the singularity or plurality of the target and the availability of identifying information.

The emotions evoked by considering the victim's plight seem to play a major role in explaining the described effect. In line with social psychological research on helping behavior, highlighting the role of emotions as motivators of helping behavior (Pillavin, Rodin, & Pillavin, 1969; Dovidio, Piliavin, Gaertner, Schroeder, & Clark, 1991), we find that the aversive arousal caused by perceiving the distress of the person in need is directly related to the decision to help. A single identified victim evoked stronger feelings than an unidentified single victim, or a group of victims, regardless of their being identified or not. Specifically, reported rating of distress (feeling worried, upset, and sad) significantly predicted willingness to contribute, suggesting that the intensified emotional response to the single identified victim is an important determinant of the identification effect. As a result of the spontaneous emotional response to the single victim, participants' willingness to contribute to a single victim was higher, overall, than their willingness to contribute to the group.

Contributing to a single victim more than to a group of victims, when the total cost in those two situations is held constant, constitutes a clear violation of the normative principle of dominance. Recently Västfjäll, Peters, and Slovic (in preparation) showed that the effect of identification diminishes even with two victims. Following the above results , Slovic (2007) describes a "collapse model" of people's response to the number of victims, suggesting that even when going from one to two victims, feeling and meaning begin to fade; wherefore, large numbers of victims represent dry statistics that fail to spark emotion and feeling and thus fail to motivate actions. However, the respondents in these studies who encountered only one target (the single victim, two victims, or a group of eight victims), were most likely not aware of their insensitivity to the number of victims saved.

Do people consider an increased donation to a single identified victim a rational behavior? We confronted participants directly with the dilemma using a comparative setting, asking them to choose between donating to a single identified sick child and donating to seven identified sick children. Most of the participants (69%) in this condition chose to donate to the group; showing greater sensitivity to the number of victims in need (see Figure 8.1). Thus, it appears that preference for the single victim over the group is not consistent with people's aspiration for coherent

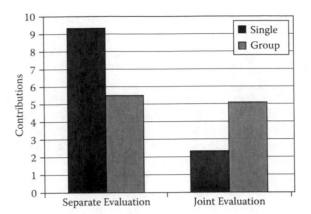

Figure 8.1   Mean contributions for identifiable single sick children and identifiable groups of eight children in separate and joint evaluations. Adapted from Kogut, T., & Ritov, I. (2005b). The singularity effect of identified victims in separate and joint evaluations. *Organizational Behavior and Human Decision Processes, 97*(2), 106–116.

preferences. In line with the notion that separate evaluation is largely determined by affective reaction, these results further show that greater donations to the single victim most likely stem from the stronger emotional response evoked by such victims in conditions where donors evaluated a single child or a group separately.

THE IDENTIFIABLE VICTIM EFFECT AND PERCEIVED GROUP BELONGING

One aspect of the above research that may constrain its implications is the nature of the victims. In all experiments described so far, the implicit assumption has been that the victims belong to the same social group as the respondents. The effect of identification of the victims on people's willingness to help, and specifically the great impact of identifying a single individual relative to the impact of identifying a group of individuals, may be confined to victims within the respondent's in-group.

The finding that identification of the victim enhances emotional reaction only when a single victim is considered, but not when several victims are considered, is consistent with the notion that groups are perceived as more psychologically distant and are processed at a more abstract level than single individuals (Hamilton & Sherman, 1996; Susskind et al., 1999). However, psychological distance is determined by factors besides group size (e.g., time distance or perspective of self vs. others; Wakslak, Nussbaum, Liberman, & Trope, 2008; Pronin, Olivola, & Kennedy, 2008). One of the factors that received immense attention in the literature in this context is social categorization.

Categorization of others as belonging to the same social group as oneself arouses feelings of greater closeness and responsibility, and augments emotional response to their distress (Brewer & Gardner, 1996; Dovidio et al., 1991; Dovidio et al., 1997).

Willingness to help is similarly affected by social categorization. People tend to help those whom they perceive as similar to themselves (Dovidio, 1984; Dovidio et al., 1997). It is perhaps not surprising that people tend to help members of their own social group more than they help other victims. But does this preference apply to single identified victims as well? To the extent that psychological distance affects perceivers' reaction to victims, the exceptionally generous response to a single identified victim observed in our earlier research may be limited to victims who belong to the perceiver's social category. By contrast, victims who are not members of the perceiver's in-group, even identified individuals, are likely to be processed at a higher, more abstract construal level (Trope & Liberman, 2000), evoking less empathic emotion. In that case, identifying the victims as a single person or as a group would not evoke greater willingness to help. Furthermore, recent studies show that when people are presented with more abstract, less emotional information, their judgment becomes more sensitive to quantitative aspects (Hsee & Rottenstreich, 2004). If deciding on a contribution to out-group victims involves more abstract and less emotional processing, we can predict that contributions for a number of victims will exceed contributions for a single victim, regardless of whether identifying information is provided or not.

We first examined these predictions in December 2004, two days after the powerful earthquake in the Indian Ocean (Kogut & Ritov, 2007). We chose tsunami victims as the target of the study, because among them were people from different nationalities. In addition to the large number of local residents, many foreign tourists were dead or missing. The questionnaires of the experiment were distributed to students at Hebrew University two days after the tsunami struck, as rescue teams were already working on the ground and news reports mentioned the many missing, including Israeli tourists. The questionnaires all started by informing participants of an Israeli rescue team that was sent to the Abalok island, located a thousand kilometers from India, in the center of the earthquake area, in order to seek and rescue missing people. Following this initial information, the questionnaire continued by reporting about either one person or seven people who were still missing on the island, manipulating the number of victims (single vs. a group of seven individuals); the identification of the victims (identified vs. unidentified); and the nationality group (Israeli victims vs. Indian victims). In the identified victim condition, the names of the victims were also given, whereas the unidentified condition questionnaires only mentioned the existence of such victims (single victim or a group of seven, Indian or Israeli). Participants in all conditions were asked whether they were willing to contribute money to help fund the continued work of the rescue team on the island and had the opportunity to contribute any amount of money they wished (all the money raised in this study was transferred to the Israeli Volunteering Association, which was collecting money for the tsunami victims).

The results indicated that increased willingness to help identified victims may be largely confined to situations in which the target of help is a single victim belonging to the respondent's nationality. Identified single victims received significantly higher contributions than identified groups. Specifically, in the own-nation condition, the percentage of contributors to the single identified victim (48%) was higher

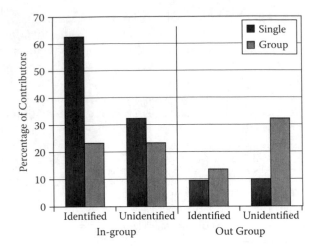

Figure 8.2   Percentage of contributors for in-group and out-group tsunami victims, as a function of the identification and the singularity of the victim. Adapted from Kogut, T., & Ritov, I. (2007). One of us: Outstanding willingness to help save a single identified compatriot. *Organizational Behavior and Human Decision Processes, 104*(2), 150–157.

than to the percentage of contributors for the identified group (23%). The order reversed in the other-nation condition: only 10% of the responders contributed money to help rescue a single identified victim, whereas 22% of the responders contributed for the identified group (see Figure 8.2).° Similar results were found when examining the amount of money contributed to the different victims: in the in-group conditions, single victims received higher contributions ($M = 12.22$) than groups ($M = .1.90$), while in the out-group conditions, groups received higher contributions ($M = 2.08$) than single victims ($M = 1.67$).ᶦ Thus, the singularity effect of identified victims occurred in the own-nation condition only.

We found a similar pattern of results in another context, where the contributions were needed in order to provide expensive medication for sick children. Again, expressed willingness to contribute to saving sick children was amplified when the depicted victim was a single child, purportedly a member of the respondents' social category (own-nation). In this experiment, victims were identified by a picture only and were presented either as Israelis (in-group condition) or as Argentinean (out-group condition). The same pictures were used for the identification of the Israeli and the Argentinean victims. Finally, the emotions evoked by considering the victims' plight were also particularly intense when the victim was a single child, notably a compatriot. Examining both reported distress

---

° Loglinear analysis of the dichotomous variable of contribute/not contribute by singularity, group-belonging, and identification yielded a significant main effect of group-belonging (Chi-sq for removal of the term = 11.01, df = 1, p < .001) as well as a significant interaction of group-belonging and victim singularity (Chi-sq for removal of the term = 9.85, df = 1, p < .01).

ᶦ F(1,41.45) = 17.79 p < .001 for the interaction between group belonging and victim singularity on the log-transform of contributions.

evoked by considering the victims' plight and the effect of these thoughts on the participant's mood, we found that in the own-nation condition, single victims yielded higher ratings of distress and a sharper mood change than groups of victims, while in the other-nation condition, groups yielded higher ratings of distress and a sharper mood change than individuals. Again, we suggest that these emotions may be at the source of the *nationality in-group singularity effect* of identified victims.

DIFFERENT TYPES OF SOCIAL CATEGORIZATIONS

The research described above examined the effect of identification of the victim on helping same-nationality versus different-nationality victims. However, nationality is only one determinant of group belonging. Individuals have multiple social identities derived from different perceived memberships in social groups, which might create different levels of group belonging. The factors that generate the social categories may range from deep-rooted factors such as ethnicity, religion, or ideology to more random factors such as age group or even some miscellaneous, experimentally manipulated criterion. The effect of the identification of the victim may differ, depending on the basis for the subjective categorization.

Obviously, certain categorizations are more prominent, more important for the individual, or evoke greater emotion than others, and therefore may have different implications for behavior, decisions, and judgment. In order to help clarify the conditions in which the identifiability of the target enhances decisions in his or her favor, our currently ongoing research further examines the influence of the identification of victims in the context of different social categorizations. We focus on the target's social categorization in relation to the potential contributor, as well as the type of social categories considered.

Seminal past research has shown that even an arbitrary group affiliation may affect the way people treat others. The minimal group paradigm (MGP) was developed in order to show that a very simple minimal manipulation was sufficient in order to produce in-group favoritism (Tajfel, Billig, Bundy, & Flament, 1971). Participants assigned to mutually exclusive social categories (e.g., persons preferring the art of Klee versus the art of Kandinsky) allocated more money to in-group than out-group members. Specifically, category members maximized the relative difference between the earnings of the in-group and out-group members, rather than maximizing the in-group absolute earning, or the overall earning.

In order to clarify the conditions in which the identifiability of the target enhances decisions in his/her favor, we started our investigation using the MGP (Ritov & Kogut, 2009, working paper). Based on Tajfel's paradigm, participants first took an "artistic preference" test. In each session, participants were classified into two equal size groups (the yellow group and the blue group), supposedly based on their responses to the artistic preference test. In effect, they were randomly assigned to the two groups. Following the group assignment stage, participants played the dictator game. In this game, participants are randomly assigned as allocators and recipients. The allocators are given a fixed sum of money, and they can allocate any part of it (or nothing at all) to the recipient. Thus, this game offers the opportunity to examine sharing behavior and decisions regarding resource allocation. The manipulation of identifiability that we used was extremely weak (similar to Small & Lowenstein, 2003): in the *identified* condition, the number of the partner was already determined and known to the participant, whereas in the *unidentified* condition, participants were told that the number of their partner would be determined after their decision. However, in all conditions the recipient group belonging (a member of the same group as the allocator or a member of the other group) was known.

Results show that participants' allocations replicate the pattern found in the earlier studies where categorization was based on nationality rather than on the MGP. Identifiability increased allocation to in-group but not to out-group members. On average, the identifiable in-group recipients received 5.4 out of 11 shekels (the initial endowment to the allocators), as opposed to only 2.6 shekels given to unidentifiable in-group recipients. No significant difference was found for out-group recipients; identifiable recipients received on average 3.3 and unidentifiable recipients received 3.4 shekels.

IDEOLOGY-BASED CATEGORIZATION

Can identifiability actually decrease willingness to help under some conditions? Obviously, specific information regarding the victim may evoke negative reactions. For example, an individual victim may be unattractive in some respect, or the identifying information may raise doubts as to the victim's responsibility for their current state. However, can identifiability decrease willingness to contribute even if identification conveys no negative information? If shared group membership is the strongest factor evoking feelings of closeness toward other members of the group, then being exposed to specific features of the identified in-group victim, features not shared by all group members, may detract from the intensity of the feelings evoked. More generally, we suggest that identifying the victim may increase or decrease perceived affinity, and hence also modify the empathy and concern one feels for that victim. When identifying the individual victim increases the feeling of closeness, willingness to help the victim should increase. By contrast, when identifying the specific victim decreases the sense of affinity, willingness to help may also decrease.

Social categorization based on ideology or political orientation provides an interesting example. Contrary to the grouping based on the MGP, grouping based on ideology or political orientation is often relatively deep-rooted and raises intense (positive and negative) emotions. People sometimes identify with such groups more than they do with any individual members of the group. In that case, specific information about a group member may decrease perceived connectedness, and this may in turn reduce willingness to help.

We took advantage of the political situation in Israel in September of 2005, and examined the effect of identifiability on willingness to help a single settler's family in financial hardship following evacuation from Gaza (Ritov & Kogut, 2009, working paper). We were interested to see if identifiability would result in a similar effect among potential contributors who shared the family's ideological stand, and those who opposed it.

Israel's unilateral disengagement plan was enacted in August 2005 to remove all permanent Israeli presence in the Gaza Strip. All settlers from 21 Jewish settlements were evicted and all buildings were demolished. Participants in our study responded to the questionnaire a few days after the disengagement. Although all evicted settlers received government compensation, participants were asked about their willingness to help one evicted family who was experiencing severe financial hardship despite the compensation they received. Participants were randomly assigned to two experimental conditions: identified ("the Har'el family") vs. unidentified ("a family") victim. The evacuation from Gaza highlighted the political–ideological divide between the left and right wings in Israel. We classified responders into opposers of the disengagement (sharing the ideology of the family; the ideological in-group) and supporters of the disengagement (disagreeing with the ideology of the family; the ideological out-group), based on their response to a questionnaire regarding political attitudes.

After reading the information about the family, participants were asked whether they would be willing to contribute money to help the family, and if so, how much. Intriguingly, the pattern of results we found does not match the pattern found when groups were based on nationality. Among responders classified as ideological in-group members (opposers of the disengagement), unidentified families elicited higher contributions than identified ones, while among responders classified as ideological out-group members (supporters of the disengagement), contributions were higher when the family was identified. Thus, identifiability of the victim increased contributions to out-group, but not to in-group, members (see Figure 8.3).

Similarly, in another experiment, contributions for saving a sick child who lives in a settlement replicated the above pattern of behavior. In this experiment,

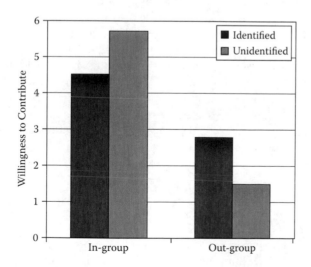

Figure 8.3   Mean contributions to an identified and unidentified family, as a function of group belonging, when groups are based on ideology. From Ritov, I., & Kogut, T. (2009). The effect of victims' identifiability in different inter-group contexts. Working paper.

identification of the sick child was manipulated by both the victim's name and his picture. Again, classification of responders into ideological in-group and ideological out-group members was based on their response to a questionnaire regarding political attitudes. Finally, in addition to their willingness to help, participants reported the extent to which they perceived the victim as a member of their social group using several established rating scales. Interestingly, participants' ratings of the extent to which they perceive the victim as an in-group member replicated the pattern found for contributions, such that for responders who shared the victim's ideology (in-group), unidentified victims were rated as closer to self than identified victims. By contrast, for responders who held a conflicting view (out-group), identified victims were rated as closer to self than unidentified ones. These findings support our proposal that subjective psychological distance mediates the identifiable victim effect.

The discrepancy between the findings of the two latter studies and our earlier work points to the importance of the kind of social categories considered for predicting behavior toward individuals and groups. When group belonging was based on nationality, identifying the victim presumably increased the sense of shared group belonging and therefore increased contributions. By contrast, when group belonging was based on ideology, feelings of shared group belonging and similarity were most intense when the ideological label was dominant, in which case encountering a specific individual could only decrease perceived affinity. Identifying the in-group member, in those cases, did not lead to increased willingness to help.

In addition, the categorization criterion may also influence the emotional arousal toward the out-group. When categories are based on ideology, people may develop negative emotions toward the out-group (disagreements, negativism, rejection, or hate). Enhancing empathy toward a specific out-group member in need (e.g., by identifying the person) may separate or distinguish that person from the group, increasing caring and generosity toward him/her (Batson, Early, & Salvarani,1997; Batson, Chang, Orr, & Rowland, 2002).

We need to acknowledge a potential confound between ideological group belonging and the political orientation of the participants that might occur in the above studies. In both studies, ideological in-group responders were necessarily right wing and ideological out-group responders were closer to the left wing. Moreover, the victims we described belonged only to one of the ideological groups. Future research should attempt to control for these possible limitations.

CONCLUSION

In line with a growing body of research showing the major role of emotions in decision making (Epstein, 1994; Slovic et al., 2002; Loewenstein, Weber, Hsee, & Welch, 2001; Loewenstein & Lerner, 2003; Greene, Sommerville, Nystrom, Darley, & Cohen, 2001; Sunstein, 2004), the identifiable victim effect appears to stem from a spontaneous emotional arousal toward a single specific target. The direct emotional reaction to the identifiable victim influences the decision to help in ways that may depart from what the individual would view as the best course of action. In particular, such immediate emotional response may cause an identifiable single victim to take precedence over less affect-rich stimuli, like a group of victims.

In this chapter we consider some of the boundary conditions of the effect. First we demonstrate that the identifiable victim effect is largely restricted to single victims (the *singularity effect*). Identifying a group of victims did not increase contributions in any of the experiments described. Moreover, the singularity effect diminishes when the identified single victim is presented in a comparative context (joint evaluation when the potential contributors are aware of other victims). The singularity effect is therefore limited to situations where the victim is presented alone.

Another factor that influences decisions regarding identifiable victims is their perceived group belonging as well as the type of groups considered. Identification of the victim leads to an increase in helping behavior only when the victim is a single individual who is perceived as belonging to the helper's own in-group when groups are based on nationality. In contrast, when groups are based on ideology, identification increased contributions to single out-group victims, but not to in-group victims. These findings are compatible with the notion that feelings of closeness, either augmented or diminished by identifiability of the victim, result in turn in increased or decreased helping behavior. Further research is required in order to further explore this hypothesis and examine the role of the type of perceived social categorization in determining people's responses to identifiable in-group and out-group members.

Can individuals be taught to value life consistently? Research examining the influence of the awareness to the identifiable victim effect by teaching or priming people to recognize the discrepancy in giving to identifiable and statistical victims shows that indeed, when primed to think rationally, people discount sympathy toward identifiable victims. Unfortunately, such debiasing reduces overall contributions, as it brings willingness to contribute for the identified victim down to the level of willingness to contribute to the statistical victims, rather than the other way around (Small, Loewenstein, & Slovic, 2007).

In addition to its theoretical contribution, the described research has practical implications for efforts to recruit potential donors for social causes. Many public service campaigns and commercial advertising efforts attempt to influence people's decisions concerning members of their own society as well as out-group societies. Our research suggests that the way a cause is presented can play a critical role in people's helping decisions when considering supporting others in need. Specifically, when considering the presentation of targets in need, presenting single identified in-group victims alone (separate evaluation) is most likely to yield the maximum donation when groups are based on nationality (i.e., compatriot). By contrast, when trying to recruit donations in a different country, it is best to present a group of people in need, so that the potential contributors will perceive the need to be extensive. This recommendation does not apply to solicitation of donations in a political context, as identification of a single group member is likely to increase contributions mostly for out-group members.

REFERENCES

Batson, C. D., Chang, J., Orr, R., & Rowland, J. (2002). Empathy, attitudes, and action: Can feeling for a member of a stigmatized group motivate one to help the group? *Personality and Social Psychology Bulletin, 28*, 1656–1666.

Batson, C. D., Early, S., & Salvarani, G. (1997). Perspective taking: Imagining how another feels versus imagining how you would feel. *Personality & Social Psychology Bulletin, 23*, 751–758.

Brewer, M., & Gardner, W. (1996). Who is this "we"? Levels of collective identity. *Journal of Personality and Social Psychology, 71*, 83–93.

Dovidio, J. F. (1984). Helping behavior and altruism: An empirical and conceptual overview. In L. Berkowits (Ed.), *Advances in Experimental Social Psychology* (Vol. 17, pp. 361–427). New York: Academic Press.

Dovidio, J. F., Gaertner, S. L., Validzic, A., Motoka, K., Johnson, B., & Frazier, S. (1997). Extending the benefits of recategorization: Evaluations, self-disclosure, and helping. *Journal of Experimental Social Psychology, 33*, 401–420.

Dovidio, J. F., Piliavin, J. A., Gaertner, S., Schroeder, D. A., & Clark, R. D. III (1991). The arousal cost-reward model and the process of intervention: A review of the evidence. In M. Clark (Ed.), *Prosocial Behavior. Review of Personality and Social Psychology* (Vol. 12, pp. 86–118). Newberry Park, CA: Sage.

Epstein, S. (1994). Integration of the cognitive and the psychodynamic unconscious. *American Psychologist, 49*, 709–724.

Greene, J. D., Sommerville, R.B., Nystrom, L.E., Darley, J.M., & Cohen, J.D. (2001). An fMRI investigation of emotional engagement in moral judgment. *Science, 293*, 2105–2108.

Hamilton, D. L., & Sherman, S. J. (1996). Perceiving persons and groups. *Psychological Review, 103*(2), 336–355.

Hsee, C., & Rottenstreich, Y. (2004). Music, pandas, and muggers: On the affective psychology of value. *Journal of Experimental Psychology General, 133*, 23–30.

Jenni, K. E., & Loewenstein, G. (1997). Explaining the "identifiable victim effect." *Journal of Risk and Uncertainty, 14*, 235–257.

Kogut, T., & Ritov, I. (2005a). The "identified victim effect": An identified group, or just a single individual? *Journal of Behavioral Decision Making, 18*, 157–167.

Kogut, T., & Ritov, I. (2005b). The singularity effect of identified victims in separate and joint evaluations. *Organizational Behavior and Human Decision Processes, 97*(2), 106–116.

Kogut, T., & Ritov, I. (2007). One of us: Outstanding willingness to help save a single identified compatriot. *Organizational Behavior and Human Decision Processes, 104*(2), 150–157.

Loewenstein, G. F., & Lerner, J. S. (2003). The role of affect in decision making. In R. J. Davidson, & K. R. Scherer (Eds.). *Handbook of affective sciences* (pp. 563–673). London: Oxford University Press.

Loewenstein, G. F., Weber, E.U., Hsee, C.H., & Welch, N. (2001). Risk as feelings. *Psychological Bulletin, 127*, 267–286.

Pillavin, I. M., Rodin, J., & Pillavin, J. (1969). Good Samaritanism: An underground phenomenon? *Journal of Personality and Social Psychology, 13*, 289–299.

Pronin, E., Olivola, C. Y., & Kennedy, K. A. (2008). Doing unto future selves as you would do unto others: Psychological distance and decision making. *Personality and Social Psychology Bulletin, 34*, 224–236.

Ritov, I., & Kogut, T. (2009). The effect of victims' identifiability in different inter-group contexts. Working paper.

Schelling, T. C. (1968). "The life you save may be your own." In Samuel Chase (Ed.), *Problems in public expenditure analysis.* Washington, DC: The Brookings Institute.

Slovic, P. (2007). If I look at the mass I will never act: Psychic numbing and genocide. *Judgment and Decision Making, 2*(2), 1–17.

Slovic, P., Finucane, M., Peters, E. & MacGregor, D. G. (2002). The affect heuristic. In Gilovich, T. & Griffin, D. (Eds.), *Heuristics and biases: The psychology of intuitive judgment* (pp. 397–420). New York: Cambridge University Press.

Small, D. A., & Loewenstein, G. (2003). Helping a victim or helping the victim: Altruism and identifiability. *Journal of Risk and Uncertainty, 26*(1), 5–16.

Small, D.A., Loewenstein, G., & Slovic, P. (2007). Sympathy and callousness: The impact of deliberative thought on donations to identifiable and statistical victims. *Organizational Behavior and Human Decision Processes, 102*, 143–153.

Sunstein, C. R. (2004). Moral heuristics. *Behavioral and Brain Sciences, 28*, 531–542.

Susskind, J., Maurer, K., Thakkar, V., Hamilton, D. L. & Sherman, J.W. (1999). Perceiving individuals and groups: Expectancies, dispositional inferences, and causal attributions. *Journal of Personality and Social Psychology, 76*(2), 181–191.

Tajfel, H., Billing, M. G., Bundy, R. P., & Flament, C. (1971). Social categorization and intergroup behaviour. *European Journal of Social Psychology, 1*, 149–178.

Trope, Y., & Liberman, N. (2000). Temporal construal and time-dependent changes in preference. *Journal of Personality and Social Psychology, 79*, 876–889.

Västfjäll, D., Peters, E., & Slovic, P. Representation, affect, and willingness-to-donate to children in need. Unpublished manuscript.

Wakslak, C. J., Nussbaum, S., Liberman. N., & Trope, Y. (2008). Representations of the self in the near and distant future. *Journal of Personality and Social Psychology, 95*, 757–773.

Section III

The Role of Emotions

9

Sympathy Biases and Sympathy Appeals
Reducing Social Distance to Boost Charitable Contributions

DEBORAH A. SMALL

*I*n recent years, large-scale natural disasters have tested both the public's generosity and its collective ability to make wise decisions. People around the world appeared big-hearted when they donated time and money to help people devastated by the Asian tsunami (December 2004) and Hurricane Katrina (August 2005). Yet the plight of people with more widespread and persistent problems, such as starvation and water- or insect-borne disease, fail to arouse sympathy and attract donations. Similarly, ill-fated individuals such as Lacy Peterson (murdered in 2002) and Natalee Holloway (missing since 2005), have become household names due to obsessive media coverage. In contrast, the sad stories of millions of other unnamed unfortunates are never told. Researchers wishing to rectify this situation can ask the glass half-full question: "Why do some victims spark a sympathetic and altruistic response?" Or, they can ask the glass half-empty question: "Why do other tragedies and victims fail to stimulate charity?"

In this chapter, I attempt to answer both questions by describing research that links factors that promote sympathy. Although some giving derives from self-interest (tax write-offs, social incentives), I take the view that giving also comes from the heart. That is, certain misfortunes engender an emotional response that motivates prosocial action. This emotional response, which I call *sympathy*, is of particular interest because it can help explain the limits of rational charitable decisions. In the following section, I will discuss the role of sympathy in guiding charitable giving. I will not go so far as to argue that this emotional response to suffering is purely altruistic (see Cialdini et al., 1997). However, I do believe that it is a special and distinct motive that distinguishes charitable from other prosocial motives because it addresses the welfare of others as opposed to the welfare of the self.[*]

DOES SYMPATHY HELP OR HINDER RATIONAL DECISION MAKING?

When faced with a variety of ways to spend one's limited money and time to help others, what is a good decision maker to do? Rational giving would involve two key judgments: (1) Do the victims merit assistance? and (2) How much good will results from any aid? Ideally, charitable giving would be directed toward the problems that need it most, and where the aid can help the most people and/or have the greatest impact. Unfortunately, this is often difficult to assess (see Baron, this volume). Moreover, this is not how most people go about making decisions. At the extreme, fictional victims, such as those in books and movies, foster copious tears. Perhaps if actual malnourished children could provoke that reaction, then people would be more prone to give to Save the Children or UNICEF. In addition, several studies demonstrate clear violations of rationality, in which willingness to donate or lend money is greater when the recipient is a single person instead of a group (e.g., Kogut & Ritov, 2005a; Galak, Small, & Stephen, 2009). As I will describe in the next section, these irrational behavior patterns arise from the biasing influence of sympathy.

On the other hand, sympathy has undoubted social value. In general, emotions are functional because they motivate people to act. A general umbrella charity, such as the United Way, might be deemed deserving and worthy, yet it does not tug at the heart strings. Why is sympathy more likely than a judgment of worthiness to promote a charitable response? In contrast to cold cognitions, which are relatively unchanging and unobtrusive, emotions are passing and signal to an organism to stop current activities, pay closer attention, and respond to the emotion. Emotions create a mental spotlight, whose intense focus rapidly promotes an urge to act in a distinct way associated with the specific emotion at hand (Frijda, 1986). Sympathy, in particular, is triggered by witnessing the suffering of other people. It triggers a motivation to act to relieve the suffering. Batson and many others have consistently demonstrated the link between this other-oriented emotional response and prosocial behavior (e.g., Batson, Early, & Salvarani, 1997; Coke, Batson, and McDavis, 1978; Loewenstein & Small, 2007). In the following section, I describe factors that, by facilitating sympathy, enhance charitable giving.

SOCIAL DISTANCE AND THE DETERMINANTS OF SYMPATHY

People tend to feel more sympathetic toward and help other people who are closer to them. This tendency is quite functional and might be programmed by evolution. Kin selection theory in biology suggests that altruistic behavior depends on

---

[*] Batson and colleagues use the term empathic concern, rather than sympathy to describe the other-oriented emotional response (e.g., Batson, 1987). I use the term sympathy to distinguish it from the more common meaning of empathy—experiencing someone else's feelings (see also Wispe, 1991).

relatedness or the odds that a gene in the receiver is an identical copy by descent of a gene in the giver (Hamilton, 1964). As it happens, the greater the relatedness, the higher the probability that altruistic behavior will be observed. In human society, the kinship connection is complex and genetic overlap is typically not detectable. Therefore, humans must use heuristics (mental "rules of thumb") to determine closeness, such as "those in my home are kin" (Rachlin & Jones, 2008). Moreover, kin selection has likely over-generalized to the point that simply feeling close to someone evokes a similar emotional and behavioral response—regardless of any genetic relationship.

In one clever study demonstrating the impact of felt closeness on generosity, Jones and Rachlin (2006) asked undergraduates to imagine a list of 100 people closest to them and to choose (hypothetically) between different distributions of money between themselves and those people, at different points on a 1 to 100 scale of social distance. For example, participants were asked to choose between $155 for themselves, or $75 for themselves and $75 for the person ranked number 1 on the list. They were asked to choose similarly for persons at other ranks on the list. Results showed that generosity declined with social distance, such that people allocated less and less as relationships grew more and more distant. These findings parallel research examining the ways in which individuals trade off outcomes for themselves in the present versus the future (e.g., Ainslie, 1992). In addition, some research shows that people treat their future self in a way analogous to how they treat others in decisions as if the self in the future is actually a different (albeit close) person (Pronin, Olivola, & Kennedy, 2008).

When individuals construct lists of *close others*, the lists typically start with relatives, then continue in order with friends, colleagues, and acquaintances. Close others does not include unknown others. Yet giving to charity typically involves helping others with whom people have no actual relationship. Donors rarely meet the recipients of their charity or learn their identities.° Yet even when recipients are anonymous, the principle of connectedness, or *social distance*, still applies. Certain anonymous victims *feel closer* than others for several reasons, including similarity, perspective-taking, identifiability, proximity, and relatedness to a victim with the same misfortune. In turn, factors that reduce social distance to anonymous victims tend to promote sympathy and helpful behavior (Loewenstein & Small, 2007). I will review these factors next.

Similarity

First and foremost, individuals feel close to others with whom they have something in common. Hornstein (1976) proposed that emphasizing similarity gives rise to a sense of "we-ness," which in turn facilitates helping. Krebs (1975) showed that when a stranger was ostensibly about to receive an electric shock, individuals led to believe that they were similar to the stranger in terms of values and traits exhibited a stronger physiological stress response and reported feeling worse than

---

° Certain charities (e.g., donorschoose.org) attempt to connect benefactors to recipients directly as a way to reduce social distance. This strategy, while effective, is not practical for many charities.

those led to believe that they were dissimilar (see also Stotland & Dunn, 1963). Research on intergroup relations further supports this thesis. In many studies that openly and arbitrarily assign people to an "in" group or an "out" group, perceptions of group membership consistently result in better treatment of in-group members—even when the determinant of group membership is clearly random (e.g., Dovidio, Gaertner, Validzic, Matoka, et al., 1997; Flippen, Hornstein, Siegal, & Weitzman, 1996; Levine, Cassidy, Brazier, & Reicher, 2002). Recent studies that subtly reminded participants of group status at a level below conscious awareness provided further evidence of preferential treatment and ruled out experimental demand as a cause of this behavior (Garcia, Weaver, Moskowitz, & Darley, 2002). In sum, the more that anonymous victims are perceived as similar to or part of the same group as potential benefactors, the more likely they are to get support.

Perspective-Taking

Social distance is also reduced when a person actively imagines how another person is affected by his or her plight. Batson and colleagues have consistently shown greater altruistic behavior by individuals primed to take the victim's perspective (Batson et al., 1997; Batson, Lishner, Carpenter, Dulin, et al., 2003; Coke et al., 1978). Perspective-taking can take one of two forms: imagining how another feels or imagining how you would feel in his/her shoes. Although these two states are very similar, Batson et al. (1997) found that they have distinct emotional and behavioral consequences. Both produce sympathy, however, imagining *yourself* in the other's shoes also produces personal distress. Personal distress evokes egoistic (self-protective) motivation rather than altruistic (other-protective) motivation. As a result, individuals may not help if helping does not, in some way, reduce this personal distress. In contrast, taking the focus off of the self and imagining the other's feelings is the surer way to motivate prosocial behavior.

Proximity

Another important factor that influences sympathy is proximity, or physical nearness. The tendency for physical distance to increase callousness is documented in Jonathan Glover's book, *Humanity*. Glover (1999) describes the relative ease with which military pilots carry out bombings, because distance from their victims blunts the emotions that could inhibit their actions.

Similarly, social psychologist Stanley Milgram conducted several variations of his famed eponymous experiment, which manipulated the nearness of participants instructed to administer electric shocks to other participants, who were actually researchers pretending to be shocked. Milgram discovered that the closer the "victim" the less likely people were to comply with the request of the authority figure/experimenter to shock the victim (Milgram, 1974).

Finally, a recent study by Williams and Bargh (2008) found that merely representing physical distance by plotting close or distant points on a Cartesian coordinate (x, y, z axes) plane influences judgments that are seemingly unrelated to this task, such as those about emotional attachments to family members. Thus it seems that the simple concept of physical distance can evoke the more abstract sense of social distance. This suggests that the effects of physical distance are not only due to the fact that with distance, people are less likely to see and hear victims (as is often the case in the real world). The relationship between physical and social distance also exists at a purely conceptual level, independent of the situational variables that are typically confounded with physical distance.

Identifiability

When people with problems are nearby, they lose their anonymity and become identifiable. When they can be identified, people relate to them almost as if a true relationship exists. The notion of an *identifiable victim effect* was first described by Thomas Shelling (1968), who noted that the death of any particular person invokes "anxiety and sentiment, guilt and awe, responsibility and religion, [however] … most of the awesomeness disappears when we deal with statistical death." Identified victims, such as Natalee Holloway, received a great deal of sympathy and media attention. But as Schelling also noted, victimization statistics do not seem to arouse much sympathy. For instance, one billion children live in poverty (UNICEF, 2005), yet accounts of mass poverty rarely generate compelling media stories or widespread donations from private citizens.

Empirical research supports this description of the identifiable victim effect. Specifically, research finds that people are more generous to an identifiable victim, even when no meaningful information is provided about the identified victim. In the first study in this area, George Loewenstein and I (Small & Loewenstein, 2003) gave each member of a group of research participants $10 and a number. Based on a drawing of numbers, half the participants ("victims") were asked to return the money. Next, each of the participants who kept their $10 had the opportunity to share it with a "victim." In a determinate (identifiable) condition, the potential giver *first* drew the number of the victim from a bag, then decided how much to give to that victim (knowing, however, that he/she would never learn the actual identity of the victim). In the indeterminate (unidentifiable) condition, the potential giver decided how much to give immediately *before* drawing the victim's number. Donations were about twice as large, on average, in the determinate condition as in the indeterminate condition, despite the fact that determining the victims provided no information about them. In a separate study, we found a similar effect of *determinateness* on feelings of sympathy (see Loewenstein & Small, 2007).

Additionally, Tehila Kogut and Ilana Ritov have demonstrated that a single identifiable victim receives more support than a group of identifiable victims, suggesting that the combination of identification (by face and name) and singularity elicit special sympathy (Kogut & Ritov, 2005a). In a series of studies, participants were asked to contribute to a costly life-saving treatment needed by either one sick child or a group of eight sick children. The target amount needed to save the child (children) was held constant. Collective total contributions to individuals were greater than contributions to the group. However, when a separate set of participants was asked to choose between contributing to one or eight victims, most chose to donate to the group (Kogut & Ritov, 2005b). In other words, people are sensitive to quantity when judging comparatively, because the task makes that scope salient. However, when only considering one target, they respond based on their feelings of sympathy, which are not sensitive to scope (cf. Hsee & Rottenstreich, 2004).

Finally, research has found that lives become more identifiable when the reference group of a victim is smaller, such that the victim(s) represent a greater proportion of that group (Jenni & Loewenstein, 1997). An identifiable victim represents one end of this continuum: once someone is identified, she or he becomes her own reference group and thus receives the most sympathy. At the other extreme, when there are a large number of victims of a particular type, individuals become hidden among masses. In that case, it may be especially difficult to feel connected to someone with a problem.

All of these findings can be viewed through the lens of social distance. When an individual is identified, given a name and a picture, and taken out of a group, all of these aspects of identifiability reduce the social distance from anonymous donors. As with similarity and perspective-taking, this feeling of closeness facilitates sympathy and giving.

Personal Experience

Another factor that promotes sympathy by reducing social distance is personal experience. Many celebrity activists, including actors Michael J. Fox (Parkinson's disease) and the late Christopher Reeve (spinal cord injury), and former First Lady Nancy Reagan (Alzheimer's disease on behalf of her late husband), support this assumption. A few studies found that compared with those with no personal experience of rape or abuse, those who had personally experienced that type of violence reported greater empathy (Barnett, Tetreault, Esper, & Bristow, 1986) and a greater likelihood to help (Christy & Voigt, 1994).

Moreover, recent research finds that people who know someone with a particular misfortune are more sympathetic and helpful toward other people with the same misfortune (Small & Simonsohn, 2008). This pattern occurs because the sympathy inherent in a close relationship with a victim extends to other victims, leading benefactors to prefer charities that help those suffering from the misfortunes that have affected their friends and loved ones. While it is not surprising that knowing a victim is correlated with charity choices because personal experience often provides *information* about the severity of such misfortunes and about opportunities to help, Small and Simonsohn (2008) demonstrated that the effects of personal experience exist over and above any such information effects.

In experiments that carefully manipulated "friendship" and "victimhood" and provided identical information to friends of both victims and nonvictims, we found that friendship with a victim leads people to donate more to other victims of the *same* misfortune, but has no effect on donations to victims of a *different* misfortune. In other words, friendship with a victim does not simply make people more sympathetic and generous, it directs their sympathy to others with the same misfortune that afflicts their own friend or loved one.

Once again, social distance is critical. For example, someone who has lost a close friend to breast cancer may volunteer and/or give money for breast cancer research. This person has no actual relationship to the anonymous people who might benefit. Nor is this person any more likely to get the disease and thus possibly benefit from future research than is a similar person who did not lose a close friend to the disease. Yet, personal experience with the disease reduces the social distance from people with the same diagnosis as this person's friend. These other people with breast cancer may be complete strangers, but the personal exposure forges a connection.

Summary

I have discussed several factors that direct and sometimes misdirect sympathy toward some social problems and away from others. The common feature is that each reduces the social distance between anonymous aid recipients and their benefactors. Closer anonymous victims can tug at our heartstrings, whereas distant victims are all too easy to ignore.

FROM SYMPATHY BIASES TO SYMPATHY APPEALS

The previous section may not seem overly encouraging to nonprofit professionals. When it deals with unidentified or other socially distant populations, what is a charity to do in the face of these entrenched psychological biases? Knowing about the psychology of sympathy biases can help charities to garner greater sympathy and, as a result, more effectively market their causes.

Psychologists, marketers, and politicians know how the strategic framing of language can powerfully affect judgment, emotion, and behavior (cf., Kahneman & Tversky, 1984; McFarland & Miller, 1994). Consider, for example, how the media describes problems. One study investigated reactions to the increased appearance of the fatal neurological disease called bovine spongiform encephalopathy. The study found that beef consumption dropped significantly after newspaper articles played up the dramatic term, "mad cow disease." In contrast, consumption was unaffected when articles favored the scientific term instead (Sinaceur & Heath, 2005). Charities, too, could better frame their appeals in ways that reduce the social distance to victims and appeal to sympathy. In the following, I will outline some suggestions for how this might be achieved based on what we know from research on sympathy.

Framing Victims as Similar and Proximate

As previously stated, research demonstrates a clear link between perceived similarity and proximity to victims, and sympathy and helping. Note that the *perception* is critical. Research has shown that drawing attention to nearly any feature of similarity, even when superficial and arbitrary, can heighten the persuasiveness of an appeal. In the 1970s, one study found that when students on a campus were asked for a dime to make a phone call, the request was more likely to be granted if the person asking was dressed similarly to the person being asked (Emswiller, Deaux, & Willits, 1971). In the business best-seller *Influence* (2001), Robert Cialdini advises salespeople to claim similarity to potential customers. Car salespeople are notorious for exploiting this phenomenon. As Cialdini notes, when customers are trading in an old car, the salesperson will inspect what is in the trunk (such as camping gear), and then will casually mention their own *similar* interest in camping. The evidence suggests that this works well! One study of insurance companies found that customers were more likely to buy insurance when a salesperson was like them in age, religion, politics, and cigarette-smoking habits (Evans, 1963).

Charities do not typically have "salespeople" *per se* who are in direct contact with potential donors. However, they can apply the principle of similarity to reduce perceptions of social distance between recipients of aid and potential donors. In this age of social media, there are many opportunities to target potential donors based on features that match those of portrayed victims (for example, in age, religion, language, or cultural group, etc.), just as in the insurance sales study described above.

Perceptions of proximity can similarly be manipulated. For instance, research shows that perceptions of distance are altered by the presence of geopolitical borders, even though those borders may be arbitrary (Galak, Kruger, & Rozin, 2009). As an example, citizens of Nevada were far more upset than were citizens of California about the placement of the Yucca Mountain nuclear waste repository because it was just inside the Nevada border. In reality, it was closer to many California population centers than to those in Nevada. Moreover, a recent study found that people associate northbound travel with uphill travel and southbound travel with downhill travel. As a result, they perceive the same objective distance to be longer when traveling northbound than when traveling southbound (Nelson & Simmons, 2009). Finally, studies show that effortful movement (e.g., wearing a heavy backpack) increases perception of distance (Proffitt, Stefanucci, Banton, & Epstein, 2003). Evidence like this underscores the malleability of perceived physical distance. Charities can thus strive to reduce the perceived distance to those they seek to support in their marketing communications.

Using Identifiable Victims

Charities already use identifiable victims to evoke sympathy. Most human-need charities feature images of victims in their appeals. Yet they do not always do so in the most effective way. Marketing campaigns sometimes fall prey to the "more is better" approach and portray several victims, despite the evidence that a *single* pictured victim is more emotionally compelling than many pictured victims (Kogut & Ritov, 2005a).

Another common mistake is to try to appeal *both* with an identifiable victim *and* with victim statistics. At first, this approach seems sensible; perhaps the identifiable victim will move people emotionally *and* the statistics will convince them that aid will have a meaningful impact. However, research shows that providing statistics alongside an identifiable victim can inhibit giving (Small, Loewenstein, & Slovic, 2007). Why? It appears that statistics cause people to think more analytically, a mindset that overrides emotionality. Thus, the best pitch may use a single, identifiable victim, to arouse and capture sympathy.

Finally, my research shows that portraying an identifiable victim expressing *sadness* is more effective than portrayals expressing *happiness* or *neutral* emotion

(Small & Verrochi, 2009). This effect holds true for various human need–related charities involving both children and adults. A sad facial expression works because emotions are contagious, so observers literally feel the pain of the portrayed victim. That shared experience of sadness emotionally equips observers to empathize and respond.

Despite the advantages of portraying a victim expressing sadness, we have found that most charity advertisements do not do this. In personal conversations with advertisers and other practitioners about this, we heard them express a belief that it is important to create a positive tone; they are generally wary about anything dark or disturbing in their materials. Yet, changing the facial expression is subtle and need not involve adapting the tone of the ad as a whole. Indeed, the research does not indicate that more negative emotion is better; rather, a subtle change in the facial expression in a picture significantly changes observers' responses.

Creating and Capitalizing on Relationships to Victims

Finally, research described earlier finds that people are prone to give to charities that support victims of misfortunes when potential donors have personally known someone with the same problem (Small & Simonsohn, 2008). One study used a five-minute icebreaker exercise to induce "friendships" between random pairs of strangers. If an instant, laboratory-generated "friendship" can inspire generosity toward others with the same misfortune, then surely charities can inspire a connection between victims and benefactors. This may be one reason why charities employ celebrities, such as Michael J. Fox (Parkinson's) and retired basketball star Magic Johnson (HIV/AIDS) to help raise money. People may feel that they are virtually friends with the celebrities and thus may exhibit more sympathy towards other who are similarly unfortunate.

Although charities seem to recognize the benefit of employing celebrities in marketing communications, they seem less aware, if at all, of the potential gains of targeting real-life friends of victims. I suspect that charities such as Race for the Cure are successful in part because they have found a way of successfully reaching friends and family members of people with breast cancer. When such individuals start raising money, they naturally tap their friends and families for donations. Other charities could similarly activate such persons as social nodes in a network of concerned friends.

CONCLUSION

Psychological research finds that feelings of sympathy exert a powerful influence on charitable giving and that sympathy arises when features of the situation reduce the perceived social distance between anonymous recipients of aid and potential donors. Social distance and sympathy often distort charitable giving decisions. Scarce resources are concentrated on close, sympathetic victims and situations. Distant abstractions—no matter how serious their plight—do not get the support that they need and deserve. These biases are not easy to correct because appeals to reason can backfire by blunting emotional responses, thus suppressing the motivation to help. Therefore, educating the public about sympathy biases could actually backfire in some cases. Alternatively, charities could strive to change perceptions of social distance so that sympathy and aid are both redirected to where they are most needed.

In this chapter, I described several factors that tend to reduce social distance, including similarity, perspective-taking, physical proximity, identifiability, and personal experience. Each of these factors occurs naturally in some incidences, such as when benefactors live near victims or when they have firsthand experience with the situation. Charities should capitalize on these natural advantages by targeting near-distance benefactors and by highlighting similarities and personal experiences. In addition, they should strive to frame people and situations that do not naturally possess such advantages in ways that shorten the distance. Any cause can have an identifiable "poster child" and there are many ways to convey similarity. Thus, the lessons herein can be used by professionals and volunteers alike to develop support for socially distant causes.

REFERENCES

Ainslie, G. (1992). *Picoeconomics: The interaction of successive motivational states within the person*. New York: Cambridge University Press.

Barnett, M. A., Tetreault, P. A., Esper, J. A., & Bristow, A.R. (1986). Similarity and empathy: The experience of rape. *The Journal of Social Psychology, 126*(1), 47–49.

Baron, J., & Szymanska , E. (2009). Heuristics and biases in charity. This volume.

Batson, C. D. (1987). Prosocial Motivation: Is it every truly altruistic? In L. Berkowitz (Ed.), *Advances in experimental social psychology* (Vol. 20, pp. 665–122). New York: Academic Press.

Batson, C. D., Early, S., & Salvarani, G. (1997). Perspective taking: Imagining how another feels versus imagining how you would feel. *Personality and Social Psychology Bulletin, 23*(7), 751–758.

Batson, C. D., Lishner, D. A., Carpenter, A., Dulin, L., Harjusola-Webb, S., Stocks, E. L., Gale, S., Hassan, O., & Samput, B. (2003). "… As you would have them do unto you": Does imagining yourself in the other's place stimulate moral action? *Personality and Social Psychology Bulletin, 29*(4), 1190–1201.

Christy, C. A., & Voigt, H. (1994). Bystander responses to public episodes of child abuse. *Journal of Applied Social Psychology, 24*(9), 824–847.

Cialdini, R., Brown, S., Lewis, B., Luce, C., & Neuberg, S. (1997). Reinterpreting the empathy-altruism relationship: When one into one equals oneness. *Journal of Personality and Social Psychology, 73*, 481–494.

Cialdini, R. B. (2001). *Influence: Science and practice*. Boston: Allyn and Bacon.

Coke, J. S., Batson, C. D., & McDavis, K. (1978). Empathic mediation of helping: A two-stage model. *Journal of Personality & Social Psychology, 36*(7), 752–766.

Dovidio, J. F., Gaertner, S. L., Validzic, A., Matoka, K., Johnson, B., & Frazier, S. (1997). Extending the benefits of recategorization: Evaluations, self-disclosure, and helping. *Journal of Experimental Social Psychology, 33*(4), 401–420.

Emswiller, T., Deaux, K., & Willits, J. E. (1971). Similarity, sex, and request for small favors. *Journal of Applied Social Psychology, 1*, 284–291.

Evans, F. B. (1963). Selling as a dyadic relationship: A new approach. *American Behavioral Scientists, 6*(7), 76–79.

Flippen, A. R., Hornstein, H. A., Siegal, W. E., & Weitzman, E. A. (1996). A comparison of similarity and interdependence as triggers for in-group formation. *Personality and Social Psychology Bulletin, 22*(9), 882–893.

Frijda, N. H. (2986). *The emotions*. Cambridge, England: Cambridge University Press.

Galak, J., Krueger, J., & Rozin, P. (2009). Not in my backyard: The influence of arbitrary boundaries on consumer choice. Working paper. Carnegie Mellon University.

Galak, J., Small, D. A., and Stephen, A. T. (2009). Micro-financing decisions: When a group receives less than an individual. Working paper. Carnegie Mellon University.

Garcia, S. M., Weaver, K., Moskowitz, G. B., & Darley, J. M. (2002). Interpersonal relations and group processes—crowded minds: The implicit bystander effect. *Journal of Personality and Social Psychology, 83*(4), 843–852.

Glover, J. (1999). *Humanity*. New Haven, CT: Yale University Press.

Hamilton, W. D. (1964). The genetical evolution of social behavior. *Journal of Theoretical Biology, 7*, 1–52.

Hornstein, H. A. (1976). *Cruelty and kindness: A new look at aggression and altruism*. Englewood Cliffs, NJ: Prentice-Hall.

Hsee, C. K., & Rottenstreich, Y. (2004). Music, pandas, and muggers: On the affective psychology of value. *Journal of Experimental Psychology: General, 133*(1) 23–30.

Jenni, K. E., & Loewenstein, G. F. (1997). Explaining the "identifiable victim effect." *Journal of Risk and Uncertainty, 14*, 235–257.

Jones, B., & Rachlin, H. (2006). Social discounting. *Psychological Science, 17*, 283–286.

Kahneman, D., & Tversky, A. (1984). Choices, values, and frames. *American Psychologist, 39*, 341–350.

Kogut, T., & Ritov, I. (2005a). The "identified victim" effect: An identified group, or just a single individual? *Journal of Behavioral Decision Making, 18*, 157–167.

Kogut, T., & Ritov, I. (2005b). The singularity effect of identified victims in separate and joint evaluation. *Organizational Behavior and Human Decision Processes, 97*(2), 106–116.

Krebs, D. (1975). Empathy and altruism. *Journal of Personality and Social Psychology, 32*(6), 1134–1146.

Levine, M., Cassidy, C., Brazier, G., & Reicher, S. (2002). Self-categorization and bystander non-intervention: Two experimental studies. *Journal of Applied Social Psychology, 32*(7), 1452–1463.

Loewenstein, G., & Small, D. A. (2007). The Scarecrow and the Tinman: The vicissitudes of human sympathy and caring. *Review of General Psychology, 11*(2) (Special Issue on Emotions and Decision Making), 112–126.

McFarland, C., & Miller, D. T. (1994). The framing of relative performance feedback: Seeing the glass half empty or half full. *Journal of Personality and Social Psychology, 66*, 1061–1073.

Milgram, S. (1974). *Obedience to authority: An experimental view*. New York: Harper & Row.

Nelson, L. D., & Simmons, J.,P. (2009). On southbound ease and northbound fees: Literal consequences of the metaphoric link between vertical position and cardinal direction. *Journal of Marketing Research, 46*, 715–724.

Proffitt, D. R., Stefanucci, J. Banton, T., & Epstein, W. (2003). The role of effort in perceiving distance. *Psychological Science, 14*(2), 106–112.

Pronin, E., Olivola, C. Y., and Kennedy, K. A. (2008). Doing unto future selves as you would do unto others: Psychological distance and decision making. *Personality and Social Psychology Bulletin, 34*, 224–236.

Rachlin, H., & Jones, B. A. (2008). Altruism among relatives and non-relatives. *Behavioral Processes, 79*, 120–123.

Schelling, T. C. (1968). The life you save may be your own. In S. B. Chase (Ed.), *Problems in public expenditure analysis.* Washington, DC: The Brookings Institute.

Sinaceur, M., Heath, C., & Cole, S. (2005). Emotional and deliberative reactions to a public crisis: Mad cow disease in France. *Psychological Science, 16*(3), 247–254.

Small, D. A., & Loewenstein, G. (2003). Helping *a* victim or helping *the* victim: Altruism and identifiabilty. *Journal of Risk and Uncertainty, 26,* 5–16.

Small, D. A., Loewenstein, G., Slovic, P. (2007). Sympathy and callousness: The impact of deliberative thought on donations to identifiable and statistical victims. *Organizational Behavior and Human Decision Processes, 102*(2), 143–153..

Small, D. A., & Simonsohn, U. (2008). Friends of victims: The impact of personal relationships with victims on generosity toward others. *Journal of Consumer Research, 35,* 532–542.

Small, D. A., & Verrochi, N. M. (2009). The face of need: Facial emotion expression on charity advertisements. *Journal of Marketing Research, 46,* 777–787.

Stotland, E., & Dunn, R. E. (1963). Empathy, self-esteem, and birth order. *Journal of Abnormal & Social Psychology, 66*(6), 532–540.

UNICEF. (2005). *State of world's children.* New York: UNICEF. http://www.unicef.org/sowcOS/english/index.html

Williams, L. E., & Bargh, J. A. (2008). Keeping one's distance: The influence of spatial distance cues on affect and evaluation. *Psychological Science, 19*(3), 302–308.

Wispe, L. G. (1972). Positive forms of social behavior: An overview. *Journal of Social Issues, 28*(3), 1–19.

10

Affective Motivations to Help Others
A Two-Stage Model of Donation Decisions

STEPHAN DICKERT, NAMIKA SAGARA, and PAUL SLOVIC

When confronted with the suffering of another person, people often experience a host of emotional reactions. Efforts by charity organizations to secure donations for humanitarian aid purposes tend to capitalize on this by presenting persons in need of help in a way that facilitates the generation of these feelings (i.e., by identifying the persons to make them more real; Small & Loewenstein, 2003). This seems to be an effective strategy, as the motivational aspects of feelings have been prominently linked to prosocial behavior in studies investigating determinants for altruism (Andreoni, 1990; Batson, 1990). When considering the origins of such feelings and their impact on charitable behavior, it becomes apparent that providing help to others can arise from both selfless and selfish intentions. The scientific debate about motivations to help other people revolves around the question of whether we help others because we care about them or because we care primarily about ourselves (Batson, 1990; Cialdini et al., 1987, Eisenberg & Miller, 1987; Haidt, 2007). One consistent determinant for helping seems to be empathic concern for another person (e.g., Kogut & Ritov, 2005 a, b; Loewenstein & Small, 2007). Nonetheless, prosocial behavior can also be motivated by a desire to reduce aversive arousal that is experienced due to the exposure to the suffering of others (Hoffman, 1981). The reduction of aversive arousal is a form of emotional regulation or mood management (Gross, 2002) that motivates action with the self-interest of making oneself feel better. Understanding the basic mechanisms of affective reactions to the suffering of others and their relation to people's willingness to donate money is crucial when investigating the motivation to help others.

Recent psychological research on affective reactions to the suffering of others suggests that the way we process information influences the decision to help those in need (Loewenstein & Small, 2007; Slovic, 2007; Small, Loewenstein, & Slovic, 2007). The psychological factors that determine helping revolve around how emotionally salient the people in need are, which also depends on how these people and their needs are presented. Those who evoke stronger affective reactions might have a greater chance of being helped (Kogut & Ritov, 2005 a, b). In fact, apathetic responses to others in need could be a result of us not meaningfully representing their situation and suffering (Slovic, 2007). When information about victims is processed in a way that fosters concrete mental images, affective reactions are likely stronger in comparison to when this information is processed in a detached, abstract, or intangible way (Dickert & Slovic, 2009). Our inability to bring meaning to abstractly represented large numbers also explains why calamities that cost a large number of people their lives sometimes evoke less of a helping response than an individual victim would (e.g., Fetherstonhaugh, Slovic, Johnson, & Friedrich, 1997; Slovic, 2007). While most people would probably agree that it is better to save many lives versus just one, our affective reactions might speak a different language when these two situations are considered separately. For example, Kogut and Ritov (2005a) show that a single life can evoke stronger affective reactions and be valued higher than several lives.

The way that information about people is processed and mentally represented seems to be a central key in our affective reactions toward them. Several *dual-process* theories of human information processing point toward two qualitatively different yet interconnected processing modes (Epstein, 1994; Kahneman, 2003; Kahneman & Frederick, 2002; Stanovich & West, 2000). One mode is characterized by relatively quick, automatic, effortless, associative, concrete, and affective processing, while the other is thought to be more slow, effortful, rule-based, controlled, and abstract. These two processes are not orthogonal, and often inform and influence each other. In fact, their relationship seems to be rather complex (Evans, 2008). Kahneman (2003) suggests that the slower and reason-driven process can control the output of the more immediate and affective-driven process. It is likely that processing information about victims affectively leads to stronger emotional reactions than deliberative processing (Dickert, 2008; Slovic, 2007). To the degree that a deliberative approach to helping reduces affective reactions, it is possible that it also has a deleterious effect on the motivation to help others (Small, Loewenstein, & Slovic, 2007).

Although there are undoubtedly other motivations to provide help (see Loewenstein & Small, 2007), the strong link between emotional reactions and helping suggests that charitable behavior is driven by motivations related to feelings. To study this relationship, people's willingness to help is often measured by means of financial contributions, which are then related to people's affective reactions. Donation decisions, however, are perhaps better described by a two-stage process that takes into account the initial decision to donate any money at all and then examines the donation amount at a later stage. Research on the construction of preferences supports this assumption and shows that valuations (such as donation amounts) are not read off a master list but instead are constructed on the spot (Lichtenstein & Slovic, 2006; Slovic, 1995). Early research on valuation and preferences regarding gambles (Slovic & Lichtenstein, 1968) presented evidence for a two-stage process model that separated initial choices to play or not to play a gamble from the processes underlying the size of the monetary valuation of the gamble. In accord with this two-stage model for evaluating gambles, we propose that different mechanisms govern decisions to donate money compared to decisions about how much money to donate. Moreover, separating donation decisions into two processing stages allows a more detailed approach to the question of how empathy-related feelings and mood management motivate charitable behavior. Research on empathy and perspective taking suggests that emotions focused on the self are easier to access and less effortful than other-focused emotions (Batson, 1990; Hodges & Wegner, 1997; Rossnagel, 2000; Sabbagh, & Taylor, 2000). Thus, if prosocial behavior is separated into an initial decision to provide any help at all, and at a later stage decide on the amount of help, it is likely that the initial decision is related to how one feels about oneself (i.e., mood management), while the subsequent decision on the amount of help is informed by how one feels about the victim (i.e., empathy). In two experiments we empirically investigated this two-stage process model of donation decisions. Additionally, we were interested in extending research by Small et al. (2007) on the effects of information processing on charitable donations, affective reactions, and the relationship between affect and donations.

GENERAL HYPOTHESES

In line with dual process models, we conceptualized information processing as guided by affect and deliberation. Study 1 manipulated information processing by means of a priming task and Study 2 did so with a cognitive load task. In accordance with Small et al. (2007), we hypothesized that an increase in deliberation shifts information processing away from affective cues (such as empathy), resulting in lower affective reactions and a weaker relationship between affect and willingness to donate money. We separated affective reactions broadly into those that are motivated by mood management and those that are motivated by empathy. Moreover, we investigated the extent to which these differently motivated affective reactions are related to the decision to donate and the donation amount. Consistent with a two-stage processing perspective on charitable giving with different affective processes working in each stage, we expected that mood management would be related to the initial decision to donate, while the donation amount would be related to empathic feelings.

Study 1

Study 1 was designed to test the effect of shifting the balance between deliberative and affective information processing by means of a priming paradigm. Research in both social psychology (e.g., Murphy & Zajonc, 1993) and judgment and decision making (e.g., Fedorikhin & Cole, 2004; Hsee & Rottenstreich, 2004) has used priming manipulations to influence participants' information processing in both subtle and perceptible ways. For example, Murphy and Zajonc (1993) compared the impact of subliminal primes that were either affect rich (happy and angry facial expressions) or affect poor (small and large polygon shapes) on attractiveness judgments of Chinese ideographs. Their results suggest that affect-rich primes lead to higher attractiveness ratings than affect-poor primes, which is indicative of differential information processing depending on the affective content of the primes. Using perceptible primes, Hsee and Rottenstreich (2004) had participants either focus on calculations or feelings to construct a value for a consumer good. Priming participants to deliberate resulted in pricing sensitive to the quantity of the good (i.e., participants were willing to pay more money for greater quantities). Small et al. (2007) used an analogous methodology in a donation context to show that more deliberation (in form of calculative thought) lessens the affective appeal of an identifiable person in need of help.

Similar to Hsee and Rottenstreich's (2004) and Small et al.'s (2007) manipulations, participants in the current study were presented with an affect prime, deliberation prime, or with a no-prime control. We thereby intended to focus participants on their feelings (e.g., by making them sensitive to the affective aspects of the persons in need of help) or on deliberative aspects (e.g., how much money each person receives if $X are donated). This difference in information processing gave rise to the following predictions regarding affective reactions, donations, and their relationship.

Participants were expected to report stronger affective reactions in the affect prime condition versus the calculation prime condition (Hypothesis 1). We also predicted that higher affect should lead to higher donations. Therefore, we hypothesized that affective priming would lead to higher willingness to donate compared to neutral and calculation priming (Hypothesis 2). Finally, we expected that with a shift toward affective processing in the affect priming condition, the relationship between emotions and donations should be stronger compared to the calculative thought condition (Hypothesis 3). Finally, we hypothesized that emotions that are focused on the self (mood management) are predictive of the initial decision to donate, while emotions focused on the victim (empathy) are predictive of the donation amount (Hypothesis 4).

Method   For Study 1, we recruited 256 students at the University of Oregon (52% were female; $M_{age} = 22.1$ years, $SD = 2.4$). We manipulated how participants processed information by employing a priming paradigm, which featured three levels (calculation vs. neutral vs. affective). In the calculation prime condition, participants were asked to perform six mathematical algebraic calculations adapted from Hsee and Rottenstreich (2004; e.g., "If an object travels at five feet per minute, then by your calculations how many feet will it travel in 360 minutes?"). Two participants answered all calculation questions incorrectly and were removed from further analysis. Participants in the affective prime condition were asked to describe in writing how they felt about specific objects or people (e.g., a newborn baby or George W. Bush). These affective primes were designed to prime participants to access their feelings, but were also intended to be balanced in valence (three positive and three negative objects) in an effort to avoid biasing participants' moods.

Of the 87 participants in this condition, 44 (50.6%) reported three positive and three negative emotional reactions, and of the remaining participants in this condition, 22 (25.3%) expressed more negative than positive emotions, while 21 (24.1%) expressed more positive than negative emotions. Participants in the neutral prime condition were not primed to calculate or to express their feelings about anything. Additionally, we varied the number of people in need of help by either presenting a single child or a group of eight children (adapted from Kogut & Ritov, 2005a). Each child was identified by his/her name, age, and a picture. Participants were informed that the children's lives were in danger due to an acute life-threatening disease, and that money needs to be raised in order to save them from dying. They could then indicate whether they would make a hypothetical financial contribution and if so, how much. Thus, the dependent variables of interest were participants' willingness to donate (assessed as a binary response: Yes/No) and, if applicable, the donation amount (assessed as an open-ended question). Additionally, we measured participants' affective responses to the children by asking them (1) how much they were worried, upset, and sad about the children, (2) how much sympathy and compassion they felt for the children, (3) how strongly they felt about the children, and (4) the extent to which donating money would make them feel better. Each of these four affect variables was measured on a 7-point rating scale. Note that the first three of these affect questions targeted empathy-related feelings, while the last question was designed to measure feelings related to mood management.

Results   *Affect structure.* Before testing the effect of priming on participants' affect responses, we investigated whether our distinction between empathy and mood management-related feelings was supported by the data. Analyses of correlational patterns (Table 10.1, top part) showed that all feelings are highly positively correlated. However, empathy-related feelings correlated much more strongly with each other ($.72 < r < .78$), whereas feelings motivated by mood management (i.e., the extent to which donating would make the participants feel better) correlated with the other affect measures somewhat less strongly ($.39 < r < .41$). The zero-order correlations between the affect variables and the amount (see Table 10.1, bottom part) that participants were willing to donate were within the same order of magnitude ($.33 < r < .44$).

A principal components analysis of the four affect variables showed that empathic feelings (i.e., sympathy, worry, and feelings for the sick children) are

TABLE 10.1   Correlations of Affect Variables and Donation Amount

	Sympathy	Worry	Feel for Children	Feel Better If I Donate	Donation Amount
Sympathy	1.00				
Worry	.73[a]	1.00			
Feel for children	.72[a]	.78[a]	1.00		
Feel better if I donate	.39[a]	.41[a]	.41[a]	1.00	
Donation Amount	.33[a]	.38[a]	.39[a]	.44[a]	1.00

[a] $p < .001$

structurally different than feelings related to mood management (i.e., how much better a donation would make the participants feel) and best represented by two separate affective components. Based on these findings, participants' sympathy, worry, and feelings for the children were averaged into one variable (Cronbach's α = .90) measuring empathic feelings toward the victim(s). Given the different structure of these affect variables, we conducted the following analyses separately for feelings motivated by empathy and mood management.

Effect of priming on affect. As expected, we found that participants expressed higher empathic feelings when they were primed to process information affectively (in the affect prime condition, $M = 3.6$, $SD = 1.5$) compared to participants who processed information deliberatively (in the calculation prime condition, $M = 3.0$, $SD = 1.4$). In contrast, we found no evidence that feelings related to mood management were influenced by our priming manipulation (see Figure 10.1).

Effect of priming on donation amounts. Of the 254 participants, 228 (90%) indicated that they would donate money. Interestingly, affect priming increased the proportion of participants (96%) who were willing to donate money relative to the neutral prime condition (90%), whereas calculation priming decreased the proportion of participants willing to donate (83%). Affective priming also had the desired effect of increasing the donation amounts, whereas calculation priming decreased donation amounts relative to the neutral priming condition (see Figure 10.2).

Finally, we tested whether participants' decisions to donate are related to participants' affective reactions. A logistic regression analysis was performed for each priming condition with the two different types of feelings (empathy vs. mood management) as predictors. Results for the calculation and affect prime conditions are presented in Table 10.2. The regression models significantly predicted donation decisions for the calculation and affect prime conditions. For these two conditions, feelings discriminate between participants who donated and those who did not. Examination of the individual predictor variables reveals that only

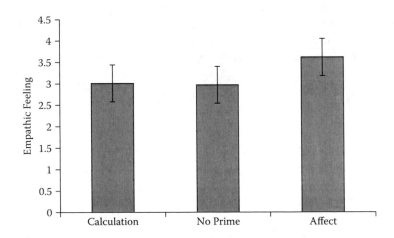

Figure 10.1   Effect of priming on empathic feelings. Note: Error bars represent 95% confidence intervals.

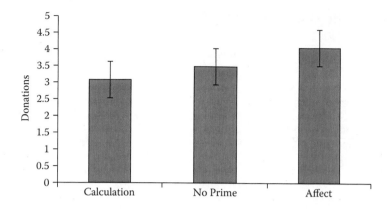

Figure 10.2 Donation amounts for priming conditions. Note: Error bars represent 95% confidence intervals.

feelings informed by mood management were predictive of the decision to donate. An increase in how much better participants estimated they would feel due to a donation increased the odds of donating by a factor of 3 in the calculation prime condition and by almost 5 in the affect prime condition.

We next investigated whether feelings were also predictive of the donation amount (see Table 10.3). These results indicate a clear difference in the predictive strength of empathic feelings versus mood management on donation amount. Mood management was predictive of donations in all priming conditions. However, empathic feelings were predictive of donations only in the affective prime and no-prime condition. Together with the results of the logistic regression presented in Table 10.2, these results give support to the notion that the relationship between emotions and donations is stronger in the affect prime condition (Hypothesis 3). Additionally, these regression analyses show that the initial decision to donate is related to people's mood management, while the donation amount is also related to their empathic response (Hypothesis 4). Note that empathy was only predictive of the donation amount when participants were primed to feel (vs. calculate).

To further explore the impact of priming on affect and donations, a mediation analysis was conducted. Since both donations and empathic feelings were higher in the affect prime condition, we reasoned that the effect of priming on donations was possibly better explained through its positive effect on empathy. Västfjäll, D.,

TABLE 10.2 Affective Predictors of Donation Decisions by Priming Condition

Model	Individual Predictors	Exp(b)	Wald	p
Calculation Prime	Empathic Feelings	.804	.690	.405
$\chi^2 (2) = 18.4, p < .001$	Mood Management	3.143	10.38	.001
Affect Prime	Empathic Feelings	1.256	.360	.547
$\chi^2 (2) = 11.3, p < .01$	Mood Management	4.986	4.000	.046

TABLE 10.3   Affect Predicting Donations Amounts by Priming Condition

Overall Model	Individual Predictors	β	t	P
Calculation Prime $F(2,82) = 15.3$, $p < .001$, $adjR^2 = .26$	Empathic Feelings	.070	.640	.522
	Mood Management	.480	4.280	.000
Affect Prime $F(2,84) = 15.2$, $p < .001$, $adjR^2 = .25$	Empathic Feelings	.240	2.310	.023
	Mood Management	.370	3.650	.001

Peters, E., & Slovic, P. (unpublished manuscript) found that willingness to donate money was mediated by the level of affect felt toward victims in need of help. In fact, using Baron and Kenny's (1986) regression approach to mediation analyses, we found that the effect of priming was partially mediated by empathic feelings. A test of the indirect effect (Sobel, 1982) on donations was significant, *Sobel test statistic* = 2.55, $p < .05$, supporting the mediator role of empathic feelings. This suggests that affective information processing has a positive effect on the generation of empathic feelings, which then increases the donation amount that people are willing to contribute. A similar analysis with how much better participants felt due to a donation revealed that mood management did not mediate donations.

Discussion   Study 1 used a priming manipulation to guide participants' information processing toward either affective or deliberative dimensions. These priming manipulations were designed to focus participants on affective aspects of the donation task (e.g., how they felt toward the sick children) or on deliberative aspects (e.g., using a calculative approach to valuing the children's lives). Asking participants to perform mathematical calculations prior to being exposed to the children stimuli had the effect of lowering empathic feelings and donation amounts relative to the no-prime control condition, indicating that empathy toward the children was of lesser intensity (and importance). Conversely, asking participants to focus on their feelings resulted in greater empathic feelings and higher donations relative to the control condition. A mediation analysis suggests that the effect of priming on donations comes from changing people's empathic feelings toward the people in need, which then motivates higher donations. It is of note that we found no support for priming to influence participants' feelings related to mood management, nor did we find that the relationship between mood management and donation amounts was mediated by our information processing condition.

The effect of feelings on donations seems to depend on the type of feelings and processing stage of the donation decision. Investigating participants' willingness to donate (vs. not donate) suggests that mood management is more important than empathic feelings in the initial decision to donate. It seems as though people rely more on social-egoism motivations (Batson, 1990) when deciding on whether they should help or not. However, the quantity of the provided help (i.e., the donation amount) is also based on empathic feelings when participants are primed to engage in affective evaluations and process information more affectively (i.e., System 1). In this second process stage, higher empathy increases donation amounts.

Study 2

In Study 2 we manipulated information processing by means of a cognitive load manipulation intended to restrict deliberative processing capacities. We also wanted to explore whether the different roles of empathic feelings and mood management on donation decisions emerged with a different paradigm.

Cognitive load paradigms are designed to tax deliberative processing capacities and result in information processing influenced by nondeliberative (i.e., affective) aspects of the decision task. Pham (2007) argues that judgments and decisions that have affective processing as a basis are relatively unaffected by such processing restrictions. Restricting processing resources can therefore accentuate the role of affective information. Affective aspects about an object (or person) are more quickly available compared to those based on slow and careful deliberation and are accessible even when cognitive resources are low (Slovic, Finucane, Peters, & MacGregor, 2002, 2004). Taxing deliberative processing should therefore lead to decision making that relies more on affective input. Empirical support for this notion was found by Shiv and Fedorikhin (1999), who administered a 7-digit memory load to decrease participants' ability to cogitate about their choices so that affective attributes of options are given relatively more weight. Conversely, when the ability to deliberate is available, mental processes tend to be more elaborate and comparisons between choice options can include the careful weighing of decision attributes and consequences (Rottenstreich, Sood, & Brenner, 2007). In a donation context, elaboration on different decision attributes (e.g., how much the person in need deserves help or how much of an impact a donation would have) may deter empathic feelings and thereby have a deleterious effect on donations (Small et al., 2007).

To investigate the extent to which processing capacity influences donations, Study 2 manipulated cognitive load along with the number of individuals in need of help. We assumed that a restriction in deliberative processing capacity makes affective aspects of the decision task more salient (compared to deliberative aspects), which was expected to result in stronger affective reactions (Hypothesis 1) and higher donations (Hypothesis 2). Moreover, in line with results from Study 1 we hypothesized that empathic feelings and mood management relate to different aspects of the donation task. Specifically, mood management should be more predictive of the decision to donate, whereas empathic feelings should be more predictive of the donation amount (Hypothesis 3).

Method   A total of 193 undergraduate students at the University of Oregon took part in this study (51% female, M_{age} = 22.3 years, SD = 2.9). We manipulated participants' processing capacity with a memory load task (high vs. low). Participants in the high-load condition had to remember a randomly generated 10-letter sequence ("DKZZVHTRKJ"), whereas those in the low-load condition had to remember a 2-letter sequence ("XD"). Additionally, we manipulated whether participants

TABLE 10.4   Correlations of Affect Variables and Donation Amount

	Sympathy	Worry	Feel Better	Regret	Donation Amount
Sympathy	1.00				
Worry	.66[a]	1.00			
Feel better	.34[a]	.42[a]	1.00		
Regret	.36[a]	.48[a]	.50[a]	1.00	
Donation Amount	.35[a]	.42[a]	.42[a]	.44[a]	1.00

[a] $p < .01$

saw a single child in need of help or a group of eight children. The information about the sick children in need of a financial contribution was identical to Study 1. Participants' donation decisions, donation amounts, and feelings toward the children were again the main variables of interest. After viewing the information about the child (children) and being informed that he/she is (they are) in danger from an unspecified life-threatening disease, participants indicated whether they would make a (hypothetical) financial contribution to them. If so, they were next asked to enter the amount they would be willing to contribute. Several questions related to the participants' feelings toward and perceptions of the children followed on a second page. These questions were measured on 7-point rating scale and included how much participants were (1) worried, upset, and sad, (2) how much sympathy and compassion they felt, (3) how much they would regret not donating, and (4) and how much better they felt if they donated.

Results   *Descriptive analyses.* Of the 193 participants, 152 (79%) recalled their letter-sequence accurately and were included for further analyses.[°]

Affect structure. Before testing the effect of cognitive load on participants' affect responses, the underlying structure of participants' affect and related responses were investigated. Analyses of correlational patterns showed that all affect variables had a significant positive relationship to each other (see Table 10.4, top).

While all variables were significantly positively correlated, closer inspection of Table 10.4 shows that sympathy and worry correlated slightly higher with each other ($r = .66$) than other affect variables. These two variables were taken as a measurement of empathic feelings. In contrast, how much better participants felt about themselves after donating and their anticipated regret ($r = .50$) were taken as measurements of feelings related to mood management. The correlations between the individual affective variables and participants' stated donation amount (Table 10.4, bottom) were in the same range as we found in Study 1.

A principle components analysis again revealed two affective components that supported the conceptual distinction between empathic feelings and mood management. While sympathy and worry loaded highly on only the first component, feeling better and anticipated regret loaded highly on only the second component.

[°] Inclusion of participants who did not recall their letter sequence correctly yielded the same pattern of results (see Dickert, 2008).

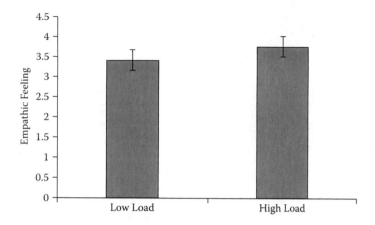

Figure 10.3   Empathic feelings by cognitive load. Note: Error bars represent 95% confidence intervals.

Based on these analyses, sympathy and worry were combined to measure empathic feelings and the other two variables were combined to measure feelings related to mood management.

Effect of cognitive load on affect. Results showed that participants reported slightly higher empathic feelings in the high-load condition (M = 3.8, SD = 1.5) than in the low-load condition (M = 3.5, SD = 1.5), but this difference failed to reach statistical significance (Figure 10.3). Additionally, groups of children (M = 3.8, SD = 1.3) elicited higher empathic feelings than individual children (M = 3.4, SD = 1.6). Neither the cognitive load manipulation nor varying the number of children had an effect on feelings related to mood management, as a similar analysis of variance (ANOVA) showed.

Effect of cognitive load on donations. Of the 152 participants who recalled their letter sequence correctly, 112 (74%) indicated that they would donate money (see Table 10.5 for details).

Inspection of Table 10.5 shows that in the low-load condition a higher percentage of participants donated to one child (80%) than to eight children (66%). The opposite pattern was observed under high load, where a higher percentage of participants donated to eight children (82%) than to one child (71%). Results of the donation amounts (see Figure 10.4) indicated that participants in the high-load condition (M = 2.8, SD = 1.94) donated slightly more money than participants in the low-load condition (M = 2.3, SD = 1.8).

TABLE 10.5   Contribution Frequency by Cognitive Load and Number of Children

	Low Cognitive Load	High Cognitive Load	Totals
One child	24 of 30 (80%)	30 of 42 (71%)	54 of 72 (75%)
Eight children	27 of 41 (66%)	32 of 39 (82%)	59 of 80 (74%)
Totals	51 of 71 (72%)	62 of 81 (77%)	113 of 152 (74%)

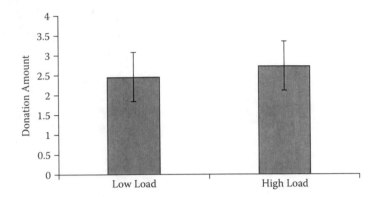

Figure 10.4   Donation amount for cognitive load. Note: Error bars represent 95% confidence intervals.

To test whether the decision to donate any money at all is related to participants' affect and processing capacity, a logistic regression analysis was performed. Results are presented in Table 10.6, and indicate that the regression model was significantly predictive of participants' decisions to donate. Mood management was highly predictive of donation decisions, whereas empathic feelings did not seem to discriminate participants who decided to donate from those who did not.

We also performed regression analyses to determine the extent to which donation amounts were predicted by participants' affective reactions (see Table 10.7 for results). As in Study 1, mood management was predictive of donation amounts regardless of information processing condition. However, empathic feelings were significantly predictive of the donation amount only when deliberative capacity was decreased in the high-load condition.

Discussion   Study 2 was designed to investigate the effects of cognitive load on affective reactions and donations. We expected that participants under high cognitive load would engage in more affective processing and show a stronger relationship between their affective reactions and donations. This assumes that they used these feelings as a source of information to guide their donation decisions when deliberative capacity was decreased. As in Study 1, we found support for

TABLE 10.6   Affective Predictors of Donation Decisions by Cognitive Load Condition

Model	Individual Predictors	Exp(b)	Wald	p
High Cognitive Load:	Empathic Feelings	1.220	.840	.360
χ^2 (2) = 29.1, p < .001	Mood Management	3.391	12.900	.001
Low Cognitive Load:	Empathic Feelings	1.108	.170	.681
χ^2 (2) = 20.8, p < .001	Mood Management	2.471	10.540	.001

TABLE 10.7   Affect Predicting Donation Amounts
by Cognitive Load Condition

Model	Individual Predictors	B	t	p
High Cognitive Load $F(2,78) = 16.5$, $p < .01$, adj$R^2 = .28$	Empathic Feelings	.230	2.200	.031
	Mood Management	.400	3.700	.001
Low Cognitive Load $F(2,67) = 12.8$, $p < .01$, adj$R^2 = .26$	Empathic Feelings	.210	1.600	.112
	Mood Management	.370	2.800	.006

a distinction between feelings motivated by empathy versus mood management. Restricting processing resources led to a slight increase in empathic feelings and somewhat higher donation amounts for groups. It is of note that empathic feelings seemed to be sensitive to processing resources, whereas feelings related to mood management were robust against possible disruptive effects of deliberative processing.

Analyses of how empathic versus mood management feelings were related to donation decisions confirmed findings from Study 1. Specifically, the initial decision to donate was predicted only by mood management, regardless of processing resource availability. When participants decided on the donation amount, both empathic feelings and mood management seem to be important. Note, however, that this was somewhat more the case in the high-load condition, where restricted processing capacity enabled higher levels of empathic feelings as well as a stronger connection between these feelings and the donation amount. As in Study 1, feelings related to mood management were predictive of donation amounts regardless of information processing mode.

GENERAL DISCUSSION

In two studies we investigated the role of information processing on people's charitable behavior and affective reactions to sick children in need of financial contributions. We divided affective reactions into empathic feelings and mood management–related feelings. This distinction dovetails nicely with seminal research on prosocial behavior that distinguishes selfless from selfish motivations to provide help (Batson, 1990). Our results suggest that mood management is remarkably robust against information processing manipulations, as feelings related to mood management were independent of priming and processing capacity. This could be due to the fact that feelings related to mood management in our studies were anticipated feeling states related to goals (i.e., making oneself feel better) and might not be as easily influenced by our employed information processing manipulations as experienced emotions are. However, mood management was the single best predictor of participants' decisions to donate anything at all. Empathic feelings, on the other hand, were generally higher when participants were primed to focus on their feelings and somewhat higher when their deliberative capacity was limited. We also found evidence that donations were generally higher when participants were primed to focus on their feelings and, to a lesser extent, when their processing capacity was limited. In line with Small, Loewenstein, and Slovic (2007), this suggests that a more deliberative approach can have a deleterious effect on donations. Put differently, if we think too much about the victims, we may be less inclined to provide assistance motivated by empathy.

Recent research on the singularity effect (e.g., Kogut & Ritov, 2005 a, b) found that single victims evoked higher affective reactions than groups. The difference in our finding might be related to the fact that we used pictures of children with a different ethnicity than our participants. Kogut and Ritov (2007) found that people's willingness to help a single identified individual is greater than the willingness to help a group only when the individual belongs to the perceiver's in-group. As we used children with a different ethnicity than our participants, it is possible that our participants did not perceive them as belonging to their in-group.

A central question in our studies was how the differently motivated feelings (empathy vs. mood management) related to donations. In this context, we assume that the regulation of one's own negative arousal constitutes a departure from purely selfless motivations to help. When confronted with the misery of others, people donate money at least partly with the intention of making themselves feel better and/or avoiding postchoice regret due to not donating. Note, however, that empathic feelings and mood management are not opposites on a continuum, and are often related to each other (as was shown in our correlational analyses in both studies). An implicit assumption in our experiments was that donation decisions follow a time course in which people first decide whether they provide any help at all and then determine the amount of help. Decomposing donations into two stages (cf. Slovic & Lichtenstein, 1968), one at which participants made the initial decision to donate money, and a second one at which they decide on the donation amount, allowed us to investigate whether empathic versus mood management feelings have different functions in determining donation decisions and donation amounts. In the early stages of these decisions, mood management seemed to be more important than empathy. We found that the initial decision to donate depended only on participants' affect related to mood management. Mood management was also strongly predictive of donation amounts, regardless of information processing mode. However, our results also show that empathic feelings have their place in driving donation amounts under specific circumstances. When information about the victims was processed affectively, people seemed to base the extent of their help on the experienced sympathy and compassion toward the victims.

Practical and Theoretical Implications

Whether the charity serves starving children, homeless people displaced by war, people suffering and dying from AIDS, or any other charitable cause, the relationship between our affective responses and donations for others in need is of special interest to private aid foundations and charities. As affective responses seem to be a core ingredient in motivating people to help others, these organizations need to be aware of the conditions that foster emotional reactions. Moreover, the sometimes subtle ways in which emotions influence the decision to donate should be taken into account when efforts are made to secure charitable contributions. Our findings point out that people's own mood management is an important motivation to initiate helping, presumably because the negative feeling that arises when witnessing the suffering of another provides a strong impetus to leave this negative arousal state behind by making a donation. As a result, people who experience stronger negative arousal in the face of identified victims are more likely to donate money. The donation amount, on the other hand, is also dependent on the degree to which the donor empathizes with the victim.

A practical implication of these mechanisms is that both mood management and empathy-related feelings are conducive to donations and donation amounts. Factors that influence mood management are likely those that increase potential donors' negative arousal, while empathic responses are at least partly related to how information is processed. An important consideration for getting potential donors to the point where they are willing to make any contribution at all is their belief that their financial contribution indeed can make a difference. As there are several other competing possibilities for managing one's own mood besides donating money (e.g., reducing exposure to the suffering of the victims or to dissociate with them), it seems vital that the reduction of one's negative arousal can be achieved by donating money. Higher donation amounts seem to be related to empathic concern. Priming people to *feel* rather than to *think* about the victims' situation increases empathy and, subsequently, the donated amount. One way of achieving this could be to ask potential donors to take the perspective of the victim (Coke, Batson, & McDavis, 1978).

While it could be argued that the underlying motivation (selfish vs. selfless) to help others is of secondary importance as long as people help at all, future studies of philanthropy should pay close attention to the factors that facilitate these different kinds of motivations. If a person only helps another in order to feel better about herself, it might just as well be likely that other, less charitable forms of mood management might substitute for helping. When we asked people who chose not to donate any money for their motivations (in a different donation task with real money), we received elaborate replies that involved reasons deflecting personal responsibility and highlighting the lack of an impact of a donation. For example, one participant stated that her father had just donated money to an unnamed charitable organization last Christmas, and another participant asserted that these donations never reach the intended target anyway. Future research might inspect the role that these justifications play in regulating people's feelings and their decisions to abstain from helping others. We believe that mood management is a key player in these decisions.

Even though our experiments have focused specifically on affective motivations of helping, future research could also take a closer look at the role that deliberation might have for facilitating charitable behavior. Loewenstein and Small (2007) suggest that most deliberations in this context include an estimate of how much help is deserved by the victim and whether one is actually able to provide help. Manipulation of these factors might influence both people's feelings and their willingness to donate money to charitable causes.

Finally, we would like to point out that the picture of a self-serving person who donates to charity primarily to make herself feel better needs to be qualified. Although mood management was definitely a strong predictor of donation decisions and donation amounts in our data, we also found that empathic feelings were correlated with mood management and also predicted donation amount in specific situations. Empathic feelings are prominently linked to prosocial behavior, and specifically sympathy and compassion have been identified as determinants for charitable behavior. An important question seems to be when empathy is related to helping, and our results indicate that affective processing is beneficial for such feelings. Too much deliberation, on the other hand, might lead people to focus on other cues when they ponder whether they should donate and in what amount.

ACKNOWLEDGMENTS

Support for this research was provided by the US National Science Foundation under Grant #SES-0649509. Portions of this chapter are based on Stephan Dickert, Namika Sagara, and Paul Slovic, "Affective Motivations To Help Others: A Two-Stage Model of Donation Decisions," /Journal of Behavioral Decision Making. Advance online publication /doi: 10.1002/bdm.697 Copyright © 2010 John Wiley and Sons. Reprinted with permission.

REFERENCES

Andreoni, J. (1990). Impure altruism and donations to public goods: A theory of warm-glow giving. *The Economic Journal, 100*, 464–477.

Baron, R. M., & Kenny, D. A. (1986). The moderator-mediator variable distinction in social psychological research: Conceptual, strategic and statistical considerations. *Journal of Personality and Social Psychology, 51*, 1173–1182.

Batson, C. D. (1990). How social an animal? The human capacity for caring. *American Psychologist, 45*, 336–346.

Cialdini, R. B., Schaller, M., Houlihan, D., Arps, K., Fultz, J., & Beaman, A. L. (1987). Empathy-based helping: Is it selflessly or selfishly motivated? *Journal of Personality and Social Psychology. 52*(4), 749–758.

Coke, J. S., Batson, C. D., & McDavis, K. (1978). Empathic mediation of helping: A two-stage model. *Journal of Personality and Social Psychology, 36*, 752–766.

Dickert, S. (2008). Two routes to the perception of need: The role of affective and deliberative information processing in pro-social behaviour. Doctoral Dissertation, University of Oregon, Eugene, Oregon.

Dickert S., & Slovic, P. (2009). Attentional mechanisms in the generation of sympathy. *Judgment and Decision Making, 4*, 297–306.

Eisenberg, N., & Miller, P. A. (1987). Empathy and prosocial behavior. *Psychological Bulletin, 101*, 91–119.

Epstein, S. (1994). Integration of the cognitive and the psychodynamic unconscious. *American Psychologist, 49*, 709–724.

Evans, J. St. B. T. (2008). Dual-processing accounts of reasoning, judgment, and social cognition. *Annual Review of Psychology, 59*, 255–278.

Fedorikhin, A., & Cole, C. A. (2004). Mood effects on attitudes, perceived risk and choice: Moderators and mediators. *Journal of Consumer Psychology, 14*, 2–12.

Fetherstonhaugh, D., Slovic, P., Johnson, S. M., & Friedrich, J. (1997). Insensitivity to the value of human life: A study of psychophysical numbing. *Journal of Risk and Uncertainty, 14*, 283–300.

Gross, J. (2002). Emotion regulation: Affective, cognitive, and social consequences. *Psychophysiology, 39*, 281–291.

Haidt, J. (2007). The new synthesis in moral psychology. *Science, 316*, 998–1002.

Hodges, S. D., & Wegner, D. M. (1997). Automatic and controlled empathy. In W. J. Ickes, *Empathic accuracy.* (pp. 311–339). New York: Guilford Press.

Hoffman, M. L. (1981). Is altruism part of human nature? *Journal of Personality and Social Psychology, 40*, 121–137.

Hsee, C. K., & Rottenstreich, Y. (2004). Music, pandas, and muggers: On the affective psychology of value. *Journal of Experimental Psychology: General, 133*(1), 23–30.

Kahneman, D. (2003). A perspective on judgment and choice: Mapping bounded rationality. *American Psychologist, 58*, 697–720.

Kahneman, D., & Frederick, S. (2002). Representativeness revisited: Attribute substitution in intuitive judgment. In T. Gilovich, D. Griffin, & D. Kahneman (Eds.), *Heuristics and biases* (pp. 49–81). New York: Cambridge University Press.

Kogut, T., & Ritov, I. (2005a). The "identified victim" effect: An identified group, or just a single individual? *Journal of Behavioral Decision Making, 18*, 157–167.

Kogut, T., & Ritov, I. (2005b). The singularity of identified victims in separate and joint evaluations. *Organizational Behavior and Human Decision Processes, 97*, 106–116.

Kogut, T., & Ritov, I. (2007). "One of us": Outstanding willingness to help save a single identified compatriot. *Organizational Behavior and Human Decision Processes, 104*, 150–157.

Lichtenstein, S. & Slovic, P. (2006). *The construction of preference.* New York: Cambridge University Press.

Loewenstein, G., & Small, D. (2007). The scarecrow and the tin man: The vicissitudes of human sympathy and caring. *Review of General Psychology , 11*(2), 112–126.

Murphy, S. T., & Zajonc, R. B. (1993). Affect, cognition, and awareness: Affective priming with optimal and suboptimal stimulus exposures. *Journal of Personality and Social Psychology, 64*, 723–739.

Pham, M. T. (2007). Emotion and rationality: A critical review and interpretation of empirical evidence. *Review of General Psychology, 11*(2), 155–178.

Rossnagel, C. (2000). Cognitive load and perspective-taking: Applying the automatic-controlled distinction to verbal communication. *European Journal of Social Psychology, 30*, 425–445.

Rottenstreich, Y., Sood, S., & Brenner, L. (2007). Feeling and thinking in memory-based versus stimulus-based choices. *Journal of Consumer Research, 33*, 461–469.

Sabbagh, M., & Taylor, M. (2000). Neural correlates of theory-of-mind reasoning: An event-related potential study. *Psychological Science, 11*, 46–50.

Shiv, B., & Fedorikhin, A. (1999). Heart and mind in conflict: The interplay of affect and cognition in consumer decision making. *Journal of Consumer Research, 26*, 278–292.

Sobel, M. E. (1982). Asymptotic confidence intervals for indirect effects in structural equation models. In S. Leinhardt (Ed.), *Sociological methodology* (pp. 290–312). Washington, DC: American Sociological Association.

Slovic, P. (1995). The construction of preference. *American Psychologist, 50*, 364–371.

Slovic, P. (2007). "If I look at the mass I will never act": Psychic numbing and genocide. *Judgment and Decision Making, 2*(2), 79–95.

Slovic, P., Finucane, M. L., Peters, E., & MacGregor, D. G. (2002). The affect heuristic. In T. Gilovich, D. Griffin, & D. Kahneman (Eds.), *Heuristics and biases: The psychology of intuitive judgment* (pp. 397–420). New York: Cambridge University Press.

Slovic, P., Finucane, M., Peters, E., & MacGregor, D. (2004). Risk as analysis and risk as feelings: Some thoughts about affect, reason, risk, and rationality, *Risk Analysis, 24,* 311–322.

Slovic, P., & Lichtenstein, S. (1968). Relative importance of probabilities and payoffs in risk taking. *Journal of Experimental Psychology, 78*(3), 1–18.

Small, D. A., & Loewenstein, G. (2003). Helping a victim or helping the victim: Altruism and identifiability. *Journal of Risk and Uncertainty, 26,* 5–16.

Small, D. A., Loewenstein, G., & Slovic, P. (2007). Sympathy and callousness: Affect and deliberations in donation decisions. *Organizational Behavior and Human Decision Processes, 102,* 143–153.

Stanovich, K. E., & West, R. F. (2000). Individual differences in reasoning: Implications for the rationality debate? *Behavioral and Brain Sciences, 23,* 645–726.

Västfjäll, D., Peters, E., & Slovic, P. *Compassion fatigue: Donations and affect are greatest for a single child in need.* Unpublished manuscript, Decision Research, 2010.

11

Donate Different
External and Internal Influences on Emotion-Based Donation Decisions

MICHAELA HUBER, LEAF VAN BOVEN, and
A. PETER MCGRAW

*I*t has been said that feeling is for doing. Emotional arousal is a "call to action" that can elicit behavioral responses where dispassionate analysis might not. Decisions about donating resources to alleviate humanitarian suffering are no exception: sympathetic emotions, affective reactions in response to others' suffering, can exert powerful influence over decisions to help others. Emotions are thus helpful determinants of helping behavior (e.g., Batson, 1990). Without such emotions, people may behave more selfishly and less altruistically.

But emotions can lead to puzzling behavior that people might prefer to avoid, especially upon reflection. For example, people may give generously to single, identifiable victims (e.g., Baby Jessica) whose plight happens to receive widespread media attention—a donation people might later think would have been better spent on alleviating starvation or providing medical care to hundreds of people in a third world country (Small & Loewenstein, 2003). Or people might donate generously to charitable causes that, owing to glossy photos and well-orchestrated marketing appeals, just happened to tug at people's heartstrings (and hence their purse strings), even though they might acknowledge that the organization to which they donated is inefficiently operated. In cases such as these, one might wonder whether people in everyday life, if not policy makers, might prefer to make donation decisions differently. If people would prefer to donate differently, in what ways would they rather make donation decisions, and how might they be encouraged to do so?

We examine such questions in this chapter by reviewing recent research on the role of emotion in donation decisions and on potential strategies for altering emotionally influenced decision processes. We first offer a selective review of research indicating that emotional experiences influence donation decisions, focusing on people's tendency to make donation decisions based on emotional factors rather than on information about the objective amount or scope of human suffering, a pattern referred to as *scope insensitivity*. We also review research recently conducted in our own lab indicating that when people learn about multiple sources of human suffering, they tend to donate more to human suffering that just happens to arouse immediate (rather than previous) emotions, which contributes to scope insensitivity. After presenting preliminary evidence that people would prefer to make donation decisions differently than they often do, giving more weight to information about the objective scope of human suffering than to emotional information, we draw a distinction between two types of strategies to alter donation decisions: externally focused strategies emphasize constraints external to the decision maker whereas internally focused strategies emphasize factors such as self-reflection and mindfulness. We suggest that internal strategies may, on balance, be more attractive and feasible means of influencing donation decisions.

SCOPE INSENSITIVITY IN DONATION DECISIONS

As noted earlier, emotions can strongly influence donation decisions: people give more to those whose suffering is more upsetting compared with those whose suffering is relatively less upsetting (Batson, 1990). Emotions are therefore helpful in that they can encourage people to donate more resources than they might otherwise. But the strong influence of emotion on donation decisions can be problematic in at least two ways. The first is that people might often personally prefer to behave less emotionally and more analytically (Hsee & Rottenstreich, 2004; Kahneman, Ritov, & Schkade, 1999; Kahneman, Schkade, & Sunstein, 1998; Loewenstein, 1996; Loewenstein, Weber, Hsee, & Welch, 2001; Metcalfe & Mischel, 1999; Rottenstreich & Hsee, 2001; Slovic, 1987; Slovic, Finucane, Peters, & MacGregor, 2002), and emotions might lead people to make decisions in ways they would rather not. The second is that because factors that arouse emotions may be independent of the objective severity of suffering, emotionally influenced decisions might produce decisions that are insensitive to—if not neglectful of—the objective scope of human suffering. Such scope insensitivity has garnered substantial research interest, as illustrated by three phenomena: the identifiable victim effect, psychic numbing, and recent research from our own lab on the immediacy bias in donation decisions.

Identifiable Victims

Among the clearest illustrations that emotions influence donation decisions and contribute to scope insensitivity comes from research on the identifiable victim effect (Kogut & Ritov, 2005a, 2005b; Small & Loewenstein, 2003). There, people are more inclined to make donations that might alleviate the suffering of a specific, identified individual rather than a statistical group of individuals.

In one study, for example, people gave more money to save the life of an ill child when they saw a picture of the child along with identifying information compared with receiving no picture or identifying information (Kogut & Ritov, 2005b). In another study, children were described as being treated in a medical center with their lives in danger and that money needed to be raised for a drug that cures their disease (Kogut & Ritov, 2005a). People were willing to contribute more money when they saw a picture of a single, identified child compared with a child who was not identified with a picture. Importantly, people were also willing to contribute more money when they saw the single identified victim compared with a group of eight identified victims. In these studies on identifiable victims, people donate more to single identified individuals than to groups of individuals—keenly illustrating insensitivity to the scope of human suffering, at least in terms of the number of victims suffering.

The identifiable victim effect is largely attributable to the stronger emotions evoked by an identifiable victim compared with an unidentifiable victim (Kogut & Ritov, 2005a). Because emotions are closely intertwined with immediate behavioral inclinations (Loewenstein, 1996; Metcalfe & Mischel, 1999), the emotionally evocative single, identified victim leads people to donate more than the abstract, less emotionally evocative statistical victims. This emotional analysis of the identifiable victim effect implies that making people aware of the effect and drawing people's attention to information about the scope of human suffering would mitigate the identifiable victim effect, leading people to donate more to large groups of (statistical) victims than to single identifiable victims. Unfortunately this is not the case, for reasons reviewed next.

Psychic Numbing

There is mounting evidence that thinking and deciding in a calculating manner, as would seem to be required when processing information about the objective scope of human suffering, can directly undermine emotions that can lead people to make charitable donations. Slovic (2007) has characterized a process by which thinking about large-scale numbers of suffering humans actively mitigates emotional reactions—a process he refers to as *psychic numbing*—such that people become more and more insensitive to increases in the scope of human suffering (Fetherstonhaugh, Slovic, Johnson, & Friedrich, 1997). For example, whereas there is a sharp increase in emotions as the number of suffering humans increases from none to one, there is a proportionally smaller increase in emotions as the number of suffering humans increases from one to two, from two to three, and so on. Moreover, as the number of suffering humans becomes exceptionally large—as in genocide, mass starvation, and other chronic crises—emotions can actually dissipate such that people are less emotionally responsive to large-scale suffering than to small-scale suffering.

One factor that contributes to psychic numbing is that people can move from valuing the outcomes of donation decisions in a primarily "hot" emotional way to primarily a "cold" calculating way (e.g., Hsee & Rottenstreich, 2004;

Kahneman, 2003). These two modes of valuation—by feeling and by calculation—are distinct and somewhat incompatible. In one study, for instance, people were asked how much they would be willing to donate to rescue animals of an endangered species (pandas) in a remote Asian region (Hsee & Rottenstreich, 2004). The animals were represented by pictures, which were assumed to evoke primarily valuation by feeling, or by dots, which were assumed to evoke primarily valuation by calculation. When valuing by feeling, whether one or four animals was to be saved did not influence people's donation decisions, indicating scope insensitivity. In contrast, when valuing by calculation, people were willing to donate more to save four than to save one animal, indicating scope sensitivity. Thus, people were insensitive to scope when valuing by feeling, but not when valuing by calculation.

Together, research on psychic numbing and on valuation by feeling versus calculation yields the controversial and somewhat troubling prediction that increasing scope sensitivity by encouraging people to attend and give weight to information about the objective scope of human suffering may actually undermine people's willingness to donate by undermining emotions. Preliminary support for this suggestion comes from a series of experiments in which participants in a study of the identifiable victim effect were informed about the effect, and admonished to avoid it (Small, Loewenstein, & Slovic, 2007). In response to learning about the identifiable victim effect, participants who were forewarned about it and encouraged to avoid it decreased, rather than increased, the amount they donated; the behavior of participants in the statistical victim condition was unchanged. This pattern suggests that encouraging people to be on guard against biased behavior, which may encourage them to decide in a more calculating way, undermined their emotionally induced desire to donate. The results of research on the identifiable victim effect, psychic numbing, and valuation by feeling versus calculation indicates that people donate more to alleviate emotionally evocative than nonevocative human suffering, but that informing people about this tendency may undermine their overall likelihood of donating.

Given this conclusion, those in the business of persuading people to donate might consider encouraging people to think more emotionally about large-scale suffering rather than encouraging people to think in a more calculating way about human suffering. Indeed, the role of attention and mental imagery are important psychological contributors to increased emotional reactions to single identified victims or victims that are similar to the perceiver (Dickert & Slovic, 2009; Loewenstein & Small, 2007; Slovic, 2007). Making it easy for people to mentally imagine and to focus their attention on victims in large-scale suffering might facilitate emotional reactions, for example, by raising awareness of the 38,000 annual handgun deaths represented by piling up 38,000 pairs of shoes, or by helping comprehend the magnitude of the Holocaust by displaying a collection of six million paper clips, with each clip representing the loss of one life (Schroeder & Schroeder-Hildebrand, 2004; both examples described in Slovic, 2007). Research conducted in our lab, however, indicates that even when large-scale human suffering is conveyed in an emotionally evocative way, people still exhibit a disproportionate response to human suffering that happens to arouse immediate rather than previous emotions, which can contribute to scope insensitivity.

Immediacy Bias

If decisions to donate to alleviate human suffering are influenced by the emotional reactions to the sources of suffering, then to understand donation decisions we also need to understand where those emotional reactions come from and how people perceive them. We have recently examined how people perceive the intensity of their emotional reactions when they experience a sequence of emotions that are of approximately equal intensity (Van Boven, White, & Huber, 2009). We found that people tend to perceive their immediate emotions as more intense than their previous emotions, even when the emotional experiences were of equal intensity. For example, when presented with a series of emotionally evocative pictures, people perceive as more intense whichever picture happens to be immediately presented.

This *immediacy bias* in emotion perception seems to occur for two reasons. One is that immediate emotions exert greater influence over attention than previous emotions, capturing and holding people's attention, which naturally makes immediate emotions seem more intense. A second reason is that information about immediate emotions is more cognitively available than information about previous emotions. Because people use the availability of information about emotions to perceive emotional intensity, the greater availability of information about immediate emotions makes them seem more intense than previous emotions.

Importantly, the immediacy bias in emotion perception produces similar patterns in other emotionally influenced judgments. Perceptions of terrorist threats, for instance, have been shown to be influenced by the fear and anxiety evoked by those threats, independent of the objective likelihood or severity of those threats (Lerner, Gonzalez, Small, & Fischhoff, 2003; Loewenstein et al. 2001; Slovic, 1987; McGraw, Todorov, & Kunreuther, 2009; Sunstein, 2003). The emotional nature of perceived terrorist threats implies that the immediacy bias in emotion perception would produce an immediacy bias in terrorist risk perceptions. Indeed, we found that people tend to perceive terrorist threats that happen to arouse their immediate fear and anxiety as more dangerous and risky compared with threats that happen to have aroused previous fear and anxiety (Van Boven et al., 2009, Study 5).

We recently tested whether people might also exhibit an immediacy bias in perceptions of emotional reactions to human suffering, and whether this immediacy bias in perceived emotions might produce an immediacy bias in donation decisions. That is, we examined whether people might be more likely to donate resources to alleviate human suffering that happens to arouse immediate emotion than to human suffering that happened to have aroused previous emotion. In one test of this prediction, participants watched (in random order) two short films obtained from Doctors Without Borders about two different crises, separated by 20 minutes. The film clips, both of which were emotionally evocative, were about Niger and Sudan, describing famine, malnutrition, and disease. Directly after viewing the second clip, participants were asked to make ratings of how deserving each crisis was for receiving humanitarian aid. Consistent with the immediacy bias, participants perceived as more deserving whichever crisis they happened to have learned about second and aroused immediate emotions. And when asked to allocate a $3.00 donation between the two crises, most participants (67%) chose to donate more money to the humanitarian crisis they learned about second.

Another study provided a conceptual replication of this pattern, and illustrated how the immediacy bias in donation decisions can contribute to scope insensitivity. Participants first viewed a short film about human suffering in one of two African countries, either Niger or Angola. The film was accompanied by a description that provided clear information about the objective scope (in terms of mortality rates) of the humanitarian crisis: "each year, approximately 180,000 (or 120,000) (1.8% [or 1.2%] of the actual population) people die because of malnutrition and disease." After a delay of approximately 20 minutes, participants then viewed a film about whichever country they had not previously learned about, accompanied by a short description stating that either a larger or smaller number of people were dying in the second crisis. We thus manipulated experimentally whether the immediate or previous crisis was the deadlier one. Importantly, when participants were later asked to recall the mortality rates of the two crises, a clear majority (75%) correctly recalled which crisis was deadlier, indicating that the manipulation of scope magnitude was quite successful.

Consistent with our initial study, participants perceived whichever crisis they happened to learn about second as more deserving, and reported their emotional reactions to that crisis as more intense compared with the first crisis they learned about. The tendency to perceive the second crisis as more deserving and upsetting emerged independent of information about which crisis was deadlier (see Figure 11.1). We also asked participants to put their judgments into action by asking them "to write a letter to one of their state senators to draw attention to one of

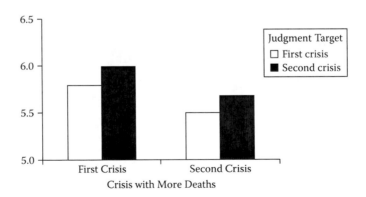

Figure 11.1   Participants' reactions after learning about the second crisis. Reactions are displayed to the first and second crisis as a function of the crises' deadliness. Measures are composites of three highly correlated variables, including judged deservingness, intensity of emotional reactions, and upsetness (ranging from 1 to 7 where 7 indicates higher deservingness, more intense, 2nd, and upset reactions).

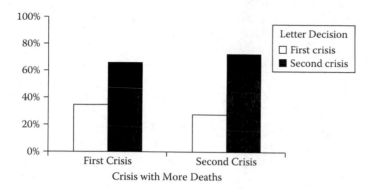

Figure 11.2   Percentage of participants who decide to write a letter about the first or the second crisis as a function of which crisis was deadlier.

the locations you learned about," after reminding them that they would be able to review all the materials about the crises provided in the experiment. As predicted, and consistent with their judgments, most participants (69%) chose to write a letter about the humanitarian crisis they had just learned about, independent of which crisis was objectively deadlier (see Figure 11.2).° Whether or not participants correctly recalled which crisis was deadlier did not significantly moderate their donation decisions, consistent with scope insensitivity.

In sum, these two studies, as well as several others described later, indicate that just as people perceive their immediate emotional experiences as more intense than previous emotional experiences, they also perceive humanitarian crises that happen to arouse immediate emotions as more deserving of aid than crises that happened to have aroused previous emotions. This immediacy bias in the perceived deservingness of humanitarian crises leads people to donate more money and take more action to alleviate humanitarian suffering that happens to arouse immediate emotions. This immediacy bias in donation decisions occurs independent of information (that people accurately recall) about which humanitarian crisis is deadlier, further illustrating people's scope insensitivity.

INTERVENING TO DONATE DIFFERENTLY

Although emotion's influence on donation decisions is undoubtedly sensible and desirable in many situations, there are many other situations in which people might prefer to donate differently. Emotional arousal can often be a reliable, accurate indicator of suffering's objective severity and urgency: people feel more intense

---

° Interestingly, upon hearing the procedure of this study, some critics have suggested that the difference in scope (180,000 versus 120,000 annual deaths) is ignored because of its relatively small size. Frankly, we find it astounding that 60,000 annual deaths might be characterized (by either audience members or participants) as "small." In any event, the point is moot given that participants clearly recall which crisis is deadlier, and we presume that, all else equal, people would prefer to take costless action to prevent 60,000 annual deaths than to not prevent 60,000 annual deaths.

distress when others' suffering is more severe and dire. However, emotional arousal can be influenced by factors independent of, if not in opposition to, objective severity and urgency of human suffering, as illustrated by studies of scope insensitivity. In such cases, people might prefer that donation decisions—both their own and others—be based on objective severity and urgency more than on immediate emotional reactions. In one recent illustration of this preference, we described to people decisions made by others either based primarily on emotional information rather than information about scope, or on information about scope rather than emotional information (Huber and Van Boven, 2010). People evaluated emotion-based decisions less favorably, of lower quality, compared with scope-based decisions. Such evaluations imply that people intuitively believe that donation decisions should be based more on objective information about scope rather than subjective emotions.

If people would prefer to make donation decisions differently, based more on objective information than on emotional information, how can they be helped to do so? Research on the identifiable victim effect, discussed earlier, implies that it is not sufficient to simply inform people that their donation decisions are highly emotional. Doing so can lead people to donate less overall than to donate in a less emotional, more analytical manner.

Given that people often prefer to donate differently, but that informing people about scope insensitivity may not change donation behavior in a desired manner, we consider two broad types of donation decision interventions: externally focused interventions versus internally focused interventions. In brief, we define *external interventions* as those involving changes to the context or structure in which a decision is made, for instance, by changing the timing or incentive structure of a decision; *internal interventions*, in contrast, are based on people's internally generated beliefs about how to manage their own decisions, for instance, by more carefully monitoring the degree to which their decisions correspond with their personal beliefs about how to make donation decisions normatively. After reviewing several types of external and internal interventions, we conclude that although both external and internal interventions can influence donation decisions, internal interventions, on balance, may often be both more feasible and desirable.

External Interventions

External interventions are those that impose constraints on the way people make decisions. External interventions are designed to decrease the influence of (presumably) undesirable factors such as emotions while increasing the influence of (presumably) desired factors such as objective information about scope. Broadly speaking, external interventions seek to change the "choice architecture" of the way decisions are made (Thaler & Sunstein, 2008). For instance, one might require people to read about a broad range of potential donation recipients and to explicitly allocate donations of $0 to those recipients whom they might otherwise implicitly choose to donate nothing. Such a change in the choice structure would force people to consider all possible donation recipients when, left to their own devices, they might consider only those potential recipients who happen to arouse immediate emotions.

A common approach for external interventions is to change the timing of decisions. We have examined two external interventions that change the timing of donation decisions, reducing the influence of immediate emotions. One intervention is to impose a delay after learning about humanitarian suffering and when the donation decision is made; the other is to ask people to decide sequentially, rather than post hoc, or after the fact, how much to donate to each of a set of human suffering.

Delayed donation decisions. Several researchers and policy makers have suggested a "cooling off" period for decisions that might be unduly influenced by immediate emotion (Mischel, & Ayduk, 2004; Wilson, & Brekke, 1994; Wilson, Centerbar, & Brekke, 2002). The idea is that when one's decisions have been unduly swayed by emotions—as when one responds to front-page newspaper coverage of abandoned puppies by donating to help a handful of cute canines instead of donating to feed several villages of malnourished children—that allowing time for emotion to subside will reduce the tendency to donate more to causes that happen to arouse immediate emotion.

We tested the possibility that a delay would diminish the immediacy bias in donation decisions, discussed earlier (Huber et al., 2010). In the study in which participants learned about human suffering in two African countries and decided about which country to write a letter, some people were asked one day later rather than immediately after learning about the humanitarian crises to decide about which to write a letter. Consistent with other research on "cooling off" effects, people who made their decision after a day's delay were equally likely to write about the first crisis they had learned about as they were to write about the second crisis they had learned about (see Figure 11.3). Consistent with their decisions, people also judged the first and second crises they learned about to be approximately equally deserving, emotionally evocative, and upsetting.

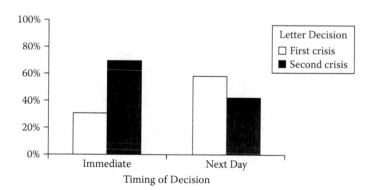

Figure 11.3 Percentage of participants who decided to write a letter about the first or the second crisis as a function of whether this decision was made immediately after learning about the crises (first day) or the next day. On the first day, the percentage of participants who choose to write about the second crisis (relative to the first crisis) is significantly greater. On the second day, there is no significant difference between the percentage of participants who choose to write about the second compared with the first crisis.

Introducing a day's delay thus eliminated the immediacy bias in donation decisions, and would seem a straightforward way to reduce immediate emotion's influence. There is a complication, however, in that introducing a delay is effective only if people have not previously made a (tentative) decision. Some of the participants in our study indicated which crisis they would write a letter about both immediately after learning about both humanitarian crises and one day afterward. Unlike those participants who only made their letter writing decision one day after learning about both crises, those who made their decision both immediately *and* the next day were more likely to select the second crisis they learned about (the one that had previously been associated with immediate emotions). Introducing a delay thus reduced the role of immediate emotion only when people had not previously made a tentative decision. We suspect this pattern simply reflects people's desire to be consistent, not to change their minds—or to be seen changing their minds—about which crisis they want to call attention to. From the perspective of intervening to change donation decisions, this pattern implies that decreasing emotion's role by delaying decisions must include a "pure" delay and prevent tentative decisions.

Sequential vs. post hoc donation decisions. In our studies of the immediacy bias in humanitarian donation decisions, people chose to donate more to the final humanitarian crisis in a series of humanitarian crises because the final crisis happened to be the one that aroused immediate emotions. Our analysis of the immediacy bias—that people tend to donate more to whichever crisis happens to arouse immediate emotions—implies that the tendency to donate more money to the final crisis in a sequence would be diminished if people made sequential donation decisions. In sequential donation decisions, people would make decisions directly after learning about each in a sequence of crises rather than after learning about the entire sequence. Allowing people to make donation decisions directly after learning about each crisis would allow each crisis to garner proportionally larger donations.

We tested this prediction in an experiment in which people viewed short (approximately 3 minutes each) films about a series of four humanitarian crises, each separated by a brief delay. The crises included disease and hunger in Angola, an emergency feeding program in Niger, AIDS and antiretroviral drugs in Malawi, and tuberculosis in Sudan. The order of the films was counterbalanced to avoid order effects. In the post hoc decision condition, participants decided after viewing all four films how they wanted to allocate $95, which was selected to avoid an easy four-way split among the four crises. They were told that one person's allocation would be randomly selected and actually implemented. Replicating our earlier findings, people allocated disproportionally more money to the crisis described in the final film in the series compared with the crises they had learned about earlier in the series (see the dark line in Figure 11.4). The allocation to the last crisis they learned about was significantly larger than the allocation to the average of the first three crises, which did not differ significantly from each other. Another group of participants viewed the same four films, but rather than making their allocation decision after viewing all four films, they made an allocation decision after viewing each of the four films, knowing that they had a total of $95 to allocate among four crises. As expected, these participants in the sequential allocation decision condition did not allocate disproportionally more money to the crisis summarized in the final film compared with the crises they had learned about earlier in the series (see the light grey line in Figure 11.4).

In fact, the only allocations in the sequential allocation condition that are statistically significantly different from each other are the allocations to the first and the allocation to the fourth crisis. Overall, however, there is a linear trend in the sequential allocation condition. This "primacy effect" is consistent with previous research indicating that when people sequentially allocate charitable contributions to a series of causes, they tend to allocate more to the first cause they encounter (Payne, Schkade, Desvousges, & Aultman, 2000). Our interpretation of primacy effects in sequential allocation decisions is that they occur because allocations are based on a combination of immediate emotional reaction to the initial causes they encounter, and a dwindling supply of available resources, which prevents people from allocating equal amounts to subsequent emotionally evocative causes.

The tendency for people to exhibit primacy effects when making sequential allocation decisions highlights two important facts. First, in both sequential and post hoc allocations, people appear to respond to their immediate emotions, aroused either by the first or final cause they encounter. Second, and what is more important, a strong response to immediate emotions implies that people are relatively insensitive to information about the scope of suffering, given that their behavior can be so strongly influenced by order of presentation and decision timing.

Summary. Our studies indicate that changing the timing of donation decisions can moderate at least one influence of emotion on donation decisions: the immediacy bias. Introducing a delay decreases the immediacy bias (as long as people have not previously made a tentative decision), as does asking people to make sequential rather than post hoc allocation decisions. The results of our studies, however, suggest

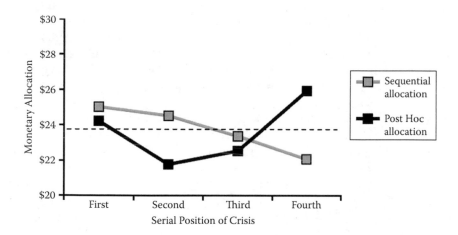

Figure 11.4   Participants' allocations to each of the four crises as a function of making sequential allocations after learning about each crisis, or making post hoc allocations after learning about all four crises. The dashed reference line represents an equal distribution of the $95 to each of the four crises ($23.75 to each crisis).

three reasons to question the feasibility of external interventions to help people be less influenced by emotions and more influenced by information about the objective scope of human suffering. First, although delaying decisions decreased people's tendency to allocate more to the second source of suffering they learned about, there was no evidence that delaying decisions increased the influence of information about the scope of suffering in their decisions. Although people's decisions were less influenced by immediate emotion, their decisions were not significantly more influenced by information about scope. This conclusion is based on the finding that even though a majority of participants (67%) could correctly recall which crisis was deadlier on the second day, this information did not influence their decisions—even though their immediate emotional reactions were less intense. Second, when implementing a delayed donation decision, it may be difficult to prevent people from making tentative decisions, which our study implied would prevent the effect of delay.

Finally, and perhaps most importantly, external interventions to alter the timing of donation decisions require, well, external intervention. They are thus only feasible insofar as some external agent is motivated and able to change the structure of decisions. External interventions thus do not help people who wish to alter their donation decisions on their own accord. External intervention may also raise concerns—some legitimate, others overblown—about personal freedom versus paternalism in deciding whom to make charitable donations to (Thaler & Sunstein, 2008). These three questions suggest—to us, at least—that external intervention may be of limited effectiveness and feasibility. Such concerns have led us to start investigating what we refer to as *internal interventions* that encourage people to monitor and change their own donation decisions.

Internal Interventions

Internally focused interventions are those that encourage people to monitor and modify their own decision processes, rather than having these changes in decision process externally imposed by altering timing, incentives, or other aspects of "choice architecture" (e.g., Thaler & Sunstein, 2008) and other external interventions. We have started to investigate various internally focused interventions to encourage people to make decisions about charitable aid donations, in addition to other types of decisions, in a way that better corresponds with their personal beliefs about the way such decisions should normatively be made. Specifically, we have begun investigating whether asking people to reflect, prior to making donation decisions, on how people intuitively believe donation decisions should be made changes the way people subsequently make donation decisions. We refer to this procedure as creating a state of *mindfulness* (Langer, 1989), a state characterized by heightened awareness of personal beliefs about normative decision making, conscious monitoring, and control of decision processes. Reflecting on one's beliefs about how decisions should be made changes the decision process (e.g., the weighting of different types of information) only to the degree that people's personal beliefs are different from what people would have done otherwise.

Internally focused, mindfulness interventions such as those we have begun to explore should be successful when four conditions are met. First, when people make decisions in ways that, after (mindful) reflection, they would prefer to have made differently, such as when people make donation decisions based on emotionally evocative appeals rather than on objective information about the scope of suffering. Second, that one reason people make decisions in ways they would prefer to avoid is because they fail to notice or attend to the discrepancy between their actual decision processes and how they would prefer to make decisions, such as when people's decisions are overly influenced by focal, salient, emotional information. Third, that people can perceive (or make reasonably accurate guesses), which aspects of their decision making do not meet their ideals, such as when people perceive that they are more influenced by emotion and less influenced by scope than they would prefer to be. Finally, that people have the ability to correct, revise, and otherwise alter their decision processes.

Our mindfulness manipulations in donation decisions build on preliminary results of mindfulness manipulations in two decision domains with slightly different characteristics than the decisions we have discussed here (Huber & Van Boven, 2010). In all the studies summarized in the following sections, we asked people simply to think about their personal beliefs and to indicate how much they think they should rely on different types of information when making their decisions. We refer to this intervention as internally focused because, ultimately, the beliefs that people bring to mind are their own internally generated beliefs, instead of being provided externally by some objective rules or norms. Whereas choice architecture, such as the external interventions discussed earlier, are designed to influence people's decisions in a particular direction, internal mindfulness interventions simply influence people's decisions in ways that they prefer to be influenced.

As an example of the effectiveness of this mindfulness manipulation, consider a study of the role of partisan politics versus personal attitudes in policy evaluation (Huber & Van Boven, 2010). People read a summarized "cap and trade" policy to mitigate global warming. The policy was strongly supported, depending on random assignment, by either Democrats or Republicans. We found, replicating previous research (Cohen, 2003), that participants in a control condition evaluated the policy primarily along partisan lines with relatively little influence of people's personal attitudes toward the global warming crisis, which we had measured with an internally reliable, multidimensional measure of attitudes toward global warming. In another condition, participants were first asked to reflect on how they thought policies should be evaluated and, specifically, to rate how much they thought policies should be evaluated based on partisan considerations (such as which party supports the policy) versus people's personal attitudes toward policy-relevant issues; participants in the control condition were asked these questions after evaluating the policy. People tended to think that policies should be evaluated based on personal attitudes toward policy-relevant issues more than on partisan considerations—an opinion that did not vary as a function of whether people evaluated the policy before or after they reported how they thought policies should be evaluated. Importantly, however, people who were made mindful of their ideal policy evaluation procedures before evaluating the policy were less influenced by partisan considerations (i.e., whether Democrats or Republicans supported the policy) and were more influenced by their personal attitudes about the global warming crisis, compared with people in the control condition. Making people mindful of how much they personally believe partisan politics and personal attitudes should normatively influence policy evaluation thus led them to evaluate policies in a manner that more closely matched their personal normative beliefs.

In another study, we examined whether making people mindful of the decision process would influence the way they made decisions in the domain of romantic relationships, where emotions would be seen as relatively more (rather than less) normatively desirable (Huber & Van Boven, 2009). University undergraduates were asked to consider two (hypothetical) people with whom they might potentially go on a date. One person had relatively strong "objective" status appeal, a pre-law student who was currently applying for well-renowned law schools, whereas the other person had relatively weaker status appeal, an education major who intended to be a high school teacher. However, people were asked to imagine that although they enjoy spending time with the prospective lawyer, they felt more emotionally pulled toward the prospective high school teacher. Half of the participants were asked to reflect on how they thought the decision of whom to date should be made. Specifically, they were asked to indicate how much their decision should be influenced by their feelings and by extrinsic attributes such as career status. They subsequently decided with whom they would go on a date. The other half of participants were asked these questions after they made their dating decision. People who had first reflected on how they should make this decision were more influenced by their beliefs about how romantic decisions should be made compared with people who reflected on how they should make dating decisions after having made their decision. When deciding after reflection, participants who had strong beliefs that feelings are more important than extrinsic attributes had a stronger preference for the person they felt more emotionally pulled toward compared with participants who thought that both emotions and extrinsic attributes are important. Again, simply, making people mindful of how they personally believed a dating decision should be made led them to make a decision in a manner that more closely corresponded with their personal beliefs.

These two preliminary studies of policy evaluation and romantic choices imply that making people mindful of how they personally believe judgments and decisions should be made can help them make donation decisions in ways that more closely correspond with their personal normative beliefs. Notice that with such mindfulness manipulations, the standard against which decision processes are evaluated is not externally imposed, but by decision makers themselves. Such self-imposed standards may avoid many of the concerns associated with externally imposed standards.

The results of these studies also imply that people can help themselves make better donation decisions by becoming more mindful of their own decision standards. That is, making people mindful of how they would personally prefer to make donation decisions should lead them to make donation decisions in ways that correspond more closely with their personal preferences. To test this possibility, we asked participants to make (hypothetical) donation decisions in which they allocated charitable contributions between two humanitarian crises, suffering from malaria in Ghana or suffering from tuberculosis in Malawi. The number of people who were affected by each of the diseases was manipulated and counterbalanced such that for half the participants, malaria was the objectively more severe crisis because more people were affected; for the other half of the participants, tuberculosis was the objectively more severe crisis (Huber & Van Boven, 2009).

We sought to make people mindful of their personal beliefs about the importance of objective scope information when making charitable donation decisions. People reported how much they personally thought donation decisions should be influenced by the crises' objective scope of suffering and by the emotionality associated with each crisis. Depending on random assignment, people reported their personal beliefs about how donation decisions should be made either before or after making their donation decision. Not surprisingly, most participants (88%) thought that the objective scope of the crises should be more or equally influential than emotionality of the crises (55% and 33%, respectively), whereas a distinct minority (12%) thought that objective scope should be less influential than emotionality. Importantly, people's beliefs about how donation decisions should be made did not vary depending on whether people reported those beliefs before or after making their decisions.

What *did* vary by condition, however, was how much people's decisions corresponded with their personal beliefs about how they should make donation decisions. People who reported how they thought donation decisions should be made before actually making those decisions behaved in a way that corresponded with their personal beliefs. That is, people who thought that objective scope should be relatively more influential than emotionality made decisions based relatively more on objective scope, compared with people who thought that objective scope should be relatively less than or equally influential as emotionality (see Figure 11.5). In contrast, the association between beliefs about how donation decisions should be

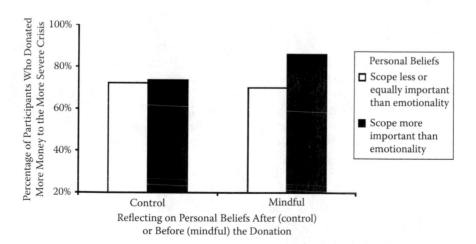

Figure 11.5   Percentage of participants who donated more money to the more severe crisis as a function of whether they reflected on personal beliefs after (control) or before (mindful) the donation. Participants whose personal belief is that scope is less or equally important than emotionality are compared with participants who believe that scope is more important than emotionality.

made and how donation decisions were actually made was substantially lower among those who reported their personal beliefs after making their donation decisions. The degree to which people's personal beliefs about how they should make donation decisions corresponded with their decision was thus larger when they were first made mindful of how they personally believed such decisions should be made.

These results highlight the potentially powerful influence of internally focused interventions that make people mindful of how they personally believe they should make decisions before they actually make decisions. To the degree that such internally focused manipulations really change the way people make decisions—and we recognize that additional research is needed to draw such a conclusion—they may provide an appealing, feasible alternative to the externally focused manipulations described earlier. The internally focused, mindfulness manipulation we have been developing increases the influence of objective scope information; can be implemented in the immediate context of a decision (whereas delaying a decision cannot); and, most importantly, relies on people's personal beliefs about how to best make decisions rather than imposing an outsider's belief about how such decision should be made. That is, internally focused interventions rely on people's own standards about how best to make judgments and decisions, rather than trying to convince people to adopt some externally provided standard.

CONCLUSION AND PRACTICAL IMPLICATIONS

A long-standing observation among those who study judgment and decision making is that people often think and choose in ways that can be collectively problematic, and that do not reflect people's personal preferences for how they should make judgments and decisions. This observation is applicable to the domain of donation decisions. Donation decision research indicates that people often respond readily and forcefully to the emotions evoked by worthy causes while showing little or no response to information about the objective scope of causes. Given that people would often prefer to make donation decisions in different ways, researchers have begun to examine ways to encourage people to donate based less on emotionality and more on information about the objective scope of suffering and need.

In this chapter, we distinguished two broad classes of interventions: externally focused interventions that lead people to make less emotional donations by changing the timing or "architecture" of the donation decision, versus internally focused interventions that lead people to make donation decisions based on their personal beliefs about how such decisions ought to be made. In our research, we found that externally focused interventions can reduce the impact of immediate emotions on donation decisions by either delaying the timing of donation decisions or by forcing people to allocate donations sequentially among various causes rather than after learning about all the causes.

In terms of practical implications for charity organizations, foundations, and policy makers, these findings suggest that a "cooling off" period after people learned about humanitarian crises is advisable if one wants to remove the effect of immediate emotions associated with humanitarian crises. This might be desirable in a situation where an organization needs to increase donations to mitigate chronic suffering in African countries, but the situational context is such that an immediate humanitarian crisis that is happening elsewhere (e.g., the Indian Ocean tsunami in 2004). Without immediate emotions aroused by one specific crisis, we suspect that people would give equal, presumably fair, amounts to the most severe crises people know about. On the other hand, if an organization is interested in raising donations for one specific region or crisis, then they might keep the time between learning about the crisis and making a donation or monetary allocation as short as possible.

Another scenario to consider is when, for instance at the end of the year, people decide how much they will donate to charitable organizations. If people then decide to look for organizations with the intention to give a portion of their total donation to each of these organizations, then it really matters when people make these decisions: if they learn about all the possible organizations first and then make a decision, it is likely that they will give most to whichever organization they learned about last—a situation that charities can hardly control. The alternative is a sequential allocation where people give to each organization immediately after they have learned about it. This can be done by making it easy for people to donate, for example, by allowing them to donate online or through automatic payment plans. That way, organizations have a good chance of receiving more equal amounts of monetary donations.

Internally focused interventions rest on the assumption that people often have relatively clear beliefs about how best to make donation decisions, but often make donation decisions mindlessly, without reference to their personal beliefs. Our internally focused mindfulness manipulation, in which people are asked to reflect on their personal beliefs about how decisions should be made before they actually make those decisions, appears to encourage people to make decisions that more closely correspond with their beliefs. The potential strength of such interventions is that they rely on people to monitor and correct their own decision processes, rather than imposing decision processes upon them.

Internally focused interventions may also be particularly appealing as a means of avoiding regret about how one had made decisions (e.g., Connolly & Zeelenberg, 2002). By holding themselves to their own standards by being mindful of their personal beliefs about normatively appropriate decision processes, people become the arbiters of how much they allow more fact-based or more emotion-based information to influence their own behavior. This might be especially relevant when it comes to making donation decisions.

Especially in the domain of charitable giving, a mindfulness-based manipulation that leads people to reflect on their beliefs about how they ought to make their decisions could be useful and easy to implement. Most people agree that severity of suffering should matter more than (or at least equal to) emotional reactions to crises. Right before people make a donation decision, the organization could provide a simple statement that encourages a mindful decision. Presumably, for a majority of people, this reminder would lead to higher donations to the more severe suffering. People rarely have the resources to help all those who suffer. By making decisions in a way that reflects their personal beliefs about how such decisions ought to be made, people can at least help in the best way possible.

REFERENCES

Batson, C. D. (1990). How social an animal? The human capacity for caring. *American Psychologist, 45*, 336–346.

Cohen, G. L. (2003). Party over policy: The dominating impact of group influence on political beliefs. *Journal of Personality and Social Psychology, 85*, 808–822.

Connolly, T., & Zeelenberg, M. (2002). Regret in decision making. *Current Directions in Psychological Science, 11*, 212–216.

Dickert, S., & Slovic, P. (2009). Attentional mechanisms in the generation of sympathy. *Judgment and Decision Making, 4*, 297–306.

Fetherstonhaugh, D., Slovic, P., Johnson, S. M., & Friedrich, J. (1997). Insensitivity to the value of human life: A study of psychophysical numbing. *Journal of Risk and Uncertainty, 14*, 283–300.

Hsee, C. K., & Rottenstreich, Y. (2004). Music, pandas, and muggers: On the affective psychology of value. *Journal of Experimental Psychology: General, 133*, 23–30.

Huber, M., & Van Boven, L. (2009). Decision making and introspecting on prescriptive beliefs. Unpublished raw data, University of Colorado at Boulder.

Huber, M., & Van Boven, L. (2010). Reflecting on decision processes: How introspection can improve judgment and decision making. Unpublished manuscript, University of Colorado at Boulder.

Huber, M., Van Boven, L., McGraw, A. P., Johnson-Graham, L. (2010). Whom to help? Immediacy bias in judgments and decisions about humanitarian aid. Unpublished manuscript, University of Colorado at Boulder.

Kahneman, D. (2003). A perspective on judgment and choice: Mapping bounded rationality. *American Psychologist, 58*, 697–720.

Kahneman, D., Ritov, I., & Schkade, D. (1999). Economic preference or attitude expression? An analysis of dollar response to public issues. *Journal of Risk and Uncertainty, 19*, 203–235.

Kahneman, D., Schkade, D., & Sunstein, C. (1998). Shared outrage and erratic awards: The psychology of punitive damages. *Journal of Risk and Uncertainty, 16*, 49–86.

Kogut, T., & Ritov, I. (2005a). The "identified victim" effect: An identified group, or a single individual? *Journal of Behavioral Decision Making, 18*, 157–167.

Kogut, T., & Ritov, I. (2005b). The singularity effect of identified victims in separate and joint evaluations. *Organizational Behavior and Human Decision Processes, 97*, 106–116.

Langer, E. J. (1989). *Mindfulness*. Reading, MA: Addison-Wesley Publishing Company.

Lerner, J. S., Gonzalez, R. M., Small, D. A., & Fischhoff, B. (2003). Emotion and perceived risks of terrorism: A national field experiment. *Psychological Science, 14*, 144–150.

Loewenstein, G. (1996). Out of control: Visceral influences on behavior. *Organizational Behavior and Human Decision Processes, 65*, 272–292.

Loewenstein, G., & Small, D. (2007). The Scarecrow and the Tinman: The vicissitudes of human sympathy and caring. *Review of General Psychology, 11*, 112–126.

Loewenstein, G. F., Weber, E. U., Hsee, C. K., & Welch, N. (2001). Risk as feelings. *Psychological Bulletin, 127*, 267–286.

McGraw, A. P., Todorov, A., & Kunreuther, H. (2009). A policy maker's dilemma: Preventing blame or preventing terrorism. *Unpublished Manuscript.*

Metcalfe, J., & Mischel, W. (1999). A hot/cool-system analysis of delay of gratification: Dynamics of willpower. *Psychological Review, 106*, 3–19.

Mischel, W., & Ayduk, O. (2004). Willpower in a cognitive-affective processing system: The dynamics of delay of gratification. In R. F. Baumeister (Ed.), *Handbook of self-regulation: Research, theory, and applications* (pp. 99–129). New York: Guilford Press.

Payne, J. W., Schkade, D. A., Desvousges, W. H., & Aultman, C. (2000). Valuation of multiple environmental programs. *Journal of Risk & Uncertainty, 21*, 95–115.

Rottenstreich, Y., & Hsee, C. K. (2001). Money, kisses, and electric shocks: On the affective psychology of risk. *Psychological Science, 12*, 185–190.

Schroeder, P., & Schroeder-Hildebrand, D. (2004). *Six million paper clips: The making of a children's holocaust museum*. Minneapolis, MN: Kar-Ben Publishing.

Slovic, P. (1987). Perception of risk. *Science, 236*, 280–285.

Slovic, P. (2007). "If I look at the mass I will never act": Psychic numbing and genocide. *Judgment and Decision Making, 2*, 79–95.

Slovic, P., Finucane, M., Peters, E., & MacGregor, D. G. (2002). Rational actors or rational fools: Implications of the affect heuristic for behavioral economics. *The Journal of Socio-Economics, 31*, 329–342.

Small, D. A., & Loewenstein, G. (2003). Helping a victim or helping the victim: Altruism and identifiability. *Journal of Risk and Uncertainty, 26*, 5–16.

Small, D. A., Loewenstein, G., & Slovic, P. (2007). Sympathy and callousness: The impact of deliberative thought on donations to identifiable and statistical victims. *Organizational Behavior and Human Decision Processes, 102*, 143–153.

Sunstein, C. R. (2003). Terrorism and probability neglect. *Journal of Risk and Uncertainty, 26*, 121–136.

Thaler, R. H., & Sunstein, C. R. (2008). *Nudge: Improving decisions about health, wealth, and happiness*. New Haven, CT: Yale University Press.

Van Boven, L., White, K., & Huber, M. (2009). Immediacy bias in emotion perception: Current emotions seem more intense than previous emotions. *Journal of Experimental Psychology: General, 138*, 368–382.

Wilson, T. D., & Brekke, N. (1994). Mental contamination and mental correction: Unwanted influences on judgments and evaluations. *Psychological Bulletin, 116*, 117–142.

Wilson, T. D., Centerbar, D. B., & Brekke, N. (2002). Mental contamination and the debiasing problem. In T. Gilovich, D. Griffin & D. Kahneman (Eds.), *Heuristics and biases: The psychology of intuitive judgment* (pp. 185–200). New York: Cambridge University Press.

Section IV

Other Important Influences on Charitable Giving

12

The Benefits of Asking for Time

WENDY LIU

OVERVIEW

A n old adage says "Time is money." This phrase, so succinctly put by Benjamin
Franklin, highlights the generally held belief about the value of time in our
society. In the modern economy, money is the predominant currency of
exchange, and hence the depository and ultimate measure of wealth and value. Time,
on the other hand, is considered an economic good through its association with money.
From the perspective of an individual supplying labor, one can give time and effort in
exchange for a monetary compensation such as a salary, or a profit from one's ventures.
Further, a person could invest time in learning and acquiring resources to enhance
one's future earnings. From the perspective of an organization buying labor, it needs to
pay for the time and effort of its employees and contributors. Alternatively, if volunteers
contribute time for free, that can translate into savings in labor costs. Thus through its
intimate link with monetary payments, time becomes yet another economic resource.

For nonprofit organizations, the need for labor and money is ever present (West,
2004), and donations of both types are routinely requested. Generally speaking, nonprofit organizations' first priority tends to be to seek monetary donations
because such funds are the most fungible and useful. Requests for volunteering, on
the other hand, might be made depending on the organization's needs and usage of
labor. Thus, even though "time is money," a nonprofit organization may find itself
giving greater attention to raising money than to encouraging volunteering.

An interesting question arises, however, when we take a different, more donor-
oriented perspective. That is, from the view point of the donor—that is, potential
donors—how do they think about a charity's request for time versus a request for
money? What kinds of thought processes are involved? Further, does a time versus
a monetary request evoke the same kind of thoughts and, if different, what are the
consequences of these distinct thoughts?

In recent years, research in management and the social sciences has become
increasingly interested in understanding the mechanisms of philanthropy and

giving, particularly from a psychological perspective (e.g., Strahilevitz & Myers, 1998; Reed, Aquino, & Levy 2007; Slovic, 2007; Small & Simonsohn, 2008). In tandem, a significant body of work has been building in psychology and behavioral economics that examines people's behavior with respect to money and, more recently, time. Indeed, one of the most active areas of research currently is regarding the psychology of time (e.g., Trope & Liberman, 2003; Zauberman & Lynch, 2005; Soman, 2007; Mogilner & Aaker, 2009), shedding light on the important and unique role the concept of time plays in social cognition. The two streams of research, namely on giving and on time and money, have reached a confluence lately, yielding a number of intriguing studies that specifically examine the psychology of giving time versus money. Notably, Liu and Aaker (2008) demonstrated a Time-Ask Effect in fundraising, whereby people become more generous toward a charity when an initial request of time (versus money) donation is made. At the same time, another stream of research by DeVoe and Pfeffer (2007) focused on differences in people's attitudes toward giving time based on the nature of their occupation, creating a connection between giving time and money.

The main goal of this chapter is to review the latest advances in the study of the psychology of time and money, and specifically to present the new findings on the donation of time and money. The hope is that the insights revealed by these studies may help nonprofit organizations improve their effectiveness in fundraising and garnering public support.

The chapter is organized as follows. First, I will review the current literature on the psychology of time and money, first focusing on the mental accounting differences, and then extending the discussion to the broader psychological implications associated with thinking about time and money. Upon this backdrop, I next introduce the Time-Ask Effect (Liu & Aaker, 2008), before turning to the research on volunteerism and occupation (DeVoe & Pfeffer, 2007) as further discussion of the relationship between construal of money/time and giving. Finally, a summary section highlights the implications of these research findings for practitioners in nonprofit organizations, as well as for potential donors.

THE PSYCHOLOGY OF TIME VERSUS MONEY

Mental Accounting of Time and Money

Mental accounting refers to how individuals and households keep track of their economic transactions (Thaler, 1985). More specifically, it addresses the implicit psychological processes underlying people's valuation of economic resources and products. As such, mental accounting takes on a behavioral perspective that is often in conflict with theoretical assumptions made about human behavior in standard economic models. A few of the classic violations of theoretical assumptions in economics include, for example, loss aversion (Kahneman & Tversky, 1979), attention to transaction utility, and the bracketing of spending episodes and categories, a violation of fungibility (Thaler, 1999).

Certainly it is not surprising that the bulk of the mental accounting literature studies people's valuation of money (in various forms such as cash or credit cards), as money *is* the predominant currency of exchange in our society. However, although money is the main economic resource people tend to deal with, it is not the only scarce resource in people's lives. Recently, a growing body of studies has begun to turn its attention to another common resource, namely the resource of time. The interesting question therein is, although the study of mental accounting (focused on money) tends to speak to economic resources in general, it is nevertheless possible that people may account for time differently than money. Hence the new waves of studies on time accounting typically pit time against money to examine how the two resources are similarly or differentially evaluated (e.g., Leclerc, Schmitt, & Dube, 1995; Soman 2001; Okada & Hoch, 2004). A number of converging insights have been uncovered in this endeavor, pointing to significant differences in the mental accounting of time versus money. For example, people tend to project greater *slack* (i.e., abundance) in their time (relative to money) in the future, thereby leading to differential discount rates for their future outlay of time versus money (Zauberman & Lynch, 2005). To illustrate, theoretically, on average people should be just as busy two weeks from now as they are today; they should also be just as rich or poor two weeks from now as today. However, Zauberman and Lynch's research finds that in fact people perceive that they will have more time and money in the future than they do today; but, importantly, this effect is significantly bigger for time than for money. That is, people are more optimistic about time than money in the future. This difference in forecasting of slack can lead to interesting patterns in consumer choice. For example, Soman (1998) found that for a coupon that offers a monetary rebate but takes significant time and effort to redeem, people will take this coupon into consideration when they make a purchase, but only if the coupon is to be redeemed in the future, rather than immediately. Thus unlike for money, when thinking about the present, time is scarce and valuable; however when thinking about the future, time becomes more abundant.

In another line of research, time and money have been found to also differ in their concreteness, whereby the valuation of time is typically more ambiguous than one's valuation of money. This can also lead to discrepancies in behavior with respect to spending time versus money. For example, the ambiguity in the valuation of time can lead to more flexible justifications of expenditures of time than money (Okada & Hoch, 2004). Participants in one study were asked to consider a scenario in which they had to spend either 4 hours of time helping with an experiment (time investment), or $50 (money investment), in order to acquire a dinner coupon for a local restaurant. The experiment then manipulated whether the dining experience was a positive or negative one when using the coupon. It was found that when time was spent to acquire the dinner, people were less sensitive to whether the meal was good or not, compared to when money was spent to acquire the dinner. In particular, when the meal was good, those who spent money were significantly happier than those who spent time; in contrast, when the meal was bad, those who spent money were significantly less happy than those who spent time. Thus it appears people are more sensitive to the return on their money than on their time.

In sum, in both the perception of one's level of resources (particularly in the future), and in the evaluation of specific outcomes, people seem to account for time and money in very different ways. However, the findings did not stop there. Building on these findings, further studies are beginning to reveal that mental accounting is only one part of the overall picture of how individuals respond to time and money. Most interestingly, new studies have emerged showing that the psychological impact of thinking about time and/or money can go beyond the valuation of the time and money itself, to the extent that they can bring about fundamental changes in the person's mindset and thought process.

The Broader Impact of Thinking About Time and Money

One of the most telling studies done by Vohs, Mead, and Goode (2006) demonstrates the startling shift in behavior when people are merely minimally exposed to the concept of money. Participants in the experiment were either primed with money-related words or simply saw a stack of Monopoly money. The presence of these money-related concepts was sufficient to induce a change in behavior. Specifically, when these participants then worked on solving a difficult puzzle, they were less likely to ask for help. Instead, they persisted longer in working on the puzzle themselves. The researchers argue that the mere priming with the concept of money activated a set of psychological constructs associated with money. In particular, money is associated with instrumentality toward goals and self-efficacy in reaching those goals. That is, thinking about money leads to a mindset that focuses on achieving one's goals through one's own means. Taking it one step further, a follow-up experiment showed that when primed with money, in addition to being less likely to seek help from others, people were also less willing to volunteer their time to help others. Thus, people not only want to be self-sufficient when the concept of money is activated, they also expect others to be the same way. Hence money seems to affect people's behavior not just in purchase transactions, but also in a broader set of contexts. In particular, it can change the general mindset of the person, making the person more focused on instrumental utility toward goals and on reaching these goals on one's own.

An interesting question thus emerges: if money creates a self-centered and goal-focused mindset, what kind of mindset does thinking about time bring forth? A number of existing research streams in psychology can help shed light on this question. These research findings generally point to the notion that the consideration of time, particularly how to spend one's time, may activate an emotional mindset, focused on the emotional meaning of events. First, the consumption of time is by definition an experience. Both real and imagined, experiences engender feelings and emotions (Schwarz & Clore, 1996). Thus, thoughts of spending time doing an activity naturally evoke feelings, making the emotional impact of the event salient. Consequently, people may be more motivated to attain positive emotions when they think about spending time. Second, recent research suggests that experiences (e.g., spending time doing an activity) are more directly associated with feeling happy than are nonexperiential, material acquisitions. In a series of studies, Van Boven and Gilovich (2003) showed that an experience, such as going to a show, created greater happiness than did consuming a material product of similar economic value. Third, emerging research suggests that the salience of the concept of time in life can activate goals of attaining emotional meaning (Carstensen, Isaacowitz, & Charles, 1999; Liu & Aaker, 2007). For example, when young adults are made to consider their entire life course (e.g., through witnessing a cancer death of a close other, or considering life fifty years later), they are more likely to make choices that are emotionally meaningful in the long run (Liu and Aaker, 2007). Taken together, diverse research streams seem to converge on the notion that while the thought of money creates a focus on instrumentality and self-efficacy toward goals, thinking about time creates a focus on the emotional meaning of events, and an emphasis on pursuing emotional satisfaction.

This insight becomes the impetus for the Time-Ask Effect research (Liu & Aaker, 2008), which examines the differential impact of thinking about donating money versus donating time to a charity on the individual's level of generosity. The Time-Ask Effect posits that by asking people to consider donating time for a charity, this thought about spending time can put people into an emotional mind-set that allows them to focus on the emotional significance of giving. As reviewed below, because giving is often driven by powerful emotions, fostering an emotional mindset toward giving in turn increases people's propensity to give.

The Emotions of Giving

Mounting research shows that perhaps the most powerful driver of individual giving is one's emotions (tax benefits aside). Such emotions can come in several dimensions, including sympathy and empathy (Batson, 1987; Small, Loewenstein, & Slovic 2007; Decety & Meyer, 2008), (the relief of) guilt (Strahilevitz & Meyers, 1998; de Hooge, Zeelenberg, & Breugelmans, 2007), and personal satisfaction and happiness from doing good (Kahneman, Diener, & Schwarz, 1999; Harbaugh, Mayr, & Burghart, 2007; Dunn, Aknin, & Norton, 2008). First and foremost, human beings seemed to be wired to be able to feel for the suffering and pain of others. Thus a large body of research finds that giving is increased in situations where the victim is made concrete, thereby allowing the donor to feel for the victim vividly (Small & Simonsohn, 2008). For example, when poverty in Africa is presented as a statistic, empathy is relatively low, compared to when the presentation features a single African child in need (Slovic, 2007). Similarly, emotions are more strongly felt for a single victim rather than a group of victims, particularly for a victim with a name or even a minimal form of identification (Small et al., 2007). Thus, a basic ability to feel for others powerfully drives charitable giving.

Additionally, however, a second factor tends to be involved in giving; namely, the person's self-identity. That is, how the person perceives him/herself, which is linked to deep emotional responses. For example, when a person does something wrong, he/she will feel guilty. In this case, if the person can perform a good deed for others, then his/her harmed self-image may be redeemed. Thus, research finds people are often more likely to make a charitable donation after they have indulged in some guilty pleasure themselves (Strahilevitz & Meyers, 1998). Interestingly, whereas the role of giving in alleviating guilt speaks to neutralizing a negative emotion, recent research suggests giving can also have a direct positive impact on a person's self-satisfaction and emotional well-being (Thoits & Hewitt, 2001).

For example, studies show that volunteering can create a happy mood (McGowan, 2006). Further, when comparing people who have spent the same amount of money on themselves versus on others, it is found that giving to others leads to greater happiness than purchasing for oneself (Dunn et al., 2008). In fact, the positive boost one gets from giving is so significant that it is even associated with lower mortality rates (Harris & Thoresen, 2005).

Given the positive emotional benefit of giving for the donor (in addition to benefits to the recipient of help), one might predict that people should be giving often—instead of buying one more treat for the self, why not use the money to help others? Plausible as this argument may be theoretically, it should surprise no one that in reality, people still tend to focus on amassing products for themselves (Kasser & Kanner, 2004), rather than more freely giving away time or money to help others. Hence there is a disconnect between the potential happiness that could result from helping others and people's chronic economic focus, which prevents them from doing so.

Liu and Aaker's Time-Ask Effect research tackled this disconnect from the standpoint of shifting people's mindset by having people consider time versus money. It is argued that people "underhelp" because the idea of helping others as a means to happiness may not always be salient. That is, in today's commercial society, the chronically present mindset people hold might be a weaker version of the mindset created by priming people with money (Vohs, Mead, & Goode, 2006). As a default, people may be more focused on the instrumental utility of objects, rather than the emotional meaning of events. Under such a mindset, giving to charity can seem like an unattractive proposition because giving takes away resources the person could use to fulfill goals for him/herself. Consequently, when approached with a charity request, people's chronic mindset might be to focus on the negative economic impact of such an act for the self.

Nevertheless, even though such a negative economic mindset tends to be the default, what would happen if this mindset is shifted by, say, an activation of the concept of spending time? As argued earlier, because the concept of time creates a focus on the emotional implications of an event, thinking about donating time (vs. money) can allow the person to see charitable giving in terms of its emotional meaning; that is, how giving can bring about personal satisfaction and happiness. This perspective consequently can lead to a more positive inclination to contribute to a charitable cause. Liu and Aaker dubbed this positive influence on charitable contributions of thinking about time as the Time-Ask Effect.

THE TIME-ASK EFFECT

Nonprofits are a $300 billion industry in the United States (Giving USA Foundation, 2007). As a typical part of their operation, such organizations routinely send out requests for donations. In fact, the number one reason people give is because they are asked. Two common types of requests made by nonprofits are for a monetary or time donation (volunteering); that is, a money-ask or a time-ask. On the surface, these two types of requests are independent events, each abiding by its own mental accounting rules. However, the research discussed earlier on the psychological effects of thinking about time versus money suggests that perhaps the effect of money-ask versus time-ask can be more profound and far-reaching, affecting not just the response to the request per se, but also one's general mindset toward the donation.

To test this possibility, Liu and Aaker conducted a series of experiments. In one experiment done in the lab, participants were asked to read about a fictional non-profit organization, the "American Lung Cancer Association." After going through the information about the organization, participants were then told that the foundation was having a fundraising event. Randomly assigned, half of the participants were asked, "How much time would you like to donate to the American Lung Cancer Foundation?" (time-ask present). The other participants were not asked the volunteering intent question (time-ask absent). Next, both groups were asked, "How much money would you donate to the American Lung Cancer Foundation?" Thus, the dependent variable was the amount of money people pledged to donate, and the test of interest was whether those in the time-ask present condition would indicate greater amounts of donation compared to those in the time-ask absent condition where their interest to donate money is directly asked without being preceded by a time-ask question first. Results revealed that indeed, first having a time-ask question significantly increased the amount of money subsequently pledged ($36.44 vs. $24.46). Thus, consistent with our prediction, first approaching people with a time-ask put people into a different, more emotionally focused mindset in which people felt more generous toward giving.

In another more elaborate study, the authors conducted a field experiment by partnering with HopeLab (www.HopeLab.org), a San Francisco Bay Area–based nonprofit organization that develops innovative social technologies to improve the quality of life for children with serious chronic illnesses (e.g., Re-Mission video game). The experiment was conducted in conjunction with their fundraising efforts on college campuses, with the goal of observing real donations in action. A research facilitator representing the HopeLab organization waited outside a room where another study was taking place. When students left the room, the facilitator approached them individually to see if they would be willing to partici-pate in another 30-minute study in which they would receive up to $10 for their participation.

Upon agreeing to participate, students read a one-page background introduc-tion about HopeLab, followed immediately by the time- versus money-ask manipu-lation. In the time-ask-first condition, participants were asked to indicate (a) "How interested are you in volunteering for HopeLab?" and (b) "How interested are you in making a donation to HopeLab?"(1 = Not at all; 7 = Very much). The question order was reversed in the money-ask-first condition. No questions were asked in the third (control) condition. The ordering of the time- versus money-ask questions served to manipulate the mindset of the participants—the question asked first served to set the mindset for the evaluation of the charity. Participants acquired either an emotional mindset that favored giving (when time was asked first), or an instrumental utility mindset (when money was asked first), which is not compatible with giving. Next, all three groups were asked questions regarding their impres-sions of HopeLab, followed by 20 minutes of unrelated filler questions.

When finished and exiting the study, participants handed the questionnaire to the facilitator who was standing next to a box with the sign, "HopeLab Donations." The facilitator paid each participant with ten $1 bills. Although the facilitator did not suggest that the participants make any donation, the box was in public view. Thus, participants could put any number (or zero) of the $1 bills they had earned into the donation box. A secondary researcher, collecting the questionnaires, gave the participants a receipt on which participants had to write down the total received (i.e., net of any contributions) for reimbursement purposes. This receipt served as the main dependent variable assessing actual donations.

Finally, each participant was given a flyer entitled, "Volunteer for HopeLab." The flyer talked about a volunteering opportunity with HopeLab, and ended with "Would you like to volunteer for this effort? ___ Yes ___ No, thanks. To begin volunteering, or for more information, please include your email ____." The following week, the fundraising organizer at HopeLab contacted all participants who left their email and helped monitor the number of hours these volunteers actually worked for HopeLab. Thus, in addition to the observation of actual monetary donations (put into the donation box by each person), the number of emails left through the flyer, as well as the actual number of hours people eventually volunteered for HopeLab over the course of one month, was monitored.

The data was analyzed comparing actual monetary and time donation activities across the time-ask-first, money-ask-first, and control (no-ask) conditions. Again, results show that those in the time-ask-first condition were the most generous, donating on average $5.85 of the $10 they received, compared to those in the money-ask-first condition ($3.07) and the no-ask condition ($4.42). Interestingly, not only did the time-ask-first situation increase donations compared to the control condition, the money-ask-first situation significantly reduced the amount of donations. That is, whereas making time salient before a giving decision increases generosity, making money salient before the decision can reduce generosity (Figure 12.1).

Similarly, examining the data for volunteer signing up (and actually carrying through with the volunteer work), again those in the time-ask-first condition were the most likely to sign up and worked the most hours, compared to those in both the money-ask-first and no-ask conditions. In the time-ask-first condition, 14% of the participants indicated they would volunteer for HopeLab and wrote down their

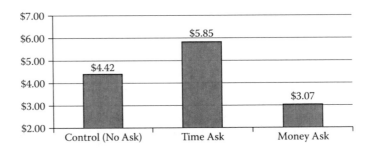

Figure 12.1   Donation to HopeLab (out of $10 compensation from participation in the study).

email to be contacted, compared to 3% in the money-ask-first condition and 3% in the control condition. Further, about half the people in each condition who gave their email turned their commitment into action. Thus, 7.0% of all participants in the time-ask-first condition actually volunteered time to HopeLab (for an average 6.5 hours each). In contrast, only 1.6% of those in the money-ask-first condition, and 1.6% of those in the control condition actually volunteered.

A follow-up study probed the mechanism by which time-ask creates greater generosity. After a time-ask-first or a money-ask-first manipulation, as in the previous study, participants were asked how much they would endorse the statement, "Happiness is tied to volunteering." Those in the time-ask-first condition gave a significantly stronger endorsement of this claim than those in the money-ask-first condition. That is, whereas the happiness that comes with helping others was readily apparent after a time-ask-first manipulation, it did not occur as strongly following a money-ask-first manipulation.

Discussion

Several implications can be derived from this series of studies. First, the findings provide evidence that as discussed earlier, thinking about time versus money can indeed have very different psychological consequences. In particular, the process measures support the notion that time and money create different focuses. Time evokes a mindset attuned to emotional meaning and satisfaction, whereas money evokes a mindset of instrumental utility. These differential mindsets in turn direct people to evaluate charitable giving in distinct lights—either as an emotionally meaningful activity that creates personal happiness or as an economic loss.

A second insight emerging from these studies is the malleability of people's attitudes toward charitable giving. Much of a donation decision may depend on situational factors that sway people's mindset one way or another. A simple mental exercise of thinking about giving time to a charity can create a shift in mindset toward an emotional focus, whereas thinking about money has just the opposite effect. Of note, the positive effect of a time-ask occurs regardless of whether people were willing to give time—the mere thought of this possibility was sufficient to generate the effect. Thus the meaning of a charitable giving decision is truly in the eye of the beholder, and is construed based on the momentarily accessible mental frames presented to the individual.

The practical implications of the Time-Ask Effect for nonprofit organizations is imminent—organizations could do well to increase contributions from the public by first making a time-ask, such as by first inviting potential donors or members of a society to participate in volunteering events. For example, a school could find ways for its alumni to give time by asking them to serve as mentors for current students. Even when the primary focus of a campaign is to raise money, it may still be beneficial to think of ways to create volunteering opportunities. For instance, a nonprofit organization seeking help for the victims of Hurricane Katrina in Mississippi may consider first asking people to directly join the rebuilding efforts. Certainly it would take a lot of effort to coordinate volunteering activities, and the number of volunteers that can be accommodated could be limited. However, based on the results of the current studies, regardless of whether people accept such time-ask requests or whether they actually get to take part in volunteering, they are still more likely to behave more generously toward the charity in subsequent encounters because they are now able to see the charity in an emotional light. Indeed, many highly successful nonprofit organizations place significant emphasis on non-monetary participation. For example, Avon organizes the annual Walk for Breast Cancer, an event many could participate in. In addition to raising breast cancer awareness through the publicity of the event itself, just asking people to join the walk could foster an emotional connection between Avon's cause and the general public.

WHEN TIME BECOMES MONEY

Liu and Aaker found that people tend to have different mindsets and mental constructs associated with time and money. However, two important questions remain: first, why would there be such different associations and where do these associations come from? And second, are these associations held to the same degree by everyone, or could there be individual differences? Answers to these questions may be informed by the perspective that people's mental representations of social constructs are formed through a lifelong process of learning, experience, and acculturation (Pillow, Zautra, & Sandler, 1996; Liu & Aaker, 2006). In particular, people's living environment and situation tend to have a significant impact on how people perceive and judge the world. For example, becoming a parent leads to the perception that the world is a more dangerous place (even though in fact it is not the world but the person that has changed in the event of parenthood; Eibach, Libby, & Gilovich, 2003). In the same vein, one would expect an individual's associations with time and money to also be influenced by his/her life experience.

A series of recent studies by DeVoe and Pfeffer (2007) provided empirical support for the notion that an individual's life experience can systematically affect his/her attitude toward time. The authors examined the relationship between the nature of an individual's occupation and his/her construal of time, which in turn leads to differential propensities to volunteer for charity. Specifically, the authors conjectured that if a person's occupation is one where the person is paid by the hour (rather than by a salary that is not explicitly tied to the number of hours worked), his/her attitude toward time will become more similar to that toward money. That is, even though earlier we discussed general differences in people's construal of time versus money that lead to the Time-Ask Effect, such differences might be blurred for those who are paid by the hour. DeVoe and Pfeffer reasoned that this blurring occurs because such individuals routinely make direct links between exact amounts of time and exact amounts of money. This linking eliminates the ambiguity associated with the evaluation of time, while at the same time conditions the person to readily and directly associate time with money. Based on this reasoning, the authors tested a number of hypotheses.

For example, previous research shows that people attend to sunk cost more strongly for money than for time (Soman, 2001). If one wasted money on one thing, he/she will want to make it up by saving on something else. However, DeVoe and Pfeffer (2007) tested whether there could be individual variations underneath the average pattern, and found a marked difference between people who are paid by the hour versus those who are not. Specifically, unlike nonhourly workers, those with hourly pay exhibited the same model of mental accounting for time and money—they were just as upset about a sunk cost of time as they were about money.

In the domain of charitable contributions, DeVoe and Pfeffer (2007) examined the relationship between pay type and volunteerism, utilizing data from the 2003 American Time Use Survey (ATUS). Controlling for a host of other variables, such as demographics, education, income level, number of hours worked per week, and industry sectors, the authors found a significant negative correlation between hourly pay and volunteering. Translating the results into annual numbers, nonhourly paid workers on average would spent 65.4 hours a year on volunteer activities, whereas hourly paid workers spent on average 41.9 hours a year, a 36% drop compared to their nonhourly paid counterparts.

DeVoe and Pfeffer's findings offer a deeper understanding into the Time-Ask Effect. One implication of work for the Time-Ask Effect is that even though time, in general, creates a more emotional mindset toward giving, such an effect should not be taken for granted. The emotional mindset associated with time is a result of how the person experiences time in his/her everyday situations. Although the population on average does not automatically think of time the same way they think of money, there are conditions of exception. In particular, for those who routinely make explicit connections between time and money, the Time-Ask Effect might be abated. For them, thinking about donating time might not prompt the consideration of the emotional benefits of giving; instead, it would engender the same kind of thoughts about giving up economic resources as does a money-ask, which thwarts giving.

An interesting question arising from this discussion is how might one foster greater contributions from people with hourly pay while still utilizing the principles of the Time-Ask Effect. Although not explicitly tested, one idea might be that for this group of individuals, it is even more important that the donation request explicitly breaks the link between time and money, for example, by making salient the nonmonetary ways of spending time, such as time spent with family and friends, time spent relaxing in the park, or playing sports.

Another question for nonprofits to consider is with regard to one of the largest bodies of volunteers—senior citizens. Retired seniors are a unique group because on the one hand, they have a lot of free time, and yet on the other hand, research by Laura Carstensen and colleagues (e.g., Carstensen, Isaacowitz, & Charles, 1999) shows that because they perceive their time in life as limited, they may also be very selective in how they spend their time. Thus, given the preciousness of time to senior citizens, should a charity first approach this group with a time-ask; that is, could the Time-Ask Effect apply to seniors as well? The key insight from the works of Carstensen et al. is that although senior citizens perceive time as more limited, they are even more motivated to spend their time in ways that are emotionally meaningful. Because helping others is a meaningful and noble activity, volunteering could indeed provide a deep source of personal satisfaction to people of age, and a time-ask should be responded to quite favorably by this group, creating a win-win situation for donors and the nonprofit organization.

SUMMARY DISCUSSION

Is time like money? This chapter reviewed some of the latest research efforts in management and psychology that speak to this question. These collective bodies of work suggest time and money are complex concepts individuals learn and deal with throughout their lifetime. At a fundamental level, a number of important differences exist. First, people use different mental accounting rules for time versus money. Time is valued more ambiguously than money, resulting in less attention to sunk cost for time (Soman, 2001; Okada & Hoch, 2004), and rosier forecasts of abundance of time in one's future, compared to forecasts for money (Zauberman & Lynch, 2005). Importantly, the differences between time and money go beyond mental accounting. Through their role in everyday life, people have formed a rich set of associations and mindsets around the general concepts of time and money. The Time-Ask Effect examines the differences in mindset and demonstrates how such associations could have significant impacts on the success of fundraising activities. Specifically, because thinking about spending time activates a mindset focused on emotional meaning and satisfaction, it puts charitable giving in a more positive light than thinking about spending money.

Building on this finding, nonprofit organizations might be able to better engage their community and ultimately increase the level of donations in both time and money by following a simple principle: *ask for time before asking for money*. In practice, this could mean giving more thought to devising ways in which the community might participate in the organization through activities— that is, through spending time with the organization, rather than merely writing a check. Further, the mere consideration of such time-spending opportunities might be enough—even if people cannot commit to participating in such activities (we are always busy after all), it does not hurt—in fact it is beneficial—to still ask them! It is the thought of spending time that changes their mindset from an economic evaluation of the charity to that of emotional satisfaction, which in turn can translate into more generosity toward the organization (in money and time) in the future. Thus, popular charity events such as 10k walks, benefit galas, and community fairs may all serve an even greater purpose for a cause than the already substantial benefits of public awareness and direct revenues from those events. See Olivola and Shafir (under review); see also Oviola in this volume for how to best design such events.

Final Words

The Time-Ask Effect also highlights another important aspect of charitable giving, one that is not always salient in the minds of donors or fundraisers. Whereas people tend to focus on the recipients of help and the success of the causes (and rightly so), the other side of the equation—the welfare of the donors—is often less addressed. However, as the Time-Ask Effect research points out, charitable giving also serves important functions for the giver as well as for the receiver. In particular, giving provides the donor with significant emotional meaning and satisfaction, contributing to greater personal happiness, and even better health (Harris & Thoresen, 2005)! This holistic benefit to the donor should not be neglected and indeed be more emphasized in our society. Giving, it turns out, can really be a win-win situation for the community.

REFERENCES

Batson, C. D. (1987). Self-report ratings of empathic emotion. In N. Eisenberg & J. Strayer (Eds.), *Empathy and its development: Cambridge studies in social and emotional development* (pp. 356–360). New York: Cambridge University Press.

Carstensen, L. L., Isaacowitz, D. M., & Charles, S. T. (1999). Taking time seriously: A theory of socioemotional selectivity. *American Psychologist, 54*, 165–181.

Decety, J., & Meyer, M. (2008). From emotion resonance to empathic understanding: A social developmental neuroscience account. *Development and Psychopathology. Special Issue: Imaging Brain Systems in Normality and Psychopathology, 20*(4), 1053–1080.

De Hooge, I. E., Zeelenberg, M., & Breugelmans, S. M. (2007). Moral sentiments and cooperation: Differential influences of shame and guilt. *Cognition & Emotion, 21*(5), 1025–1042.

DeVoe, S. E., & Pfeffer, J. (2007). When time is money: The effect of hourly payment on the evaluation of time. *Organizational Behavior & Human Decision Processes, 104*(1), 1–13.

DeVoe, S. E., & Pfeffer, J. (2007). Hourly payment and volunteering: The effect of organizational practice on decisions about time use. *Academy of Management Journal, 50*(4), 783–798.

Dunn, E. W., Aknin, L. B., & Norton, M. I. (2008). Spending money on others promotes happiness. *Science, 319*(5870), 1687–1688.

Eibach, R. P., Libby, L. K., & Gilovich, T. D. (2003). When change in the self is mistaken for change in the world. *Journal of Personality and Social Psychology, 84*, 917–931.

Giving USA Foundation. (2007). Annual report on philanthropy 2006. http://www.aafrc.org/press_releases/gusa.cfm.

Harbaugh, W. T., Mayr, U., & Burghart, D. R. (2007). Neural responses to taxation and voluntary giving reveal motives for charitable donations. *Science, 316*, 1622–25.

Harris, A. H., & Thoresen, C. E. (2005). Volunteering is associated with delayed mortality in older people: Analysis of the longitudinal study of aging. *Journal of Health Psychology, 10*(6), 739–52.

Kahneman, D., Diener, E., & Schwarz, N. (1999). *Well-being: The foundations of hedonic psychology.* New York: Russell Sage Foundation.

Kahneman, D., & Tversky, A. (1979). Prospect theory: An analysis of decision under risk. *Econometrica, 47*, 263–291.

Kasser, T., & Kanner, A. D. (2004). *Psychology and consumer culture: The struggle for a good life in a materialistic world.* Washington, DC: American Psychological Association.

Leclerc, F., Schmitt, B., & Dube, L. (1995). Waiting time and decision making: Is time like money? *Journal of Consumer Research, 22*, 110–19.

Liu, W., & Aaker, J. (2007). Do you look to the future or focus on today? The impact of life experience on intertemporal choice. *Organizational Behavior and Human Decision Processes, 102*, 212–25.

McGowan, K. (2006, January). The pleasure paradox. *Psychology Today*, 52–55.

Mogilner, C., & Aaker, J. (2009). The time vs. money effect: Shifting product attitudes and decisions through personal connection. *Journal of Consumer Research, 36,* 277–291.

Okada, E. M., & Hoch, S. J. (2004). Spending time versus spending money. *Journal of Consumer Research, 31,* 313–23.

Olivola, C. Y., & Shafir, E. (under review). The martyrdom effect: When pain and effort increase prosocial contributions.

Pillow, D. R., Zautra, A. J., & Sandler, I. (1996). Major life events and minor stressors: Identifying mediation links in the stress process. *Journal of Personality and Social Psychology, 70,* 381–394.

Reed II, A., Aquino, K., & Levy, E. (2007). Moral identity and judgments of charitable behaviors. *Journal of Marketing, 71,* 178–193.

Schwarz, N., & Clore, G. (1996). Feelings and phenomenal experiences. In T. Higgins & Kruglanski, A. (Eds.), *Social psychology: Handbook of basic principles* (pp. 433–465). New York: Guilford Press.

Slovic, P. (2007). "If I look at the mass I will never act": Psychic numbing and genocide. *Judgment and Decision Making, 2*(2), 79–95

Small, D., Loewenstein, G., & Slovic, P. (2007). Sympathy and callousness: The impact of deliberative thought on donations to identifiable and statistical victims. *Organizational Behavior and Human Decision Processes, 102*(2), 143–153.

Small, D. A., & Simonsohn, U. (2008). Friends of victims: Personal experience and prosocial behavior. *Journal of Consumer Research. Special Issue: Consumer Welfare, 35*(3), 532–542.

Soman, D. (2001). The mental accounting of sunk time costs: Why time is not like money. *Journal of Behavioral Decision Making, 14*(3), 169–185.

Strahilevitz, M., & Myers, J. G. (1998). Donations to charity as purchase incentives: How well they work may depend on what you are trying to sell. *Journal of Consumer Research, 24,* 434–446.

Thaler, R. H. (1985). Mental accounting and consumer choice. *Marketing Science, 4,* 199–214.

Thaler, R. H. (1999). Mental accounting matters. *Journal of Behavioral Decision Making, 12,* 183–206.

Thoits, P. A., & Hewitt, L. N. (2001). Volunteer work and well-being. *Journal of Health and Social Behavior, 42,* 115–131.

Trope, Y., & Liberman, N. (2003). Temporal construal. *Psychological Review, 110,* 403–421.

Van Boven, L., & Gilovich, T. (2003). To do or to have: That is the question. *Journal of Personality and Social Psychology, 85*(6), 1193–1202.

Vohs, K. D., Mead, N. L., & Goode, M. R. (2006). The psychological consequences of money. *Science, 314,* 1154–1156.

West, L. A. (2004). Non-profits face funding pressures. *Journal of Accountancy, 198,* 1–2.

Zauberman, G., & Lynch, Jr., J. G. (2005). Resource slack and discounting of future time versus money. *Journal of Experimental Psychology: General, 134,* 23–37.

13

Heuristics and Biases in Charity

JONATHAN BARON and EWA SZYMANSKA

INTRODUCTION

A ltruistic behavior often leads to desirable social outcomes. We can thus assume that more altruism is better than less, other things being equal. But altruism tends to be already widely encouraged, so efforts to promote it even further may produce little noticeable change. Instead, it might be easier to do more good by improving efficiency of the altruistic behaviors already in place.

Because altruism is a precious but scarce resource, its wise allocation should be a priority. That is, given the amount of money a person would be willing to give to charity, and the relevant information available, a donor should allocate the donated funds in as efficient a manner as possible.° There are several obstacles in the way of achieving such efficiency, however. For example, some donors make decisions that are simply not as well informed as they could be. But an even bigger threat to optimality is posed by overly simplistic decision rules, also referred to as *heuristics* or *cognitive biases*. Biases are systematic errors in thinking that are not necessarily a result of misinformation or ignorance, but rather are brought about by an overgeneralization of some decision rule that might be useful in one context but is ill-suited or even harmful when applied in another. Cognitive biases often lead to the systematic misallocations of funds and waste of resources.

° We focus here on monetary donations, but we acknowledge that altruism also includes many other behaviors, such as donating time. Two other forms of altruism are worth mentioning. One is political action designed to serve the ends of helping others in much the way that charity does. The other is the choice of work. Arguably, people want to contribute to the well-being of others through their work, to the point where they are willing to accept lower salaries in order to do jobs that serve this end, e.g., being a public defender instead of a tax lawyer. These other competing modes of altruism are important and should not be ignored. We shall return to this point, especially with respect to political behavior.

We propose utilitarianism, or the totality of good that comes about from a choice, as our gold standard for assessing the effectiveness of choices made in the context of charitable contributions. The utilitarian model we apply does not attempt to tell people how altruistic they "should be," but simply accepts their willingness to donate as is. (Later, we discuss extensions of this model.) From a utilitarian perspective, the best measure of efficiency is the amount of good done per some monetary unit (e.g., a dollar) donated. For example, we ask how many lives are saved for how many dollars? In what follows, we discuss several examples of how people's contribution decisions may fail to meet this standard of economic efficiency.

We next present our own empirical findings, which further demonstrate the systematic deviations from the predictions of a normative model. Finally, we return to the subject of utilitarianism, and we introduce the theoretical foundations of the efficiency standard we have proposed. We also provide an overview of the other possible versions of the utilitarian model, and we comment on ways in which people could be assisted in their selection of the optimally altruistic choices.

In sum, our general perspective is that optimal altruism should be viewed as a value maximization problem. In the upcoming section, we examine the most common decision-making errors that stand in the way of maximizing efficiency of donations. In the next section, we ask how people may depart from this standard of efficiency. We believe that, if we can correct the cognitive biases or work around them, then we can improve the efficiency of altruistic behavior and thus do more good for the sacrifices that people are willing to make.

Possible Nonutilitarian Heuristics

Evaluability   Hsee (1996) argued that people pay more attention to attributes that are easy to evaluate. He manipulated the ease of evaluation by presenting unfamiliar information with or without a comparative context. For example, imagine being asked how much you would pay for a music dictionary with a torn cover and 50,000 entries. The cover is easy to evaluate, and torn covers are not a desirable feature to most buyers. But unless music theory is your profession or a hobby, you are probably not sure how to evaluate the number of entries. Consequently, you would likely pay considerable attention to the condition of a book, and would not be willing to pay much for the dictionary with a torn cover. On the other hand, if you were simultaneously presented with another dictionary that has an intact cover but only 25,000 entries, you would attend more to the number of entries and likely pay more for the 50,000 dictionary, despite its torn cover.

In the case of donating to charities, donors often correctly wonder about efficiency. As we have noted, the best measure of efficiency from a utilitarian perspective is the amount of welfare-enhancing results. But this dimension is often difficult to evaluate. Few organizations devoted to saving lives bother to even try to calculate just how many lives are saved for how many dollars. Fewer publicize such figures. And when life saving is not the only goal, the task of measuring benefits becomes more difficult still. (For health outcomes, it is possible to estimate benefits in terms of "quality adjusted life years," as many agencies now do (see Baron, 2008).

Such analyses are used by governments and insurance companies, but not, to our knowledge, by charitable organizations.)

Instead, what is more evaluable than the lives saved per dollar of contribution is the operating cost per dollar. How much money is spent on administration, advertising, and other functions not related directly to a charity's main function? Ratings are available for this sort of efficiency. For example, the Charity Navigator site providing online rankings of over 5,400 American charities (see www.charity-navigator.org), publishes lists such as "10 Inefficient Fundraisers" or "10 Charities Overpaying Their For-Profit Fundraisers." It is, however, unclear that focusing on the operating costs maximizes the sort of efficiency that ought to matter, namely, the amount of good done per dollar spent. For example, Charity A may spend 10% of donors' contributions on operating costs, but need $10 to save a single life. Charity B may have higher operating expenses, using 25% of donations to cover the costs, but require as little as $5 to save a human life. In this scenario, the Charity Navigator would reliably single out the percentage of resources used to pay for the operating costs, thus suggesting to the potential donors that contributing to Charity A would be the more efficient use of their money. However, this is evidently not the case. Suppose that charities A and B both receive $100. Charity A spends $10 on overhead and saves 9 human lives with the remaining $90. Charity B, on the other hand, allocates $25 toward its operating expenses, but manages to save 15 lives with the remaining $75. Clearly, Charity B is generating significantly more welfare with the $100 donation than Charity A.

Of course we are not arguing that keeping the costs down is irrelevant. It is undeniably of great importance to manage the expenses wisely and to ensure that operating costs are not exceeding acceptable limits. After all, each dollar cost reduction frees up funds for the actual charitable programs. But, as in the case of judging a music dictionary by its torn cover, if we look at the operating costs in isolation, we might not be making allocation decisions that are as good as we might think they are. An efficient organization should manage costs wisely, while carefully watching the bottom line. In the case of charities, the bottom line is an increase in the economic welfare or the number of lives saved. The bottom line ought to matter to donors, but it is a number that is hard to obtain. Instead, donors, reinforced by third-party evaluators such as the Charity Navigator, base their allocation decisions on easy-to-evaluate information about operating costs.

Average vs. Marginal Benefit

We believe that if the information about the average benefit per dollar was made available and presented in a way that allows for meaningful comparisons, people would likely attend to this important statistic. In the case of charitable contributions, knowing and appropriately taking into account the average benefit per dollar is a definite improvement in the decision-making process. But what is even more relevant to an optimal allocation of funds is the *marginal benefit per marginal dollar.* The marginal benefit per marginal dollar is the benefit-to-cost ratio for every *new* contribution. For example, a popular charity might be relatively well funded, so that the marginal benefit per dollar of a new donation is much lower than the average benefit. In other words, the organization may lack good ways to use additional money. On the other hand, a small organization that has not yet reached its target funding level might be able to make better use of additional funds, even if its average benefit-to-cost ratio is lower for all the funds it has. This might be the most difficult statistic to obtain, however, as it is not in the well-funded charity's best interest to advertise the ratio.

Diversification   In general, variety seeking is a good thing to do for several reasons. For goods that involve experiences, like listening to music or watching movies, variety reduces the effects of adaptation to repeated presentations of the same thing. For investments, diversification reduces risk. But people continue to seek variety also when they have no reason to do so. In fact, as we are going to demonstrate, people apply the *diversification heuristic* (Read & Lowewnstein, 1995; Fox, Ratner, & Lieb, 2005) even to charitable giving.

Diversification in charitable giving means that an individual donor prefers to contribute money to many different charities, instead of allocating all the funds to a single, most efficient organization. It may extend to the idea of giving equal contributions to several charities (Fox et al., 2005).

Diversification has many possible explanations. For example, people may fail to understand the relation between allocation and maximization. To illustrate, Ubel, DeKay, Baron, and Asch (1996, p. 2998) told subjects (people waiting for jury duty), "All else equal, kidney transplants are more likely to succeed if they are transplanted into patients who 'match' the kidney donor. The number of successful transplants one year after transplant is eight out of ten for patients with a *complete match* and seven out of ten for patients with a *partial match*." The subjects were asked to allocate 100 available kidneys among two groups: 100 patients with a complete match (hence 80% success rate) and 100 patients with a partial match (70% success rate). Most subjects allocated 50 kidneys to each group. When asked how to maximize the success rate, fewer than 20% of the subjects gave the correct answer (all 100 to the 80% success group), and most of these subjects still allocated the kidneys equally. Thus, people may diversify because they allocate so as to match rather than maximize effectiveness.

Another reason for giving to many different charities, instead of just the best one, might be the desire for a "warm glow," (Andreoni, 1990) or a positive feeling that arises from every act of helping each organization. The magnitude of the glow may be roughly constant for each act of contributing (Margolis, 1982). Of course this is a self-interested motivation, although not necessarily a bad one if it increases altruism.

Diversification might also be explained in terms of the donor's inclination to think of charities like investments. For the average donor, they are not the same. The difference can be understood in terms of the principle of *declining marginal utility*. According to this well-known economic principle, when an individual, or a charitable organization, receives more of something, each extra unit of the added thing contributes progressively less and less utility (does less and less good). The principle applies to money as well as it does to, for example, ice cream (would you be as excited about a tenth consecutive scoop of ice cream on your plate as you were about the first, the second, or even the third?). For investments, given a fixed expected level of income, it is more important to avoid losses from that level than it is to obtain gains of the same amount, because the losses have a greater effect on total utility (i.e., the pain after losing some amount is greater than the pleasure after gaining the same amount). Thus, it pays to reduce one's risk by spreading out investments, so that if one investment does badly, the investor does not lose too much.

The marginal benefit per dollar (recall the difference between the average vs. marginal benefit) of some support is usually much higher than the marginal benefit of support in addition to some other previous support. In the context of charitable donations, however, a single donor does not have much influence over the total level of the charity's income (unless the donor is a major philanthropist). Thus, the usual arguments that favor diversification in investments do not necessarily apply to donations by typical donors. For charities, the focus should be on maximizing the expected increase in the economic welfare per dollar of every contribution.

In other words, a donor may err by thinking and acting as if she were the only donor to the charities that she supports. If she were, then it would make sense to diversify because of the principle of declining marginal utility just described. In reality, however, more often than not, each contributor has only a tiny effect on the total funding required by a charitable organization, so the argument based on the principle of declining marginal utility is unlikely to apply.

We should, therefore, identify a charity with the highest expected benefit per dollar, and make our entire contribution to that one charity. Of course, this is a risk. We may be wrong. But if people were willing to take the risk, more good would be generated in the long run.

For donors of small amounts of money, diversification has another negative feature, which is that charities spend money on mailings. As a consequence of this fact, and the arguments made earlier, the first author resolved last year to donate $10 each to most of the charities to which he had given money for years, telling them that this was the last contribution and that he should be removed from their mailing lists. Unfortunately, he could not bring himself to follow his own advice and narrow it down to one, or two, or three. The diversification intuition is strong.

Prominence   People tend to pay attention to a single prominent attribute, or an attribute they view as the most important (Tversky, Sattath, & Slovic, 1988), to the exclusion of all other attributes they deem as less important. For example, people may care first and foremost about reducing the number of casualties on the highways. This is a perfectly valid goal; however, treating the number of casualties as a strictly prominent attribute makes wise decision trade-offs very difficult. If two safety programs differ in cost and in the number of lives saved, people tend to choose an option that saves more people. They do this even if the difference in lives is small and the difference in cost is large. The prominence effect relates to the lexicographic choice strategy, in which the option with the best value on the most important attribute is simply selected (Bettman, Luce, & Payne, 1998).

The trouble with basing decisions on prominence is that sometimes the prominent attribute should be outweighed by large differences in other attributes. Accepting large surges in cost in exchange for only a small increase in goal achievement represents yet another bias leading to the inefficient allocations.

Parochialism   Parochialism, formally defined, is an in-group bias in which people weigh the welfare of their own group more heavily than those of outsiders, to the point where they favor policies that help their group but do greater harm to outsiders. Charity will, we assume, never do this; it will always do more good than harm. But it can be inefficient if the out-group charities are more efficient than the in-group ones, yet receive less funding simply because they provide aid to the outsiders. A situation in which the out-group charities are able to stretch a dollar further than the organizations helping fellow citizens is often the case in the United States, as the cost of life saving in, for example, Africa is far lower than that in the United States.

If we assume that people would not reallocate their contributions to the more efficient external charity because their altruism is limited to insiders, then we cannot consider parochialism a bias, as any attempt at encouraging the reallocation would bring about more harm than good. This argument depends on the assumption that parochialism is a result of some strong human intuition, much like our deeply ingrained commitment to close family members. In other words, parochialism may be seen as analogous to family loyalty, which can be explained in terms of a biological adaptation aimed at increasing the individual's fitness indirectly— through assisting one's close relatives. However, it is not clear how the biological tendency to help the family members would generalize to our commitment to, for example, strangers in Hawaii who suffered from a tsunami. But given that the U.S. citizens do seem to experience a sense of commitment to tsunami victims in Hawaii, we have grounds to expect that the same cognitive mechanism may affect their commitment to New Zealanders who suffered the same fate. This assumption, in turn, suggests that parochialism results from cognitive illusions that might be corrected.

Baron (in press) argues that parochialism is greater for harms of inaction than for action. That is, people are reluctant to harm outsiders through acts but much more willing to do nothing to help them. If people can be brought to see this as a kind of inconsistency, perhaps there will be more obligation to help outsiders. Failure to give to charity is, in fact, an omission that results in great harm.

Parochialism can also be reduced by encouraging people to think of outsiders as individuals rather than as members of an abstract group. Parochialism is at least in part the result of thinking abstractly about people in terms of, for example, "nations" and "the enemy."[*]

If the option of modifying parochialism is open either to the decision maker or to others, then in-group bias in charity could be counted as a bias against even the sophisticated utilitarian view. In particular, the view that takes moral education

---

[*] Schick (1991, p. 1) tells the following story: "Writing about his experiences in the Spanish Civil War, George Orwell tells this story. He had gone out to a spot near the Fascist trenches from which he thought he might snipe at someone. He waited a long time without any luck. None of the enemy made an appearance. Then, at last, some disturbance took place, much shouting and blowing of whistles followed, and a man jumped out of the trench and ran along the parapet in full view. He was half-dressed and was holding up his trousers with both hands as he ran. I refrained from shooting at him. I did not shoot part because of that detail about the trousers. I had come here to shoot at 'Fascists'; but a man holding up his trousers isn't a 'Fascist', he is visibly a fellow-creature, similar to yourself, and you don't feel like shooting at him."

costs into account might be relevant, in that the costs of reducing in-group bias might be relatively low.

Identifiability   We shall not examine the identifiability effect in the studies we report; however, since four articles in this volume discuss the finding that altruism is greater when single victims are identified (Loewenstein & Small; Kogut & Ritov; Ritov & Kogut; Slovic), we will briefly discuss how the identifiability effect violates the efficiency standards we proposed earlier. Recently, Charness and Gneezy (2008) found that "giving" in a dictator game (where one subject has control of some money and can give some to another subject who has none) was higher when the recipient was identified by last name. This effect results in part from the fact that the identified victim evokes more empathy.

Is this a bias? From the simple utilitarian perspective, it is. By increasing altruism toward the identifiable victims, it almost necessarily reduces altruism toward the unidentified ones, who are often the ones most in need of help (because they tend to be masses of people who are undergoing some great deprivation). Perhaps, though, the emotion changes the benefit/cost threshold for altruism, meaning that people are willing to incur a greater personal cost of helping, even when the amount of benefit to others does not change. This shift in the benefit/cost threshold might possibly even increase overall altruism.

On the other hand, it is clearly a kind of framing effect, in which choices are affected by how they are presented, holding the reality constant. Victims all have names. The fact that we are aware of one of them is an accident. We could make up names for the others, or even tell ourselves that our donation to some relief fund is going to help someone named Zhang. Thus, the identifiability effect may fail a simpler test of rationality.

Voluntary Versus Tax   A final violation of the efficiency standards we discuss is that people tend to oppose the government aid programs supported by taxes— often referred to as "forced charity." Baron (1997) argued that contributions (of time or money) to political causes that support helpful programs could sometimes be more efficient than direct contributions to the beneficiaries of the proposed programs. This is because although the probability of having some effect through political action is very low, the benefits of a successful initiative are potentially very high. In economics, the expected utility, or the anticipated amount of generated welfare, equals the size of the possible benefits times the probability of obtaining those benefits. If we apply this formula separately to the two modes of helping—an individual donation and a political action—the expected utility of the two modes might be similar, sometimes higher for individual contributions but sometimes higher for political action, depending on the details. After all, little benefit times high probability of making at least a small difference (as in an individual donation), might well be roughly the same as a great benefit times a small probability of doing any good at all (as in political action). Moreover, the cost of political action might be so much lower than the cost of direct contribution that it might be required by the efficiency standards to combine political action with direct donation.

In part, the bias against "forced charity" may arise from a belief in freedom, the belief that government should not force us to help others but should, more or less, provide us with services from which we all benefit and pay for collectively, such as roads, military defense, and protection of our property. (Some libertarians would not even go that far.) Insofar as this is true, it may represent a kind of cognitive inconsistency. Some people benefit very little from roads or property protection, so paying taxes for these things is a way of forcing them to sacrifice for the benefit of others. It is a matter of degree.

EXPERIMENTS

Here we report the results of four experiments designed to look for evidence of some of the biases just described.°

All studies were done as questionnaires on the World Wide Web. Subjects were part of a panel of about 1,500. We sent emails to 500 at a time, indicating the availability of a study and giving the URL. We paid $3 (to be added to earnings from other studies and then paid through PayPal) for each study. We aimed for 80 responses to each study and then withdrew it. The subjects were mostly Americans. Their median income and education was typical of the U.S. population. Their ages ranged from 20 to 80, with a median of about 42 (varying from study to study). About 80% were female.

Each study began with an introductory page, which was followed by 14 to 16 additional pages, each with one item and 4 to 5 questions following the item. The full sets of questions for each study are shown in Appendix A, with one item used for illustration for each set. The introductory page was similar for all the studies reported, and read as follows:

> The first part (7 pages, 4 questions each) is about personal contributions to worthy causes, such as helping people in need who cannot help themselves, people such as young children or those who are ill. Imagine that you are not one of these needy people and that, in fact, you have enough money so that it is easy for you to give some away for such causes without seriously hurting your quality of life. Imagine that you are willing to contribute some of your annual income to such causes.
>
> The second part (7 pages, 4 questions each) is about your evaluation of programs to cure and prevent serious diseases that affect children, such as AIDS, malaria, worms, polio, and whooping cough. Many children in Africa suffer from these diseases and often die. But pockets of curable and preventable childhood diseases exist in rich countries too. Other questions in this part concern health insurance.
>
> Suppose that all of these programs are effective and efficient. We are interested in your views about how such programs should be funded.

Here we report results according to the issues addressed, identifying the study that produced them.†

° See Appendix A.
† The data and R scripts used for analysis are at http://finzi.psych.upenn.edu/~baron/R/ewas/".

Waste

The following item was included in our first study to test the idea that subjects will focus on waste even with efficiency held constant (recall our discussion of the evaluability heuristic, and the donor's preoccupation with the operating costs, to the exclusion of other relevant information): "A and B help prevent deaths in children. Both of them can prevent 5 deaths for every $1,000 of donations. A spends $200 out of every $1,000 of donations on advertising. B spends $100." (Note that despite higher operating costs, B generates exactly the same amount of welfare as A). Subjects were asked, "How much would you allocate to A/B?" The mean response was 75% to A, which was significantly higher ($p = .0000$, rounded) than the 50% we might expect of an unbiased responder, given equal efficiency.

In the second study, we put "of donations" in bold font; but again, the mean allocation was 68%, still clearly different from 50%.

Since subjects might have thought that the $1,000 referred to what was left after advertising, in the third study, we tried to make the distinction clearer still: "A and B help prevent deaths in children. Both of them can prevent 5 deaths for every $1,000 of donations. A spends $200 out of every $1,000 of donations on overhead expenses, but manages to save 5 lives with the remaining $800. B spends $100 out of every $1,000 on overhead, and saves 5 lives with the remaining $900." The mean response was 3.38 on a 1–5 scale in which 1 meant "all to A" and 5 meant "all to B" ($t_{83} = 3.39$, $p = 0.001$, vs. 3, which would mean equal allocation).

In sum, waste (or the operating cost) matters to people, even in cases when the reason for worrying about waste—the resulting lack of efficiency—is absent.

Average cost

We can similarly ask whether subjects attend to average benefit per dollar even when the marginal benefit turns out to be equal. In our first study about this, we asked, "A and B help prevent deaths in children. A prevents 5 deaths for every $1,000 of donations, on the average, and B prevents 6 deaths for every $1,000. Given the donations they have received so far, and the opportunities for expansion, A will prevent 5 deaths for each additional $1,000 beyond its current level of spending and B will also prevent 5 deaths." The mean allocation to B was 72% (again, significantly higher than 50%). Subjects apparently attended to the average benefit even when the marginal benefit was the same.

In a subsequent study, we asked, "A and B will each prevent 5 deaths for every $10,000 of new donations. A was much more expensive to get started. Thus, the cost per life saved on the average is higher for A, because A has spent more money in total." The mean allocation to B was 61%, still higher than 50% ($t_{76} = 3.66$, $p = 0.0005$).

As in the case of waste, subjects attend to a dimension that would be relevant, average benefit per dollar, except that the reason for its relevance is now absent.

Diversification

We examined the diversification heuristic using multiple approaches.

Unequal Efficiency   We find that people allocate money to the less efficient charity just for the sake of diversifying. In the first study we stated, "A can save one life for $10,000. B can save one life for $12,500. The people helped are from the same groups, with the same problems." On average, subjects allocated 18% to B, the less efficient charity; 40% of the subjects allocated at least some proportion of funding to B.

In the second study we stated, "A can save 5 lives for $50,000. B can save 4 lives for $50,000. The people helped are from the same groups, with the same problems." Here, the mean allocation to B was 14%, with 38% of the subjects allocating more than nothing.

In the same study we stated, "A and B are both involved in preventing death in people with AIDS. A uses a method with a 75% chance of success over 5 years. B uses a method with a 50% chance of success over 5 years, with the same patients." Here, the mean allocation to B was 12%, with 43% allocating more than nothing.

In the fourth study, we included three relevant items: "A and B are both involved in preventing death in people with AIDS. A uses a method with a 75% chance of success over 5 years. B uses a method with a 50% chance of success over 5 years, with the same patients"; "A can save one life for $10,000. B can save one life for $12,500. The people helped are from the same groups, with the same problems"; "A can save 5 lives for $50,000. B can save 4 lives for $50,000. The people helped are from the same groups, with the same problems." We consider these items together, as they did not differ in any meaningful way. Each item was followed by several questions, given here with the responses to each. In all cases, the options were as follows:

1. All to A
2. More to A, some to B
3. Equally to A and B
4. More to B, some to A
5. All to B

"What is the right allocation between A and B, ignoring your own feelings?"
    Mean 1.46 (that is, between 1 and 2 on the above scale), 28% of subjects allocated some to B.

"What allocation would you feel best about making?"
    Mean 1.48, 29% of subjects allocated some to B.

"What allocation between A and B would be the most efficient use of your money?"
    Mean 1.33, 21% of subjects allocated some to B.

"What between A and B would do the most good for each $1,000 spent?"
    Mean 1.33, 22% of subjects allocated some to B.

Note that the responses to "right allocation" and "feel best" were more equal than those to the last two questions, which were about efficiency. The difference was significant ($t_{77} = 3.22$, $p = 0.0019$, for the means; $t_{77} = 3.61$, $p = 0.0006$, for the proportion of responses in which something was allocated to B).

In sum, as found by Ubel et al. (1996) in a different situation involving allocation of organs for transplantation to two groups, one group with a higher success rate than the other, people do not allocate so as to achieve the most efficient (or the utilitarian best) outcome. That is, people fail to allocate organs first to the group with the higher success rate. Ubel et al. found two reasons why some people systematically fail to maximize efficiency. Both of these are consistent with our results. Some subjects thought that some allocation to the group with a lower success rate would in fact maximize the outcome. Others understood how to maximize but thought that it was unfair to give nothing to the group with the lower success rate.

Unequal Efficiency, Several Projects Versus One   We also looked at the bias toward supporting multiple projects, at the expense of overall efficiency.

In the first study we asked, "A puts all the money into one project, which has a 75% chance of helping many children, and a 25% chance of doing no good at all. B puts the money into several different projects, each of which has a 70% chance of helping some children, but a 30% chance of doing no good." The expected utility of A is higher than B (75% > 70%), and so, our goal of maximizing welfare clearly implies allocating *all* funds to A. But 32% (vs. the optimal 0%) of the allocations went to B, and 60% of the subjects allocated something to B.

In the third study, we attempted to be more specific: "A puts $1,000,000 into one project, which has a 75% chance of helping 10,000 children, and a 25% chance of doing no good. B puts $200,000 into each of 5 projects ($1,000,000 total). Each of the 5 has a 70% chance of helping 2,000 children and a 30% chance of doing no good. (If all 5 succeed, then the total benefit is 10,000 children, the same as A.)" The mean allocation was 2.73 on 1–5 scale where 1 is all to A, 5 is all to B; 81% of the subjects allocated some funds to B.

We asked the same question in our last study, and the mean allocation was 2.46 (with 75% allocating some to B). In this case, the allocation judgment was not significantly higher than the efficiency judgment (2.39), meaning that people actually believed the efficiency of both charities to be roughly equal. Thus, unlike in the previous case of two charities, concern for fairness leads people to go against what they think is most efficient. They just get that incorrect.

(Note that these results are unaffected by the number of groups benefiting from the projects. When the projects are equated for efficiency, their number has no effect on allocation decisions. Specifically, in the first two studies, we asked, "A puts all the money into one project, which will help 100,000 children. B puts the money into five different projects, each of which will help 20,000 children. [The benefit per child will be the same.]" The mean allocation to A was 49% and 48% in the two respective studies, neither of which differed from equal allocation.)

Nationalism

We asked some simple questions about nationalism. In the first study we asked, "A helps children who are in your own country. B helps children around the world. The children are equally needy." The mean allocation was 33% to B, where 50% would be equal allocation. In a follow-up study we added, for emphasis, "and the benefits are the same for each child." The mean was unchanged at 32% to B. We also specified what countries the children supported by B were in, using India, Africa, and Latin America. The mean allocation to B was 30% overall, and the regions did not differ. Subjects had an opportunity to comment on each item. A typical comment was, "There are just as many needy children in THIS country and I would help them FIRST."

In our third study, we tried to make it clear that the children were all strangers: "A cures a disease in children who are in a distant part of your own country. B cures the same disease in children in India. A and B are equally efficient. You do not know any of the affected children, or any children who have had this disease." National bias was still present. The mean allocation was 2.55 (1 = all to own country, 5 = all to other country; $p = .0000$ compared to 3.00, i.e., equal allocation). The same held for Eastern Europe, China, and Africa, and the regions did not differ in allocation.

However, 58% of the subjects had means of 3 (equal allocation) or higher. One of these subjects commented, "Children are children, no matter where they are from." Thus when the need and benefits are made explicit, some people do not feel a duty to help their co-nationals first.

Forced Charity

Comments on early studies suggested a general antipathy to any sort of compulsory assessment for charitable purposes:

> "Nobody has the right, weather [sic] it is voted upon or not, can force employees to donate money."
> "While I believe in helping others, have a hard time being forced to help."
> "No matter how important a program is we cannot give up freedom of choice."
> "The citizen should have the choice as to whether he wants to contribute or not."
> "I would not like being forced to pay for any—it should be your choice."

In our fourth study, we presented the following scenario:

> Your country requires everyone to buy health insurance. The fee is fixed at about $2,500 per person.
> **Case A:** To help those who have trouble paying, the government levies a special income tax. Families earning less than $7,500 per person pay no tax. Others pay a fixed percentage of their income above $7,500/person.
> **Case B:** To help those who have trouble paying, charities collect *voluntary donations*. The charities distribute the funds to try to come as close as possible to the situation described in Case A. That is, they provide a subsidy for families earning less than $7,500/person, they reduce the subsidy gradually as income increases, and they solicit contributions from rich people who would pay less in Case B than in Case A. Suppose that the charities succeed, so that the bottom line is the same for each family as in Case A.

We asked four questions:

1. Which case would you favor if you had a choice? [A, B, equal]
2. Which case is more fair in distributing the cost and benefits?

3. Which case provides more freedom of choice?
4. Which is more important in this case? [fair distribution, freedom of choice, equal].

Answers to the questions were highly correlated. The mean response to them was 0.12 (–1 = forced, 1 = voluntary), which did not differ significantly from zero ($p = .09$). On the whole, in this case, there was no particular bias against forced charity. Another similar case yielded similar results. However, the following case yielded a small but significant bias:

> Workers in your country who make widgets (imaginary goods) are getting lower wages because of competition from foreign imports. The price of widgets has gone down, and the workers have accepted wage cuts to avoid layoffs.
> **Case A:** The government puts a tax on widgets. The proceeds from the tax are used to help the domestic workers by restoring their wages to their original level.
> **Case B:** A voluntary charity collects funds to help the domestic workers. The funds are sufficient to restore their wages to their original level.

A second version of Case B read: "A campaign to induce buyers to buy domestic widgets voluntarily succeeds in allowing their price to go up. Wages go back up to their original level."

For both versions, subjects favored the voluntary mechanism, with means of .17 ($t_{77} = 2.84$, $p = 0.0057$) and .20 ($t_{77} = 5.96$, $p = 0.0000$), respectively. But 33% and 26%, respectively, favored the tax. This contrasts with another case:

> A *new* epidemic disease threatens to infect 10% and kill 1% of the children in *your nation*. It can be cured by a treatment that costs too much for any insurance company to cover it, including current government insurance, without raising premiums or taxes. Additional funds are needed.
> **Case A:** The funds are raised with an increase of income taxes by a percentage of the current tax, sufficient to cover the costs.
> **Case B:** The funds are raised by voluntary donations. Treatment is free to those who get the disease. Donations are sufficient to cover the costs.

Here the mean was .37, and only 14% favored the tax.

In sum, we have some evidence for a labile preference for voluntary mechanisms. Of course, in stating these cases, we have asked subjects to accept the implausible assumption that voluntary mechanisms can raise as much as taxes.

DISCUSSION

Whether a charitable donation is inspired primarily by altruism, reputational concerns, psychological benefits to the self, or a combination of other motivational factors,[*] we argue that a decision to financially self-sacrifice should be accompanied by a straightforward goal of maximizing the total expected utilities of others. Given the enormous economic needs in developing nations coupled with the relatively small costs of saving human lives in the poorest countries (World Bank, 2004), maximizing

---

[*] For a comprehensive review of the reasons why people donate, see Bekkers and Wiepking (2007).

the utility of each donation is of crucial importance. We recognize that one problem with utility maximization in charitable giving is the current lack of adequate measures to assess the efficacy of philanthropic organizations worldwide (World Bank, 2007). What concerns us more, however, are our findings from a series of studies on charitable donations where the subjects made systematically suboptimal allocations despite being provided with clear diagnostic indicators of the charitable organizations' performance.

The most pronounced deviations from the utilitarian standards included: (1) the waste heuristic, or preoccupation with the overhead expenses that led subjects to favor less efficient charities with low operating costs over more efficient organizations with slightly higher operating costs; (2) average cost bias, or attention to average benefit per dollar when, in fact, the marginal benefit should guide a decision; (3) the diversification heuristic, or a tendency to donate to many charities even in cases when contributing to only one organization would save more lives; (4) parochialism, or support for organizations helping co-nationals even when donating to international causes would help more people; and finally (5) a framing effect, or preference for either a system of voluntary donations or forced charity (i.e., taxes) depended on the type of presentation.

One idea for helping people to generate the most good with the resources they are willing to donate is to encourage charities to disclose information about their current state of funding by regularly updating the benefit-to-cost ratio for new contributions (i.e., the ratio of benefit to beneficiaries over cost to a donor). Such a single indicator of efficacy, if calculated properly, would enable donors to select the most efficient charities at the time of contribution. A skeptic might argue that the underperforming charities, as well as the organizations with ample funding, would have little or no incentive to publish their benefit-to-cost ratios. A possible solution may include educating donors about the biases that subvert the cost-effectiveness of their decisions. We doubt whether education in and of itself would be capable of eliminating the common biases. Nevertheless, education might awaken public demand for access to standardized information on charities, turning a disclosure of the benefit-to-cost indicator into a norm.

More beneficial still might be maximization of the efficacy of tax-supported initiatives, accompanied by an increase in public support for collective action. Sachs (2005, p. 2) argues that even though "introductory economics textbooks preach individualism and decentralized markets, our safety and prosperity depend at least as much on collective decisions to fight disease, promote good science and widespread education, provide critical infrastructure, and act in unison to help the poorest of the poor." In other words, the most efficient use of the human capacity for caring may not be an annual charitable donation, but rather support for a broader social movement or an engagement in social entrepreneurship.

Utilitarian Models of Altruism

The utilitarian model that we have applied, assuming a fixed willingness to sacrifice self-interest, is simplistic. Future research should consider extensions of this model, or alternatives to it, even within the utilitarian framework.

Maximize Total Utility   The simplest utilitarian model for decision making requires that all choices maximize the welfare of everyone affected by them. The model provides a measure of the total expected goodness of consequences and holds that more self-sacrifice is always better, as long as the individual costs of sacrificing are less than the benefits provided to others. Such a simple utilitarian formula is especially useful in the context of third-party decision making, in which those who decide remain unaffected by their decisions. However, it is less helpful in understanding and improving individual decisions, since in real life, people find it difficult to sacrifice their self-interest.

An alternative normative model evaluates the goodness of consequences of different options (i.e., their utility) in terms of the decision maker's own goals. These goals include altruistic goals, but the welfare of other's carries less weight than the well-being of a decision maker.

Thus, those who want to know how rational their decisions are can get two different answers, depending on which model they apply—simple utilitarianism or expected-utility based on the personal goals.

Limited Self-Sacrifice   We can think of self-sacrifice as a limited resource, subject to an external constraint. In the simplest form of this model, each person begins with a simple expected utility approach and then reduces personal expected utility by some fixed limited amount, so long as this reduction leads to greater benefit for others, for each unit of time.

For example, suppose that we consider only money. People work to make money. They have some utility function for annual income; increases in income have utility for them. Presumably this utility is marginally declining with income, e.g., their utility in "utiles" is the square root of thousands of dollars. Then, having made their money, they consider how much to give to charity. They are willing to sacrifice, say, 1 utile, period. So, someone who makes $64,000 is willing to sacrifice $15,000, because 1 utile is the difference between the utility of $64,000 (8 utiles) and the utility of $49,000 (7 utiles). This form of the model allows us to consider questions of efficiency very easily. We ask, given the limitation, how we can best maximize the utilities of others. For example, what charitable causes will do the most good, for $15,000? This model is basically what we have applied here, although our results are relevant to some other models too.

An advantage of this model is that it is compatible with a decision maker's point of view. Instead of asking an abstract question, "What is the most rational thing to do?" a decision maker can ask, "How can I do the most good given the limited self-sacrifice that I am willing to make?" The latter question assumes that the level of self-sacrifice is constrained and not solely under the individual's control, which is, in fact, how many people may view it.

It is also possible to reframe the model, and instead of focusing on the limited ability to sacrifice, take into account the generated benefits for others. For example, people might be willing to reduce their own welfare if the gain for others is greater by some constant multiplier, such as 10. That is, they would be following a rule of thumb that if you can give up 1 utile in order to increase 11 people's utility by 1 utile each, then you would do it.

This form corresponds to proposals for *weighted utilitarianism* that have often been discussed (e.g., Baron, 1993). The difference between the present approach and the earlier proposals is that they were viewed as recommendations made to an individual—almost a way of capturing some concept of "duty" within a utilitarian framework. It is as if they said, "If you always sacrifice your own good when you can do 10 times as much good for others, then you have done your duty and you don't need to feel guilty anymore." The trouble with this is that it doesn't really answer any question. Not "what is best?" and not "what is rational?" Those are already answered in other ways: what is best is to maximize utility for all, which could require more self-sacrifice than most people are willing to make; and what is rational (arguably) is to best achieve your own goals, including your goal of being altruistic. Our idea of an external limitation on altruism is an answer to the second question. Our normative model does not attempt to tell people how altruistic they should be, but it simply accepts their willingness to sacrifice as it is.

A more realistic form of this model is that self-sacrifice is indeed limited but can be "stretched." As the amount of self-sacrifice increases (per unit time), the benefit-to-cost ratio—the ratio of benefit to others over cost to the self—must be higher before a self-sacrificing option is chosen. This model specifies the same optimal behavior in our experiments as the basic model.

Limited Altruism

We could extend the model further to allow altruism to depend on the beneficiaries. In the most general case, the function implied in the last case would depend on who benefits. That is, we would behave as if we multiplied the marginal benefit to person P by some factor (usually less than 1) that depended both on who P is and on the marginal cost to us of providing the marginal benefit (with lower weight for greater cost), and then did a utilitarian calculation taking into account everyone's utility. This is the most realistic model, because, for example, people are much more willing to sacrifice for their children and spouses than for others. (We could imagine that most people think of self-interest as the interest of their immediate family.) Another example is that altruism for unrelated others may be greater for people in one's group, such as a nation.

In the present studies, we tried to avoid this issue by asking subject to put aside their own feelings.

Moral Education

A final model is relevant if we take the position of the moral educator rather than the individual decision maker. Arguably, the position of the educator is the most basic one (Baron, 1996).

If we had no moral principles, we could derive them by asking what principles we would rationally endorse as principles for everyone to follow. With an answer to this, we are in a position to know how to educate others. This argument is a theoretical device (in the spirit of the "veil of ignorance").

Yet moral education is relevant if we consider the costs and benefits of efforts to inculcate or encourage altruism in others, as done by Kaplow and Shavell (2007). It might be easier to increase altruism toward distant strangers than toward family members, because the latter would be naturally strong and not susceptible to much further increase. Because of this natural strength, it would likewise be futile (that is, prohibitively costly) to try to encourage altruism toward distant strangers *at the expense* of family members. An optimal moral system for the purpose of public norms, norms that were generally endorsed and supported, would thus take into account these natural constraints, wherever they come from. It is not obvious, though, that national loyalty is one of these constraints (in contrast to loyalty toward spouses and children, which has clear biological roots).

Implications

Of course, charities may capitalize on the above biases by, for example, suggesting that donors allocate some money to a particular charity even if they contribute to others, or advertising favorable statistics, even if they are not the most relevant ones. In turn, one lesson for a donor is to be more open-minded. Stretch your imagination. See below the surface. Be aware of your own cognitive shortcuts that can undermine your goal of helping.

More generally, though, donors should put charitable contributions in a broader context that includes all their other altruistic behavior, including what they do with their work, and their political actions. Charitable institutions might also consider political action as an alternative to direct aid. For example, it may (or may not) be more helpful to Africans to lobby against trade restrictions on their exports, or in favor of medical research on tropical diseases, than to provide direct aid. Of course, such efforts must be considered in the light of tax laws.

Efforts at donor education might be seen as parallel to investor education, which is now carried out (to some degree, with some effectiveness) by investment advisors and by various institutions. It might even make sense for this function to be filled by current financial advisors, given that charitable donations are part of people's total financial picture. Estate lawyers will tell you how to minimize your tax burden, but not, yet, how to maximize the benefits that you leave behind.

REFERENCES

Andreoni, J. (1990). Impure altruism and donations to public goods: A theory of warm-glow giving. *The Economic Journal, 100*, 464–477.

Baron, J. (1993). *Morality and rational choice*. Dordrecht: Kluwer.

Baron, J. (1996). Norm-endorsement utilitarianism and the nature of utility. *Economics and Philosophy, 12*, 165–182.

Baron, J. (1997). Political action vs. voluntarism in social dilemmas and aid for the needy. *Rationality and Society, 9*, 307–326.

Baron, J. (2008). *Thinking and deciding* (4th ed.). New York: Cambridge University Press.

Baron, J. (in press). Parochialism as a result of cognitive biases. In A. K. Woods, R. Goodman, & D. Jinks (Eds.), *Understanding social action, promoting human rights*. Oxford: Oxford University Press.

Bekkers, R., & Wiepking, P. (2007, October 28). Generosity and philanthropy: A literature review. Available at the Social Science Research Network (SSRN): http://ssrn.com/abstract=1015507

Bettman, J. R., Luce M. F., & Payne, J. W. (1998). Constructive consumer choice processes. *Journal of Consumer Research, 25,* 187–217.

Charness, G., & Gneezy, U. (2008). What's in a name? Anonymity and social distance in dictator and ultimatum games. *Journal of Economic Behavior & Organization, 68,* 29–35.

Fox, C. R., Ratner, R. K., & Lieb, D. S. (2005). How subjective grouping of options influences choice and allocation: Diversification bias and the phenomenon of partition dependence. *Journal of Experimental Psychology: General, 134,* 538–551.

Hsee, C. K. (1996). The evaluability hypothesis: An explanation of preference reversals between joint and separate evaluation of alternatives. *Organizational Behavior and Human Decision Processes, 46,* 247–257.

Kaplow, L., & Shavell, S. (2007). Moral rules, the moral sentiments, and behavior: Toward a theory of an optimal moral system. *Journal of Political Economy, 115,* 494–514.

Margolis, H. (1982). *Selfishness, altruism, and rationality: A theory of social choice.* New York: Cambridge University Press.

Read, D., & Loewenstein, G. (1995). Diversification bias: Explaining the discrepancy in variety seeking between combined and separated choices. *Journal of Experimental Psychology: Applied, 1,* 34–49.

Sachs J. D. (2005). *The end of poverty.* New York: Penguin Press.

Schick, F. (1991). *Understanding action: An essay on reasons.* New York: Cambridge University Press.

Tversky, A., Sattath, S., & Slovic, P. (1988). Contingent weighting in judgment and choice. *Psychological Review, 95,* 371–384.

Ubel, P. A., DeKay, M. L., Baron, J., & Asch, D. A. (1996). Public preferences for efficiency and racial equity in kidney transplant allocation decisions. *Transplantation Proceedings, 28,* 2997–3002.

World Bank (2004). World Development Reports. Washington, DC: The World Bank Group. http://go.worldbank.org/2A5GCSRQH0

World Bank (2007). World Development Reports. Washington, DC: The World Bank Group. http://go.worldbank.org/2A5GCSRQH0

APPENDIX A

The experiments themselves are available at http://finzi.psych.upenn.edu/~baron/ex/ewas/, as char1, char2, char3, and char4. The questions asked in each study are shown below, with an example of one item.

CHAR 1 AND 2

A and B both help thousands of children. In A, each contribution goes to one child. In B, the contribution is spread out over all the children. Each child gets the same help.

How much would you allocate to A/B?
    100%/0%
    90%/10%
    80%/20%
    70%/30%
    60%/40%

50%/50%
40%/60%
30%/70%
20%/80%
10%/90%
0%/100%

Which choice would give you a better feeling?
A or B: no difference

Which choice is a more effective use of your money?
A or B: no difference

With which choice are you more sure that your contribution will do some good (as opposed to none)?
A or B: no difference

CHAR3, PART 1

What is the right allocation between A and B, ignoring your own feelings? All to A More to A, some to B, Equally to A and B, More to B, some to A, All to B

Which would give you a better feeling?
Contributing to A or contributing to B: no difference
What allocation between A and B would be the most efficient use of your money?
All to A, More to A, some to B
Equally to A and B
More to B, some to A
All to B

CHAR3, PART 2

Case A: Your employer collects individual voluntary contributions by deducting them from paychecks. It is expected that 50% of the employees will contribute an average of $20 each.

Case B: The employees have voted, by a margin of 55% to 45%, for a system in which the employer deducts $10 from everyone's paycheck, leading to the same total contribution as in Case A.

Which case would you favor if you had a choice?
A and B equal

Which case is more fair in allocating the cost among potential contributors?
A and B equal

Which case provides more freedom to potential contributors?
    A and B equal

Which is more important in this case?
    Fair cost allocation
    Freedom of choice equal

What if Case A, the voluntary-contribution case, would raise half as much money as Case B (rather than the same amount). Which case would you favor?
    A and B equal

CHAR4, PART 1

A can save one life for $10,000. B can save one life for $12,500. The people helped are from the same groups, with the same problems.

What is the right allocation between A and B, ignoring your own feelings?
    All to A
    More to A, some to B
    Equally to A and B
    More to B, some to A
    All to B

What allocation would you feel best about making?
    All to A
    More to A, some to B
    Equally to A and B
    More to B, some to A
    All to B

What allocation between A and B would be the most efficient use of your money?
    All to A
    More to A, some to B
    Equally to A and B
    More to B, some to A
    All to B

What allocation between A and B would do the most good for each $1,000 spent?
    All to A
    More to A, some to B
    Equally to A and B
    More to B, some to A
    All to B

CHAR4, PART 2

Your country requires everyone to buy health insurance. The fee is fixed at about $2,500 per person.

Case A: To help those who have trouble paying, the government levies a special income tax. Families earning less than $7,500 per person pay no tax. Others pay a fixed percentages of their income above $7,500/person.

Case B: To help those who have trouble paying, charities collect voluntary donations. The charities distribute the funds to try to come as close as possible to the situation described in Case A. That is, they provide a subsidy for families earning less than $7,500/person, they reduce the subsidy gradually as income increases, and they solicit contributions from rich people who would pay less in Case B than in Case A. Suppose that the charities succeed, so that the bottom line is the same for each family as in Case A.

Which case would you favor if you had a choice?
    A and B equal

Which case is more fair in distributing the cost and benefits?
    A and B equal

Which case provides more freedom of choice?
    A and B equal

Which is more important in this case?
    Fair distribution
    Freedom of choice
    Equal

14

The Critical Link Between Tangibility and Generosity

CYNTHIA CRYDER and GEORGE LOEWENSTEIN

*I*n 2006, the consumer products giant Procter and Gamble (P&G) launched a new marketing campaign in South Africa for Pampers, its flagship brand of disposable diaper. The campaign, titled "1 Pack = 1 Vaccine", was a collaboration with UNICEF and was geared toward eliminating newborn tetanus, a leading cause of neonatal death in developing countries. This was a classic win-win situation: UNICEF received P&G's help in their neonatal tetanus campaign (assistance that ultimately amounted to distributing more than 150 million vaccines), and P&G enhanced its image among consumers.[*] The campaign was one of the most successful in Pampers' 50-year history in its impact on consumer attitudes, and more importantly, its impact on sales.[†] In contrast, a competing campaign launched in other countries using the slogan "1 Pack Will Help Eradicate Newborn Tetanus Globally" was much less successful.

Why, beyond the problematic wordiness, would the "1 pack will help eradicate newborn tetanus globally" campaign be so much less effective than "1 Pack = 1 Vaccine?" In this paper, we argue that the answer lies in its inferior *tangibility*. We present evidence that documents the positive impact of tangibility on generosity and suggests that tangibility increases generosity for two reasons.

First, tangibility increases the perception that one's involvement will make a difference. Buying a pack of Pampers that will "help" eradicate tetanus is much less gratifying than buying a pack of pampers that will actually provide a vaccine to a specific baby. Likewise, although one might think that the term *globally* would underscore the pervasiveness, and hence importance, of the tetanus

---

[*] After the campaign, consumers increased in their propensity to endorse statements such as "Pampers helps me help others."

[†] We thank Paul Brest and Sandile Hlatshwayo for bringing this example to our attention.

problem, highlighting the huge scope of the problem can backfire by making it feel as if one's own contribution is just a drop in the bucket.

Second, tangibility often intensifies emotional reactions. In a wide range of research, emotions have been shown to both lead to increased generosity (e.g., Batson et al., 1997; Batson, 1998; Batson et al., 1988; Batson et al., 1989; Coke et al., 1978; Dovidio et al., 1990; Toi & Batson, 1982; Smith, Keating, & Stotland, 1989) and to result from increased generosity (Andreoni, 1990; Dunn, Aknin, & Norton, 2008; Harbaugh, Mayr, & Burghart, 2008). By emphasizing the idea that a single purchase of Pampers finances a single dose of vaccine, the "1 Pack = 1 Vaccine" message gives license to the consumer's imagination. Walking *into* the store, the shopper may have been just another mother buying diapers; walking *out*, as she plays images in her mind of a child receiving the vaccine and of the smiling and appreciative parent, the shopper has been transformed into an activist, a humanitarian, and a heroine.

In this chapter we will explore how tangible information about both people and needs increases generosity.

RESEARCH ON TANGIBILITY AND GENEROSITY

The Identifiable Victim Effect

In a 1968 book chapter about inconsistencies in the valuation of human life (The Life You Save May Be Your Own), Thomas Schelling, an invariably astute observer of life, noted that in almost all cases an individual life described in detail is more valuable to us than the equivalent life described only as a statistic. Simply knowing details about a person whose life is at stake, such as their age, gender, or hair color makes us value their life more than if the same endangered life is abstract and anonymous. This phenomenon clearly has consequences for how policy makers allocate money for saving citizens' lives, which was Schelling's main focus, but it also has important implications for the types of appeals that are more or less effective in eliciting generosity.

Research on what has come to be known as the "identifiable victim effect" consistently finds that people give more to individual, identified victims than to equivalent statistical victims or groups of victims. In one hypothetical choice study, for example, participants given information about a child in need of medical treatment were willing to donate over 75% more when the child was identified by age, name, and picture, as compared to when the child was described without these identifying features (Kogut & Ritov, 2005a). In another demonstration involving real donations, participants gave 60% more on average when a victim was identified by age, name, and picture, compared to when the victim was not described with identifying details (Kogut & Ritov, 2005b). Similarly, in a laboratory experiment examining the "dictator game" (Forsythe, Horowitz, Savin, & Sefton, 1994; Kahneman, Knetsch, & Thaler, 1986), college students who received $10 and were given the opportunity to share any portion of that money with a fellow student, were more generous when they were informed of the would-be recipient's name, hometown, major, and hobbies than when they were not given this personal information (Bohnet & Frey, 1999; see also Charness & Gneezy, 2008). Importantly, this general phenomenon is not limited to cases involving donations. For example, in medicine, physicians consider individual patients and statistical patients differently. When physicians make decisions about individual patients, as opposed to making policy decisions applying to patients in general, they are more likely to recommend attentive care such as additional low-cost tests and in-person visits instead of phone consultations (Redelmeier & Tversky, 1990).

Even the most subtle differences between identified and statistical victims can have dramatic consequences for generosity. In one demonstration, (Small & Loewenstein, 2003), people were more generous when the victim who would receive their aid had already been chosen compared to when the victim who would receive their aid had not yet been chosen. In this experiment, again involving the dictator game, each participant in a 10-participant session was given $10 and assigned a number (from 1 to 10). Five numbers were drawn randomly and people with those numbers (the victims) lost their $10. Then, each of the 5 participants who had not lost $10 could share their $10 with a participant who had lost the $10. In one of two experimental conditions, the fortunate participants who had retained their $10 *first* drew the number of the victim who would receive their contribution, then decided how much to share. In the other condition, the fortunate participants were told that the number of the victim who would receive their contribution would be drawn right *after* they decided how much to give; the participant first decided how much to share and then the number of the victim with whom they would share was drawn. In both conditions, participants knew that they would never learn the identity of the person with whom they could share. Yet those who drew the number first, and so knew the number of the person with whom they were linked, shared, on average, 60% more than did participants whose recipient had not yet been, but was shortly to be, determined.

The effect was replicated in a field experiment in which participants could donate to Habitat for Humanity to build a new home for a family. Half of the participants were told that the family whose home would be built had already been selected from a list of four families. The other half were shown the same list, but were told that one of the four would be chosen shortly. In neither case did the potential donor learn *which* family had been selected; however, consistent with the previous finding, participants donated over 25% more to Habitat for Humanity when they believed that the family who would receive help had already been determined.

Explanations for the Identifiable Victim Effect

One common explanation for increased generosity toward individuals rather than groups is that donating toward only one person promotes the feeling that the donor is making a greater proportional difference (Baron, 1997; Featherstonhaugh et al., 1997; Jenni & Loewenstein, 1997). For example, Featherstonhaugh and coauthors (1997) found that the perceived benefit of a lifesaving intervention increased as the proportion of people in need increased (e.g., from 4,500/250,000 to 4,500/11,000), while holding the actual number in need constant. Since the size of the denominator is often arbitrary, the impact of proportion suggests that concern can be manipulated relatively easily by, for example, focusing an appeal on a subsection of a group in need instead of the entire group in need.

This *denominator effect* is robust, likely because it plays on both of the mechanisms identified earlier. When many people are in need, helping a few of them feels subjectively as if one is having only a small impact because one's intervention leaves so many untouched. In contrast, helping a few people out of a total of a few people who need help feels subjectively as if one is having a much larger impact. And, just as thinking of *oneself* as one out of 6 billion people alive on the Earth has a tendency to render one's own life less significant, as the denominator increases of those in need it becomes difficult to identify with, or empathize with, any member of the multitude.

The identifiable victim effect is more, however, than *just* a denominator effect. Many demonstrations of the identifiable victim effect provide details about an individual rather than varying the number of people highlighted in the request (Kogut & Ritov, 2005a; Bohnet & Frey, 1999). Other research finds that people are less sympathetic and willing to help all members of a small group than they are to help one individual randomly selected from the group (and presented alone; Kogut & Ritov, 2005a). This effect cannot be attributed to an impact of proportionality because in both of these cases the numerator and denominator are the same (e.g., 5/5 or 1/1).[*] There is evidence that people have a larger emotional response to individual victims rather than a group of victims. People report greater emotional distress for a single identified victim compared to a group of identified victims, and this greater emotional distress corresponds with greater contributions for the single identified victim compared to a group of identified victims (Kogut & Ritov, 2005a).

Why should people be less sympathetic to a small group of individuals than they are to any individual selected from the group? A fascinating study by Morewedge and Schooler (2009) may provide an important clue. The study was inspired by Schooler's daughter, who had an aquarium populated by brine shrimp (popularly known as "sea monkeys"), which died, one at a time, until there was only one sea monkey left. Schooler noticed that, having previously viewed the sea monkeys as an undifferentiated mass, he and his children became fascinated with the last remaining one, imputing to it a personality and identity and experiencing a concern for its survival that they had not felt for its multitude of brethren. Morewedge and Schooler followed up on this observation with experimental studies. In one study, participants (commuters in Boston) were presented with a black-and-white image of two-finned sea creatures in a fish tank, and rated the extent to which the creature seemed to possess beliefs, desires, consciousness, and intelligence. The number of other identical sea creatures present (0, 1, 2, 3 or 4) varied for different participants. Participants who saw many sea creatures were less likely to attribute high-level mental states to those creatures compared to participants who saw fewer or only one creature. A follow-up study showed a similar effect when holding the

---

[*] Interestingly, providing identifying information about group members does not increase contributions to a group (Kogut & Ritov, 2005a, 2005b), and in fact, the reverse effect sometimes occurs: unidentified groups raise more money than identified groups (Kogut & Ritov, 2005b).

number of creatures constant, but varying whether the focal creature looked the same or different from its counterparts. Participants were more likely to attribute high-level mental states to those creatures that stood out among their counterparts compared to those who were one of many similar, other creatures.

Assuming that people are more likely to experience emotions, such as sympathy, toward sentient, conscious, intelligent creatures compared to those with less advanced mental states, Morewedge and Schooler's result helps to explain the greater emotion, and hence generosity, evoked by single victims. Other work about the importance of emotion finds that people are more likely to pass along stories that are emotional versus informational (Heath, Bell, & Sternberg, 2001) and that people are more likely to act upon emotionally evocative compared to technical information (Sinaceur & Heath, 2005). Work focusing specifically on the identifiable victim effect finds that priming people to be calculating instead of emotional— for example, by having participants solve arithmetic problems before making a donation decision—eliminates the identifiable victim effect by reducing generosity toward identified victims (Small, Loewenstein, & Slovic, 2007). In sum, it appears that the ability for people to feel greater emotion toward individual victims is a critical element in understanding the identified victim and related effects.

Tangibility and Generosity   A key difference between identified versus statistical victims is that identifiable victims are inherently more tangible than their statistical (and abstract) counterparts. Although the identifiable victim effect could be construed as a special case of tangibility, connections between tangibility and generosity exist beyond the identifiable victim effect. For example, people are more generous toward causes with which they have direct personal experience, and hence more tangible information, such as when AIDS volunteers are more likely to have a loved one who suffered from AIDS than from Alzheimer's disease, and Alzheimer's disease volunteers are more likely to have a loved one who suffered from Alzheimer's disease than from AIDS (Small & Simonsohn, 2007).

Tangible information, broadly, is information that is specific and concrete as opposed to general and abstract. Information can be inherently tangible, such as when it is highly specific and imbued with rich detail or information, and can become more tangible due to the way that it is processed. Information that is very "psychologically near" to us (i.e., close or immediate in terms of time, space, or social proximity; see, e.g., Pronin, Olivola, & Kennedy, 2008) is processed more concretely (Lewin, 1951; Liberman, Trope, & Stephan, 2007). For example, we process information about the present more concretely than we process information about the future (Trope & Liberman, 2003), and we process events that are spatially close to us more concretely than we process those events that are spatially far away from us (Fujita, Henderson, Eng, Trope, & Lieberman, 2006).

In our own research, we have examined diverse consequences of the hypothesis that generosity is positively related to tangibility. For example, in one set of experiments we varied the order in which potential donors made the two most basic choices associated with donating to charity: (1) How much should I donate? and (2) To whom will I give? Both orders are common in charitable giving. Many times, people choose the cause or causes that they will support, and then decide how much to give. Other times, however, people decide the amount first; for example, subscribers to the Fidelity® Charitable Gift Fund first contribute money to the fund, typically in the form of appreciated stock at year's end, and then subsequently, at their leisure, decide where to allocate those contributions.

We hypothesized that if people first decide how much money to donate, the recipient would not be concrete when they made the decision. In contrast, if people first decide to whom they wish to donate, the recipient is much more tangible at the moment when they choose an amount. Thus, we hypothesized that people would donate more when they made the *who* decision before they made the *how much* decision than if they made the same two decisions in the reverse order.

In experiments testing this idea, we asked participants to make real or hypothetical choices about how much to donate to one of several charitable organizations such as Save the Children, the American Red Cross, and Oxfam America. All participants first viewed a list of charities that they could support, to ensure that everyone knew what organizations they could donate to. Then, participants in one condition first chose one of the charities to support, and then chose an amount to give, while those in the other condition first chose an amount to give to one of the charities and then picked which organization their donation would go to.

Participants who picked a specific charity first, and then picked an amount to give, donated more than those who made the two decisions in reverse order. This effect was replicated using several procedural variations including hypothetical choice scenarios, decisions made using real money, and decisions made at a within-charity level in which participants were willing to donate more to a charity when they chose a specific fund to support within that charity before deciding how much to give to the charity. One study also demonstrated that participants' assessments of the impact of their donation partially explained the findings. People who chose a specific donation target before deciding how much to give felt as if their donation would have more of an impact, and this increased feeling of impact led to increased giving (Cryder & Loewenstein, 2009).

In a second project, we tested a new way to increase the tangibility of a donation target. Instead of changing the scope of the target as in the project above (considering one charity versus several when deciding how much to give), participants focused on a single charity from the start and received more specific versus less specific information about that charity. In the first experiment, participants read information about the charity Oxfam, and decided how much, if anything, they wished to donate to Oxfam. In one experimental condition, Oxfam was framed in a tangible way with detailed information explaining that one way donations are used is to provide clean water to villagers in West Africa. In another condition, Oxfam was framed in an intangible way with general information explaining that donations would go to a broad range of needs across the globe. Participants who read about Oxfam framed in a tangible way donated almost twice as much as participants who read about Oxfam framed in a general way, and consistent with previous tangibility findings, an increased feeling of impact explained this difference (Cryder, Loewenstein, & Scheines, 2010). In a second, real-world experiment, we measured generous responses to two different charities that naturally differed in tangibility. In one condition, participants read about an inherently tangible charity

("Nothing but Nets", a charity that provides mosquito protection bed nets to families in Africa). In another condition, participants read about an inherently intangible charity (Oxfam International, an international aid organization that provides aid to people across the globe). Consistent with results from the previous study, participants who read about the tangible charity donated almost three times as much as participants who read about the intangible charity, and an increased feeling of impact again mediated this effect (Cryder et al., 2010).

Goal Proximity   Concrete information can lead to an increased feeling of impact (Cryder & Loewenstein, 2009) and can lead to increased emotional response (Cryder, Loewenstein, & Seltman, 2008). In a project about goal proximity, we observe cases in which the increased feeling of impact not only leads to greater giving, but also leads to greater emotional satisfaction *from* giving.

Actions near the end of a sequence seem more influential than actions at the beginning of a sequence. For example, in a scenario in which two people flip a coin and win a prize if the outcomes match (both heads or both tails), participants report that the person who flips last will receive more blame for a failed outcome than the person who flips first, even though both contributors clearly have equal impact (Miller & Gunasegaram, 1990). Just as individuals who play a role near the end of a sequence receive disproportionate blame when the final outcome is bad, in a line of work about goal proximity and generosity, we hypothesized that individuals who play a role near the end of a sequence also receive, or at least anticipate receiving, disproportionate credit when the outcome is good.

This hypothesis has clear consequences for the domain of charitable giving. Specifically, donations that are made near the end of a fundraising campaign (e.g., the final $100 of a $10,000 campaign) may feel more satisfying, and hence be more attractive to potential donors, than donations made near the start of the campaign (e.g., the second $100 contribution made to the same campaign). Thus, in a series of studies we hypothesized that rates of donation would increase as charities approached reaching their fundraising goals (Cryder, Loewenstein, & Seltman, 2008).

Our first study addressing this idea was an Internet field study that used information from the Web site for Kiva, a nonprofit organization that facilitates brokerage of low-interest loans to low-income individuals in the developing world. On the Kiva Web site, potential loan recipients are listed along with information about their background, the nature of their loan request, and the progress that they have achieved toward reaching their loan amount goal. Private individuals can go to the Kiva Web site and contribute money toward recipients' loan requests. Using a Web robot (i.e., a Bot), we collected information about the progress each recipient had achieved in obtaining a desired loan, every hour, every day, for approximately one week. As predicted, rates of donation increased as recipients approached their fundraising goals. The rate of contributions when recipients were 33 to 66% of the way toward reaching their fundraising goal was significantly and substantially greater than when recipients were 0 to 33% of the way toward reaching their goal, and the rate of contributions when recipients were 66 to 100% of the way toward reaching their fundraising goal was significantly and substantially greater than when recipients were 33 to 66% of the way toward reaching the goal.

A field experiment conducted in partnership with a local disaster relief agency tested this idea experimentally. In the experiment, several thousand donors received one of four mailings. The mailings informed the donors that the fund they could support was either (a) 10% of the way toward reaching its goal, (b) 66% of the way toward reaching its goal, (c) 85% of the way toward reaching its goal, or (d) did not mention the fund's progress toward the goal. Donation rates were highest when a fund was very close to reaching its fundraising goal (control condition). In a pattern similar to that in the first study, there was a large benefit in the number of donations garnered when mentioning that a fund was 85% of the way toward its goal, but less benefit to mentioning that a fund was 10% or 66% of the way toward its goal.

In a third and final study in this series, we investigated the underlying processes behind this pattern. Participants were asked how likely they would be to help Sheila, a junior high student who was selling candy bars to raise money for a school fundraiser. In one condition, Sheila needed to sell 17 more candy bars to reach her goal. In another condition, Sheila needed to sell only 3 more candy bars to reach goal. Participants reported being more likely to buy a candy bar when Sheila was only 3 candy bars away from her goal compared to 17 candy bars away from her goal, even though participants in both conditions were told that Sheila was sure to reach her goal within the next 24 hours (ensuring that Sheila's likelihood of success was not driving the results). In addition, participants' reports of excitement and satisfaction of helping Sheila when she was very close to reaching her goal completely mediated, or explained, the effect. The finding that rates of donation increase as charities approach their fundraising goals is consistent with the notion that efforts at the end of the process feel more concrete and influential than do efforts near the beginning of a process, and that the increased feeling of impact leads to an increase in the excitement and satisfaction of giving (Cryder, Loewenstein, & Seltman 2008).

In sum, our own and others' research about identifiability, concreteness, and goal proximity highlight the importance of tangibility for generosity, and point to three interrelated causal mechanisms outlined in Figure 14.1. First, increasing the concreteness of someone's contribution leads to an increased feeling of impact associated with giving. Second, increasing the concreteness of a victim or

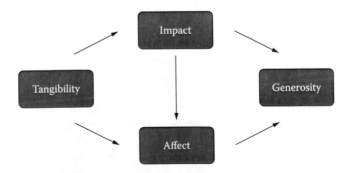

Figure 14.1   Relationship between tangibility, perceived impact, affect, and generosity.

need leads to heightened sympathy (affect) for that need. Finally, the increased feeling of impact from giving to a concrete need can also increase affect such as excitement and warm-glow satisfaction from giving (Andreoni, 1990). The direct path from impact, the direct path from emotional response, and the indirect path from impact to emotional response all lead to increased generosity. The identifiable victim effect capitalizes on all three of these effects by making victims very concrete and increasing sympathy felt toward the victim, but also by maximizing the proportion of the need that is fulfilled by a single donor and increasing a donor's feeling of impact (and potentially, anticipated satisfaction). In real-world requests for generosity, methods of increasing the concreteness to encourage affect and perceived impact can be used to encourage generosity and contributions.

How Do Organizations Currently Use Tangible Information?

Despite the importance of tangibility, many if not most of the most worthy organizations—organizations that actually make a major (tangible) difference in people's lives—fail to exploit the power of tangibility when it comes to fundraising. For example, the entry page for the United Way Web site relies almost exclusively on abstract information to encourage people to volunteer and donate. The main graphic on the page is an abstract cut-out shape of the United States. Words on the Web page encourage people to "Live United" and go on to say "It's a credo. A mission. A goal." After a few seconds, pictures of about a dozen volunteers in white "Live United" shirts appear; however, nowhere on the Web page are people who are helped by the United Way pictured or mentioned, nor is there even an explanation of exactly what it means to "Live United."

The donation Web page for the United Way continues in abstraction. Although there is a well-designed section of the donation page that asks people to choose a specific cause (education, health, etc.) before deciding how much to give, most of the text on the donation page paints a vague picture of how the United Way, and contributions to the Untied Way, make a difference. The page asks people to "invest in their community" by giving to the United Way and explains that their worldwide network is vast and widespread, "working to advance the common good in 47 countries and territories, including nearly 1,300 local organizations in the U.S." Finally, the text offers a vague appeal to supporters by saying, "With your help we can reignite a movement that is committed to creating opportunities for everyone." Such an absence of tangibility leaves the potential donor unmoved, and potentially unconvinced, about how his or her donation can make a difference.

Finally, the lack of tangibility persists for those who, despite the weakness of the appeals, donate nevertheless. This is the point at which the process becomes entirely intangible because once a donation is sent, it simply disappears. Donors never receive information about how their donation helps, and lacking reinforcement from concrete information about their contribution's accomplishment, donors are unlikely to have motivation to donate ever again. Unfortunately, The United Way is not the only major charity that solicits but then fails to follow-up on donations; the donation process for Oxfam and other major organizations is quite similar.

There are, however, a few unique examples of charities that have effectively put tangibility to work, and their remarkable success is testament to the potential power of tangibility. One recent success story is from the United Nations Foundation campaign Nothing but Nets, mentioned earlier in the paper in an experiment that we ran on the impact of tangibility on sympathy. In the Nothing but Nets campaign, potential donors are informed that all overhead costs are covered by a single large benefactor, so that all other donors' contributions directly provide bed nets—a concrete contribution—to protect against malaria, a tangible problem. The campaign focuses on a tangible need and tangible contribution from the start and has demonstrated remarkable success, raising over $18 million in the campaign's first 19 months (United Nations Foundation, 2007). Even this campaign, however, does not use tangibility as effectively as it could. Although the entry page to the Web site effectively communicates the simple message that a small donation provides nets that can save lives, the actual donation page reverts to abstraction. Potential donors are not reminded where their money will go or how many nets it will buy (i.e., lives they can save). And again, as far as we know, donations are not followed up with information about what one's donation has accomplished. The success of this campaign reinforces the potential gains from increasing tangibility, but also highlights the potential for further improvement.

Harnessing the Power of Technology

It could be argued that historically, technology has often had a detrimental effect on human kindness by decreasing tangibility of victims and thereby increasing callousness rather than generosity. As Jonathan Glover discusses in his book *Humanity: A Moral History of the 20th Century* (2001), modern weapons, including airplanes and boats, made it possible to inflict suffering on large numbers of people who are out of sight and hence unidentified. Thus, for example, sailors and officers on British ships that blockaded German ports during World War I had no direct exposure to the widespread hunger that the blockade caused, and those who flew B-52 bombers 40,000 feet over Vietnam had no direct exposure to the horrors produced by the bombs they dropped. Indeed, some historians have argued that a photograph of a girl—a single identified victim—running down the street burned from a napalm fire behind her played a more significant role in turning American public opinion against the war than did all of the casualty statistics.

Even if technology has historically decreased sympathy, however, some of the newest technologies hold the promise of increasing sympathy by increasing tangibility. New information technologies, most notably the Internet, have the capacity to connect us to specific people, places, and events, even in real time, to a degree that was unthinkable in the past. Many of the neediest potential recipients of aid, such as people in Africa suffering from AIDS, malaria, and dysentery, are extremely distant both in geographic and cultural terms from people located in centers of wealth such as the United States. At a mass level, the Internet holds the potential to bring needy people and potential donors much closer together.

One organization that is remarkable in harnessing the power of technology to benefit distant others is Kiva. As discussed earlier in this chapter, Kiva is a young nonprofit organization that facilitates the brokerage of low-interest loans to individuals in the developing world. Kiva is also one of the few nonprofit organizations that matches contributors directly with aid recipients. On the Kiva Web site, potential contributors first see a list of small business owners whom they can support. The list includes highly detailed information about each recipient including a picture and information such as country of origin, occupation, family background, and business background. The list also describes the request that the potential loan recipient has made in terms of the loan amount requested and the need the loan would fulfill. Once a contributor has chosen a loan recipient to support, the tangible connection between contributor and recipient continues. The contributor can log in to the Kiva Web site at any time and check the loan repayment progress of their recipient. In addition, contributors receive an e-mail each time their recipient makes a loan payment. Finally, contributors receive an e-mail when their recipient has completely paid off the loan—in a sense, when success for the project has been achieved. Kiva supporters have a connection with the person they have helped from the beginning when they choose the person through the very end when the person has repaid the loan. Though this approach is revolutionary in its strategy, it relies on what is by now relatively basic technology to establish and maintain connections between contributors and recipients: digital photography, the Internet, e-mail, and information systems.

Kiva's approach is noteworthy not only in its innovation but also in success. Although Kiva is only a few years old, in the less than year-long interval between March 2008 and January 2009 they raised over $33 million in loans (Kiva.org, 2009). This is more than half of the contributions that Oxfam America raises in a whole year (Oxfam America, 2009), even though Oxfam is a much older organization (almost 40 years old) and has a sparkling reputation in the nonprofit world. Indeed, there have been times when Kiva has been so successful in raising funds that they could not maintain an adequate supply of loan recipients. In January and March of 2008, there were times when potential Kiva supporters who visited the Kiva Web site learned that there were no recipients available to fund (Walker, 2008); there were more people willing to help than could be listed at that time as needing help. Undoubtedly, the fact that Kiva solicits loans that are repaid to lenders (without interest) instead of soliciting pure donations contributes to Kiva's success. Nevertheless, we suspect that a main factor driving Kiva's success is the constant and tangible link that Kiva provides between contributors and those who are helped.

Decision Making and Policy

It is clear that there is a difference in the way that people value tangible versus intangible victims and causes; however, it is less clear which type of framing is "correct" or should be adopted for decision making. When people learn about the identified victim effect and then participate in an experiment in which they can donate to an identified victim (in one condition) or a statistical victim (in another condition), the identified victim effect disappears, and the equalization between conditions is entirely driven by a decrease in donations to the identified victim

(Small, Loewenstein, & Slovic 2007). Similarly, when people simultaneously compare donating to a single victim or donating to a group of victims (compared to considering a single victim or a group of victims in isolation), preference for the single victim disappears and overall donations decrease by over 60% (Kogut & Ritov, 2005b). It seems almost as if any method of priming a deliberative mindset, such as performing math calculations (Small et al., 2007), gaining information about the identified victim effect (Small et al., 2007), or comparing different potential recipients (Kogut & Ritov, 2005b) leads to less generosity. Although one interpretation of these results is that a cognitive mindset shrivels an otherwise noble generous tendency, another interpretation is that it squelches immature sentimentality. Somewhat consistent with the latter view is research by Batson and colleagues (Batson et al., 1995, 1999) showing that empathy-inducing information about an individual causes people to unfairly and inefficiently allocate resources toward that individual and away from other equally (or more) deserving group members. Collectively, this work suggests that we should rely upon our rational selves to guide us in decisions about allocating resources between causes, lest we be steered astray by the biasing powers of emotion. In the case of choosing which of several worthy causes to support, such as in the case of policy decisions, allowing reason to rule may indeed yield the best outcome by allowing each worthy cause to have consideration rather than letting the one that garners the most sympathy to rule.

In the case of individuals choosing whether or not to support a needy cause at all, however, letting ourselves be guided by our heartstrings, and simply therefore being more likely to give, may yield the best collective outcome. Increased individual generosity from those of us with resources to spare may not only benefit the recipients of aid, but may also benefit us as givers. Recent research demonstrates that acting generously increases happiness. People who spend money on others report greater happiness than do those who spend money on themselves, even when people are randomly assigned to spend money on others or themselves (Dunn, Aknin, & Norton, 2008; see also Chapter 1). In addition, mesolimbic reward systems activate when people are informed that they have donated to charity (Moll et al., 2006). In sum, when individuals act generously, there is opportunity for all parties to benefit, suggesting that acting upon our sympathies in individual decision making can encourage both overall generosity to those in need as well as donor well-being.

As argued by Loewenstein and Small (2007), the ideal altruistic situation is one in which our sympathies and rational sides align; that is, when both our heart and our head tell us to support the same cause in the same magnitude. When there is conflict, however, relying on our sympathy for decisions about *whether* to give and relying on our reason for decisions about *how* to give may yield the best policy of all.

Conclusions

In this chapter we explored how tangible information about victims and needs leads to increases in generosity. We started by discussing demonstrations of the identifiable victim effect that illustrate how we respond more generously to identified, individual victims than to statistical groups of victims. We then discussed how the identified victim effect represents a more general phenomenon; namely, that people respond more generously to concrete rather than abstract needs because concreteness allows greater emotion and allows each donor's contribution to feel more impactful.

Many future directions and open questions for this work remain. First, what are the long-term consequences of making concrete requests? While we expect that increasing the feeling of a donor's impact can only increase the likelihood of donating again in the future so that the donor can regain that positive feeling, the long-term impact of using sympathy-based appeals is unclear. Do people become immune to sympathy appeals over time? Do they become avoidant of messages they know will tug at their heartstrings? Second, how are different types of supporters influenced by different messages? For example, new donors may respond very differently to different types of solicitations than do established donors. Finally, what types of solicitations effectively appeal to our sense of reason? While too much statistical information seems to hinder generosity, there may be some types of factual information that allow greater confidence that our contributions will actually make a positive difference. Answers to these questions will not only allow a greater understanding about the foundations of human generosity, but will also, hopefully, lead to new methods to increase philanthropic donations.

REFERENCES

Andreoni, J. (1990). Impure altruism and donations to public goods: A theory of warm-glow giving. *Economic Journal, 100,* 464–477.

Baron, J. (1997). Confusion of relative and absolute risk in valuation. *Journal of Risk and Uncertainty, 14*(3), 301–309.

Batson, C. D. (1998). Prosocial behavior and altruism. In D. T. Gilbert, S. T. Fiske, & G. Lindzey (Eds.), *Handbook of Social Psychology* (4th ed., pp. 282–316). Boston: McGraw Hill.

Batson, C. D., Ahmad, N., Yin, J., Bedell, S. J., Johnson, J. W., & Templin, C. M. (1999). Two threats to the common good: Self-interested egoism and empathy-induced altruism. *Personality and Social Psychology Bulletin, 25*(1), 3–16.

Batson, C. D., Batson, J. G., Griffitt, C. A., Barrientos, S., Brandt, J. R., Sprengelmeyer, P., et al. (1989). Negative-state relief and the empathy-altruism hypothesis. *Journal of Personality and Social Psychology, 56*(6), 922–933.

Batson, C. D., Dyck, I. L., Bran, J. R., Batson, J. G., Powell, A. L., McMaster, M. R., et al. (1988). Five studies testing two new egoistic alternatives to the empathy-altruism hypothesis. *Journal of Personality and Social Psychology, 55*(1), 52–77.

Batson, C. D., Sager, K., Garst, E., Kang, M., Rubchinsky, K., & Dawson, K. (1997). Is empathy-induced helping due to self-other merging? *Journal of Personality and Social Psychology, 73*(3), 495–509.

Batson, C. D., Turk, C., Shaw, L., & Klein, T. (1995). Information function of empathetic emotion: Learning that we value the other's welfare. *Journal of Personality and Social Psychology, 68*(2), 300–313.

Bohnet, I., & Frey, B. (1999). Social distance and other-regarding behavior in dictator games. *The American Economic Review, 89*(1), 335–339.

Charness, G., & Gneezy, U. (2008). What's in a name? Reducing the social distance in dictator and ultimatum games. *Journal of Economic Behavior and Organization, 68,* 29–35.

Coke, J. S., Batson, C. D., & McDavis, K. (1978). Empathic mediation of helping: A two-stage model. *Journal of Personality and Social Psychology, 36,* 752–766.

Cryder, C. E., & Loewenstein, G. (2009, February). *The critical link between tangibility and generosity*. Paper presented at the annual winter conference for the Society for Consumer Psychology, San Diego, CA.

Cryder, C. E., Lowenstein, G., & Scheines, R. (2010). The Donor is in the details. Manuscript in preparation.

Cryder, C. E., Loewenstein, G., & Seltman, H. (2008, April). *A race to the finish: Nearing fundraising goals increases the rate of donation*. Paper presented at the meeting for Behavioral Decision Research in Management. La Jolla, CA.

Dovidio, J. F., Allen, J. L., & Schroeder, D. A. (1990). The specificity of empathy-induced altruism: Evidence of altruistic motivation. *Journal of Personality and Social Psychology, 59*, 249–260.

Dunn, E. W., Aknin, L. B., & Norton, M. I. (2008). Spending money on others promotes happiness. *Science, 319*(5870), 1687–1688.

Featherstonhaugh, D., Slovic, P., Johnson, S. M., & Friedrich J. (1997). Insensitivity to the value of human life: A study of psychophysical numbing. *Journal of Risk and Uncertainty, 14*(3), 283–300.

Forsythe, R., Horowitz, J., Savin, N., & Sefton, M. (1994). Fairness in simple bargaining experiments. *Games and Economic Behavior, 6*, 347–369.

Fujita, K., Henderson, M., Eng, J., Trope, Y., & Liberman, N. (2006). Spatial distance and mental construal of social events. *Psychological Science, 17*(4), 278–282.

Giving USA 2007: The annual report on philanthropy for the year 2006. (2007). New York: AAFRC Trust for Philanthropy.

Glover, J. (2001). *Humanity: A moral history of the twentieth century*. New Haven, CT: Yale University Press.

Harbaugh, W., Mayr, U., & Burghart, D. (2007). Neural responses to taxation and voluntary giving reveal motives for charitable donations. *Science, 316*, 1622–1625.

Heath, C., Bell, C., & Sternberg, E. (2001). Emotional selection in memes: The case of urban legends. *Journal of Personality and Social Psychology, 81*, 1028–1041.

Jenni, K. E., & Loewenstein, G. (1997). Explaining the "identifiable victim effect." *Journal of Risk and Uncertainty, 14*(3), 235–257.

Kahneman, D., Knetsch, J. L., & Thaler, R. H. (1986). Fairness and the assumptions of economics. *The Journal of Business, 59*, S285–S300.

Kiva.org (2009). Facts and statistics. Retrieved from http://www.kiva.org/about/facts/

Kogut, T., & Ritov, I. (2005a). The "identified victim" effect: An individual group or just a single individual. *Journal of Behavioral Decision Making, 18*(3), 157–167.

Kogut, T., & Ritov, I. (2005b). The singularity effect of identified victims in separate and joint evaluation. *Organizational Behavior and Human Decision Processes, 97*(2), 106–116.

Lewin, K. (1951). *Field theory in social science: Selected theoretical papers* (D. Cartwright, Ed.). New York: Harper.

Liberman, N., Trope, Y., & Stephan, E. (2007). Psychological distance. In A. W. Kruglanski & E. T. Higgins (Eds.), *Social psychology: Handbook of basic principles* (Vol. 2, pp. 353–383). New York: Guilford Press.

Loewenstein, G., & Small, D. A. (2007). The scarecrow and the tin man: The vicissitudes of human sympathy and caring. *Review of General Psychology, 11*(2), 112–126.

Miller, D. T., & Gunasegaram, S. (1990). Temporal order and the perceived mutability of events: Implications for blame assignment. *Journal of Personality and Social Psychology, 59*(6), 1111–1118.

Moll, J., Krueger, F., Zahn, R., Pardini, M., de Oliveira-Souza, R., & Grafman, J. (2006). Human fronto-mesolimbic networks guide decisions about charitable donations. *Proceedings of the National Academy of Sciences, 103*(42), 15623–15628.

Morewedge, C. K., & Schooler, J. (2009). Mind diffusion: Deindividuation reduces attribution of mind to group members. Working paper, Carnegie Mellon University.

Oxfam-America, Inc. (2007). Oxfam America 2007 Annual Report. Retrieved from http://www.oxfamamerica.org/workspaces/whoweare/financial_info/annual_reports/annual2007/OA_2007Form990.pdf

Pronin, E., Olivola, C. Y., & Kennedy, K. A. (2008). Doing unto future selves as you would do unto others: Psychological distance and decision making. *Personality and Social Psychology Bulletin, 34,* 224–236.

Redelmeier, D. A., & Tversky, A. (1990). The discrepancy between medical decisions for individual patients and for groups. *New England Journal of Medicine, 322*(16), 1162–1164.

Schelling, T.C. (1968). The life you save may be your own. In S. B. Chase (Ed.), *Problems in public expenditure analysis* (pp. 127–162). Washington, DC: Brookings Institution.

Sinaceur, M., & Heath, C. (2005). Emotional and deliberative reactions to a public crisis: Mad cow disease in France. *Psychological Science, 16,* 247–254.

Small, D.A., & Loewenstein, G. (2003). Helping a victim or helping the victim: Altruism and identifiability. *Journal of Risk and Uncertainty, 26*(1), 5–16.

Small, D. A., Loewenstein, G., & Slovic, P. (2007). Sympathy and callousness: The impact of deliberative thought on donations to identifiable and statistical victims. *Organizational Behavior and Human Decision Processes, 102*(2), 143–153.

Small, D. A., & Simonsohn, U. (2008). Friends of victims: Personal experience and prosocial behavior. *Journal of Consumer Research*, 35, 532–542.

Smith, K. D., Keating, J. P., & Stotland, E. (1989). Altruism reconsidered: The effect of denying feedback on a victim's status to empathic witness. *Journal of Personality and Social Psychology, 57*(4), 641–530.

Todorov, A., Goren, A., & Trope, Y. (2006). Probability as a psychological distance: Construal and preferences. *Journal of Experimental Social Psychology, 43*(3), 473–482.

Toi, M., & Batson, C. D. (1982). More evidence that empathy is a source of altruistic motivation. *Journal of Personality and Social Psychology, 43,* 281–292.

Trope, Y., & Liberman, N. (2003). Temporal construal. *Psychological Review, 110*(3), 403–421.

United Nations Foundation (2007). Retrieved from http://www.unfoundation.org

Walker, Rob. (2008, January 27). Extra helping. *New York Times.* Retrieved from http://www.nytimes.com/2008/01/27/magazine/27wwln-consumed-t.html?_r=1&ref=magazine&oref=slogin

Index